our weapon

SUBCOMANDANTE MARCOS

EDITED BY JUANA PONCE de LEÓN

FOREWORD BY JOSÉ SARAMAGO

AFTERWORD BY ANA CARRIGAN

TIMELINE BY TOM HANSEN AND ENLACE CIVIL

SEVEN STORIES PRESS
New York • London • Sydney • Toronto

A portion of the royalties for Our Word is Our Weapon *goes to Enlace Civil, based in San Cristobal de las Casas, Chiapas, Mexico.*

A SEVEN STORIES PRESS FIRST EDITION

SEVEN STORIES PRESS
140 Watts Street
New York, NY 10013
www.sevenstories.com

IN CANADA:
Hushion House, 36 Northline Road, Toronto, Ontario M4B 3E2

IN THE U.K.:
Turnaround Publisher Services Ltd., Unit 3, Olympia Trading Estate, Coburg Road, Wood Green, London N22 6TZ

IN AUSTRALIA:
Tower Books, 9/19 Rodborough Road, Frenchs Forest NSW 2086

Library of Congress Cataloging-in-Publication Data
Marcos, subcomandante.
[Selections. English. 2000]
Our word is our weapon: selected writings / Subcomandante Insurgente Marcos; edited by Juana Ponce de León.
1. cm.
ISBN: 1-58322-036-4
1. Marcos, subcomandante—Correspondence. 2. Revolutionaries—Mexico—Chiapas—Correspondence. 3. Chiapas (Mexico)—History—Peasant Uprising, 1994—Causes. 4. Ejârcito Zapatista de Liberaciân Nacional (Mexico) 5. Mexico—Politics and government—1988– I. Ponce de León, Juana. II. Title.

F1256.M285 2000
972'.75—dc21   00-030791

9 8 7 6 5 4 3 2 1

College professors may order examination copies of Seven Stories Press titles for a free six-month trial period. To order, visit www.sevenstories.com/textbook, or fax on school letterhead to (212) 226-1411.

BOOK DESIGN BY POLLEN/Stewart Cauley and India Amos

PRINTED IN THE U.S.A.

*This book is dedicated to Aureliana and
La Realidad, for helping us learn to see,
and to Nico and Ana, that they may be
touched by so much understanding.*

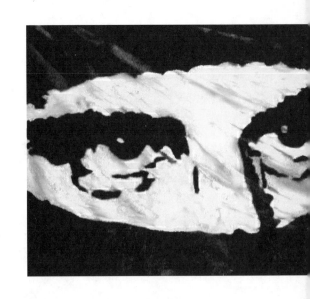

Contents

Acknowledgments xi

Foreword: Chiapas, a Name of Pain and Hope xix
JOSÉ SARAMAGO

Editor's Note: Traveling Back for Tomorrow xxiii

SECTION I
Unveiling Mexico

PART ONE **Names the Unnamed**

1. Twelve Women in the Twelfth Year: The Moment of War 5
2. War! First Declaration of the Lacandon Jungle 13
3. Dying in Order to Live 17
4. In Our Dreams We Have Seen Another World 18
5. Votán–Zapata or Five Hundred Years of History 19
6. A Storm and a Prophecy—Chiapas: The Southeast in Two Winds 22
7. Who Should Ask for Pardon and Who Can Grant It? 38
8. Five Hundred Years of Indigenous Resistance 40
9. Second Declaration of the Lacandon Jungle 43
10. Aguascalientes: Opening Words to the National Deomocratic Convention 52
11. The Long Journey from Despair to Hope 60
12. Mr. Zedillo, Welcome to the Nightmare 70
13. Come, Brothers and Sisters 80
14. The Word and the Silence 83
15. Fourth Declaration of the Lacandon Jungle (excerpt) 86
16. Closing Words to the National Indigenous Forum (excerpt) 90
17. Today, Eighty-Five Years Later, History Repeats Itself 96
18. The Unjust Sentencing of Elorriaga and Entzin 106
19. Opening Remarks at the First Intercontinental *Encuentro* for Humanity and against Neoliberalism 109
20. Tomorrow Begins Today: Closing Remarks at the First Intercontinental *Encuentro* for Humanity and against Neoliberalism 115

21. Second Declaration of La Realidad for
Humanity and against Neoliberalism   124

22. Civil Society That So Perturbs   128

23. The Spiral from the End and the Beginning   133

24. An Urgent Telegram   138

25. Do the Pictures Lie?   139

26. For Those Who Protest with Us after Acteal   140

27. The Sea of My Insomnia: The Table at San Andres   145

28. Tlatelolco: Thirty Years Later the Struggle Continues   151

29. Under Siege: The Zapatista Community of Amador Hernandez   155

30. Why We Use the Weapon of Resistance   159

PART TWO   **One World**

31. Flowers, Like Hope, Are Harvested   167

32. From Vietnam to Chiapas, Twenty Years Before   169

33. A Call to Latin America   172

34. On Independent Media   174

35. Letter to the Indigenous Leadership of the United States   177

36. From Here to There and Back Again   179

37. On May Day and Tupac Amaru   184

38. This Ocean No Longer Separates Us   185

39. Letter to Mumia Abu-Jamal   188

40. Letter to the Supreme Court of Pennsylvania, USA   192

41. "No!" to the War in the Balkans   193

42. For Maurice Najman, Who Keeps Feigning Death   195

43. Letter to Leonard Peltier   204

SECTION II

Beneath the Mask

44. To Open a Crack in History   209

45. We Know What We're Doing; It Is Worth It   213

46. The Library of Aguascalientes   222

47. The Retreat Is Making Us Almost Scratch the Sky   226

48. Death Has Paid a Visit   236

49. A Year of the Zapatista Government 241

50. Zapatistas, Guadalupanos, and the Virgin of Guadalupe 246

51. A Land to Harvest a Future 252

52. Letter to Eduardo Galeano 254

53. Letter to John Berger 259

54. Dignity Cannot Be Studied; You Live It or It Dies 264

55. Letter to the Eureka Committee 267

56. It Continues Raining Here 271

57. Democratic Teachers and the Zapatista Dream 274

58. Closing Words at the National *Encuentro* in Defense of the Cultural Heritage 278

SECTION III

Walking Memory

PART ONE **Tales for a Sleepless Solitude— The Stories of Don Durito**

59. Ten Years Later: Durito Found Us Again 289

60. To Mariana Moguel (age ten) 291

61. The Glass to See to the Other Side 294

62. Deep Inside the Cave of Desire 297

63. Durito and Pegasus 302

64. The Story of the Tiny Mouse and the Tiny Cat 308

65. The Story of the Cold Foot and the Hot Foot 310

66. The Story of the Bean-brown Horse 314

67. Love and the Calendar 316

68. Another Cloud, Another Bottle, and Another Letter from Durito 318

69. P.S. that Fulfills Its Editorial Duty 321

70. Durito the Pirate 322

71. The Hour of the Little Ones 331

72. The True Story of Mary Read and Anne Bonny 335

PART TWO **Tales of Many Others**

73. The Tale of the Ever Never 341

74. The Parrot's Victory 342

75. Tales of the Seahorse: Beads and Accounts of Numbers   343

76. The Tale of the Little Seamstress   345

77. The Tale of the Little Newsboy   346

78. The Tale of the Little Wisp of a Cloud   347

79. The Story of the Schizophrenic Pig   349

80. The Tale of the Lime with an Identity Crisis   351

81. The Tale of the Nonconformist Little Toad   352

82. The Tale of the Pink Shoelaces   355

83. The Tale of Always and Never   356

84. The Little Tree and the Others   357

85. A Light, a Flower, and a Dawn   359

86. The Words That Walk Truths   364

PART THREE **Old Don Antonio**

87. The Story of Colors   373

88. The Story of the Mirrors   376

89. The Story of Dreams   380

90. The Story of the Seven Rainbows   383

91. The Story of Noise and Silence   386

92. Making the Bread Called Tomorrow   389

93. The Story of the Others   390

94. The Tale of the Lion and the Mirror   392

95. The Story of the Measure of Memory   395

96. The Story of One and All   397

97. The Dawn Is Heralding Heat and Flashes   399

98. The Story of the Milky Way   402

99. The Story of the False Light, the Stone, and the Corn   405

100. The Night Is Ours   407

101. The Story of the Questions   413

Afterword: Chiapas, the First Postmodern Revolution   417
ANA CARRIGAN

Zapatista Timeline   445
TOM HANSEN and ENLACE CIVIL

Bibliography   453

Contributors   455

Acknowledgments

THIS BOOK could not have been were it not for the generosity of spirit, talent, and daring of many people, more than could possibly be named in this short page or retained in this faulty memory of mine. To the dedicated people who translate the Zapatista communiqués so that they may circulate the world through the Internet, we owe a great debt for keeping the issues in Chiapas ever-present and for helping breach the Mexican government's cordon of silence and denial. A heartfelt thank you to Cecilia Rodriguez, *la irlandesa*, Michele Cheung, *la maître*, *la niña*, and the many more translators whose names never made the downloads intact. Many of the communiqués of the last two years would simply not have been available without these translators' commitment, and the ability of sleuths like Michele Cheung to locate missing texts and narratives.

In Mexico, first and foremost, to the organization of Enlace Civil for the bridges they build between the communities of resistance and civil society, and for the guidance and care they shared with us during our visits to Chiapas. To Javier Elorriaga and the FZLN for providing a valuable reference point from within the struggle. To Luis Hernandez Navarro and David Brooks of *La Jornada* for their invaluable help in piecing together the complicated Mexican political puzzle, and to Carmen Lira for opening the doors for us to that important journal's talented writers and their photography archives. To Susana Cato and Lorena Crenier for giving shape and color to the puzzle. To Lourdes Sanchez, I thank for the many insights into Mayan mythology and customs. To Lydia Neri for careful fact checking. To Armando Ponce of *Proceso* for giving me the gift of special issues of the magazine to further my research, and for giving me shelter while in Mexico. To the mysterious Nixim for her help finding images. To all the photographers, including Yuriria, Antonio Turok, Mat Jacob, and Pedro Valtierra, thank you for the amazing images that appear in this book.

Thanks to Tom Hansen of Mexico Solidarity Committee, thanks for giving us time and invaluable information. To Michael Eisenmenger and Amy Melnick for many hours of conversation and impressions and solidarity during our long journey into Chiapas. And to Juan Haro of Azul and Tamara Ford for their commentary.

At Seven Stories Press, profound thanks to Dan Simon, who understood the importance of publishing these writings. To all my colleagues and friends at the press who pitched in and made working on this an even greater delight, in particular to Jill Schoolman, who spent countless hours, late into the night, assisting me in this process. Thanks as well to Adriana Scopino for her fine-tuning and to Stewart Cauley for designing a beautiful book.

There are no words ample or deep enough to express my gratitude to Greg Ruggiero, my editor at Seven Stories Press, for having involved me in this endeavor. His profound commitment to the struggle for human rights, his boundless energy and good spirit have sustained me and the project every step along the way. And, finally, I must acknowledge Nico and Ana, my son and daughter, who endured many days of household havoc while I was engaged in this project.

Forgive me,

friend, for making you a madman, by persuading you to believe, as I did myself, that there have been formerly, and are now, knights-errant in the world.

—Miguel de Cervantes, *Don Quixote*, II.74

The word

Was born in the blood,
Grew in the dark body, beating,
And took flight through the lips and mouth.

Farther away and nearer
Still, still it came
From dead fathers and from wandering races,
From lands which had turned to stone,
Lands weary of their poor tribes,
For when grief took to the roads
The people set out and arrived
And married new land and water
To grow their words again.
And so this is the inheritance;
This is the wavelength which connects us
With dead men and the dawning
Of new beings not yet come to light.

—Pablo Neruda, from "The Word," *Fully Empowered*

Poem in Two Beats and a Subversive Ending

FIRST BEAT
I
slid
down
the smile
of
a word,
drilled.
That is my origin...
But,
I
don't remember
if
I
was expelled
or
if
I took my things
and
slid
down
thinking...

SECOND BEAT
It was
words
that
created
us.

They
shaped us,
and spread
their lines
to control
us.

A SUBVERSIVE ENDING
But
I
know
that
a few men
gather
inside caverns
in SILENCE

Never again will the Zapatistas be alone....

—Subcomandante Insurgente Marcos

Chiapas, a Name of Pain and Hope

JOSÉ SARAMAGO

IN 1721, with a feigned innocence that couldn't conceal his tart sarcasm, Charles-Louis de Secondat asked, "Persians? But how is it possible for someone to be Persian?" It's been almost three hundred years now since the Baron de Montesquieu wrote his famous *Lettres Persanes,* and even today we haven't succeeded in putting together an intelligent answer to this most essential of all questions on the historical agenda of human relationships. As a matter of fact, we still can't understand how it was ever possible for someone to have been a "Persian," and furthermore, as if such a peculiarity were not out of the question, to persist in being one today when the world seeks to convince us that the only desirable and profitable thing to be is what in very broad and artificially conciliatory terms is customarily called "Western" (in mentality, fashions, tastes, habits, interests, manias, ideas)—or, in the all too frequent case of not succeeding in reaching such sublime heights, to be "Westernized" in some bastard way at least, whether through force of persuasion or in a more radical way, if persuasion should fail.

To be "Persian" is to be someone strange, someone different—in simple terms to be the "other." The very existence of the Persian has been enough to disturb, confuse, disrupt, and perturb the workings of institutions; the Persian can even reach the inadmissible extreme of upsetting what all governments in the world are most jealous of: the sovereign tranquillity of their power.

The indigenous were and still are Persians in Brazil (where the landless now represent another type of Persians). The indigenous in the United States once were but have almost ceased to be Persians. In their time Incas, Mayas, and Aztecs were Persians, as were and still are their descendants, wherever they have lived and still live.

There are Persians in Guatemala, Bolivia, Colombia, and Peru. There is also an overabundance of Persians in that painful land of Mexico, where Sebastiao Salgado's inquiring, rigorous camera drew shudders from us with the challenging figures facing us. They ask: How can it be that you "Westerners" and "Westernized" people to the north, south, east, and west, so cultured, so civilized, so perfect, lack that modicum of intelligence and sensibility necessary to understand us, the "Persians" of Chiapas?

It is really only a matter of understanding–understanding the expression in those looks, their solemnity, the simplicity of their grouping, feeling and thinking together, weeping the same tears in common, smiling the same smile; understanding the hands of the sole survivor of a slaughter, held like protective wings over the head of her daughter; understanding this endless stream of living and dead, this lost blood, this acquired hope, this silence of one who has borne centuries of demanding respect and justice, this suppressed anger of one who has finally wearied of hoping.

Six years ago, changes were introduced in the Mexican Constitution in obedience to the neoliberal "economic revolution" directed from without, and were mercilessly applied by the government to bring agrarian reform and redistribution to an end. This reduced to nothing the possibility for landless peasants to have a parcel of land to cultivate. The indigenous thought they could defend their historic rights (or simply their common-law ones, in case it was assumed that indigenous communities had no place in the history of Mexico) by organizing into civic societies that were characterized, and still are, by their singular insistence on renouncing any kind of violence, starting with the one that was their due.

These societies had the support of the Catholic Church from the beginning, but that protection was of little use to them. Their leaders and representatives were jailed repeatedly; the systematic, implacable, and brutal persecution by the powers of the state and the large landowners increased in conjunction with and under the shadow of the interests and privileges of both. These persecutors violently expelled the indigenous from their ancestral lands, and the mountains and jungle, many times over, became the last refuge of the people displaced. There in the dense mists of the heights and the valleys, the seeds of rebellion would germinate.

The indigenous of Chiapas aren't the only humiliated and offended people in this world. In all places and at all times, regardless of race, color, customs, culture, and religious belief, the human creature we are so proud to be has always known how to humiliate and offend those whom, with sad irony, he continues to call his fellows. We have invented things that don't exist in nature: cruelty, torture, and disdain. By a perverse use of race, we've come to divide humanity into irreducible categories: rich and poor, master and slave, powerful and weak, wise and ignorant. And incessantly in each of these divisions we've made subdivisions so as to vary and freely multiply reasons for disdain, humiliation, and offense.

In recent years Chiapas has been the place where the most disdained, most humiliated, and most offended people of Mexico were able to recover intact a dignity and an honor that had never been completely lost, a place where the heavy tombstone of an oppression that has gone on for centuries has been shattered to allow the passage of a procession of new and different living people ahead of an endless procession of murders. These men, women, and children of the present are only demanding respect for their rights, not just as human beings and as part of this humanity but also as the indigenous who want to continue being indigenous. They've risen up most especially with a moral strength that only honor and dignity themselves are capable of bringing to birth and nursing in the spirit, even while the body suffers from hunger and the usual miseries.

On the other side of the heights of Chiapas lies not only the government of Mexico but the whole world. No matter how much of an attempt has been made to reduce the question of Chiapas to merely a local conflict, whose solution should be found within the strict confines of an application of national law–hypocritically malleable and adjustable, as has been seen once again, according to the strategies and tactics of economic and political power to which they are surrogate–what is being played out in the Chiapas mountains and the Lacandon Jungle reaches beyond the borders of Mexico to the heart of that portion of humanity that has not renounced and never will renounce dreams and hopes, the simple imperative of equal justice for all.

As that figure, exceptional and exemplary for many reasons, whom we know by the name of the Subcomandante Insurgente Marcos has written, it is "a world where there is room for many worlds, a world that can be one and diverse," a world, I might add myself, that for all people and all time declares untouchable the right of everyone to be a "Persian" any time he or she wants to and without obeying anything but one's own roots.

The mountainous highlands of Chiapas are without a doubt one of the most amazing landscapes my eyes have ever seen, but they are also a place where violence and protected crime thrive. Thousands of the indigenous, driven from their homes and their lands for the "unpardonable crime" of being silent or open sympathizers with the Zapatista National Liberation Army (EZLN), are crammed into camps of improvised huts, where there is not enough food, where the little water available is almost always contaminated, where illnesses like tuberculosis, cholera, measles, tetanus, pneumonia, typhus, and malaria are decimating adults and children. All this is happening in full view of the indifferent authorities and official medical administration.

Some sixty thousand soldiers–no more nor less than a third of the permanent strength of the Mexican army at present–occupy the state of Chiapas under the pretext of defending and assuring public order.

The factual reality, however, gives the lie to this justification. The Mexican army is protecting one part of the indigenous population; it is not only protecting it but at the same time teaching, training, and arming these indigenous who are generally dependent upon and subordinate to the Institutional Revolutionary Party (PRI), which for sixty years has been exercising uninterrupted and practi-

cally absolute power. These indigenous are–not by any extraordinary coinci-
dence–the ones who make up the various paramilitary groups organized with the
sole objective of undertaking the dirtiest work of suppression: the attack, rape,
and murder of their own brothers and sisters.

Acteal was one more episode in the terrible tragedy that began in 1492 with
invasion and conquest. All through the five hundred years the indigenous of
Ibero-America (and I use this term intentionally so as not to let escape judgment
of the Portuguese and later on the Brazilians, who continued the genocidal
process that reduced the 3 or 4 million Indians existent in Brazil during the
period of discovery to little more than 200,000 in 1980) were passed, in a manner of speaking, from hand to hand. They were handed from the soldier who
killed them to the master who exploited them, while in between there was the
hand of the Catholic Church, which made them exchange one set of gods for
another, but which in the end was unsuccessful in changing their spirit.

After the butchery of Acteal there began to be heard over the radio words that
said, "We're winning." Some unaware person might have thought that it was a
matter of an insolent and provocative proclamation by murderers. He would have
been mistaken. Those words were a message of hope, words of courage that like
an embrace over the airwaves united the indigenous communities. While they
wept for their dead–another forty-five added to a list five centuries old–the communities stoically lifted their heads and said to each other, "We're winning,"
because it really could only have been a victory, and a great one, the greatest of all,
surviving humiliation, offense, disdain, cruelty, and torture in that way. This was
a victory of the spirit.

Eduardo Galeano, the great Uruguayan writer, tells how Marcos went to
Chiapas and spoke to the indigenous, but they didn't understand him. "Then he
penetrated the mist, learned to listen, and was able to speak." That same mist that
prevents one person from seeing is also the window that opens onto the world of
the other, the world of the indigenous, the world of the "Persian." Let us look in
silence, let us learn to listen; perhaps later we'll finally be able to understand.

Translated from the Portuguese by Gregory Rabassa

Traveling Back for Tomorrow

JUANA PONCE de LEÓN

THIS BOOK, a testimony to the power of the word, is scripted in the impossible silence of the Lacandon Jungle. Segment by segment, it is passed secretly from hand to hand, galloped inside a saddle satchel, hidden in a cyclist's bag, slipped into a backpack, or perhaps thrust inside a sack of beans, then propped in the back of an open truck, crammed with indigenous villagers who make the hours-long journey to the closest market, or doctor, and our messenger to a contact person with Internet access. Up on Dyckman Street, where Manhattan Island narrows to a close between the Hudson and Harlem Rivers, in a room that sits above squat roofs to face the treetops of the Hudson's embankment, Greg Ruggiero surfs the net. An editor, activist, and Zapatista to the core, he connects to the various websites where the latest translations of Subcomandante Marcos's communiqués reach him, and millions others worldwide.

For five years lines accumulate, giving shape to a unique proposal for social change: to create a truly democratic space where new political possibilities can be debated and advanced. By carefully depicting Mexico, the conflict in Chiapas and the indigenous struggle for human rights, and by pointing to the threats that neoliberalism poses to all of us, Marcos manages to create a mirror where we can recognize the features of our own concerns. "What makes him remarkable," declares Greg, "is the deeply personal and at the same time deeply collective voice that emerges from the literature, poetry and tales that he prolifically generates. The Mexican government has not found anything powerful enough to counter the Zapatista Word, its vision, and the resistance and liberation it offers as a counterforce to the dehumanizing institutions of business and war."

But the words spell more than revolution. As the communiqués trail in, we come face to face with a persuasive new literary voice and an important Mexican writer. Like other Latin American writers—Pablo Neruda, Miguel Angel Asturias, or Gabriel Garcia Marquez—Marcos manages to fuse his political beliefs and his literary artistry to craft the singular beauty of his voice. Hauling what appears to be several reams of communiqués, Greg requests I read them as he invites me to become the editor of Subcomandante Marcos's selected writings.

It is in that small room, perched at the northernmost point of Manhattan, where the Zapatista Word has been heard, and where this book project is born.

THE AUGUST HOUR is black, starless, damp, and chilly. Cautiously, my companions and I break the enveloping silence to wonder if the van that will take us to La Realidad, an autonomous indigenous Zapatista community seven hours outside of San Cristobal, will really arrive. The odd hour for our journey will take us past immigration checkpoints while the guards sleep; only they have the power to abort the careful orchestration of many months, which has brought us here to a hotel lobby in a dark Chiapas night. Right on cue, at 4:00 A.M. Zapatista time, two headlights pierce the black, bounce awkwardly above the cobblestones, and stop before us.

The trip has the exaggerated feel of a dream. We leave modern Mexico and cross a bridge of time and space to enter the heart of indigenous Mexico. We leave in darkness to reach the light. Our driver has night vision; he is a nocturnal animal with a sixth sense that allows us to negotiate the many hours of unpaved road, erosion, stones, and endless potholes—more like craters, really. We slip past immigration and steadily drive towards day. Dawn reveals breathtaking mountainscapes dense with greens giving way to valleys where, unexpectedly, hamlets crop up, bordered by flowering trees, patches of cornstalks, dogs, chickens, and an occasional pig. We now share the road with men, women, and children carrying machetes or hoes and small bundles of food.

Five hours into the trip our driver announces that we are approaching the first of two military checkpoints. He describes the procedure—we are tourists on our way to the beautiful Lake Miramar—and how our papers and our baggage will be inspected. Soon armed soldiers surround our van and we are asked to step out and open our baggage for inspection. A law permits the army to stop and search vehicles for arms and explosives, but it does not authorize them to inspect our identification papers. The driver's guidance helps us veil the purpose of our journey before the glacial courtesy of the army officers, who point video cameras in our faces while jotting down the details of our identities.

Less than thirty minutes from La Realidad sits another checkpoint, Guadalupe Tepeyac, host community to the first Zapatista *encuentro*, now razed by the army, its people scattered into the mountains, their homes replaced by barracks. The unreality of this violence is heightened by the sudden appearance of an albino boy, perhaps ten years old, who seems to be governed by no one—a wayward spirit in our evolving dream-journey who rummages through our belongings, tries on straw hats, sunglasses, pries open our water bottles. On the last leg of the journey we are forced off the road by a convoy of army trucks—thirty-four strong—loaded up with soldiers, machine guns, and more video cameras, one final show of power before we reach La Realidad.

A sense of urgency brings Greg and myself on this long journey. We hope to meet Marcos—the most wanted man in Mexico, transgressor of the law, Internet guerrilla, catalyst for a new kind of revolution, poet—to speak with him about the making of this book. Political advisories in the press and on the Internet indicate that the militarization in Chiapas has escalated tenfold. The physical danger to the rebel communities and their sympathizers is grave. It is imperative to get the word out.

For the government, the issue is simple. There are vast oil reserves, exotic wood, and uranium on the autonomous indigenous lands of Chiapas; the Mexican government wants them, but the indigenous communities, who have no currency in the world's markets, are in the way. While projecting through the national and international press an image of concern for the human rights issues and the intention to resolve them, the government orchestrates the privatization of these Mayan lands and a low-intensity war to weaken and divide the communities.

After much deliberation about the impact of globalization on their lives, the indigenous communities assess that NAFTA will not bring them benefits but "a death sentence," and decide to go to war on the first day of NAFTA's implementation, January 1, 1994. When the Zapatistas rebel, the message they send to the world differs starkly from that of previous guerrilla groups. They declare war on the Mexican government, "not to usurp power, but to exercise it," sending a forceful reminder that the forgotten indigenous populations are, after all, Mexicans, and that they too are entitled to exercise their political and civil rights. It is the first show of popular resistance to globalization to actually make headlines. "The war for the word," writes Marcos, "has begun."

After twelve days of fighting and the takeover of San Cristobal de las Casas and a few neighboring towns, the Zapatistas declare a unilateral cease-fire. But before they melt back into their communities, Mexico and the international press take note of an unexpected presence among the rebels. Emerging from the multitude of brown-skinned people, an assigned spokesperson proclaims: "Through me speaks the will of the Zapatista National Liberation Army." His fair skin and green eyes, which gleam beneath a black ski mask, are as dissonant as the Zapatistas' sudden cry in a long, silent night of forgetting. When the press asks who he is, he replies: "I am Subcomandante Marcos."

Wild speculation follows as to his identity and the true purpose of his relationship with the indigenous communities. With the media trained on him and on Chiapas, a stream of rebel communiqués—often penned by Marcos—start to appear in the press, and run like wildfire through the Internet. Over time, through a campaign of misinformation and silence, the Mexican government struggles to control the situation and denies that there is a conflict. With the exception of cov-

erage in *La Jornada*—the second largest newspaper in Mexico— and *Proceso* magazine—an important news and arts weekly—and Chiapas's own *El Tiempo,* the
Zapatistas practically disappear from the national press. But not so on the Internet,
where the lifeline for the movement reaches out, grows, and spreads.

Early in that spring of 1994, the Zapatistas send out a call inviting national
and international press to meet with the rebels in the jungle. Six thousand people—Mexican and foreign journalists, activists, unaligned citizens, and the curious—arrive for a first *encuentro* in August. Already there is much criticism about
the masked *subcomandante.* I am told that when Marcos finally appears before
the immense crowd, a solitary figure masked in black, he is asked: "Why hide
your face? What are you afraid to show? Only people who have something shameful to conceal hide their faces." Right there and then, Marcos offers to remove his
mask. A stunned silence spreads through the crowd, only to be broken by a unified cry: "No! No! No!" The mask stays on. It is a crucial moment in the making
of the persona of Marcos. The mask has a transformative power that allows
Marcos to shed the idiosyncrasies of his birth and assume a communal identity.
This nonself makes it possible for Marcos to become the spokesperson for the
indigenous communities. He is transparent, and he is iconographic. He hides
his face so that he can be seen. This paradox will inform all his writing.

While no certain identity has been established for Marcos, through his writing we have been able to see the organic evolution of a revolutionary. His analysis of the structure of power and corruption in Mexico, of the social makeup of
the nation, of the threats of neoliberalism are undogmatic and creative.
Repeatedly, Marcos warns that the globalization of the economy threatens to do
away with indigenous community values, thus casting aside each man, woman,
and child whose honest daily work makes Mexico rich in material and spirit.

Juxtaposed with the descriptions of an oppressive structure of class, values, and
of the political machinery that holds it all in place, Marcos offers a window into the
indigenous world that sits at the bottom of the heap, and at the heart of the nation.
Using simple, direct, parabolic language that alludes to Mayan deities and the *Popol
Vuh,* Marcos insists that political issues are human rights issues, while creating a
consciousness of indigenous Mexico and a place for it in the political and social par-
lance of present-day Mexico. He insists that indigenous Mexico is intrinsic to the
health and survival of the nation: "A people without a past can have no future."

With equal insistence, Marcos draws attention to other communities and personalities around the world who also resist globalization and human rights injustices. Sending letters to Mumia Abu-Jamal, to Leonard Peltier, to U.S. judges, or
UN officials, he emphasizes the global nature of these issues to reinforce international solidarity efforts. A "No!" to the war in Kosovo is a "No!" to the war in
Chiapas. In his communiqués to civil society—the many millions of people who

live their everyday lives unaligned to political parties—he makes a plea for political action. It is Marcos's belief that only civil society has the power to rein in a
government that has forgotten the people while in hot pursuit of profits. Only
civil society can make government "rule by obeying."

It is not surprising that a careful scrutiny of society should engender in
Marcos questions about the individual man. In the correspondence with intellectuals around the world we see the literary and philosophical man, who at one
moment is querying John Berger about the architecture of perception, and the
next moment is in conversation with Eduardo Galeano about the inexplicable
absurdity of life for a child who is surrounded by war. Other times, he finds
solace in the prismatic logic of Jorge Luis Borges, which is held securely by the
elegance of his intellect; it is a place he can return to again and again. Throughout
his writing, reflecting mirrors and transparent glass become metaphors for self-
recognition and transcendence. Sometimes, in conversation with himself, his
poems echo the romantic tones of Pablo Neruda and the surrealist imagery of
Federico Garcia Lorca. It is in these fragments that we encounter Marcos express-
ing his sensuous, introspective, and sexual sides.

Of his writing, perhaps the most popular are the tales, which fall into three categories, each corresponding to specific areas of concern for the author. "Stories for
a Night of Asphyxia," or "Tales for a Sleepless Solitude" are reminiscent of Italo
Calvino's *Italian Folktales,* where the dilemmas of adult life— sexual desire, love,
solitude and death— are central. Often, Marcos converses with his "other self," who
plays the role of devil's advocate and cynic to the author's romanticism. These are
by far the most personal of the stories, where we glimpse something of the carnal
man, with his wants, his uncertainties, and his aloneness. In the tales of Don
Durito of the Lacandon, a knight-errant and beetle with a penchant for storytelling,
we see the world viewed from below, literally and metaphorically. Durito, which
means "the little hard one," gets his name not just from his hard shell; he is a ladies'
man. He is the author's Don Quixote and, as with Cervantes's character, his adventures of chivalry and valor are spun around issues of dignity, values, proper behavior, and civic duty. Marcos, the beetle's lackey, endures verbal abuse, sleepless
nights, and many hours of dictation with great humor and a healthy dose of self-
mockery. Through his tales of Old Don Antonio, a Mayan shaman Marcos comes
to know in the course of a decade, the author passes on the oral tradition that has
been kept by the indigenous communities. These serve to highlight the indigenous
belief that only by asking questions do we begin the process of change and that
everyone is needed to ask and answer questions together....

Finally, we arrive at La Realidad to ask our questions. We wait close to an hour
at the edge of the hamlet, while our proposal is reviewed by the Zapatista leadership to see if we may enter, before we are brought to Posada 18, a tin-covered

open space that houses a large adobe mound, which turns out to be the community oven. Children and women mill around, looking at the new show in town, as we struggle to hang our hammocks and mosquito netting. We are hopelessly ineffectual, all left hands, often eliciting laughter from our spectators. No sooner are we done slinging our hammocks than a masked rebel rides up on horseback. We recognize him from photographs and documentaries—Comandante Tacho. He dismounts his horse and approaches Posada 18 to greet us.

Suddenly, the Zapatista myth has gained human proportions. We are all stunned. I hardly understand what this man is saying to us, and of the group, I am the one who speaks Spanish. Tacho is a small brown man, perhaps five-foot-five, his strong frame laden with the accessories of war—rows of bullets strapped across his chest, pistols, ropes—their purpose unmistakable. His ski mask creases above what must be a broad smile and his eyes bounce from face to face. Graciously, he shakes hands with each of us, and informs us that el Sup will come and see us sometime in the next couple of days. He thanks us for having come, and disappears as quickly as he appears.

There are many visitors about. Unbeknown to us, there is soon to be an *encuentro* for the protection of cultural heritage, which is bringing many students and anthropologists to La Realidad. There is, as well, a group of thirty or so international observers who have come to create a civilian buffer between the military and the indigenous Zapatistas.

Certain that all that can possibly happen in a given day has already transpired, Greg and I decide to stroll about the community. There are flowering trees and a bounty of ripe white guavas, mangoes, and avocados fallen on the ground. Children run around, playing; young girls carry younger siblings cradled in cloth slings around their backs or bellies, their gold earrings glinting in the sunlight. At the river, a swift current that wends its way through the center of the settlement, women wash their clothes or bathe. Hopelessly emaciated, flea-ridden dogs wander aimlessly about, incapable of creating even a stir in the chickens that scratch the earth in the heat of the afternoon. Aside from a few men walking past on some errand, the community seems mainly populated by women. Seated by the river's edge, our feet immersed in the cold, clear water, we share impressions of this little corner of paradise. For the first time in my life, I get a glimpse of why time and space are one and the same concept for the Mayans. Only the fatigue from so many sleepless hours lets us know we should return to our *posada* and get some rest.

As we make our way back, from a distance Greg notices a saddled horse in front of our dwelling, I am hopelessly myopic. Accelerating our pace, Greg can make out a masked guerrilla speaking with our companions, who have stayed behind. We hurry along, and as we get closer, we see the signature pipe, the mended cap and red bandanna. It's Marcos. We enter the *posada* and are greeted by our companions' startled, delighted, and excited expressions. We gather they have been using broken Italian and hand signs in an attempt to communicate. "You almost missed him!" they exclaim. Marcos turns to face us and in flawless English says, "Yes, you almost missed me," and follows it with a laugh. He too thanks us for visiting La Realidad and informs us he has read our proposal and feels it is important. As he speaks, his hands—pale, delicate, a contradiction to his life in the mountains—move about the air for emphasis. He appears relaxed and focused, and listens intently to what we have to say. I am surprised at the low tone of his voice. Several times he tells us: "You are cultural workers. I want the community to see you are different from the journalists who come here." At the end of our conversation, we make plans to meet again in three days.

With no electricity to be had, night comes irrefutably. The next few days give us an intimate look into the community's life. Sometime in the middle of that first night, the skies open up, and the rain pounds our tin roof. The sound is deafening, and shakes me awake to find myself far away from my life. I lie quietly and realize that not everyone is asleep. Flashlight beams dart around the dark, here and there, revealing glistening tree trunks and masked faces. I am wondering what possible purpose has them walking through the rain and the night when exhaustion claims me once again.

Dawn has not yet shown its face when the sound of a shell-horn pushes the silence. Its gentle wavering is a hollow call announcing something we do not understand. Hours later, we learn that an eleven-year-old boy has died in the night. The entire community will not work that day in order to spend time with the bereaved family. It seems death is a familiar presence here; there is no wailing or weeping to be seen. Sometime in the late afternoon a small group of people accompanies the narrow coffin, riding shoulder-high through the community en route to its gravesite. This simple, grievous scene brings to mind a rush of statistics about Chiapas and death that could be prevented had there been medicine and care available.

The days are slow with waiting. Little by little we learn about our neighbors' lives and the increasing difficulties presented by the military encirclement. They cannot go to work their small plots of land, pick coffee, or fetch wood outside the hamlet without fear of harassment by the Mexican military. Rumor has it that rodents are being dropped from helicopters into the corn, where they gnaw away at the base of the stalk, not letting the corn grow or mature. We are thankful for our meals of tortillas, eggs, and beans with coffee at Lupita's table; for our daily baths in the river; for the small tasks of washing clothes; for being able to borrow Aureliana's tattered broom to sweep out the *posada*, an excuse to sit and listen to her while sipping a treasured extra cup of coffee; for the steady stream of visitors, mostly children, who come to hang out in our hammocks and who want cookies and paper and colored pencils. Also, twice everyday we see the long, slow passage of the caravan of army trucks, soldiers, guns, and cameras as they move down the main street of the hamlet, while helicopters fly overhead. And then, again, a faithful, thundering rain pelting our tin roof at night.

This lulling daily rhythm is suddenly upset on our third day, when the village bell tolls in alarm. We are told some 500 soldiers have invaded—some by parachute—Amador Hernandez, an autonomous Zapatista village north of La Realidad. Within a matter of hours the community around us is transformed. We are no longer allowed to wander about the hamlet, nor can we bathe in the river. Red alert has been declared in La Realidad, as the community prepares to defend itself in case of attack. Tacho makes a hurried visit to let us know we will not be seeing Marcos, and I make arrangements for our group to leave the jungle that very night. Our promised rendezvous has been postponed.

Ten months have passed since that first journey, and Greg and I are back in Chiapas. San Cristobal de las Casas feels tense and empty. The presidential elections are a week off, and Mexico seems to be holding its breath, uncertain of what is coming. There are many more military and immigration checkpoints to negotiate, and new ways to avoid them. Again we make our way to La Realidad at night, our driver making turns and following an unpaved road past an uninhabited terrain. Within an hour of our arrival, we pass two brightly illuminated hamlets, an oddity here in the jungle, and soon we are at Guadalupe Tepeyac again. This time there are young, unsupervised soldiers who seem embarrassed to search through our things, and we pass through without much incident. La Realidad is asleep when we arrive.

We have come to meet again with Marcos, but he and the Zapatista leadership are deep in the jungle, far from the mounting military pressure. Things have gotten worse. There are shortages of grains and beans. There is no money. The military caravans no longer keep regular hours and the helicopters and planes are flying closer to the ground. Word spreads quickly that we have arrived, and soon old friends and many children make their way to Posada 18 to greet us. In time, Marcos radios in that it will not be possible to meet us in La Realidad, and our friends in the community console us, saying that there have not been meetings for weeks. That very midnight, we pack into the back of a seatless truck with twenty-odd polytech students who have been working on a building project, and piled on top of one another begin the seven-hour trek back to San Cristobal through the rain and mud.

The Mexican election results make the front page of major newspapers and the *New York Times* here at home. The PRI has finally been toppled, after seven decades of being in control. In Chiapas, however, the PRI has a stranglehold on the peasant population, through a mixture of intimidation and bribes. A popular radio program in Mexico City broadcasts days before the elections that the PRI is giving away a chicken to each person who agrees to vote for Labastida, their candidate. What will these ruthless people do to get back into the driver's seat? Will they attempt to destabilize Vicente Fox's new presidency by escalating the crisis in Chiapas?

A tremendous sense of urgency drives this project. Due to an international awareness of the situation in Chiapas, the Zapatistas have been able to sustain their struggle. Now more than ever, we need to spread the word, and take action. We must come to understand that each battle won for human rights and democracy is a battle won for all of us, that beneath the mask of our own personal struggles, we are all Marcos.

THE MAKING of this book raised several questions that served to underline the inherent power of the word. After making a selection of communiqués, which in our opinion best exemplify Marcos's political acuity and literary gifts, there were translation issues to sort out. Because so much of the text was culled from the Internet, there was the need to verify that author's words and meaning had been rendered faithfully into English. Because there were so many translators involved, it was important to try to unify the voice of the writer. Some words required close consideration: Should we use the word *Indian* or do we use *indigenous*? Do we use *compañero* or *comrade*? Do we italicize words like *campesino* or *huaraches* that have become part of the English vernacular?

Suddenly, emotional and political implications that could influence the meaning of the text in ways perhaps not intended by the author became apparent. In an attempt to give transparency to Marcos's voice, Greg and I spent many hours sparring over ethics, struggling to find the correspondence of cultural and political values for the Spanish in English. After much discussion, we opted to use *indigenous*—we felt it was congruent with the Zapatistas's political stance—and do away with the European term, *Indian*. Where we couldn't find the appropriate values in the English choice of word, such as *meeting, gathering* or *encounter* for the word *encuentro*—the elements of surprise, of familiarity, of the meeting of the minds, the spiritual components implied in the Spanish were simply not found in one single word—we used the Spanish. And where Spanish words were in common used here, we removed the italics.

As we reached the end of our editorial process, we became conscious of another subtle force that guided the project. As if by some sleight of hand, we found that the author had managed to infuse the book with his inclination toward the communal and the interconnection between the cultures. Leaving our hands, then, is a work that is also a literal acceptance and embracing of the "other."

Unveiling Mexico

This section, divided into two parts, deals primarily with description of and commentary on the social and political situation in Mexico, its implications for Chiapas and Mexico, and the emotional and intellectual climates that it engenders. Serving as the voice for the indigenous in Chiapas, some communiqués are "signed" by the comandancia of the Zapatista National Liberation Army, though the Marcos' imprint is everywhere evident.

PART ONE

Names the Unnamed

... in which Marcos, in an attempt to raise awareness of what is truly at stake in Chiapas and in
Mexico, points to the institutionalized corruption
of values that encourages the incursion of globalization into their nation and betrays all Mexicans.

... in which the indigenous voice of resistance
and dignity speaks through Marcos, and Marcos
speaks of the indigenous life and spiritual values
that sit at the heart of their communities and at the
heart of Mexico.

... in which war is declared against oblivion
and prejudice.

Twelve Women in the Twelfth Year

The Moment of War

MARCH 11, 1996

During the twelfth year of the Zapatistas, many kilometers and at a great distance from Beijing, twelve women meet March 8 with their faces erased . . .

I. Yesterday . . .

ALTHOUGH HER FACE is wreathed in black, still one can see a few strands of hair upon her forehead, and the eyes with the spark of one who searches. Before her she holds an M-1 carbine in the "assault" position. She has a pistol strapped to her waist. Over the left side of the chest, that place where hopes and convictions reside, she carries the rank of infantry major of an insurgent army that has called itself, this cold dawn of January 1, 1994, the Zapatista National Liberation Army.

Under her command, a rebel column takes the former capital of the southeastern Mexican state of Chiapas, San Cristobal de Las Casas. The central square of San Cristobal is deserted. Only the indigenous men and women under her command are witnesses to the moment in which the major, a rebel indigenous Tzotzil woman, takes the national flag and gives it to the commanders of the rebellion, those called "The Indigenous Clandestine Revolutionary Committee." At 02:00 southeastern time, January 1 of 1994, over the radio, the major says, "We have recovered the flag. 10-23 over."

For the rest of the world, it is 01:00 hours of the New Year, but for her, those words mark a decade-long wait. In December 1984, not yet twenty years old, she arrives in the mountains of the Lacandon Jungle, carrying the marks of the whole history of indigenous humiliation on her body. In December 1984 this brown woman says, "Enough is enough!" so softly that only she hears herself. In January 1994 this woman and several thousand indigenous people do not just say, but yell, "Enough is enough!" so loudly that all the world hears them . . .

Outside San Cristobal another column of indigenous rebels, who attack the city under the command of the only man with light skin and a large nose, has just taken the police headquarters. It frees from these clandestine jails the indigenous who were spending the New Year locked up, guilty of the most terrible crime in the Chiapanecan southeast: being poor.

The indigenous rebel Tzeltal—Capitán Insurgente Eugenio Asparuk—together with the enormous nose, is now overseeing the search and seizure of the headquarters. When the major's message arrives, Capitán Insurgente Pedro—an indigenous rebel Chol—has finished taking the Federal Highway Police Headquarters, and has secured the road that connects San Cristobal with Tuxtla Gutierrez. Capitán Insurgente Ubilio—also an indigenous rebel Tzeltal—has taken the entryways to the north of the city and with it the National Indigenous Institute, symbol of the government handouts to the indigenous people. Capitán Insurgente Guillermo—an indigenous rebel Chol—has seized the highest point of the city. From there he can observe a surprised silence peering out the windows of the houses and buildings. Insurgent and equally rebellious Capitáns Gilberto and Noe, indigenous Tzotzil and Tzeltal respectively, end their takeover of the State Judicial Police Headquarters and set it on fire before marching on to secure the other side of the city and the roads that lead to the barracks of the thirty-first Military Zone in Rancho Nuevo.

At 02:00 hours, southeastern time, January 1, 1994, five insurgent officials, indigenous rebel men, hear over the radio the voice of their commander, an indigenous rebel woman: "We have recovered the flag. 10-23 over." They repeat this to their troops, men and women, all indigenous and unconditionally rebellious, and translate the words: "We have begun . . ."

At the Municipal Palace, the major secures the positions that will protect the men and women who now govern the city, a city now under the rule of indigenous rebels. An armed woman protects them.

Among the indigenous commanders there is a tiny woman, even tinier than those around her. Her face is wreathed in black; still, one can see a few strands of hair upon her forehead, and the gaze with the spark of one who searches. A twelve-gage sawed-off shotgun hangs from her back. Wearing the traditional dress of the women from San Andres, Ramona, together with hundreds of women, walks down from the mountains toward the city of San Cristobal on that last night of 1993. Together with Susana and other indigenous people, she is part of that indigenous war command which, in 1994, gives birth to the CCRI-CG, the Clandestine Indigenous Revolutionary Committee of the General Command of the Zapatista National Liberation Army, the EZLN.

Comandante Ramona's size and brilliance will surprise the international press when she appears in the Cathedral—where the first Dialogues for Peace are held—and pulls from her backpack the national flag, seized by the major on January. Ramona does not know it then, nor do we, that she carries an illness that takes huge bites of her body, eats away at her life and dims her voice and her gaze.

Ramona and the major, the only women in the Zapatista delegation who show themselves to the world for the first time, declare, "For all intents and purposes, we were already dead. We meant absolutely nothing." With these words they can almost convey the humiliation and abandonment. The major translates to Ramona the questions of the reporters. Ramona nods and understands, as though the answers she is asked for had always been there, in her tiny figure that laughs at the Spanish language and at the ways of the city women. Ramona laughs when she does not know she is dying. And when she knows, she still laughs. Before she did not exist for anyone; now she exists, as a woman, as an indigenous woman, as a rebel woman. Now Ramona lives, a woman belonging to that race that must die in order to live . . .

The major watches as the light takes possession the streets of San Cristobal. Her soldiers secure the defense of the old city of Jovel and the protection of the men and women who are now sleeping, indigenous and mestizos, all equally surprised. The major, this indigenous rebel woman, has taken their city. Hundreds of armed indigenous people surround the old city. An armed woman commands them . . .

Minutes later the rebels will take the city of Las Margaritas; hours later the government forces that defend Ocosingo, Altamirano, and Chanal will surrender. Huixtan and Oxchuc are taken by a rebel column that heads toward the principal jail of San Cristobal. Now seven cities are in insurgent hands, following the seven words said by the major.

The war for the word has begun.

Elsewhere, other indigenous and rebellious women remake that piece of history that had been given them and that, until that January 1, had been carried in silence. They too have no name or face.

Irma. Capitán Insurgente Irma, a Chol woman, leads one of the guerrilla columns that takes the plaza at Ocosingo that January 1, 1994. From one of the edges of the central square, together with the soldiers under her command, she attacks the garrison inside the Municipal Palace until they surrender. Then Irma undoes her braid and her hair falls to her waist as though to say, "Here I am, free and new." Capitán Irma's hair shines, and continues to shine, even as the night falls over Ocosingo in rebel hands.

Laura. Capitán Insurgente Laura is a Tzotzil woman. Fierce in battle and fiercely committed to learning and teaching, Laura becomes the captain of a unit composed only of men, all novices. With the same patience as the mountain that has watched her grow, Laura teaches and gives orders. When the men under her command have doubts, she sets an example. No one carries as much or walks as far as she does. After the attack on Ocosingo, she orders the retreat of her unit. It is orderly and complete. This woman with light skin says little or nothing, but she carries in her hands a carbine that she has taken from a policeman, he who only saw someone to humiliate or rape as he gazed upon her, an indigenous woman. After surrendering, the policeman ran away in his shorts, the same one who until that day believed that women were only useful when pregnant or in the kitchen . . .

Elisa. Capitán Insurgente Elisa still carries mortar fragments that are planted forever in her body as a war trophy. She takes command of her column when the rebel line is broken and a circle of fire fills the Ocosingo market with blood. Capitán Benito has been injured and has lost his eye. Before losing consciousness, he explains: "I've had it, Capitán Elisa is in command." Capitán Elisa is already wounded when she manages to take a handful of soldiers out of the market. When Capitán Elisa, indigenous Tzeltal, gives orders, it is a soft murmur . . . but everyone obeys.

Silvia. Capitán Insurgente Silvia was trapped for ten days in the rathole that Ocosingo became after January 2. Dressed as a civilian, she scuttled along the streets of a city filled with federal soldiers, tanks, and cannons. Stopped at a military checkpoint, she is let through almost immediately. "It isn't possible that such a young and fragile woman could be a rebel," say the soldiers as they watch her pass. When she rejoins her unit in the mountains, the indigenous Chol rebel woman appears sad. Carefully, I ask her the reason why her laughter is dampened. "Over there in Ocosingo," she answers me, lowering her eyes, "I left my backpack, and with it all the music cassettes I had collected. Now we have nothing." Silence and her loss lie in her hands. I say nothing. I add my own regrets to hers, and I see that in war each loses what he or she most loves.

Maribel. Capitán Insurgente Maribel takes the radio station in Las Margaritas when her unit assaults the municipality on January 1, 1994. For nine years she has lived in the mountains so she could sit in front of that microphone and say, "We are the product of five hundred years of struggle; first we fought against slavery . . . "[1] The transmission fails due to technical difficulties. Maribel takes another position and covers the back of the unit that advances toward Comitan. Days later she will serve as guard for a prisoner of war, General Absalón Castellanos Domínguez.[2] Maribel is Tzeltal and was not yet fifteen years old when she came to the mountains of the Mexican Southeast. "The toughest moment in those nine years was when I had to climb the first hill, called 'the hill from hell.' After that, everything else was easy," said the insurgent official. When General Castellanos Domínguez is released, Capitán Maribel is the first rebel to have contact with the government. Extending his hand to her, Commissioner

Manuel Camacho Solís asks her age. "Five hundred and two," replies Maribel, who is as old as the rebellion . . .

Isidora. Capitán Insurgente Isidora, on that first day of January, a buck private, goes into Ocosingo. After spending hours rescuing her unit made up entirely of men, forty of whom were wounded, she leaves Ocosingo in flames, mortar fragments in her arms and legs. When Isidora arrives at the nursing unit and hands over the wounded, she asks for a bit of water and gets up again. "Where are you going?" they ask her as they try to treat the bleeding wounds that paint her face and redden her uniform. "To get the others," answers Isidora as she reloads her gun. They try to stop her and cannot. Buck Private Isidora says she must return to Ocosingo to rescue their *compañeros* from the dirge of mortars and grenades. They have to take her prisoner to stop her. "The only good thing about this punishment is that, at least, I can't be demoted," says Isidora, and she waits in a room that to her appears to be a jail. Months later, given a star and a promotion to infantry official, Isidora, Tzeltal and Zapatista, looks first at the star and then at her commander and asks, "Why?" As though she were being scolded, she does not wait for an answer . . .

Amalia. First lieutenant in the hospital unit. Amalia has the quickest laughter in the Mexican Southeast. When she finds Capitán Benito unconscious, lying in a pool of blood, she drags him to safety. She carries him on her back and takes him past the circle of death that surrounds the market. When someone mentions surrender, Amalia, honoring the Chol blood that runs through her veins, gets angry and begins to argue. Notwithstanding the ruthless explosions and the flying bullets, everyone listens. No one surrenders.

Elena. Lieutenant in the hospital unit. When Lieutenant Elena joined the Zapatistas, she was illiterate. There she learned to read, to write, and to administer medicine. Dealing with diarrhea and giving vaccines, she goes on to care for the wounded in a small hospital, which is also a home, a warehouse, and a pharmacy. With difficulty, she extracts from the Zapatistas' bodies mortar fragments. "Some I can take out, some I can't," says Elenita, an insurgent Chol, as though she were speaking of memories and not of pieces of lead.

In San Cristobal, that morning of January 1, 1994, she communicates with the great white nose: "Someone just came here asking questions, but I don't understand the language, I think it's English. I don't know if he's a photographer, but he has a camera."

"I'll be there soon," answers the nose as he rearranges the ski mask. Putting the weapons that have been taken from the police station into a vehicle, he travels to the center of the city. They take the weapons out and distribute them among the indigenous who are guarding the Municipal Palace. The foreigner is a tourist who asks if he may leave the city. "No," answers the ski mask with the oversize nose. "It's better that you return to your hotel. We don't know what will happen." The tourist leaves after asking permission to film with his video camera. Meanwhile the morning advances, and with the curious arrive the journalists and questions. The nose responds and explains to the locals, tourists, and journalists. The major is behind him. The ski mask talks and makes jokes. A woman who is armed watches his back.

A journalist, from behind a television camera, asks, "And who are you?"

"Who am I?" repeats the ski mask hesitantly, fighting off sleep after a long night.

"Yes," insists the journalist. "Are you 'Commander Tiger' or 'Commander Lion'?"

"No," responds the ski mask, rubbing his eyes, which are now filled with boredom.

"So, what's your name?" asks the journalist as he thrusts his camera and microphone forward. The big-nosed ski mask answers, "Marcos. Subcomandante Marcos."

Overhead, Pilatus planes begin to circle.

From that moment on, the impeccable military action of the taking of San Cristobal is blurred, and with it the fact that it was a woman—a rebel indigenous woman—who commanded the entire operation is erased. The participation of other rebel women in the actions of January 1, and during the ten-year-long road since the birth of the Zapatistas, become secondary. The faces covered with ski masks become even more anonymous when the lights focus on Marcos. The major says nothing, and she continues to watch the back of that enormous nose, which now has a name for the rest of the world. No one asks her name.

At dawn on January 2, 1994, that same woman directs the retreat from San Cristobal and the return to the mountains. Fifty days later, she comes back to San Cristobal as part of the escort that safeguards the delegates of the CCRI-CG of the Zapatista National Liberation Army to the Dialogues for Peace at the Cathedral. Some women journalists interview her and ask her name. "Ana Maria, Mayor Insurgente Ana María," she answers with her dark gaze. She leaves the cathedral and disappears for the rest of the year, 1994. Like her other *compañeras*, she must wait, she must be silent . . .

In December 1994, ten years after becoming a soldier, Ana María receives the order to prepare to break out of the military blockade established by government forces around the Lacandon jungle. At dawn on December 19, the Zapatistas take positions in thirty-eight municipalities. Ana María leads the action in the municipalities of the Altos of Chiapas. Twelve women officers are with her: Monica, Isabela, Yuri, Patricia, Juana, Ofelia, Celina, María, Gabriela, Alicia, Zenaida, and María Luisa. Ana María herself takes the municipality of Bochil.

After the Zapatista deployment, the high command of the federal army sur-rounds their ruptured blockade with silence, and, represented by the mass media, declares it is pure propaganda on the part of the EZLN. The *federales'* pride is deeply wounded: the Zapatistas have broken the blockade and, adding insult to injury, various municipalities have been taken by a unit headed by a woman. Much money is spent to keep this unacceptable event from the people. Due to the involuntary actions of her armed *compañeros*, and the deliberate actions of the government, Ana María and the Zapatista women at her side are ignored and kept invisible.

II. Today . . .

I HAVE ALMOST finished writing this when someone arrives . . .

Doña Juanita. After Old Don Antonio[3] dies, Doña Juanita allows her life to slow down to the gentle pace she uses when preparing coffee. Physically strong, Doña Juanita has announced she will die. "Don't be silly, grandmother," I say, refusing to meet her eyes. "Look, you," she answers. "If we must die in order to live, noth-ing will keep me from dying, much less a young brat like yourself," says and scolds Doña Juanita, Old Don Antonio's woman, a rebel woman all her life, and apparently, a rebel even in response to her death.

Meanwhile, on the other side of the blockade, she appears.

She. Has no military rank, no uniform, no weapon. Only she knows she is a Zapatista. Much like the Zapatistas, she has no face or name. She struggles for democracy, liberty, and justice, just like the Zapatistas. She is part of what the EZLN calls "civil society"—a people without a political party, who do not belong to "political society," made up of leaders of political parties. Rather, she is a part of that amorphous yet solid part of society that says, day after day, "Enough is enough!"

At first she is surprised at her own words. But over time, through the strength of repeating them, and above all living them, she stops being afraid of these words, stops being afraid of herself. She is now a Zapatista; she has joined her destiny with the new delirium of the Zapatista National Liberation Army, which so terrorizes political parties and Power's intellectuals. She has already fought against everyone—against her husband, her lover, her boyfriend, her children, her friend, her brother, her father, her grandfather. "You are insane," they say. She leaves a great deal behind. What she renounces, if one is talking about size, is much greater than what the empty-handed rebels leave behind. Her everything, her world, demands she forget "those crazy Zapatistas," while conformity calls her to sit down in the comfortable indifference that lives and worries only about itself. She leaves everything behind. She says nothing. Early one dawn she sharpens the tender point of hope and begins to emulate many times in one day, at least 364 times a year, the January 1 of her sister Zapatistas.

She smiles. Once she merely admired the Zapatistas, but no longer. Her admiration ended the moment she understood that they are a mirror of her rebellion, of her hope.

She discovers that she is born on January 1, 1994. From then on she feels that her life—and what was always said to be a dream and a utopia—might actually be a truth.

In silence and without pay, side by side with other men and women, she begins to knit that complex dream that some call hope: "Everything for everyone, nothing for ourselves."

She meets March 8 with her face erased, and her name hidden. With her come thousands of women. More and more arrive. Dozens, hundreds, thousands, millions of women who remember all over the world that there is much to be done and remember that there is still much to fight for. It appears that dignity is contagious, and it is the women who are more likely to become infected with this uncomfortable ill . . .

This March 8 is a good time to remember and to give their rightful place to the insurgent Zapatistas, to the women who are armed and unarmed.

To remember the rebels and those uncomfortable Mexican women now bent over knitting that history which, without them, is nothing more than a badly made fable.

III. Tomorrow . . .

IF THERE IS to be one, it will be made with the women, and above all, by them . . .

From the mountains of the Mexican Southeast
SUBCOMANDANTE INSURGENTE MARCOS

NOTES

1.   Opening lines of the Zapatista Declaration of War.

2.   General Absalón Castellanos Domínguez, governor of Chiapas from 1982 to 1988, was believed to be responsible for many deaths in the state. He was kidnapped by the Zapatistas in an effort to send a message out to the Mexican government and the people.

3.   Old Don Antonio was a Mayan shaman who befriended Marcos. Their decade-long relationship is the inspiration for the Old Don Antonio tales, in which Marcos passes on many of the creation myths that are written in the *Popol Vuh*, a sacred Mayan text.

2

War!

First Declaration of the Lacandon Jungle

JANUARY 2, 1994

To the people of Mexico

Mexican brothers and sisters:

WE ARE A PRODUCT of five hundred years of struggle: first, led by insurgents against slavery during the War of Independence with Spain; then to avoid being absorbed by North American imperialism; then to proclaim our constitution and expel the French empire from our soil; later when the people rebelled against Porfirio Diaz's dictatorship, which denied us the just application of the reform laws, and leaders like Villa and Zapata[1] emerged, poor men just like us who have been denied the most elemental preparation so they can use us as cannon fodder and pillage the wealth of our country. They don't care that we have nothing, absolutely nothing, not even a roof over our heads, no land, no work, no health care, no food or education, not the right to freely and democratically elect our political representatives, nor independence from foreigners. There is no peace or justice for ourselves and our children.

But today we say: ENOUGH IS ENOUGH!

We are the inheritors of the true builders of our nation. We are millions, the dispossessed who call upon our brothers and sisters to join this struggle as the only path, so that we will not die of hunger due to the insatiable ambition of a seventy-year dictatorship led by a clique of traitors who represent the most conservative and sellout groups. They are the same ones that opposed Hidalgo and Morelos,[2] the same ones that betrayed Vicente Guerrero,[3] the same ones that sold half our country to the foreign invader, the same ones that imported a European prince to rule our country, the same ones that formed the "scientific" Porfirista dictatorship,[4] the same ones that opposed the Petroleum Expropriation,[5] the same ones that massacred the railroad workers in 1958 and the students in 1968, the same ones that today take everything from us, absolutely everything.

To prevent the continuation of the above and as our last hope, after having tried to utilize all legal means based on our Magna Carta, we go to our constitution, to apply Article 39, which says:

13

National Sovereignty essentially and originally resides in the people. All political power emanates from the people and its purpose is to help the people. The people have, at all times, the inalienable right to alter or modify their form of government.

Therefore, according to our Constitution, we declare the following to the Mexican federal army, the pillar of the Mexican dictatorship from which we suffer, monopolized by a one-party system and led by Carlos Salinas de Gortari, the maximum and illegitimate federal executive that today holds power.

According to this Declaration of War, we ask that other powers of the nation advocate to restore the legitimacy and the stability of the nation by overthrowing the dictator.

We also ask that international organizations and the International Red Cross watch over and regulate our battles, so that our efforts are carried out while still protecting our civilian population. We declare, now and always, that we are subject to the Geneva Accord, forming the EZLN as the fighting arm of our struggle for liberation. We have the Mexican people on our side, we have the nation and the beloved tricolored flag, highly respected by our insurgent fighters; our uniforms are black and red, symbol of our working people on strike; and we will always carry our flag, emblazoned with the letters "EZLN," the Zapatista National Liberation Army, into combat.

From the outset, we reject all intentions to disgrace our just cause, accusing us of being drug traffickers, drug guerrillas, thieves, or other names that might be used by our enemies. Our struggle adheres to the Constitution and is inspirited by its call for justice and equality.

Therefore, according to this Declaration of War, we give our military forces, the EZLN, the following orders:

First: Advance to the capital of the country, overcoming the Mexican federal army, protecting in our advance the civilian population, and permitting the people liberated to elect, freely and democratically, their own administrative authorities.

Second: Respect the lives of our prisoners and turn over all wounded to the International Red Cross.

Third: Initiate summary judgments against all soldiers of the Mexican federal army and the political police who have received training or have been paid by foreigners—they are accused of being traitors to our country—and against all those who have repressed and mistreated the civil population, or robbed from or attempted crimes against the good of the people.

Fourth: Form new troops with all those Mexicans who show interest in joining our struggle, including those who, being enemy soldiers, turn themselves in without having fought against us, and promise to take orders from the General Command of the Zapatista National Liberation Army.

Fifth: We ask for the unconditional surrender of the enemy's headquarters, before we begin to combat, in order to avoid any loss of lives.

Sixth: Suspend the robbery of our natural resources in the areas controlled by the EZLN.

To the people of Mexico:
We—men and women, whole and free—are conscious that the war that we have declared is a last—but just—resort. For many years, the dictators have been waging an undeclared genocidal war against our people. Therefore, we ask for your decided participation to support this plan by the Mexican people who struggle for work, land, housing, food, health care, education, independence, freedom, democracy, justice, and peace. We declare that we will not stop fighting until the basic demands of our people have been met, by forming a government for our country that is free and democratic.

JOIN THE INSURGENT FORCES OF THE ZAPATISTA NATIONAL LIBERATION ARMY.

GENERAL COMMAND OF THE EZLN
1993

NOTES

1. Pancho Villa and Emiliano Zapata were two rebel leaders during the Mexican Revolution in 1911. Pancho Villa was a volatile, controversial man capable of great deeds and of much cruelty. With his men, he helped secure the northern part of Mexico for the revolution against President Porfirio Diaz. Emiliano Zapata, a charismatic peasant leader, brought the revolution up from the south of the country and marched into Mexico City to take over the presidency of Francisco Madero. Zapata was instrumental in the creation of the Constitution of 1917, in which indigenous lands are declared autonomous, and which set up the parameters for agrarian reform in Mexico.

2. Miguel Hidalgo y Costilla (1753–1811), a priest in the Roman Catholic Church who produced illegitimate children in defiance of his clerical vows, is considered the father of his country. He never took his priestly vows too seriously, reading the anticlerical works of the French encyclopedic philosophers and apparently regarding the Church as a sort of sinecure that would provide him with a regular income. Hidalgo's impulse toward freedom for his people was also fed by a strong egalitarian instinct, which resulted in Hidalgo's famed grito ("shout") from his pulpit at 11 p.m. of September 15, 1810. Though the grito is hailed today as a declaration of independence from Spain, in reality it was a declaration of defiance against Joseph Bonaparte and the Spaniards resident in Mexico as well as allegiance to the very undeserving Ferdinand VII. With Ignacio Allende, an intellectual comrade, Hidalgo gathered a force of 80,000 to march against royalist forces. They were ultimately defeated, but when they heard of a new rebellion in San Antonio de Bejar (today San Antonio, Texas), they moved north to join it. On March 21, in

the mountains of Coahuila, they were ambushed by a traitor and turned over to the Spanish authorities. Because he was a priest, albeit an excommunicated one, Hidalgo was turned over to the bishop of Durango for an official defrocking. On July 30, 1811, he was shot in Chihuahua.

Father Francisco Morelos offered his services as a priest to Hidalgo's army. Hidalgo refused, instead instructing Morelos to go back to the south and lead the rebellion on the Pacific Coast. At one point, in 1813, his forces controlled Acapulco and most of Southwest Mexico. They even surrounded and cut off Mexico City from reinforcements and supplies. However, Morelos realized that he could not defeat the royalist army of New Spain in direct combat. He altered his strategy, and turned his attention to instructing his followers in the art of guerrilla warfare. His followers became masters of small group engagements. In 1813 Morelos helped to create a Revolutionary Congress, whose purpose was to draft a constitution and to design laws for the new country; he was a signatory of the new constitution. As the conflict wore on in New Spain, the government's armies became vicious, and Morelos instructed his followers to do the same to all whites and mixed bloods. Thus what began as a noble cause, concerned with the civil rights of all people, degenerated into a vicious killing circle. Morelos was finally captured on November 5, 1815, at Tesmalaca. He was sentenced to death, and executed on December 22, 1815, at San Cristobal Ecatepec, a village just to the north of Guadalupe.

3. Vicente Guerrero (1782–1831), Mexican revolutionary leader, won guerrilla victories over Spanish forces. Guerrero served briefly (1829) as president, but he was forced to retreat and was finally captured and shot.

4. "Porfirista dictatorship" refers to Porfirio Díaz, absolute ruler of Mexico for thirty-five years, serving as president from 1876 to 1880 and from 1884 to 1911. (In the four-year interim, the post of president was held by a Díaz puppet named Manuel González.) An indigenous Oaxacan, Díaz was born in 1830 to José de la Cruz Díaz and Petrona Mori. He came to power as a champion of liberal principles—more municipal democracy, limited terms, and so on—but once he assumed the presidency, it soon became clear that his main concerns were internal stability and foreign investment. Anxious to create a climate of confidence for investors, Díaz addressed the problem of internal security with a simple solution: co-opting the most notorious bandits and putting them into the dreaded Rurales ("Rural Police"), a paramilitary force that was far better trained and paid than the unwilling conscripts dragooned into the army. The bandit problem disappeared overnight, and as time went by, the Rurales would also serve as an effective force against peasant revolts. Having brutally achieved domestic tranquility, Díaz opened the country up to foreign capital, both U.S. and European.

5. In 1938 Lázaro Cárdenas, the most left-wing president in Mexican history, became a national hero by expropriating the big foreign oil companies—such as William Doheny's Mexican Petroleum Company and the Waters Pierce Company, with links to Standard Oil—that had dominated in the petroleum-producing regions of the Gulf Coast of Mexico. Even though such political enemies as the church and business conservatives applauded this nationalistic gesture, Mexico faced a grim two-year period when the United States, Great Britain, and Holland agreed on a boycott of Mexican oil. Mexico's oil industry was saved only by World War II; disturbed because Cárdenas was selling petroleum to Hitler—which he had to do to keep Mexico from drowning in its own oil—the boycotting powers lifted the ban.

3

Dying In Order to Live

JANUARY 6, 1994

Here we are, the dead of all times, dying once again, but now in order to live.

DURING THESE PAST TEN years more than 150,000 indigenous have died of curable diseases. The federal, state, and municipal governments and their economic and social programs do not take into account any real solution to our problems; they limit themselves to giving us charity every time elections roll around. Charity resolves nothing but for the moment, and again death visits our homes. That is why we think no, no more; enough dying this useless death; it is better to fight for change. If we die now, it will not be with shame but with dignity, like our ancestors. We are ready to die, 150,000 more if necessary, so that our people awaken from this dream of deceit that holds us hostage.

SUBCOMANDANTE INSURGENTE MARCOS

In Our Dreams We Have Seen Another World

MARCH 1, 1994

To the Mexican people
To the people and governments of the world:

IN OUR DREAMS we have seen another world, an honest world, a world decidedly more fair than the one in which we now live. We saw that in this world there was no need for armies; peace, justice and liberty were so common that no one talked about them as far-off concepts, but as things such as bread, birds, air, water, like book and voice. This is how the good things were named in this world. And in this world there was reason and goodwill in the government, and the leaders were clear-thinking people; they ruled by obeying. This world was not a dream from the past, it was not something that came to us from our ancestors. It came from ahead, from the next step we were going to take. And so we started to move forward to attain this dream, make it come and sit down at our tables, light our homes, grow in our cornfields, fill the hearts of our children, wipe our sweat, heal our history. And it was for all. This is what we want. Nothing more, nothing less.

Now we follow our path toward our true heart to ask it what we must do. We will return to our mountains to speak in our own tongue and in our own time.

Thank you to the brothers and sisters who looked after us all these days. May your footsteps follow our path. Good-bye.

Liberty!
Justice!
Democracy!

Respectfully,
SUBCOMANDANTE MARCOS
from the mountains of the Mexican Southeast

Votán-Zapata or Five Hundred Years of History

APRIL 10, 1994

ON THE ANNIVERSARY OF ZAPATA'S ASSASSINATION.

Brothers and sisters:
The Clandestine Indigenous Revolutionary Committee–General Command of the
Zapatista National Liberation Army speaks to you to give you its words.

AT THIS MOMENT, many thousands of men, women, children, and elders—all indigenous Mexican—find themselves gathered in hundreds of *ejidos*,[1] ranches, localities, and communities in Mexico's countryside. Our hands also reach into the concrete heart of the cities. We are brought together with all those people before the tricolored flag where the eagle devours the serpent,[2] united by our common misery, by the collective oblivion into which we were cast 501 years ago, by the useless death we endure, by our being faceless, with our name ripped from us, by our having bet our lives and deaths for someone else's future. We are united by one common hope before that flag: to change, once and for all, the ground and sky that today oppress it. To do this, we, the ones without a face and name who call ourselves the "professionals of hope," the most mortal of all, the "transgressors of injustice," we who are the mountain, we of the nocturnal walk who have no voice inside the palaces, we the foreigners in our own land, the ones completely dead, history's dispossessed, the ones without a homeland and a tomorrow, the ones with a tender fury, the ones of the unmuffled truth, the ones of the long night of scorn, the true men and women . . . the smallest of people . . . the most dignified . . . the last . . . the best. We must open again the door to the brother heart so that it can receive our word.

We must speak the truth, we must put the heart in our hands. Brothers and sisters, we want you to know who is behind us, who guides us, who walks in our shoes, who rules our heart, who rides our words, who lives in our deaths.

Brothers and sisters, we want you to know the truth. And it is like this:

From the first hour in this long night of our death, our most distant grandfathers say there was someone who gathered up our pain and our oblivion. There was a man who, walking his word from afar to our mountains, came and spoke with the tongue of the true men and women. His walk was and was not from these lands.

From the mouths of our dead, from the mouths of the most knowing of our ancient ancestors, his word walked from him to our heart. There was and is, brothers and sisters, he who—being and not being seed from these lands— arrived to the mountain, dying in order to live again, who lived with his heart dying from his walk, a foreigner when he first arrived to the mountain with its nocturnal roof. He was and is a man. His tender word halts and walks in our pain. He is and is not in these lands: Votán Zapata, guardian and heart of the people.[3]

Votán Zapata, light that came from afar and was born here from our land. Votán Zapata, named again forever a man of our people. Votán Zapata, a timid fire who lived our death 501 years. Votán Zapata, the name that changes, the man without a face, the tender light that watches over us. Death was always with us, and with death hope died. Death arrived with Votán Zapata. The name without a name, Votán Zapata looked in Miguel, walked in José María, was Vicente, was named in Benito, flew in a bird, rode in Emiliano, shouted in Francisco, visited Pedro.[4] We lived dying, named without a name in our own lands. Votán Zapata arrived in our lands. Speaking, his word fell into our mouth. He arrived and is here. Votán Zapata, guardian and heart of the people.

He is and is not everything in us . . . He is walking . . . Votán Zapata, guardian and heart of the people. Keeper of the night . . . Master of the mountain . . . us . . . Votán, guardian and heart of the people. He is one and all. No one and all. Being, he is here. Votán Zapata, guardian and heart of the people.

That is the truth, brothers and sisters. You should know it, he will not die again in our life, in our death he lives already and forever. Votán, guardian and heart of the people. Without a name he is named, the faceless face, all and no one, one and all, alive in death. Votán, guardian and heart of the people. *Tapacamino* bird,[5] always before us, walking behind us. Votán, guardian and heart of the people.

He took a name in our being nameless, he took a face in our being faceless, he is sky in the mountain. Votán, guardian and heart of the people. And in our nameless, faceless path, he took a name in us: the Zapatista National Liberation Army.

With this new name we name the nameless. With this flag covering our face, we have a new face, all of us. With this name we name the unnameable: Votán Zapata, guardian and heart of the people.

The Zapatista National Liberation Army. Arming a tender fury. A nameless name. An unjust peace made war. A death that is born. An anguish made hope. A pain that smiles. A silent shout. A personal present for a foreign future. Everything for everyone, nothing for us. We, the nameless, the always dead. We, the Zapatista National Liberation Army. We, the red-and-black flag beneath the tricolored eagle. We, the red star, at last in our skies, never alone, but one more star, yes, the smallest one. We, only a gaze and a voice. We, the Zapatista National Liberation Army. We, Votán, guardian and heart of the people.

It is the truth, brothers and sisters. We come from there. We are going there. Being here we arrive. Dying death we live. Votán Zapata, father and mother, brother and sister, son and daughter, old and young, we are living . . .

Receive our truth in your dancing heart. Zapata lives, also and for always in these lands.

HEALTH TO YOU, MEXICAN BROTHERS AND SISTERS!

HEALTH TO YOU, CAMPESINOS OF THIS HOMELAND!

HEALTH TO YOU, THE INDIGENOUS OF ALL THE LANDS!

HEALTH TO YOU, ZAPATISTA FIGHTERS!

ZAPATA, IN BEING ARRIVES!

IN DEATH HE LIVES!

VIVA ZAPATA!

NOTES

1. The autonomous indigenous lands guaranteed by the Mexican Constitution of 1917.

2. The Mexican flag's imagery illustrates evil, represented by the serpent, being defeated by the Mexican state, represented by the eagle.

3. For the Mayan Tzeltales, Votán represents the third day in the Tzeltal calendar, and corresponds to "the heart of the people." He is also the first man sent by God to distribute land among the indigenous. Zapata refers to Emiliano Zapata, who helped ensure that the indigenous territories be autonomous, and beyond the reach of the Mexican government.

4. Miguel Hidalgo, José Maria Morelos, Vicente Guerrero, Benito Juarez, Emiliano Zapata, Francisco Villa, and Pedro Páramo are revolutionary heroes in Mexico, "inhabited" by the spirit of Votán Zapata.

5. Tapacamino bird, "the bird that hides the path."

6

A Storm and a Prophecy

Chiapas: The Southeast in Two Winds

WRITTEN IN AUGUST 1992,
THIS ESSAY BY MARCOS WAS NOT RELEASED PUBLICLY UNTIL JANUARY 27, 1994.

The First Wind: The One from Above

ONE

Which narrates how the supreme government, touched by the poverty of the indigenous peoples of Chiapas, lavished the area with hotels, prisons, barracks, and a military airport. It also tells how the beast feeds on the blood of the people, as well as other miserable and unfortunate happenings.

SUPPOSE THAT YOU live in the north, center, or west of this country. Suppose that you heed the old Department of Tourism slogan: "Get to know Mexico first." Suppose that you decide to visit the southeast of your country and that in the southeast you choose to visit the state of Chiapas. Suppose that you drive there (getting there by airplane is not only expensive but unlikely, a mere fantasy: there are only two "civilian" airports and one military one). Suppose that you take the Transístmica Highway. Suppose that you pay no attention to the army barracks located at Matías Romero and that you continue on to Ventosa. Suppose that you don't notice the government's immigration checkpoint near there (the checkpoint makes you think that you are leaving one country and entering another). Suppose that you decide to take a left and head toward Chiapas. Several kilometers farther on you will leave the state of Oaxaca, and you will see a big sign that reads: "WELCOME TO CHIAPAS." Have you found it?

Good, suppose you have. You have now entered by one of the three existing roads into Chiapas: the road into the northern part of the state, the road along the Pacific coast, and the road by which you entered are the three ways to get to this southeastern corner of the country by land. But the state's natural wealth doesn't leave just by way of these three roads. Chiapas loses blood through many veins: through oil and gas ducts, electric lines, railways; through bank accounts, trucks, vans, boats, and planes; through clandestine paths, gaps, and forest trails. This land continues to pay tribute to the imperialists: petroleum, electricity, cattle, money, coffee, banana, honey, corn, cacao, tobacco, sugar, soy, melon, sorghum, mamey, mango, tamarind, avocado, and Chiapaneco blood all flow as a result of the thousand teeth sunk into the throat of the Mexican Southeast. These raw materials, thousands of millions of tons of them, flow to Mexican ports, railroads, air and truck transportation centers. From there they are sent to different parts of the world—the United States, Canada, Holland, Germany, Italy, Japan—but all to fulfill one same destiny: to feed imperialism. Since the beginning, the fee that capitalism imposes on the southeastern part of this country makes Chiapas ooze blood and mud.

A handful of businesses, one of which is the Mexican state, take all the wealth out of Chiapas and in exchange leave behind their mortal and pestilent mark: in 1989 these businesses took 1,222,669,000,000 pesos from Chiapas and only left behind 616,340,000,000 pesos worth of credit and public works.[1] More than 600,000,000,000 pesos went to the belly of the beast.

In Chiapas, Pemex[2] has eighty-six teeth sunk into the townships of Estación Juárez, Reforma, Ostuacán, Pichucalco, and Ocosingo. Every day they suck out 92,000 barrels of petroleum and 517,000,000,000 cubic feet of gas. They take away the petroleum and gas and, in exchange, leave behind the mark of capitalism: ecological destruction, agricultural plunder, hyperinflation, alcoholism, prostitution, and poverty. The beast is still not satisfied and has extended its tentacles to the Lacandon Jungle: eight petroleum deposits are under exploration. The paths are made with machetes by the same campesinos who are left without land by the insatiable beast. The trees fall and dynamite explodes on land where campesinos are not allowed to cut down trees to cultivate. Every tree that is cut down costs them a fine that is ten times the minimum wage, and a jail sentence. The poor cannot cut down trees, but the petroleum beast can, a beast that every day fells more and more into foreign hands. The campesinos cut them down to survive, the beast cuts them down to plunder.

Chiapas also bleeds coffee. Thirty-five percent of the coffee produced in Mexico comes from this area. The industry employs 87,000 people. Forty-seven percent of the coffee is for national consumption, and 53 percent is exported abroad, mainly to the United States and Europe. More than 100,000 tons of coffee are taken from this state to fatten the beast's bank accounts: in 1988 a kilo of pergamino coffee was sold abroad for 8,000 pesos. The Chiapaneco producers were paid 2,500 pesos or less.

After coffee, the second most important plunder is beef. Three million head of cattle wait for middlemen and a small group of businessmen to take them away to fill refrigerators in Arriaga, Villahermosa, and Mexico City. The cattle are sold for 400 pesos per kilo by the poor farmers and resold by the middlemen and businessmen for up to ten times the price they paid for them.

The tribute that capitalism demands from Chiapas has no historical parallel. Fifty-five percent of national hydroelectric energy comes from this state, along with 20 percent of Mexico's total electricity. However, only a third of the homes in Chiapas have electricity. Where do the 12,907 kilowatts produced annually by hydroelectric plants in Chiapas go?

In spite of the current trend toward ecological awareness, the plunder of wood continues in Chiapas' forests. Between 1981 and 1989, 2,444,777 cubic meters of precious woods, conifers, and tropical trees were taken from Chiapas to Mexico City, Puebla, Veracruz, and Quintana Roo. In 1988, wood exports brought a revenue of 23,900,000,000 pesos, 6,000 percent more than in 1980.

The honey that is produced in 79,000 beehives in Chiapas goes entirely to the United States and European markets. The 2,756 tons of honey produced annually in the Chiapaneco countryside is converted into dollars that the people of Chiapas never see.

Of the corn produced in Chiapas, more than half goes to the domestic market. Chiapas is one of the largest corn producers in the country. Sorghum grown in Chiapas goes to Tabasco. Ninety percent of the tamarind goes to Mexico City and other states. Two-thirds of the avocados and all of the mameys are sold outside of the state. Sixty-nine percent of the cacao goes to the national market, and 31 percent is exported to the United States, Holland, Japan, and Italy. The majority of the bananas produced are exported.

What does the beast leave behind in exchange for all it takes away?

Chiapas has a total area of 75,634.4 square kilometers, some 7.5 million hectares. It is the eighth largest state in Mexico and is divided into 111 townships. For the purposes of looting, it is organized into nine economic regions. Forty percent of the nation's plant varieties, 36 percent of its mammal species, 34 percent of its reptiles and amphibians, 66 percent of its bird species, 20 percent of its freshwater fish, and 80 percent of its butterfly species are found in Chiapas. Seven percent of the total national rainfall falls in Chiapas. But its greatest wealth is the 3.5 million people of Chiapas, two-thirds of whom live and die in rural communities. Half of them don't have potable water, and two-thirds have no sewage service. Ninety percent of the rural population pays little or no taxes.

Communication in Chiapas is a grotesque joke for a state that produces petroleum, electricity, coffee, wood, and cattle for the hungry beast. Only two-thirds of the municipal seats have paved-road access. Twelve thousand communities have no other means of transport and communication than mountain trails. Since the days of Porfirio Díaz, the railroad lines have serviced capitalism rather than the people.[3] The railroad line that follows the coast (there are only two lines: the other crosses the northern part of the state) dates back to the turn of the century, and its tonnage is limited by the old bridges that cross the canyons of the Southeast. The only port in Chiapas, Puerto Madero, is just one more way for the beast to extract the state's resources.

And education? It is the worst in the country. At the elementary school level, 72 out of every 100 children don't finish the first grade. More than half of the schools only offer up to a third-grade education, and half of the schools have only one teacher for all the courses offered. There are statistics, although they are kept secret of course, that show that many indigenous children are forced to drop out of school due to their families' need to incorporate them into the system of exploitation. In any indigenous community it is common to see children carrying corn and wood, cooking, or washing clothes during school hours. Of the 16,058 classrooms in 1989, only 96 were in indigenous zones.

And industry? Look, 40 percent of Chiapas' "industry" consists of nixtamal[4] mills, tortillas, and mills to make wood furniture. The large companies (petroleum and electricity), which represent 2 percent of the total industry, belong to the Mexican government (and soon to foreigners). Medium-size industry, 4 percent of the total industry, is made up of sugar refineries and fish, seafood, flour, milk, and coffee processing plants. In the state of Chiapas, 94 percent of the area's industry is micro-industry.

The health conditions of the people of Chiapas are a clear example of the capitalist imprint: 1.5 million people have no medical services at their disposal. There are 0.2 clinics for every 1,000 inhabitants, one-fifth of the national average. There are 0.3 hospital beds for every 1,000 Chiapanecos, one-third the amount in the rest of Mexico. There is one operating room per 100,000 inhabitants, one-half of the amount in the rest of Mexico. There are 0.5 doctors and 0.4 nurses per 1,000 people, one-half of the national average.

Health and nutrition go hand in hand in poverty. Fifty-four percent of the population of Chiapas suffers from malnutrition, and in the highlands and forest this percentage increases to 80 percent. A campesino's average diet consists of coffee, corn, tortillas, and beans.

This is what capitalism leaves as payment for everything that it takes away.

This part of the Mexican territory, which willingly annexed itself to the young independent republic in 1824, became part of the national geography when the petroleum boom reminded the country that there was a Southeast (82 percent of Pemex's petrochemical plants are in the Southeast; in 1990, two-thirds of public investment in the Southeast was in energy). Chiapas' experience of exploitation goes back for centuries. In times past, wood, fruits, animals, and men went to the metropolis through the veins of exploitation, just as they do today. Like the banana republics, but at the peak of neoliberalism and "libertarian revolutions," the Southeast continues to export raw materials, just as it did 500 years ago. It continues to import capitalism's principal product: death and misery.

One million indigenous people live in these lands and share a disorienting nightmare with mestizos and ladinos: their only option, five hundred years after the "Meeting of Two Worlds," is to die of poverty or repression. The programs to improve the conditions of poverty, a small bit of social democracy which the Mexican state throws about and which, under the regime of Salinas de Gortari carries the name Pronasol, are a joke that brings bloody tears to those who live under the rain and sun.

Welcome! You have arrived in the poorest state in the country: Chiapas.

Suppose that you drive on to Ocosocoatla and from there down to Tuxtla Gutiérrez, the state capital. You don't stay long. Tuxtla Gutiérrez is only a large warehouse that stores products from other parts of the state. Here you find some of the wealth that will be sent to whatever destinations the capitalists decide. You don't stay long; you have just barely touched the lips of the wild beast's bloody jaws. You go on to Chiapas de Corzo without noticing the Nestle's factory that is there, and you begin to climb up into the mountains. What do you see? One thing is certain; you have entered another world, an indigenous world. Another world, but the same as that in which millions of people in the rest of the country live.

Three hundred thousand Tzotziles, 120,000 Choles, 90,000 Zoques, and 70,000 Tojolabales inhabit this indigenous world. The supreme government recognizes that "only" half of these 1,000,000 indigenous people are illiterate.

Continue along the mountain road, and you arrive in the region known as the Chiapas highlands. Here, more than 500 years ago, indigenous people were the majority, masters and owners of land and water. Now they are only the majority in population and in poverty. Drive on until you reach San Cristobal de las Casas, which 100 years ago was the state capital (disagreements among the bourgeoisie robbed it of the dubious honor of being the capital of the poorest state in Mexico). No, don't linger. If Tuxtla Gutiérrez is a large warehouse, San Cristobal is a large market. From many different routes the Tzotziles, Tzeltales, Choles, Tojolabales, and Zoques bring the indigenous tribute to capitalism. Each brings something different: wood, coffee, cloth, handicrafts, fruits, vegetables, corn. Everyone brings something: sickness, ignorance, jeers, and death. This is the poorest region of the poorest state in the country. Welcome to San Cristobal de las Casas, a "colonial city," according to the history books, although the majority of the population is indigenous. Welcome to Pronasol's huge market. Here you can buy or sell anything except indigenous dignity. Here everything is expensive except death. But don't stay too long; continue along the road, the proud result of the tourist infrastructure. In 1988 there were 6,270 hotel rooms, 139 restaurants, and 42 travel agencies in this state. This year, 1,058,098 tourists visited Chiapas and left 250 million pesos in the hands of restaurant and hotel owners.

Have you calculated the numbers? Yes, you're right: there are 7 hotel rooms for every 1,000 tourists, while there are only 0.3 hospital beds per 1,000 Chiapaneco citizens. Leave the calculations behind and drive on, noticing the three police officials in berets jogging along the shoulder of the road. Drive by the Public Security station and continue, passing hotels, restaurants, large stores, and heading toward the exit to Comitan. Leaving San Cristobal behind, you will see the famous San Cristobal caves, surrounded by leafy forest. Do you see the sign? No, you are not mistaken, this natural park is administered by . . . the army! Without leaving your uncertainty behind, drive on . . . Do you see them? Modern buildings, nice homes, paved roads . . . Is it a university? Workers' housing? No, look at the sign next to the cannons closely and read: "General Army Barracks of the 31st Military Zone." With the olive-green image still in your eyes, drive on to the intersection and decide not to go to Comitan so that you will avoid the pain of seeing that, a few meters ahead, on the hill that is called the "Foreigner," North American military personnel are operating and teaching their Mexican counterparts to operate radar. Decide that it is better to go to Ocosingo, since ecology and all that nonsense is very fashionable. Look at the trees, breathe deeply . . . Do you feel better? Yes? Then be sure to keep looking to your left, because if you don't, you will see, seven kilometers ahead, another magnificent construction with the noble symbol of SOLIDARITY on the facade. Don't look. I tell you, look the other way.

You don't notice that this new building is . . . a jail (evil tongues say that this is a benefit of Pronasol; now campesinos won't have to go all the way to Cerro Hueco, the prison in the state capital). No, brother, don't lose heart, the worst is always hidden: excessive poverty discourages tourism. Continue on, down to Huixta'n, up to Oxchuc, look at the beautiful waterfall where the Jatate River, whose waters cross the Lacandon Jungle, begins. Pass by Cuxulja and instead of following the detour to Altamirano, drive on till you reach Ocosingo: "The Door to the Lacandon Jungle."

Good, stay a while. Take a quick tour around the city . . . Principal points of interest? The two large constructions at the entrance to the city are brothels; next door is a jail; the building farther beyond, a church; this other one is a beef-processing plant; that other one, army barracks; over there is the court, the municipal building; and way over there is Pemex. The rest are small piled-up houses that crumble when the huge Pemex trucks and ranch pickup trucks pass by.

What does it look like? A Porfirista-type[5] large landed estate? But that ended seventy-five years ago! No, don't follow the road that goes to San Quintin, in front of the Montes Azules Reserve. Don't go to where the Jatate and Perlas Rivers join, don't go down there, don't walk for three eight-hour days, don't go to San Martin and see that it is a very poor and small community, don't approach that shed that is falling to pieces. What is it? A sometimes church, school, meeting room. Now it is a school. It is 11 A.M. No, don't go closer, don't look in, don't look at the four groups of children riddled with tapeworms and lice, half-naked, don't look at the four young indigenous teachers who work for miserable pay that they have to walk three days, the same three days that you just walked, to collect. Don't notice that the only division between the classrooms is a small hall. Up to what grade do they teach here? Third. No, don't look at the posters, which are the only thing that the government has sent to these children. Don't look at them: they are posters about AIDS prevention.

Better for us to move on; let's return to the paved road. Yes, I know that it is in bad condition. Let's leave Ocosingo, continue to admire the countryside . . . The owners? Yes, ranch owners. What is produced? Cattle, coffee, corn . . . Did you see the National Indigenous Institute? Yes, the one as you leave the city. Did you see those pickup trucks? They are given on credit to indigenous campesinos. They only take unleaded gas because it's better for the environment. There is no unleaded gas in Ocosingo? Well, that's not a big thing. Yes, you are right, the government is worried about the campesinos. Of course evil tongues say that there are guerrillas in these mountains and that the government's financial aid is really to buy indigenous people's loyalty, but these are rumors; surely they are just trying to undermine Pronasol.[6] What? The Citizen's Defense Committee? Oh yes! It consists of a group of "heroic" ranchers, traders, and corrupt union bosses who organize small guards to threaten the people. No, I already told you that the Porfirista large-landed estate was done away with seventy-five years ago. It would be better for us to move on . . . At the next intersection take a left. No, don't go toward Palenque. Let's go to Chilón . . . Pretty, no? Yes.

Yajalon . . . it's very modern, it even has a gas station . . . Look, there's a bank, the municipal building, the courthouse, over there the army . . . It looks like another hacienda? Go ahead and look; you won't see those other large, modern buildings on the outskirts of town, along the road to Tila and Sabanilla, with their big beautiful SOLIDARITY signs, you won't see that they are part of . . . a jail.

Good, we have arrived at the intersection. Now to Ocosingo . . . and Palenque? Are you sure? Okay, let's go. Yes, the countryside is beautiful. Are those ranches? You're correct: they produce cattle, coffee, wood. Look, we're already at Palenque. A quick tour of the city? Okay. Those are hotels, over there restaurants, the municipal building, the courthouse, those are the Army barracks, and over there . . . What? No, I already know what you're going to tell me . . . Don't say it . . . Tired? Okay, we'll stop for a bit. You don't want to see the pyramids? No? Okay.

Xi'Nich? Ah . . . an indigenous march. Yes, it's going to Mexico City. How far? One thousand, one hundred and six kilometers. The results? The government receives their petitions. Yes, that's all. Are you still tired? More? Let's wait . . . To Bonampak? The road is very bad. Okay, let's go. Yes, the panoramic route . . . This is the Federal Military Reserve, that other one belongs to the navy, the one over there belongs to the Department of Government . . . Is it always like this? No, sometimes they top it off with a campesinos' protest march.

Tired? Do you want to go back? Okay. Other places? Different places? In what country? Mexico? You will see the same. The colors will change, the languages, the countryside, the names, but the people, the exploitation, the poverty and death, are the same. Just look closely in any state in the republic. Well, good luck . . . And if you need a tourist guide please be sure to let me know. I'm at your service. Oh! One more thing. It will not always be this way. Another Mexico? No, the same . . . I am talking about something else, about other winds beginning to blow, as if another wind is picking up . . .

TWO

Which tells the story of the governor, an apprentice to the viceroy, and his heroic fight against the progressive clergy and his adventures with the feudal cattle, coffee, and business lords. It also tells other equally fantastic tales.

ONCE UPON A TIME there was a viceroy made of chocolate with a peanut for a nose. The viceroy's apprentice, Governor Patrocinio González Garrido,[7] in the manner of the old monarchs who were put in power by the Spanish crown during the Conquest, has reorganized the geography of Chiapas. The assignment of spaces to the urban and rural categories is a somewhat sophisticated exercise of power, but when directed by Mr. González Garrido's denseness, it has reached exquisite levels of stupidity. The viceroy decided that cities with services and benefits should be for those who already have everything. And he decided, the viceroy that is, that the masses are fine out in the open, exposed to wind and rough weather, and that they only deserve space in the jails, which never cease to be uncomfortable. Because of this, the viceroy decided to construct jails on the outskirts of the cities so that the proximity of the undesirable and delinquent masses would not disturb the rich. Jails and army barracks are the principal works promoted by this governor in Chiapas. His friendship with ranchers and powerful businessmen is a secret to no one. Neither is his animosity for the three dioceses that regulate the state's Catholic life. The Diocese of San Cristobal, headed by Bishop Samuel Ruiz, is a constant menace to González Garrido's reorganizing project. Hoping to modernize the absurd system of exploitation and extraction that prevails in Chiapas, Patrocinio González comes up against the stubbornness of religious and secular figures who support and preach Catholicism's option for the poor.

With the hypocritical applause of Aguirre Franco, the bishop of Tuxtla Gutiérrez, and the mute approval of the bishop of Tapachula, González Garrido sustains and gives new life to the "heroic" conspiracies of ranchers and businessmen against the members of the Diocese of San Cristobal. "Don Samuel's teams," as they are called by some, are not made up of inexperienced believers:

before Patrocinio González Garrido had even dreamed of being state governor, the Diocese of San Cristobal de las Casas preached the right to freedom and justice. For one of the country's most backward bourgeoisie—the agricultural bourgeoisie—this could only mean one thing: rebellion. These rancher and business "patriots" and "believers" know how to prevent rebellion: the existence of privately financed, armed paramilitary groups trained by members of the federal army, public security police, and state law is well known by the campesinos who suffer from their threats, torture, and gunshots.

A few months ago, Father Joel Padrón from the parish of Simojovel was arrested. Accused by the region's ranchers of initiating and taking part in land takeovers, Father Joel was arrested by state authorities and held in the Cerro Hueco jail in the state capital. The mobilization of the members of the Diocese of San Cristobal (those of Tuxtla Gutiérrez and Tapachula were conspicuous by their absence) and a federal compromise succeeded in obtaining the parish priest Padrón's freedom.

While thousands of campesinos marched in Tuxtla Gutiérrez to demand Padrón's freedom, ranchers in Ocosingo sent their paramilitary forces to clear out property-owning campesinos. Four hundred men, armed by the ranchers, destroyed and burned houses, beat indigenous women and murdered a campesino, Juan, by shooting him in the face. After the expulsion, the paramilitary forces—composed mostly of workers from local ranches and small-property owners proud of taking part in raids with the young ranchers—drove along the region's roads in pickup trucks provided by their masters. Ostentatiously displaying their arms, drunk and intoxicated, they shouted, "Ranchers are number one!" and warned everyone that it was only the beginning. Undaunted, municipal authorities in Ocosingo and soldiers stationed in the region looked on passively at the gunmen's triumphant parade.

In Tuxtla Gutiérrez, almost 10,000 campesinos marched in favor of Father Padrón's release. In a corner of Ocosingo, Juan's widow buried her husband, victim of the proud ranchers. There was no march or protest petition for Juan's death. This is Chiapas.

Recently Viceroy González Garrido was the protagonist of a new scandal, which was uncovered because the press reported the story. With the viceroy's approval, Ocosingo's feudal lords organized the Committee for Citizen Defense, a blatant attempt to institutionalize their neo-Porfirista paramilitary forces that keep order in the countryside of Chiapas. Surely nothing would have happened had it not been for the discovery of a plot to assassinate the parish priest Pablo Iribarren and the nun María del Carmen, along with Samuel Ruiz, the bishop of San Cristobal. The plot was reported by the honest Chiapaneco press, which still exists, and reached national forums. There were retractions and denials; the viceroy declared that he maintains good relations with the Church and named a special committee to investigate the case. The investigation yielded no results, and all continues as before.

During the same days, government agencies made some horrifying statistics known: in Chiapas 14,500 people die every year, the highest mortality rate in the country. The causes? Curable diseases such as respiratory infections, enteritis, parasites, amoebas, malaria, salmonella, scabies, dengue, pulmonary tuberculosis, trachoma, typhus, cholera, and measles. Many say that the figure is actually over 15,000 because deaths in marginalized zones, the majority of the state, are not reported. During Patrocinio González Garrido's four-year term more than 60,000 Chiapanecos have died, most of them poor. The war against the people, directed by the viceroy and carried out by the feudal lords, consists of methods more subtle than bombardments. There is no mention in the press of this murderous plot, which claims lives and land just as in the days of the Conquest.

The Committee for Citizen Defense continues to carry out its proselytizing work, holding meetings to convince the rich and poor of the city of Ocosingo that they should organize and arm themselves so that the campesinos won't enter the city because they will destroy everything, without respecting the rich or the poor. The viceroy smiles with approval.

THREE

Which tells how the viceroy had a brilliant idea and put it into practice. It also tells how the empire decreed the death of socialism, and then put itself to the task of carrying out this decree to the great joy of the powerful, the distress of the weak, and the indifference of the majority. It tells of Zapata and how he is said to be still be alive. It also tells of other disconcerting events.

THE VICEROY IS WORRIED. The campesinos refuse to applaud the institutional pillage written into the new Article 27 of the Constitution.[8] The viceroy is enraged. The poor aren't happy with being exploited. They refuse to humbly accept the charity that Pronasol spreads around the Chiapaneco countryside. The Viceroy is desperate. He consults his advisers. His advisers tell him an old truth: jails and military bases aren't enough to ensure continued domination. It is also necessary to control people's thoughts. The viceroy is disturbed. He paces in his palace. Then he stops and smiles.

XEOCH Radio Station: Rap and lies for the campesinos.

IN OCOSINGO and Palenque, Cancue and Chilón, Altamirano and Yajalón, the indigenous people are celebrating. A new gift from the supreme government has made life a little happier for the peons, small landowners, landless campesinos, and impoverished inhabitants of the *ejidos*. They have been given a local radio station that reaches the most isolated corners of eastern Chiapas.

The station's programming is fitting: marimbas and rap music proclaim the good news. The Chiapas countryside is being modernized. XEOCH transmits from the township of Ocosingo and can be found at 600 Mhz AM from four in the morning till ten at night. Its news shows abound with lies. They tell of the "disorientation" that "subversive" lay workers spread among the peasantry, the abundance of aid credits that are never received by the indigenous communities, and the existence of public works that have never been built. The viceroy is also given time on the air so that he can remind the population with threats that not all is lies and rap music; there are also jails and military bases and a penal code that is the most repressive in the Republic. The penal code punishes any expression of discontent. The laws against demonstrations, rebellion, inciting to riot, and so on demonstrate that the viceroy is careful to maintain everything in order.

There isn't any reason to fight. Socialism has died. Long live conformity, reform, the modern world, capitalism, and all of the cruelties that are associated with them! The viceroy and the feudal lords dance and smile euphorically in their palaces. Their joy is disconcerting for the few free thinkers who live in the area. Even they are incapable of understanding. They are without hope. It is true that one must fight, but the balance of forces isn't favorable. Now isn't the time. We must wait longer, maybe years. We must be alert against the adventurers. We must make sure that nothing happens in the cities or in the countryside, that everything continues as always. Socialism has died. Long live capitalism! Radio, the print media, and television proclaim it. It is repeated by some ex-socialists who are now amazingly changed.

Not everyone who hears the voices of hopelessness and conformity are carried away by hopelessness. There are millions of people who continue without hearing the voices of the powerful and the indifferent. They can't hear; they are deafened by the crying and blood that death and poverty are shouting in their ears. But when there is a moment of rest, they hear another voice. They don't hear the voice that comes from above; they hear the voice that is carried to them by the wind from below, a voice that is born in the indigenous heart of the mountains. This voice speaks to them about justice and freedom, it speaks to them about socialism, about hope . . . the only hope that exists in the world. The oldest of the old in the indigenous communities say that there once was a man named Zapata who rose up with his people and sang out: "Land and Freedom!" These old campesinos say that Zapata didn't die, that he must return. These old campesinos also say that the wind and the rain and the sun tell the campesinos when to cultivate the land, when to plant, and when to harvest. They say that hope is also planted and harvested. They also say that the wind and the rain and the sun are now saying something different: that with so much poverty, the time has come to harvest rebellion instead of death. That is what the old campesinos say. The powerful don't hear; they can't hear, they are deafened by the brutality that the empire shouts in their ears. "Zapata," insists the wind, the wind from below, our wind.

The Second Wind: The Wind from Below

FOUR

Which tells how dignity and defiance joined hands in the Southeast, and how Jacinto Pérez's[9] phantoms run through the Chiapaneco highlands. It also tells of a patience that has run out and of other happenings that have been ignored but have major consequences.

THESE PEOPLE WERE BORN dignified and rebellious, brothers and sisters to the rest of Mexico's exploited people. They are not just the product of the Annexation Act of 1824,[10] but of a long chain of ignominious acts and rebellions. From the time when cassocks and armor conquered this land, dignity and defiance have lived and spread under these rains.

Collective work, democratic thinking, and subjection to the decisions of the majority are more than just traditions in indigenous zones. They have been the only means of survival, resistance, dignity, and defiance. These "evil ideas," as they are seen by landholders and businessmen, go against the capitalist precept of "a lot in the hands of a few."

It has mistakenly been said that the Chiapas rebellion has no counterpart, that it is outside the national experience. This is a lie. The exploited Chiapaneco's specialty is the same as that of exploited people from Durango, Veracruz, or the plateau of northern Mexico: to fight and to lose. If the voices of those who write history speak exclusively, it is because the voice of the oppressed does not speak . . . not yet.

There is no historic, national, or regional calendar that has documented each and every rebellion against this system that is imposed and maintained with blood and fire throughout the national territory. In Chiapas, the rebel voice is only heard when it shakes the world of the landowners and business people. Indeed, the phantom of indigenous barbarism strikes government-building walls and gains access with the help of revolution, trickery, and threats. If the rebellion in the Southeast fails, like the rebellions lost in the North, Center, and West, it is not the result of bad timing; it is because the wind is fruit of the land; it comes and in time ripens, not in a book of laments, but in the ordered breasts of those who have nothing but dignity and rebelliousness.

And this wind from below, that of rebellion and dignity, is not just an answer to the wind from above. It is not just an angry response. Rather, it carries with it not just a call for the destruction of an unjust and arbitrary system but a new proposal: the hope of converting rebellion and dignity into freedom and dignity.

How will this new voice make itself heard in these lands and across the country? How will this hidden wind blow, this wind that now blows only in the mountains and canyons and hasn't yet descended to the valleys where money rules and lies govern? This wind will come from the mountains. It is already being born under the trees and is conspiring for a world so new that it is barely an intuition in the collective heart that inspires it . . .

FIVE

This chapter tells how the dignity of the indigenous people tried to make itself heard, but its voice only lasted a little while. It also tells how voices that spoke before are speaking again today, and that the Indians are walking forward once again, but this time with firm footsteps. They are walking together with other dispossessed peoples to take what belongs to them. The music of death that now plays only for those who have nothing will now play for everyone. It also tells of other frightful things that have happened and, they say, must happen.

THE INDIGENOUS MARCH called Xi'Nich, "the ant," composed of campesinos from Palenque, Ocosingo, and Salto de Agua, demonstrates the system's absurdity. These indigenous people had to walk 1,106 kilometers to make themselves heard. They had to go to the capital of the Republic in order for the central power to arrange a meeting with the viceroy. They arrived in Mexico City when capitalism was painting a frightful tragedy across the skies of Jalisco. They arrived at the capital of old New Spain, now Mexico, exactly 500 years after the foreign nightmare imposed itself in the night of this land. They arrived, and all the honest and noble people, of which there are still some, listened to them and the voices that oppress them today in the Southeast, North, Center, and West of the country also listened to them. They walked back, another 1,106 kilometers, their bags filled with promises. Again, nothing came of it . . .

In the municipal seat of Simojovel campesinos belonging to the CIOAC[11] organization were attacked by people paid by local ranchers. The campesinos in Simojovel have decided to stop being silent and to respond to the ranchers' threats. Campesinos surround the municipal seat. Nothing and no one enters or leaves without their consent. The federal army withdraws to its barracks, the police retreat, and the state's feudal lords demand arms in an attempt to restore order and respect. Negotiating commissions come and go. The conflict appears to have resolved itself. But the causes persist. With the same outward appearances, everything returns to calm.

In the town of Betania, on the outskirts of San Cristobal de las Casas, indigenous people are regularly detained and harassed by judicial agents for cutting firewood for their homes—the agents say that they are only doing this to protect the environment. The indigenous people decide to stop being silent and kidnap three judicial officials. They take the Panamerican Highway and cut off communications to the east of San Cristobal. At the intersection between Ocosingo and Comitán, campesinos are holding the judiciaries, and they demand to speak to the viceroy before they will agree to unblock the road. Business comes to a halt, tourism collapses. Negotiating commissions come and go. The conflict appears to resolve itself but the causes persist. With the same outward appearances, everything returns to calm.

In Marques de Comillas, in the township of Ocosingo, campesinos cut wood to survive. The judicial officials arrest them and confiscate the wood for their commander. The indigenous people decide to stop being silent, and they take the agents' vehicles and kidnap the agents. The governor sends Public Security police, who in turn are kidnapped in the same way. The indigenous people hold on to the trucks, the wood, and the prisoners. They let the prisoners go. There is no response. They march to Palenque to demand solutions, and the army oppresses them and kidnaps their leaders. They hold on to the vehicles. Negotiating commissions come and go. The government lets the leaders go; the campesinos return the vehicles. The conflict appears to resolve itself, but the causes persist. With the same outward appearance, everything returns to calm.

In the municipal seat of Ocosingo, 4,000 indigenous campesinos from the organization ANCIEZ[12] march from different points of the city. Three marches converge in front of the Municipal Building. The municipal president doesn't know what it's all about and flees. On the floor of his office is a calendar indicating the date: April 10, 1992. Outside indigenous campesinos from Ocosingo, Oxchuc, Huixtán, Chilón, Yajalón, Sabanilla, Salto de Agua, Palenque, Altamirano, Las Margaritas, San Cristobal, San Andres, and Cancún dance in front of a giant image of Zapata, painted by one of them, recite poetry, sing, and speak. Only they are listening. The landowners, businessmen, and judicial officials are closed up in their homes and shops; the federal garrison appears deserted. The campesinos shout that Zapata lives and the struggle continues. One of them reads a letter addressed to President Carlos Salinas de Gortari in which they accuse him of having brought all gains of the agrarian reform made under Zapata to an end, of selling the country with the North American Free Trade Agreement (NAFTA), and of bringing Mexico back to the times of Porfirio Díaz. They declare forcefully that they will not recognize Salinas' reforms to Article 27 of the Political Constitution. At two o'clock in the afternoon the demonstration disperses, in an orderly fashion, but the causes persist. With the same outward appearances everything returns to calm.

Abasolo is an *ejido* in the township of Ocosingo. For years, campesinos took land that legally belonged to them. Three of this community's leaders have been put in jail and tortured by the governor. The indigenous people decide to stop being silent, and they take the San Cristobal—Ocosingo highway. Negotiating commissions come and go. The leaders are freed. The conflict appears to resolve itself, but the causes persist. With the same outward, appearance everything returns to calm.

Antonio dreams of owning the land he works on; he dreams that his sweat is paid for with justice and truth; he dreams that there is a school to cure ignorance and medicine to scare away death; he dreams of having electricity in his home and that his table is full; he dreams that his country is free and that this is the result of the people governing themselves; and he dreams that he is at peace with himself and with the world. He dreams that he must fight to obtain this dream, he dreams that there must be death in order to gain life. Antonio dreams, and then he awakens . . . Now he knows what to do, and he sees his wife crouching by the fire, hears his son crying. He looks at the sun rising in the east and, smiling, grabs his machete.

The wind picks up, he rises and walks to meet others. Something has told him that his dream is that of many, and he goes to find them.

The viceroy dreams that his land is agitated by a terrible wind that rouses everything; he dreams that all he has stolen is taken from him, that his house is destroyed, and that his reign is brought down. He dreams, and he doesn't sleep. The viceroy goes to the feudal lords, and they tell him that they have been having the same dream. The viceroy cannot rest. So he goes to his doctor, and together they decide that it is some sort of indigenous witchcraft and that they will only be freed from this dream with blood. The viceroy orders killings and kidnappings and he builds more jails and army barracks. But the dream continues and keeps him tossing and turning and unable to sleep.

Everyone is dreaming in this country. Now it is time to wake up . . .

The storm is here. From the clash of these two winds a storm will be born. Its time has arrived. Now the wind from above rules, but the wind from below is coming . . .

The prophecy is here: When the storm calms, when rain and fire again leave the country in peace, the world will no longer be the world, but something better.

THE LACANDON JUNGLE

NOTES

1. The exchange of pesos to dollars in 1989 was 3,000 pesos for one U.S. dollar.

2. Pemex stands for Petroleum of Mexico, a government-owned company.

3. Porfirio Díaz was dictator of Mexico from 1876 to 1911 when mestizos in Chiapas accumulated enormous wealth, and the local economy was opened to international trade.

4. *Nixtamal* is cornmeal cooked with lye to make tortillas.

5. Because Porfirio Díaz favored landowners, a Porfirista-type landed estate implies a very large spread of land with many workers, feudalistic in nature.

6. Pronasol stands for Programa Nacional de Socialización, the National Program for Socialization set up by Carlos Salinas de Gortari in 1988 and active until 1994. Much like the World Bank Anti-Poverty Program, Pronasol focused on aid rather than development; it was was used as a tool to organize a new ruling party in Mexico, and as proof of Salinas's commitment to fighting poverty.

7. Patrocinio González Garrido, governor of Chiapas from 1988 to 1993 and minister of the interior during the Zapatista uprising, was forced to resign after being blamed for not having foreseen the rebellion.

8. Article 27 of the Mexican Constitution of 1917 recognized the autonomy of indigenous territories and man-dated land distribution so that the indigenous and peasants would be ensured land parcels to work and sus-tain their families. Salinas amended this article, declaring the *ejidos* to be private property, and did not enforce the redistribution of the lands taken illegally by the large landowners, as they required more space for their cattle.

9. Jacinto Pérez, an indigenous anthropologist who authored many books, was educated at Harvard University. He served as Mexico's minister of culture and was the mayor of the municipality of Chenaló during the mas-sacre at Acteal, which is within that municipality.

10. In the Annexation Act of 1824, Chiapas, then part of Guatemala, decided to become part of Mexico.

11. CIOAC—*Central Independiente de Obreros Agricolas y Campesinos* (Independent Union of Agricultural Workers and Peasants) serves as a national watchdog organization for and by the working class. It keeps an eye on industrial development to ensure the well-being of the worker.

12. ANCIEZ stands for Asociación Nacional de Campesinos Indigenas Emiliano Zapata (National Association of Indigenous Peasants Emiliano Zapata). It was founded in 1991 and disbanded in 1993, when the EZLN was formed.

7

Who Should Ask for Pardon and Who Can Grant It?

JANUARY 18, 1994

To the national weekly Proceso
To the national newspaper La Jornada
To the national newspaper El Financiero
To the local newspaper of San Cristobal de las Casas, Chiapas, Tiempo

Sirs:

I OUGHT TO START with a few apologies (a bad start, my grandmother would say). Because of a mistake by our press office, we didn't send my last letter to the weekly *Proceso.* I hope the people at *Proceso* will understand this oversight and that they'll receive this note without rancor, resentment, or re . . . etcetera.

First, I'd like to direct your attention to the enclosed communiqués from the EZLN. They refer to the federal army's repeated violations of the cease-fire,[1] the federal government's amnesty offer, and Camacho Solis' appointment as the envoy for peace and reconciliation in Chiapas.[2]

I believe you've already received the documents we sent on January 13. I don't know what reaction these documents will provoke or what the federal government's response to our demands will be, so I don't refer to them in this letter. Up to today, January 18, 1994, the only thing we've heard about is the federal government's formal offer to pardon our troops.

Why do we need to be pardoned? What are they going to pardon us for? For not dying of hunger? For not accepting our misery in silence? For not accepting humbly the historic burden of disdain and abandonment? For having risen up in arms after we found all other paths closed? For not heeding the Chiapas penal code, one of the most absurd and repressive in history? For showing the rest of the country and the whole world that human dignity still exists even among the world's poorest peoples? For having made careful preparations before we began our uprising? For bringing guns to battle instead of bows and arrows? For being Mexicans? For being mainly indigenous? For calling on the Mexican people to fight by whatever means possible for what belongs to them? For fighting for liberty, democracy, and justice? For not following the example of previous guerrilla armies? For refusing to surrender? For refusing to sell ourselves out?

Who should ask for pardon, and who can grant it? Those who for many years glutted themselves at a table of plenty while we sat with death so often, we finally stopped fearing it? Those who filled our pockets and our souls with empty promises and words?

Or should we ask pardon from the dead, our dead, who died "natural" deaths of "natural causes" like measles, whooping cough, breakbone fever, cholera, typhus, mononucleosis, tetanus, pneumonia, malaria and other lovely gastrointestinal and pulmonary diseases? Our dead, so very dead, so democratically dead from sorrow because no one did anything, because the dead, our dead, went just like that, with no one keeping count, with no one saying, "ENOUGH!" which would at least have granted some meaning to their deaths, a meaning no one ever sought for them, the dead of all times, who are now dying once again, but now in order to live?

Should we ask for pardon from those who deny us the right and capacity to govern ourselves? From those who don't respect our customs or our culture and who ask us for identification papers and obedience to a law whose existence and moral basis we don't accept? From those who oppress us, torture us, assassinate us, disappear us for the grave "crime" of wanting a piece of land, not too big and not too small, but just a simple piece of land on which we can grow something to fill our stomachs?

Who should ask for pardon, and who can grant it?

The president of the nation? Federal ministers, senators, municipal representatives, governors, or mayors? The police? The federal army? The banking, industry, commerce, and land magnates? Political parties? Intellectuals? Galio and Nexus?[3] The mass media? Students? Teachers? People in the neighborhoods? Laborers? Farm workers? Indigenous people? Those who died in vain?

Who should ask for pardon, and who can grant it?

Well, that's all for now. Health to you and a hug; in this kind of cold climate, you'll be glad for both, I think, even coming from a "professional of violence."

SUBCOMANDANTE INSURGENTE MARCOS

NOTES

1. The Zapatistas declared a unilateral cease-fire after their twelve-day takeover of San Cristobal de las Casas on January 1, 1994.

2. Manuel Camacho Solis, mayor of Mexico City from 1988 to 1993, left the PRI to join the Partido Centro Democratico (Democratic Center Party). Appointed commissioner for peace and sent to Chiapas in March 1994, he headed the negotiations between the Mexican government and the Zapatistas, held in the Cathedral of San Cristobal de las Casas.

3. Galio is a character in La Guerra de Galio (Galio's War), a novel written by Hector Aguilar Camín on the Mexican guerrilla of the 1970s. Nexus, a cultural and political magazine, was strongly aligned with Salinas.

8

Five Hundred Years of Indigenous Resistance

FEBRUARY I, 1994

To the Council of Guerrero
Chilpancingo, Guerrero, Mexico

Brothers and sisters:
WE WANT TO TELL YOU that we received your letter sent on January 24th of 1994. We are very happy to know that our indigenous brothers Amuzgos, Mixtec, Nahuatl,and Tlapanecos know of our just struggle for dignity and liberty for the indigenous and for all Mexicans.

Our heart is made strong with your words, which come from so far away, that come from the history of oppression, death, and misery that all the bad governors have decreed for our peoples, for our persons. Our heart is made big with your message that reaches us skipping mountains and rivers, cities and roads, suspicions and prejudices.

In our name, in your name, in the name of all the indigenous of Mexico, and in the name of all good people who walk a good path, we receive your words, brothers and sisters, yesterday kin in exploitation and misery, today and tomorrow brothers and sisters in a dignified and true struggle.

Today marks one month since the Zapatista light came to illuminate our night and our people.

In our heart there was so much pain, so great was our death and our shame, brothers and sisters, that they no longer fit into this world given to us by our grandfathers. So great was the pain and shame that they no longer fit inside the heart of just a few, and they spilled over and began filling other hearts with pain and shame, the hearts of the eldest and wisest of our peoples, and the hearts of the young men and women, brave ones all of them, and the hearts of the children, even the youngest ones, and filled with pain were the hearts of the animals and plants. The heart filled with stones, and our whole world was filled with pain and shame, and the wind and the sun were also pained and shamed, and the earth had pain and shame. Everything was pain and shame. Everything was silence.

The pain that gathered us made us speak, and we recognized that in our words there was truth. We understood that not only pain and shame lived in our tongue; we learned there was still hope in our chests. We spoke to ourselves, we looked inside ourselves, and we looked at our history. We saw our eldest fathers suffer and struggle, we saw our grandfathers struggle, we saw our fathers with fury in their hands, we saw that not all had been taken from us, that we still had what was most valuable, that which made us live, that which made our step rise above plants and animals, that which made the stone stay beneath our feet, and we saw, brothers and sisters, that dignity was everything we had, and we saw that our shame was big for having forgotten it, and we saw that dignity was good so that men would be men once again. And dignity came to reside once again in our heart, and we were renewed. And the dead, our dead, saw that we were renewed, and they called to us again, to dignity and to the struggle.

And so in our heart there was no longer just pain and shame. Courage and valor came to us through the mouth of our elders, who were dead but lived again in the dignity that they gave to us. And we saw that it was not good to die of shame and pain, that it was not good to die without having struggled. And we saw that we must gain a dignified death so that all could live one day with the good and with reason. And so our hands searched for liberty and justice, our hands, empty of hope, were filled with the fire to demand and shout our deep desires and our struggle. And so we rose to walk again. Our step became steady once again, our hands and our heart were armed. "For all!" says our heart, not just for some. "For all!" says our step. "For all!" shouts our spilled blood, flowering in the city streets where lies and privation govern.

We have left our lands behind, our homes are far away, we left everything and everyone, we lifted our skin to dress ourselves with war and death, we die to live. Nothing for us, everything for all, that which is rightfully ours and our children's. We have left everything, all of us.

Now they want to leave us alone, brothers and sisters, they want that our death be useless, they want that our blood be forgotten among the stones and dung, they want that our voice be hushed, they want that our step become once again distant.

Don't abandon us, brothers and sisters. Take our blood and nourish yourselves, fill the heart that is yours and of all good people in these lands, indigenous and not indigenous, men and women, elders and children. Don't leave us to ourselves. Let not this have been in vain.

Let the voice of the blood that united us when the earth and the skies were not the property of the grandees call to us once again. Let our hearts walk the same path. Let the powerful tremble. Let the heart of the small and miserable be gladdened. Let the dead of always have life.

Don't abandon us. Don't let us die alone. Don't leave our struggle in the vacuum of the powerful.

Brothers and sisters, let our path be the same, one for all.
Liberty!
Democracy!
Justice!

Respectfully,

From The Mountains Of The Mexican Southeast
CCRI-CG OF THE EZLN
SUBCOMANDANTE MARCOS

9

Second Declaration of the Lacandon Jungle

Today We Say: No! We Will Not Surrender!

JUNE 12, 1994

Those who bear swords aren't the only ones who lose blood or who shine with the fleeting light of military glory. They aren't the only ones who should have a voice in designating the leaders of the government of a people who want democracy; this right to choose belongs to every citizen who has fought in the press or in the courts. It belongs to every citizen who identifies with the ideals of the Revolution and who has fought against the despotism that has ignored our laws. Tyranny isn't eliminated just by fighting on the battlefield; dictatorships and empires are also overthrown by launching cries of freedom and terrible threats against those who are executing the people . . . Historical events have shown us that the destruction of tyranny and the overthrow of all evil governments are the work of ideas together with the sword. It is therefore an absurdity, an aberration, an outrageous despotism to deny the people the right to elect their government. The people's sovereignty is formed by all those people in society who are conscious of their rights and who, be they civilians or armed, love freedom and justice and who work for the good of the country.

—PAULINO MARTÍNEZ, (Zapatista delegate to the Revolutionary Sovereignty Convention, Aguascalientes, Mexico, on behalf of Emiliano Zapata, October 27, 1914)

To the people of Mexico
To the peoples and governments of the world

THE ZAPATISTA NATIONAL LIBERATION ARMY, at war against the bad government since January 1, 1994, addresses you in order to make known its thoughts:

Mexican brothers and sisters:
IN DECEMBER 1993 we said, "Enough!" On January 1, 1994, we called on the legislative and judicial powers to assume their constitutional responsibility and to restrain the genocidal policies that the federal executive imposes on our people. We base our constitutional right in the application of Article 39 of the Political Constitution of the United Mexican States: "National sovereignty essentially and originally resides in the people. All political power emanates from the people and its purpose is to help the people. The people have, at all times, the inalienable right to alter or modify their form of government."

The government responded to this call with a policy of extermination and lies. The powers in Mexico ignored our just demand and permitted a massacre. However, this massacre only lasted twelve days. Another force, a force superior to any political or military power, imposed its will on the parties involved in the conflict. Civil society assumed the duty of preserving our country. It showed its disapproval of the massacre, and it obliged us to hold a dialogue with the government. We understand that the ascendancy of the political party that has been in power for so long cannot be allowed to continue. We understand that this party, a party that has kept the fruit of every Mexican's labor for itself, cannot be allowed to continue. We understand that the corruption of the presidential elections that sustains this party impedes our freedom and should not be allowed to continue. We understand that this party imposes a culture of fraud with which it impedes democracy. We understand that justice only exists for the corrupt and powerful. We understand that we must construct a society in which those who rule do so through the will of the people. There is no other path.

This is understood by every honest Mexican in civil society. Only those who have based their success on the theft of the public trust, those who protect criminals and murderers by prostituting justice, those who resort to political murder and electoral fraud in order to impose their will, are opposed to our demands.

Only these fossilized politicians plan to roll back history and to erase from the national consciousness the cry taken up by the country since January 1, 1994: "Enough!"

We will not permit this. Today we do not call on those weak powers in Mexico that refuse to assume their constitutional duties and which permit themselves to be controlled by the federal executive. If the legislature and the judges have no dignity, then others who do understand that they must serve the people, and not the individual, will step forward. Our call transcends the question of presidential terms or the upcoming elections. Our sovereignty resides in civil society. Only the people can alter or modify our form of government. It is to them that we address this Second Declaration from the Lacandon Jungle.

First: We have respected the international conventions of warfare while we have carried out our military actions. These conventions have allowed us to be recognized as a belligerent force by national and foreign forces. We will continue to respect these conventions.

Second: We order all of our regular and irregular forces, both inside national territory and outside the country, to continue to obey the unilateral offensive cease-fire. We will continue to respect the cease-fire in order to permit civil society to organize in whatever forms they consider pertinent toward the goal of achieving a transition to democracy in our country.

Third: We condemn the threats against civilian society brought about by the militarization of the country, both in terms of personal and modern repressive equipment, during this time leading up to the federal elections. Without a doubt, the Salinas government is trying to impose its will by fraud. We will not permit this.

Fourth: We propose to all independent political parties that are suffering from intimidation and repression of their political rights—the same intimidation and repression that our people have suffered for the last sixty five years—that they declare themselves in favor of a transition government while we move toward democracy.

Fifth: We reject the manipulation and the attempts to separate our just demands from the demands of the Mexican people. We are Mexicans, and we will not put aside our demands nor our arms until we have democracy, freedom, and justice for all.

Sixth: We reiterate our disposition toward finding a political solution to the transition to democracy in Mexico. We call upon civil society to retake the protagonist's role that it first took up in order to stop the military phase of the war. We call upon civil society to organize itself to direct the peaceful efforts toward democracy, freedom, and justice. Democratic change is the only alternative to war.

Seventh: We call on all honest sectors of civil society to attend a National Dialogue for Democracy, Freedom, and Justice.

For this reason we say
Brothers and sisters:
AFTER THE START of the war in January 1994, the organized cry of the Mexican people stopped the fighting and called for a dialogue between the contending forces. The federal government responded to the just demands of the EZLN with a series of offers that didn't touch on the essential problem: the lack of justice, freedom, and democracy in Mexico.

The meager response by the federal government to the demands of the EZLN shows up the political party in power and the limits it imposes. It is a system that makes possible that certain sectors in the Mexican countryside, whose roots have maintained the party in power, supersede constitutional power. It is this system of complicity that has made possible the existence and belligerence of the *caciques*,[1] the omnipotent power of the ranchers and businessmen, and the spread of drug trafficking. Just the fact that the government offered us the so-called Proposals for a Dignified Peace in Chiapas provoked tremendous agitation and an open defiance by these sectors. The single-party political system is trying to maneuver within this reduced horizon. It can't alienate these sectors without attacking itself, yet it can't leave things as they are without having to face the anger of the campesinos and indigenous peoples. In other words, to go through with the proposals would necessarily mean the death of the state-party system.[2] By suicide or execution, the death of the current Mexican political system is a necessary, although not sufficient, precondition for the transition to democracy in our country. There will be no real solutions in Chiapas until the situation in Mexico as a whole is resolved.

The EZLN understands that the problem of poverty in Mexico isn't merely due to a lack of resources. Our fundamental understanding and position is that whatever efforts are made will only postpone the problem if these efforts aren't made within the context of new local, regional, and national political relationships— relationships marked by democracy, freedom, and justice. The problem of power is not a question of who rules, but of who exercises power. If it is exercised by a majority of the people, the political parties will be obligated to put their proposals forward to the people instead of merely relating to each other in the party.

Looking at the problem of power within the context of democracy, freedom, and justice will create a new political culture within the parties. A new type of political leader will be born and, undoubtedly, new types of political parties as well.

We aren't proposing a new world, but something preceding a new world: an antechamber looking into the new Mexico. In this sense, this revolution will not end in a new class, faction of a class, or group in power. It will end in a free and democratic space for political struggle born above the fetid cadaver of the state-party system and the tradition of fixed presidential successions. A new political relationship will be born, based not in the confrontation of political organizations among themselves, but in the confrontation of their political proposals with different social classes. Political leadership will depend on the support of these social classes, and not on the mere exercise of power. In this new political relationship, different political proposals (socialism, capitalism, social democracy, liberalism, Christian democracy, and so on) will have to convince a majority of the nation that their proposal is the best for the country. The groups in power will be watched by the people in such a way that they will be obligated to give a regular accounting of themselves, and the people will be able to decide whether they remain in power or not. The plebiscite is a regulated form of confrontation among the nation, political parties, and power, and it merits a place in the highest law of the country.

Current Mexican law is too constricting for these new political relationships between the governed and the governors. A National Democratic Convention is needed from which a provisional or transitional government can emerge, be it by the resignation of the federal executive or through elections.

This National Democratic Convention and transitional government should lead to the creation of a new constitution, and in the context of this new constitution, new elections should be held. The pain that this process will bring to the country will be less than the damage that would be caused by a civil war. The prophecy of the Southeast holds true for the entire country. We can learn from what has already occurred so that there is less pain during the birth of the new Mexico.

The EZLN has its idea of what system and proposal are best for the country. The political maturity of the EZLN as a representative of a sector of the nation is shown by the fact that it doesn't want to impose its proposal on the country. The EZLN demands what is shown by their example: the political maturity of Mexico and the right for all to decide, freely and democratically, the course that Mexico must take. From this historic synthesis will emerge not only a better and more just Mexico, but a new Mexico as well. This is why we are gambling our lives: so that the Mexicans of the future can inherit a country in which they are not ashamed to live.

The EZLN, in a democratic exercise without precedent in an armed organization, consulted its component bases about whether or not to sign the peace accords presented by the federal government. The indigenous bases of the EZLN, seeing that the central demands of democracy, freedom, and justice have yet to be resolved, decided against signing the government's proposal.

Under siege and under pressure from different sectors that threatened us with extermination if the peace accords weren't signed, we Zapatistas reaffirmed our commitment to achieve a peace with justice and dignity. In our struggle, the dignified struggle of our ancestors has found a home. The cry of dignity of the insurgent Vicente Guerrero—"Live for the country or die for freedom"—once again sounds from our throats. We cannot accept an undignified peace.

Our path sprang out of the impossibility of struggling peacefully for our elemental rights as human beings. The most valuable of these rights is the right to decide, freely and democratically, what form the government will take. Now the possibility of a peaceful change to democracy and freedom confronts a new test: the electoral process that will take place this August, 1994. There are those who are betting on the outcome of the elections and the post-election period. There are those who predict apathy and disillusionment. They hope to profit from the blood of those who fall in the struggle, both violent and peaceful, in the cities and in the countryside. They have found their political project in the conflict they hope will come after the elections. They hope that the political demobilization will once again open the door to war. They say that they will save the country.

Others hope that the armed conflict will restart before the elections so that they can take advantage of the chaotic situation to keep themselves in power. Just as they did before, when they usurped popular will with electoral fraud, these people hope to take advantage of a pre-electoral civil war in order to prolong the agony of a dictatorship that has already lasted decades. There are others, sterile naysayers, who reason that war is inevitable and who are waiting to watch their enemy's corpse float by—or their friend's. The sectarians suppose, erroneously, that just the firing of a gun will bring about the dawn that our people have waited for since night fell upon Mexican soil with the deaths of Villa and Zapata.

Every one of these people who steals hope supposes that behind our weapons are ambition and an agenda that will guide us to the future. They are wrong. Behind our weapons is another weapon: reason. Hope gives life to both of our weapons. We won't let them steal our hope.

The trigger brought about hope at the beginning of the year. Now it is important that the hope that comes with political mobilization takes up the protagonist's role that belongs to it by right and reason. The flag is now in the hands of those who have names and faces, good and honest people who yearn with us for the same goal. Our greetings to these men and women, and our hope that you can carry the flag to where it should be. We will be standing there waiting for you with dignity. If the flag should fall, we will be there to pick it up again.

Now is the time for hope to organize itself and to walk forward in the valleys and in the cities, as it did before in the mountains of the Southeast. Fight with your weapons; don't worry about ours. We know how to resist to the end. We know how to wait—and we know what to do should the doors through which dignity walks close once again.

This is why we address our brothers and sisters in different nongovernmental organizations, in campesino and indigenous organizations, workers in the cities and in the countryside, teachers and students, housewives and squatters, artists and intellectuals, members of independent political parties, Mexicans.

We call all of you to a national dialogue with the theme of democracy, freedom, and justice. Therefore, we extend the following invitation to a National Democratic Convention:

We, the Zapatista National Liberation Army, fighting to achieve the democracy, freedom, and justice that our country deserves, and considering that:

One: The supreme government has usurped the legality that we inherited from the heroes of the Mexican Revolution.

Two: The constitution that exists doesn't reflect the popular will of the Mexican people.

Three: The resignation of the federal executive usurper isn't enough. A new law is necessary for the new country that will be born from the struggles of all honest Mexicans.

Four: Every form of struggle is necessary in order to achieve the transition to democracy in Mexico.

Considering these things, we call for a sovereign and revolutionary National Democratic Convention from which will come a transitional government and a new national law, a new constitution that will guarantee the legal fulfillment of the people's will.

This sovereign revolutionary convention will be national in that all states of the federation will be represented. It will be plural in that all patriotic sectors will be represented. It will be democratic in that it will make decisions through national *consultas.*

The convention will be presided over, freely and voluntarily, by civilians, prestigious public figures, regardless of their political affiliation, race, religion, sex, or age.

The convention will be launched by local, state, and regional committees in every *ejido*, settlement, school, and factory. These committees will be in charge of collecting the people's proposals for the new constitution and the demands to be realized by the new government that emerges from the convention.

The convention should demand free and democratic elections and should fight for the people's will to be respected.

The Zapatista National Liberation Army will recognize the National Democratic Convention as the authentic representative of the interests of the Mexican people in their transition to democracy.

The Zapatista National Liberation Army, which now can be found throughout the national territory, is in a position to offer itself to the Mexican people as an army to guarantee that the people's will is carried out.

For the first meeting of the National Democratic Convention, the EZLN offers as a meeting place a Zapatista settlement with all of the resources to be found there.

The date and place of the first session of the National Democratic Convention will be announced when it is appropriate to do so.

Mexican brothers and sisters:
OUR STRUGGLE CONTINUES. The Zapatista flag still waves in the mountains of the Mexican Southeast, and today we say: We will not surrender!

Facing the mountains, we speak to our dead so that their words will guide us along the path that we must walk.

The drums have called, and in the land's voices our pain and our history have spoken.

"Everything for everyone," say our dead. "Until this is true, there will be nothing for us.

"Find in your hearts the voices of those for whom we fight. Invite them to walk the dignified path of those who have no faces. Call them to resist. Let no one receive anything from those who rule. Ask them to reject the handouts from the powerful. Let all the good people in this land organize with dignity. Let them resist and not sell out.

"Don't surrender! Resist! Resist with dignity in the lands of the true men and women! Let the mountains shelter the pain of the people of this land. Don't surrender! Resist! Don't sell out! Resist!"

Our dead spoke these words from their hearts. We have seen that the words of our dead are good, that there is truth in what they say and dignity in their counsel. For this reason we call on our brother Mexicans to resist with us. We call on the indigenous campesinos to resist with us. We call on the workers, squatters, housewives, students, teachers, intellectuals, writers, on all those with dignity, to resist with us. The government doesn't want democracy in our land. We will accept nothing that comes from the rotting heart of the government, not a single coin nor a single dose of medication, not a single stone nor a single grain of food. We will not accept the handouts that the government offers in exchange for our dignity.

We will not take anything from the supreme government. Although they increase our pain and sorrow, although death may accompany us, although we may see others selling themselves to the hand that oppresses them, although everything may hurt and sorrow may cry out from the rocks, we will not accept anything. We will resist. We will not take anything from the government. We will resist until those who are in power exercise their power while obeying the people's will.

Brothers and sisters

DON'T SELL OUT. Resist with us. Don't surrender. Resist with us. Repeat along with us, "We will not surrender! We will resist!" Let these words be heard not only in the mountains of the Mexican Southeast, but in the North and on the peninsulas. Let them be heard on both coasts. Let them be heard in the center of the country. Let them cry out in the valleys and in the mountains. Let them sound in the cities and in the countryside. Unite your voices, brothers and sisters. Cry out with us: "We will not surrender! We will resist!"

Let dignity break the siege and lift from us the filthy hands with which the government is trying to strangle us. We are all under siege. They will not let democracy, freedom, and justice enter Mexican territory. Brothers and sisters, we are all under siege. We will not surrender! We will resist! We have dignity! We will not sell out!

What good are the riches of the powerful if they aren't able to buy the most valuable thing in these lands? If the dignity of the Mexican people has no price, then what good is the power of the powerful?

Dignity will not surrender! Dignity will resist!
Democracy!
Freedom!
Justice!

From The Mountains Of The Mexican Southeast
CLANDESTINE REVOLUTIONARY INDIGENOUS COMMITTEE
GENERAL COMMAND OF THE ZAPATISTA NATIONAL LIBERATION ARMY

NOTES

1. *Caciques* are political bosses.

2. The state-party system refers to the predominance of one party, with the full governmental apparatus behind it, ensuring its perpetuation in power. Until the Mexican presidential elections on July 2, 2000, when Vicente Fox, candidate for the PAN (Partido Acción Nacional) won, the PRI (Partido Revolucionario Institucional) had ruled unopposed for over seven decades.

10

Aguascalientes

Opening Words to the National Democratic Convention

AUGUST 1994

To the National Democratic Convention
To the Honorable Democratic Convention
To the Democratic Convention presidency, delegates, guests, observers

Brothers and sisters:
THROUGH MY VOICE speaks the voice of the EZLN.
Aguascalientes,[1] Chiapas, headquarters, bunker, weapons factory, military training center, explosives cache. Aguascalientes, Chiapas, Noah's Ark, the Tower of Babel, Fizcarraldo's jungle nave, the delirium of neo-Zapatismo, a pirate ship.

The anachronistic paradox, the tender madness of the ones without a face, the absurdity of a civil movement in dialogue with an armed movement.

Aguascalientes, Chiapas, hope in successive steps, hope in the small palms that preside over the stairway to better reach the sky, a sea snail's hope that calls for air from the jungle, the hope of those who did not come but are here, the hope that the flowers that die in other lands may live here.

Aguascalientes, Chiapas, for the EZLN: 28 days of work, 14 hours a day, 600 men-women per hour, a total of 235,200 men-women work hours, 9,800 days of work, 28 years of work, 60,000,000 old pesos, a library, a presidium simulating the bridge of a transatlantic ship, simple benches for 8,000 conventionists, 20 guest hostels, 14 cooking fires, parking for 1,000 vehicles, an arena for assaults.

Aguascalientes, Chiapas, a common effort by civilians and military, a common effort for change, a peaceful effort by armed people.

Before Aguascalientes, they said that it was madness, that no one could, from the limits set by guns and face masks, be successful in convoking an national reunion on the eve of the elections. And before Aguascalientes, they said that no sensible person would respond to the call of a rebel group, to outlaws, to those of which little or a lot is known, to the light that lit up January, to the obsessive language that tried to recover the old and worn words: *democracy, liberty, justice*. The covered faces, the night passage, the mountains enabled as hope, the lonely indigenous glance that for centuries has pursued our barreling attempt toward modernization, the stubborn rejection of handouts to demand the apparently absurd: for everyone everything, for us nothing.

And before Aguascalientes, they said there was little time, that nobody would risk embarking on a project that, like the Tower of Babel, announced its failure from the very place and time in which it was conceived.

And before Aguascalientes, they said that fear—the sweet terror that has fed from their very birth the good people of this country—would end up imposing itself. They said that the obvious comfort of doing nothing—that of sitting and waiting to observe, that of applauding or booing the actors in this bitter comedy that is called the motherland—would reign together with other obvious things in the proverbial name of the people of Mexico, civil society.

And before Aguascalientes, they said that the insurmountable differences that fragmented us and pitted us one against the other—the omnipotent state party and the avoidable things that take form around it: presidentialism, the sacrificial bondage of liberty and democracy chained to stability and economic bonanza, of fraud and corruption as a national idiosyncrasy, of justice prostituted by handouts, of despair and conformity elevated to the status of a national security doctrine—would prevent us from turning toward a common point.

And before Aguascalientes, they said that there would be no problem, that the convocation to a dialogue between a group of transgressors of the law and a mass that is amorphous, disorganized, and fragmented down to its familial microcosm—the so-called civil society—would have no resonance nor common cause, that dispersion gathered can only cause a dispersion powered toward immobility.

And before Aguascalientes, they said that there would be no need to oppose the celebration of the National Democratic Convention, that it would abort by itself, that it was not worthwhile to sabotage it openly, that it was better that it explode from within, that it be apparent in Mexico and to the world that nonconformity was incapable of coming to an agreement, therefore, incapable of offering the country a national project that was better than the one that the institutionalized and stabilized revolution had offered us—along with the pride of now having in Mexico twenty four forefathers of International Money.

That's what they were betting on, exactly that. That's why they allowed the convocation to be sent. That's why they did not prevent you from coming here. The foreseen failure of the CND[2] should not be attributed to the powerful. Let it be evident that the weak are weak, because it is evident that they are incapable of being anything else; they are weak because they deserve it; they are weak because they desire it to be so.

And before Aguascalientes, we said yes, it was madness that from the horizon opened up by guns and face masks, it was possible to convoke a national reunion on the eve of the elections and be successful. Do you need a mirror?

And before Aguascalientes, we said that for years prudence has sat to lament the painful lessons of history, that prudence allows us today the constant drumming of doing nothing, of waiting, of despairing, that the senseless and tender fury of "For everyone everything, for us nothing" would find others who would listen, others who are transformed into us and you.

And before Aguascalientes, we said that there was enough time, that what was missing was shame for being afraid of trying to be better, that the problem with the Tower of Babel was not in the concept but in poor liaison system and a poor translation team. The failure was in not making an attempt, in sitting down to see how the tower was raised, how it stood and how it crumbled. In sitting down to see how history would give an account, not of the tower, but of those who sat down to wait for its failure.

And before Aguascalientes, we said that fear—the seductive terror that is expelled by the sewers of power and that has fed us since birth—can and should be put aside, not forgotten, not overlooked, but simply set aside. That the fear of remaining a spectator should be greater than the fear of attempting to look for a common point, something that unites, something that can transform this comedy into history.

And before Aguascalientes, we said that the differences that fragmented us and pitted us one against one another would not prevent us from focusing on the same point: the avoidable system that castrates, the system of evidences that oppress, the common places that kill, the state-party system and the absurdities within it that are invested with value and are made institutions: the hereditary dictatorship; the cornering in the arena of the impossible—as an utopia—the struggle for democracy, liberty, and justice; the electoral mockery elevated to the image of computational alchemy and to the status of national monument; misery and ignorance seen as the historical vocation of the dispossessed; democracy washed with the detergent of imports and water from antidemonstration cannons.

And before Aguascalientes, we said that there was no problem, that the convocation to a dialogue between those that are without face and armed and the disarming facelessness of civil society would find common cause, that the reunited dispersion and good dialogue could spawn a movement that might finally turn this shameful page in the history of Mexico.

And before Aguascalientes, they said that there would be no need to oppose the celebration of the CND, that it would be precisely that—no more no less—a celebration, a celebration of a broken fear, of the first teetering step toward the possibility of offering the nation an "Enough is enough!" that not only has an indigenous and campesino voice, an "Enough is enough!" that adds, that multiplies, that reproduces, that triumphs, that can be the celebration of a discovery: that of knowing ourselves, no longer with a vocation for defeat, but with the possibility of victory on our side.

That is what we are betting on. That is why the anonymous and collective will with only a red star with five points for a face—the symbol of humanity and struggle—and four letters for a name—the symbol of rebellion—has emerged in this place, forgotten by the history of governmental studies, by international treaties, by the maps and routes that money takes, this construction that we call Aguascalientes in memory of previous attempts to bring hope together.

That's why thousands of women and men with their faces covered, for the most part indigenous people, raise this tower of hope. That's why, for a time, we set aside our guns, our rancor, our pain for our dead, our conviction for war, our armed ways. That's why we constructed this place for a gathering so that, if it is successful, it will be the first step not to deny us as an alternative. That is why we raised Aguascalientes, as the seat for a reunion that, if it fails, will compel us, once again, to take up arms to pursue the right for all to a place in history.

That's why we have invited you. That's why we are happy that you have come all this way. That's why we hope that maturity and wisdom will allow you to discover that the principal enemy, the most powerful, the most terrible, is not seated here among you.

That's why, with all due respect, we address the CND to ask in the name of all men and women, of all the children and old people, of all the living and the dead of the EZLN, not to heed the words of those who predict the failure of this convention, that you search and find that which unites us, that you speak true words, that you not forget the differences that separate us and that—more often than not—pit us one against the other, that you set them aside for a moment, some days, some hours, enough minutes so you can discover the common enemy. This we ask respectfully, that you not be traitors to your ideals, your principles, your history, don't be traitors and deny each other. We ask you respectfully that you take forth your ideals, your principles, your history, that you be firm, that you be consequent, that you say "Enough is enough!" to the lies that today govern our history.

The EZLN participates in the CND with twenty delegates, each one with a single vote. Therefore, we want to make two things clear: one is our commitment to the CND; the other is our decision not to impose our point of view. We have also rejected all possibilities of participating in the presidency of the CND; this is the convention for the peaceful search for change, and should in no way be presided over by armed people. We are thankful that you give us a place, one more among the many of you, to say our words.

We want to say that if anyone doubts it, we have no misgivings of having taken up arms against the supreme government; we repeat that they left us no alternative, we do not regret taking up arms nor covering our faces, we do not lament our dead, we are proud of them and we're ready to offer more blood and more death if that is the price to achieve a democratic change in Mexico. We want to say that we are unmoved by the accusations that we are priests of martyrdom, that we are warlike. We are not attracted by the calls of sirens and angels to give us access to a world that looks upon us with disapproval and distrust, that disdains the value of our blood and offers fame in exchange for dignity. We are not interested in living as we do now.

Much has been asked with inquisitive perversity by those who seek to confirm suppositions regarding what the Zapatistas want to do with the CND, what is it that the Zapatistas hope for from this convention. Some answer: To get a civil treaty; others argue: To get eight columns in the national and international press; others say: A new justification for their warring zeal; others venture: A civil endorsement of war; an official party fears: A platform for the resurrection of a world forgotten by the system, as they put a price on the official party; the opposition murmurs: A space to enjoy the leadership of a left that appears lifeless; heard in the conspiracies beyond the grave from where eventually might come the bullet that would attempt to silence us: The endorsement of a defeat; deduced in some brilliant column by some brilliant analyst, engaged in opaque political intrigue: A platform so that Marcos might negotiate a post in modernity's next administration.

Today, before this CND, the EZLN responds to the question: What do the Zapatistas hope for from the CND? Not a sinister civilian wing that extends war to every corner of the country; not journalistic promotion that reduces the struggle for dignity to a sporadic splash on the front page; not more arguments to adorn our uniform of fire and death; not a soapbox for political calculations, for groups or subgroups in search of power; not the doubtful honor of being the historical vanguard of multiple vanguards that we are subjected to; not the pretext for being traitors to ideals and deaths that we take with pride as an inheritance; not a springboard to reach a desk, an office, in some department, in a government, in a country. Not the designation of a interim government; not the rewriting of a new constitution; not the formation of a new constitutive body, not the endorsement of a presidential candidate to the presidency of the republic of pain and conformity; not war.

Yes, to the beginning of a construction that is greater than Aguascalientes, the construction of peace with dignity. Yes, to the beginning of a greater effort than the one that lead to Aguascalientes, the effort toward a democratic change that includes liberty and justice for the majority that has been forgotten. Yes, to the beginning of the end to a long nightmare known by the grotesque name of "the history of Mexico."

The moment has come to tell everyone that we do not want and cannot take the place that some want us to take, the place from where emanate all opinions, all routes, all answers, all truths; we will not do it.

We hope that the CND will provide the opportunity to search and find some one to whom we might present this flag that we found alone and abandoned in the palaces of power, the flag that, with our blood, we snatched from its pained imprisonment in museums, the flag that we cared for day and night, the flag that accompanied us in war and that we want to keep in peace. This flag, we now present it to this CND, not so that they retain it and dole it out to the rest of the nation, not to supplant probable armed protagonisms or proven civil protagonisms, not to abrogate representative and messianic impulses. But let it stand for the struggle so that all Mexicans can call it their own, so that it can again become the national flag, your flag, *compañeros* and *compañeras*.

We hope that this CND will organize a peaceful and legal struggle, the struggle for democracy, liberty, and justice, the struggle that we found ourselves compelled to take up, armed and with our faces covered. We hope from this CND true words, the words of peace, and not the words of surrender in this democratic struggle; the word of peace, but not the word that surrenders the struggle for freedom; the word of peace, but not the word of pacifist complicity with injustice.

We hope that this CND has the capacity to understand that the right to call itself representative of the feelings of the nation it is not a resolution that will be approved by vote or consensus, but rather something that has yet to be won in the barrios, in the *ejidos*, in the colonies, in the indigenous communities, in the schools and university, in the factories, in businesses, in the centers of scientific investigation, in the artistic and cultural centers, in all the corners of the country.

We hope from this CND the clarity to realize that it is only a step, the first of many that will be necessary to take under even more adverse conditions than the present ones.

We hope that this CND has the courage to assume the color of hope that many of us in Mexico see in it, to show us that the better men and women in this country use their means and strength for a transformation towards democracy, liberty, and justice—the only possibility of survival for this nation.

We hope that this CND has the maturity to not convert this space into an internal, sterile, and castrating settling of accounts.

We hope from this CND, at last, the rise of a collective call to struggle for that which belongs to us, for that which by reason and right belongs solely to good people, for our place in history.

Our time has not come; it is not the hour for arms. We stand aside, but we will not go away. We will wait until the horizon is open, until we are no longer necessary, until we are no longer possible, we, the ever-present dead, who must die again in order to live.

We hope that this CND is an opportunity, the opportunity that was denied us by those that govern this country, the opportunity to return with dignity after having fulfilled our duty of remaining underground. The opportunity to return again to the silence which we hold quietly, to the night from whence we emerge, to the death that we inhabit. The opportunity of disappearing in the same way that we appeared at dawn, without a face, without a future. The opportunity to return to the bottom of history, to the bottom of the dream, to the bottom of the mountain.

It has been said mistakenly that the Zapatistas have placed a time limit on the resumption of war, that if on the twenty first of August things do not turn out the way the Zapatistas want, then the war will begin. They lie. Nobody, not even the EZLN, can impose time limits or give ultimatums to the people of Mexico. For the EZLN there are no time limits other than what the civil and peaceful mobilizations determine. We are subordinate to them, to the point of disappearing as an alternative.

The resumption of war will not come from us. There are no Zapatista ultimatums for civil society. We wait, we resist, we are experts at this.

Struggle. Struggle without rest. Struggle and defeat the government. Struggle and defeat us. Never will defeat be so sweet, as in a peaceful transition, when democracy, dignity, and justice are victorious.

The Clandestine Indigenous Revolutionary Committee, General Command of the EZLN, has presented you with Aguascalientes so that you may gather, so you may agree: not to immobility; not to sterile skepticism; not to the exchange of reproaches and compliments; not to a tribune for personal promotion; not to a pretext for war tourism; not to a fraudulent unconditional pacifism; not to war; and not to peace at any price.

Yes, to discuss and agree on a civil, peaceful, popular, and national organization in the struggle for freedom and justice. The CCRI-CG of the EZLN presents you now with the national flag, to remind you what it represents—motherland, history, and nation—and to commit you to what it *should* mean: democracy, liberty, and justice.

Health to you, fellow conventionists. Aguascalientes was raised for you. In the middle of an armed territory, this space for peace with justice and dignity was constructed for you.

Thank you very much.
Democracy!
Liberty!
Justice!

From the mountains of the Mexican Southeast
CLANDESTINE INDIGENOUS REVOLUTIONARY COMMITTEE
GENERAL COMMAND OF THE EZLN

NOTES

1. The site of the covention, a small village called Guadalupe Tepeyac, was renamed Aquascalientes after the place where in 1917 the first constitutional covention was held, in which Emiliano Zapata helped bring about the Queretaro Constitution, which recognized the autonomy of the indigenous population and declared their lands to be beyond the reach of the Mexican government. This constitution was a turning point in Mexican history, in which the peasants gained land and labor rights. In present-day Chiapas there are five Aquascalientes, one for each site that has been host to a Zapatista encuertro.

2. CND stands for Convención Nacional Democratica (National Democratic Convention).

The Long Journey from Despair to Hope

For Mr. Ik, Tzeltal prince, founder of the CCRI-CC of the EZLN, who died in battle at Ocosingo, Chiapas, in January 1994.
(Wherever he may be . . .)

> When He arrives we are living,
> and from the depths of the Castle of the poor
> where we had so many just like us,
> so many accomplices, so many friends
> the sail of courage is raised
> We must raise it without vacillation.
> Tomorrow we will know why
> when we triumph.
> A long chain of passion was unimprisoned.
> The ration of injustice and the ration of shame
> are truly too bitter to bear.
> Everything is not necessary to make a world.
> Happiness is necessary and nothing more.
> To be happy it is only necessary to see clearly and fight. We must not wait even an instant:
> Let us raise our heads.
> Let us take the land by force.

—PAUL ELUARD, *Mexico: Between Dreams, Nightmares and Awakenings*

One
Which speaks of the neoliberal chants of twenty four mermaids, of reefs of gold, of grounding on the sandbars of depression, and of other dangers that threaten pirates on the high seas.

The Nation and Its Sorrows Speak
They have struck me
pained,

like a piece of land,
scarred,
with wounds that do not heal,
with beatings and falls.
They have struck me
like a never-ending curse,
like a home left to ruin and bitterness.
Oh, the weight of history!
I am filled with treachery and thefts,
every added humiliation grows,
each new misery accumulates.
The imperial eagle tears at my insides
and powerful men divide among themselves
my seas and mountains,
my rivers and deserts,
my valleys and streams.
These are my afflictions,
great and never ending:
the pain of my mangled ground,
the pain of my impoverished land,
the pain of my son betrayed,
the pain of my battle lost . . .

ONE CAN REACH this country through the penthouse or through the basement. To Lower Mexico one arrives crying, on foot . . . through the mud. In 1993, in the municipality of Ocosingo, close to San Quintin, we spoke with a Guatemalan who was to begin the long and improbable journey across the Mexican lands to the American Union. To achieve this he had to risk his money, his health, his life, and his dignity.

He and his family had to traipse from Chiapas to northern Baja California, to navigate through a nightmare of misery and death.

We asked him why he was risking everything to go to the United States, and why he didn't just stay and work in one of the Mexican states that he would be crossing on his journey. He answered, laughing facetiously, "I'd have to be crazy to do that. If we are from Guate-'mala' [a 'bad' Guatemala], you guys are from Guate-'peor' [a 'worse' Guatemala]." Then he related a story about Mexico, told by those who had made it clear to the northern border and had been deported by the Border Patrol. It was about a Mexico—a far cry from its tourist attractions—with its murderous police, corrupt government functionaries, panhandlers, North American prices and Central American salaries, death squads, and a population living in misery and hopelessness.

A story we already knew. The nightmare that lives in the Basement of this country, the nightmare that finally woke us up in January of . . .

1994: REACHING THE MEXICAN PENTHOUSE

ONE ARRIVES BY PLANE. An airport in Mexico City, Monterrey, Guadalajara, or Acapulco is the entrance to an elevator that neither goes up nor down, but rides horizontally across the land of the twenty four richest men in the country, the paths of modern-day Mexico: the government offices where neoliberalism is overseen, the business clubs where the national flag fades more with each passing day, the vacation resorts whose true vocation is to mirror a social class that does not want to see what is below their feet: the long spiral stairway, the labyrinth that leads all the way down to Lower Mexico, Mexico on foot, a Mexico of mud.

Above the blood and clay that live in the basement of this country, the omnipotent twenty four are busy counting $44,100 million, a modern-day presidential gift. Penthouse Mexico simply has no time to look down; it is too busy with complicated macroeconomics calculations, exchange of promises, praises and indexes of inflation, interest rates and the level of foreign investment, import-export concessions, lists of assets and resources, scales where the country and dignity have no weight. The public debt guaranteed, long range, has gone from $3,196 million in 1970 to $76,257 million in 1989. In 1970 the private, nonguaranteed U.S. debt was $2,770 million. In 1989 it was up to $3,999 million. In 1989 the short-term public debt reached $10,295. At the beginning of the 1990s, Mexico owed $95,642 million.

Each year this country pays off more debt, yet each year it owes more. The use of International Monetary Fund credits went from $0 in 1970 to $5,091 million in 1989. The industrial and commercial economic growth takes its toll on the Mexican countryside: in agriculture, in the period of 1965 to 1980, production grew at an average national rate of 3 percent; in the period from 1980 to 1989, only by 1 percent.

Meanwhile, in foreign trade, imports speak their complicated language of numbers: grain imports in 1974 were only 2,881 thousand metric tons; in 1984 they reached 7,054 thousand. Of the total, in 1965 only 5 percent of imports were foodstuffs; in 1989 food imports reached 16 percent. On the other hand, in the same period, machinery and transportation equipment imports were reduced (50 percent in 1965, 34 percent in 1989). Exports confirm: in total, the sale of combustibles and minerals increased from 22 percent in 1965 to 41 percent in 1989. Foreign sales of machinery and transportation equipment increased from 1 percent in 1965 to 24 percent in 1989. The export of products of prime necessity were reduced from 62 percent in 1965 to 14 percent in 1989.[1]

In Penthouse Mexico Mr. Carlos Salinas de Gortari is president—but of a board of stockholders. During these modern times, Mexican neopolitics make public functionaries into a species of retail salespeople, and the president of the republic into the sales manager of a gigantic business: Mexico, Inc. The best business in the country is to be a politician in the state party in Mexico. A paternal shadow of ex-president Miguel Aleman Valdés,[2] "Mr. Amigo," protects the steps of the new generation of Mexican politicians.

The Neo-elect, Ernesto Zedillo, is repeating the fallacy of the American Dream (poor children who grow up to be rich, that is to say, to be politicians), and the modernistic economic program—which is forty eight years old!

The smokescreen about the lack of solvency, credit, and markets will again blind the heads of medium to large businesses. The "law of the jungle," free trade, will repeat its dictates: more monopolies, fewer jobs. In neoliberal politics, "growth" simply means "to sell." To practice politics, one must practice marketing technology. Sooner or later, the "citizen" of Penthouse Mexico will be named Man of the Year by some foreign institution. To achieve this he must follow:

INSTRUCTIONS TO BE NAMED MAN OF THE YEAR

1. Carefully combine a technocrat, a repentant oppositionist, a sham businessman, a union bully, a landowner, a builder, an alchemist in computational arts, a "brilliant" intellectual, a television, a radio, and an official party. Set this mixture aside in a jar and label it "Modernity."
2. Take an agricultural worker, a peasant with no land, an unemployed person, an industrial worker, a teacher without a school, a dissatisfied housewife, an applicant for housing and services, a touch of honest press, a student, a homosexual, a member of the opposition to the regime. Divide these up as much as possible. Set them aside in a jar and label them "Anti-Mexico."
3. Take an indigenous Mexican. Take away the crafts and take a picture of her. Put her crafts and the photo in a jar and set aside. Label it "Tradition."
4. Put the indigenous Mexican in another jar, set it aside, and label it "Dispensable." One must not forget to disinfect oneself after this last operation.
5. Well, now open a store and hang a huge sign that says, "Mexico 1994-2000: Huge End-of-the-Century Sale."
6. Smile for the camera. Make sure the makeup covers the dark circles under the eyes caused by the many nightmares the process has caused.

Note: Always have on hand a policeman, a soldier, and an airplane ticket out of the country. These items may be necessary at any time.

PENTHOUSE MEXICO has no foreign vocation; for this it would have to have a nationality. The only country mentioned with sincerity on that increasingly narrow top floor is the country called money. And that country has no patriots, only profit and loss indexes; history happens only within the stock markets, and its modern heroes are Good Salesmen. For some reason, due to the other history (the real history) that top floor, instead of expanding, is contracting quickly. Every day, fewer and fewer are able to reside up there. Sometimes with delicacy, other times with brutality, the incapable ones are forced to go down—those stairs. The door to Mexico's penthouse elevator opens to the great international airports; it does not go up or down. To leave the penthouse, one must descend those stairs, go down farther and farther until . . .

TO GET TO MIDDLE MEXICO . . .

. . . ONE GOES BY CAR. It is urban, and its image is a carbon copy that repeats itself throughout the country, throughout Mexico City. It is an image of concrete that cannot deny the contradiction that the extremely rich and the extremely poor coexist. Middle Mexico smells bad. Something is rotting from within, while the sense of collectivity is being diluted. Middle Mexico does have a foreign vocation. Something tells it that to rise to Penthouse Mexico, the road passes through a country that is not this one. In order to "triumph" in Mexico, one must go abroad. This does not necessarily mean to leave physically, but to leave behind history, to leave behind goals. This vocation of exile as a synonym to triumph has nothing to do with the physical crossing of a border. There are those who have left and are still with us. And there are those who, although still with us, are gone.

Only three states of the federation have very low indexes of marginalization: the Federal District (Mexico City), Nuevo Leon, and North Baja California; ten more are within the low index marginalization: Coahuila, Baja California South, Aguascalientes, Chihuahua, Sonora, Jalisco, Colima, Tamaulipas, Estado de Mexico, and Morelos; another four have a medium index of marginalization: Quintana Roo, Sinaloa, Nayarit, and Tlaxcala.

Middle Mexico survives in the worst possible way: believing that it has a life. It has all of the disadvantages of Penthouse Mexico: historical ignorance, cynicism, opportunism, and an emptiness that import products can only fill partially or not at all. It has all the disadvantages of Lower Mexico: economic instability, insecurity, bewilderment, sudden loss of hope—and what's more, on every street corner misery knocks on the windows of the car. Sooner or later, Middle Mexico must get out of the car and, if he still has some change left, get into a taxi, a collective taxi, a subway, reach a bus terminal, and start the journey down, all the way to . . .

LOWER MEXICO . . .

. . . WHICH ONE CAN REACH almost immediately. It coexists in permanent conflict with Middle Mexico. Half of the people in the seventeen Mexican states in the middle, low, and very low indexes of marginalization live in cramped conditions, in poverty, with two or more persons to a room. 50 percent of each unit earn less than two minimum wages daily. In Tlaxcala, three-quarters of the population lives in poverty.

In Aguascalientes, Chihuahua, Jalisco, Colima, Tamaulipas, Morelos, Quintana Roo, Sinaloa, and Tlaxcala, a third of the population over fifteen years old has not completed primary school; in Nayarit more than 40 percent have not. One-third of the population in Tlaxcala has no sewers or plumbing. Quintana Roo and Sinaloa have a fourth of their inhabitants living on dirt floors. The states of Durango, Queretaro, Guanajuato, Michoacan, Yucatan, Campeche, Tabasco, Zacatecas and San Luis Potosí have high indexes of marginalization. Nearly half the people over fifteen have not completed primary school; one-third have neither plumbing nor sewers; nearly two-thirds live in crowded conditions; and more than 60 percent earn less than two minimum wages per day.

Lower Mexico does not share; it battles for an urban or rural space, notwithstanding the existence of its own internal dividing lines, its borders. In rural areas, estates, haciendas, and large agricultural concerns impose upon *ejidos* and peasant communities. In urban colonies it is not necessary to state the level of income, social position, and political vocation. It is enough to say in what colony of what city one lives: the name and the location, the services, the manner of speaking of their people, the way they dress, their entertainment, education—everything limits and classifies, trying to order, to accommodate, the chaos that rules Mexican cities. Within one city there are thousands of cities, fighting, surviving, struggling. In the countryside it is the mode of transportation, the way one dresses, and the attention one receives from the bank manager that indicate one's class—a person's standing can be determined by how long it takes him or her to be received in the reception areas of the financial or political world. In Lower Mexico the manor house on the Porfirian hacienda[3] has been replaced by the inner office of the bank. This is how modern times have penetrated rural Mexico.

Lower Mexico has a fighter's vocation; it is brave, it is solidarist, it is a clan, it is the "hood," it is the gang, the race, the friend; it is the strike, the march, and the meeting; it is taking back one's land, it is blocking highways, it is the "I don't believe you!" it is the "I won't take it anymore!" it is the "*orale!*"[4] Lower Mexico is the master tradesman, the mason, the plumber, the factory worker, the driver, the employee, the subway bus shared-cab student, the street cleaner, the truck driver and logician, the housewife, the small businessman, the traveling salesman, the farmer, the mini and micro entrepreneur, the miner, the colonizer, the peasant, the tenant farmer—from the provinces, yet living in the capital—the peon, the longshoreman in port cities, the fisherman and sailor, the used-clothes dealer, the butcher, the artisan. It is all the etceteras that one finds on any bus, on any street corner, in any given nook of any given place of any Mexico . . . of Lower Mexico.

Lower Mexico is the substance of the imprisoned, of the dispossessed, of garnishments, of liens, of layoffs, of evictions, of kidnappings, of tortures, of disappeared, of hassle, of death. Lower Mexico has absolutely nothing . . . but hasn't realized it. Lower Mexico already has overpopulation problems. Lower Mexico is a millionaire if one sums up its misery and its despair. Lower Mexico shares both urban and rural space, slips and falls, battles and downfalls. Lower Mexico is really far down, so far down that it seems that there is no way to go farther down, so far down that one can hardly see that little door that leads to . . .

BASEMENT MEXICO . . .

. . . ONE ARRIVES ON FOOT, either barefoot, or with rubber-soled huaraches. To get there one must descend through history and ascend through the indexes of marginalization. Basement Mexico came first. When Mexico was not yet Mexico, when it was all just beginning, the now—Basement Mexico existed, it lived. Basement Mexico is "indigenous" because Columbus thought, 502 years ago, that the land where he had arrived was India. "Indians" is what the natives of these lands have been called from that time on. Basement Mexico is: Mazahuan, Amuzgan, Tlapanecan, Nahuatlan, Coran, Huichol, Yaqui, Mayan, Tarahumaran, Mixtec, Zapotecan, Chontal, Seri, Triquis, Kumiain, Cucapan, Paipain, Cochimian, Kiliwan, Tequistlatecan, Pame, Chichimecan, Otomi, Mazatecan, Matlatzincan, Ocuiltecan, Popolocan, Ixcatecan, Chocho-popolocan, Cuicatec, Chatino, Chinantec, Huave, Papagan, Pima, Repehuan, Guarijian, Huastec, Chuj, Jalaltec, Mixe, Zoquean, Totonacan, Kikapuan, Purepechan, Oodham, Tzotzil, Tzeltal, Tojolabal, Chol, Mam.

Basement Mexico is indigenous . . . However, for the rest of the country, it does not count—it does not produce, sell, or buy—that is, it does not exist. Check out the text of the Free Trade Agreement, and you will find that, for this government, the indigenous do not exist. Furthermore, read Addendum 1001.a-1 to the Free Trade Agreement, dated October 7, 1992 (yes, just five days before the "festivities" of the 500th anniversary of the "Discovery of America"), and you will find that Salinas' government has "forgotten" to mention the National Indigenous Institute on the list of federal government entities. We have been in the mountains a very long time, and perhaps the National Indigenous Institute has been privatized. But it is still surprising that such well-known organizations as the Patronage for Aid to Social Reintegration, and Aid for the Commercialization of the Fishing Industry, and the Doctor Andres Bustamante Gurría Institute for Human Communication appear listed as "government entities." On the other hand, in Canada there is the Department of Indian Affairs and Northern Development.

Basement Mexico amasses traditions and misery; it possesses the highest indexes of marginalization and the lowest in nutrition. Six of the thirty-two states have a very high index of marginalization, all six of which have a large indigenous population: Puebla, Veracruz, Hidalgo, Guerrero, Oaxaca, and Chiapas.

The stratification of the Mexicos is repeated in the municipalities. On a national level there are 2,403 municipalities. Of these, 1,153 have a level of marginalization considered high or very high, 1,118 have medium and low levels of marginalization and only 132 municipalities have very low levels. States with high indigenous population have the majority of their municipalities with high and very high levels of marginalization: 94 out of 111 in Chiapas; 59 out of 75 in Guerrero; 431 of 570 in Oaxaca; 141 of 217 in Puebla; 10 of 18 in Queretaro; 33 of 56 in San Luis Potosí; 130 of 207 in Veracruz; 70 of 106 in Yucatan.

In Basement Mexico one lives and dies between the mud and blood. Hidden, but in its foundation, the contempt that this Mexico suffers will permit it to organize itself and shake up the entire system. Its burden will be the possibility of freeing itself from it. For these Mexicans, the lack of democracy, liberty, and justice will be organized. It will explode and shine on . . .

JANUARY 1994 . . .

. . . WHEN THE ENTIRE COUNTRY remembered that there was a basement. Thousands of indigenous, armed with truth and fire, with shame and dignity, shook the country awake from its sweet dream of modernity. "Enough is enough!" this Mexico calls out—enough dreams, enough nightmares. Ever since steel and the gospel dominated these lands, the indigenous voice has been condemned to resisting a war of extermination that now incorporates all of the inter-galactic-technological advances. Satellites, communications equipment, and infrared rays keep watch on every move, locate rebellions, and on military maps pinpoint the places for the seeding of bombs and death. Tens of thousands of olive green masks are preparing a new and prosperous war. They want to cleanse their dignity in serving the powerful with indigenous blood. They want to be accomplices in the unjust delivery of poverty and pain.

The indigenous Zapatistas will pay for their sins with their blood. What sins? The sin of not being satisfied with handouts, the sin of insisting on their demands for democracy, liberty, and justice for all Mexico, the sin of their "Everything for everyone, nothing for us."

Those who deny the indigenous Mexican peasant the possibility of understanding the concept of Nation, who force him to look to his past—which separates him from the rest of the country—and prohibit him from looking to the future—which unites the nation and which is the only possibility for survival of the indigenous people—reiterate the division, not of social classes, but of categories of citizens. The first is the governing class, the second is the political parties of the opposition, and the third is the rest of the citizens. The indigenous would be in the very inferior category of "citizens in formation." They are Basement Mexico, the waste pile where one goes, every once in a while, to look for something that could still be used on the upper floors, or to fix some imperfection that could endanger the stability or balance in the building.

Basement Mexico is the gravest threat to the season of sales that is being organized by Penthouse Mexico. Basement Mexico has nothing to lose and everything to win. Basement Mexico does not give up, can't be bought, resists . . .

In August 1994 a voice arose from Basement Mexico, a voice that does not speak of war, that does not plan to turn back the clock of history by 502 years, that does not demand the vanguard, that does not exclude its miseries. "Everything for everyone, nothing for us," speaks the language of the millennium. The voice of those without a face, of the unnamable, became familiar in the National Democratic Convention. This voice calls to Basement Mexico, it speaks to Middle Mexico: "Don't let our blood be wasted. Don't let death be in vain," say the mountains. Through the word separate roads join. Let the rebellion also embrace . . .

THE WOMEN: DUAL DREAM, DUAL NIGHTMARE, DUAL AWAKENING

IF AMONG MEN the division of the Mexicos is evident, to a point, with women it produces novel effects that make possible submission and rebellion.

In Penthouse Mexico, women reiterate their filigree status: being a trinket for the world's executives, the wise and "efficient" administrator of familial wellbeing—that is, measuring the dosage of weekly dinners at McDonald's. In Middle Mexico, women perpetuate the ancient cycle of daughter-girlfriend-wife and/or lover-mother. In the Lower and Basement Mexicos, the duplication of the nightmare where the man dominates and determines is endemic.

With the exception of respect, for the women in the Lower and Basement Mexicos everything is duplicated: the percentage of illiteracy, the subhuman living conditions, low salaries, and marginalization. These add up to the nightmare that the system prefers to ignore or disguise under the makeup of general indexes, which hide the exploitation of women, and make general exploitation possible.

But something is beginning not to fit in this dual submission, the dual nightmare begins to duplicate an awakening.

Women from Lower and Basement Mexico awaken fighting against the present and the past, which threatens to be their future.

The conscience of humanity passes through female conscience; the knowledge of being human implies they know they're women and struggle. They no longer need anyone to speak for them; their word follows the double route of a self-propelled rebellion—the double motor of rebel women.

1. Data from International Bank for Reconstruction and Development, World Bank, July 1991.

2. Miguel Aleman Valdés was governor of Veracruz and owner of Televisa, Mexico's communications giant.

3. Porfirian hacienda means a large estate with a great deal of land, making refernce to dicator Porfirio Díaz's policy of furthering the wealthy's interests to the detriment of the vast majority of the population.

4. *Orale* is a Mexican expression equivalent to "Right on!"

12

Mr. Zedillo, Welcome to the Nightmare

DECEMBER 3, 1994

Letter to Zedillo, after his inauguration speech as the new president of Mexico.

I must conclude due to lack of time, but I will add one more observation. Sometimes it is man's lot to attack the rights of others, to take their assets, threaten the lives of those who defend their nationality, make the highest virtues appear to be crimes, and give to his own vices the luster of true virtue. But there is one thing which neither falsity nor perfidy can reach, and that is the sentence of history. History will judge us.

—BENITO JUÁREZ (to Maximilian of Hapsburg, in response to a confidential letter where Maximilian proposes a secret negotiation and a position in his government)

Mr. Ernesto Zedillo Ponce de León:

WELCOME TO THE NIGHTMARE. You should know that the political system you represent (the one to which you owe your access to power, although not to legitimacy) has prostituted language to such a degree that today "politics" is synonymous to lies, crime, and treachery. I only say to you what millions of Mexicans would like to say: We don't believe you. And I add what, perhaps, not all believe: Enough of this waiting for the day when things will change. Your words today are the same ones we have heard at the beginning of other administrations.

The nation distrusts the electoral process that fraudulently raised you toward that illusory transfer of power. So, I direct myself to you, but more so to your tutor, Mr. Salinas de Gortari, who (as seen by the cabinet that accompanies you in this new lie) refuses to retire from national political life.

How do you expect the nation to believe you will seek justice in the assassination[1] that stained Mexico's recent history and revealed the true criminal face of your state party? How can we believe you, when one of those accused of the coverup has been rewarded with the right to manage our soil's wealth?

I see that you hold onto Sedesol,[2] that government agency that dispenses alms. And what dignity can you possibly bring us in exchange for a frank dialogue and respectful negotiations, when you appoint as your conscience-buying money man a hand-me-down from Salina's team? Since May 1993, instead of extending economic assistance to the places most in need, he has been busy buying indigenous dignity, as if it were a trinket in a crafts market.

Is this your counterinsurgency plan? The proliferation of social work in order to weaken our base of popular support? It is a good strategy, found in all the North American antiguerrilla manuals (and in all its history of failures). But don't you realize that money is never spent on social work? It winds up in the pockets of the corrupt leaders and municipal presidents of the PRI[3] in the Chiapas countryside. Is this counsel from Argentina's military advisers? Will you be deceived again like the time you were told that millions and millions of old and new pesos were invested in the region that, after January 1, suddenly became a "conflict zone?" How much more money and how much more blood are necessary for you to learn that corruption—which up to now has allowed you to survive as a political system—will be your grave tomorrow?

Allow me to continue to comment. Your cabinet is proof that your inauguration speech is only a bunch of words. Rather than a governmental team, it is more like a storefront; in your economic team you have placed a team—inherited from your tutor—that distinguishes itself by its willingness to sell out in everything that concerns our national sovereignty and Mexican dignity. In the Ministry of Foreign Affairs you have someone who looks good to outsiders but not to Mexican people—have foreign affairs simply become commercial relations? In the Department of Hydraulic Resources you have guaranteed that poverty and discontent will continue to grow in the Mexican countryside.

In general, one can see in your cabinet a foreign and frenchified shadow—its cast suffered by all Mexicans during this past administration. So many lies and so much cover-up will be useless; this country will explode in your hands, no matter how much you believe that you control the resources necessary to keep the people as "put-up-with-anything" Mexicans.

I listened carefully to your speech on the radio. You are correct when you say it is not our violence that the nation fears. But your lesson is incomplete. You characterize the climate of insecurity in which the country lives as amorphous. The principal promoter of instability, insecurity, and violence is the state-party system; it is the political system that you cannot destroy, quite simply, because the power you now hold, you owe to its existence.

The cabinet you present to the country today is a small demonstration of the pending debts with which your administration commences. Your speech will crumble when your various accomplices—those whose cover-up of a state crime helped you to the presidency—come to claim their due. The crime began with the assassination of the one from whom you inherited your candidacy. It continued in the mockery of the electoral campaigns. It passed a self-test on the twenty-first of August, and it culminates in this fateful December 1, 1994.

Two "first" days now mark Mexico's history in opposite ways. The first of January was marked by the rising cries for dignity and rebellion of Mexicans of differing social origins, but suffering the same disgrace. Since that day, men, women, children and the elderly in cities and the countryside—of different colors, of different races and languages, but of a common suffering—speak with a single indigenous voice. On the other hand, the first of December concludes the burial commenced long before the twenty-first of August: the burial of a hope for the peaceful transition to democracy, liberty, and justice.

The indigenous communities suffer not only the "serious privations, injustices, and lack of opportunity" that you point out. They also suffer a serious illness that, little by little, begins to affect the rest of the population: rebellion. While your government lasts, you will be witness to this.

You say: "The government, society, the affected communities, we will all unite against poverty." Nevertheless, you appoint a cabinet along the same lines as Carlos Salinas de Gortari, the man who buried the country in misery. We do not want for Mexico your kind of unity, which will assure the permanence of the same system of oppression, now made up to look like a new administration. That is not the type of unity that Mexico needs. The one that our history reclaims is the unity against the state-party system of government, which has the nation submerged in a poverty of body and spirit.

You point out that "during this year, the spirit of all Mexicans has been darkened by the events in Chiapas, by violence, and more so, by the conditions of profound injustice, misery and negligence which fertilized that violence." Neither the conditions of profound injustice nor of violence belong exclusively to the state of Chiapas. The entire nation suffers the high social cost imposed by neoliberalism.[4] If there are no profound transformations, violence will darken the nation, and not necessarily because we promote it.

You contradict yourself when you say, "There will not be violence on the government's part," because the White Guards[5] of the large cattle ranchers and businessmen act with impunity and with government complicity. You are starting off wrong if all you can offer is half-truths. You say you are "indignant to learn that women suffer violence in public; that children and adolescents are victims of abuse outside their schools; that workers lose their salaries in muggings, and small businessmen in armed robberies; outraged to learn of the impunity resulting from the abuse of authority, venality, and corruption." Yes, and it is also outrageous to learn that there are twenty-four billionaires at the expense of a humiliating 4 percent increase in the already paltry minimum wage. It is also outrageous to learn that the theft of our national identity has been "legalized" by the North American Free Trade Agreement,[6] which only means freedom for the powerful to rob, and the freedom for the dispossessed to live in misery; it is outrageous that the one who now wears the presidential sash does so, not by the will of the people, but by the will of money and fear.

You say, "The brutal assassinations of some of the country's prominent political figures have deeply wounded the citizenry; they have sown discontent and doubt about certain institutions and, we should admit it, have divided the Mexicans." Yes, they are divided, but not only by those crimes but by those perpetrated, day and night, by all the members of the governmental apparatus—from the previous leader of the executive branch to the very last minor municipal bureaucrat.

You ask for unity and point out that: "the moment has arrived when we must gather our wills, without sacrificing our differences." But, you are only looking for the endorsement and legitimacy not given you by the popular vote. Your offer of a "permanent dialogue" has already taken shape in the repression which was set into motion in December. Perhaps you are thinking of a "Dialogue Commission" made up of grenadiers and policemen to deal with the press and the opposition.

It is not necessary to declare that as president of the republic, you will not intervene "in any way in the processes and decisions which are solely the party's to make," the party to which you belong; that will be done by Mr. Carlos Salinas de Gortari. Your cabinet and the impunity enjoyed by the PRI leadership is proof enough. Of course, we agree with you when you say that "in this historic moment, let no one run from responsibility, lessen the effort, fall into the temptation of giving up."

We, the Zapatistas, will not run from our responsibility, lessen our efforts, or give into the temptation of giving up. We will continue to struggle, with our weapons in our hands, against the state-party system, which allows us to see clearly the figure of Salinas standing behind you.

From November 17, 1994, to the present, I carry the baton of the supreme command of the rebel forces. Consequently, I assume the responsibility of responding to you in the name of our entire army.

In your first speech as president, you point out your desire to seek negotiations as a way of resolving the conflict, and you offer us that road.

Mr. Zedillo, it is my duty to say to you that we cannot believe you. You are part of a system that has arrived at the greatest aberration: to resort to assassination in order to settle its differences—as if you were a group of criminals. You do not speak to us as a representative of the nation. Your word is stained with blood from the assassination of thousands—including some from your own political circle. That stain covers the Institutional Revolutionary Party (PRI). How can we believe in the sincerity of your invitation to a negotiated solution?

From the beginning of the presidential term, the number of troops have increased, making evident a distinct disposition to annihilation. Since November 14, the intrusion of planes overhead was obvious and continuous. "Hercules" planes transported men and military supplies to the counterinsurgency commando bases on the Guatemalan border. The foreign military "advisers" (and I want to say clearly that they are not Argentinean, because these animals have no country), have prepared their pupils. The flights have stopped; I suppose you are ready. We know the number and location of your troops, your general strategy, and a few tactical plans.

Unfortunately, we can take no widespread political or armed action. The military encirclement prevents us. Our repeated declarations against the increase of your belligerent preparations have only frustrated and bored the nation.

You should know that I have given orders that all the members of the CCRI[7] remain in the rearguard, to guarantee that the political direction of our just cause not be lost. Know that, as in January, I have asked that our military leaders stay with their units. I will do the same. I have made the necessary preparations so that my successors to the military leadership can assume their responsibilities without major problems, in case I should die.

Our main strength is also our main weakness. The support of the civilian population, which allowed us to grow and become strong, now obliges us to abandon all intent to retreat without them. That is why, for us, there is no stepping back. We must fight at the side of the people who have protected us; we will be the shields and guardians of their lives. I know that takes from us all possibility of survival. To confront an army superior to ours in weapons and personnel, although not in morality, nullifies the possibilities of success. To surrender has been expressly forbidden; any Zapatista leaders who opt to surrender will be decommissioned.

No matter the outcome of this war, sooner or later this sacrifice—which today appears useless and sterile to many—will be compensated by the lightning that will illuminate other lands. For sure, the light will reach deep into the South, shimmer in the Mar de Plata, in the Andes, the land of Artigas, Paraguay, and the entirety of this inverted and absurd pyramid that is Latin America. Strength is not on our side; it has never been on the side of the dispossessed. But history's reasoning, the shame and ardor we feel in our chests that is called dignity, make of us, today's nameless, true men and women, forever.

With the dumb image of our patient waiting compensated with the aggression clothed in olive green jackets, we received your offer to make us "part of the solution," and to a secret and direct dialogue. In reference to your offer that we be "an active part in the carrying out of actions," let me make this clear. If you are referring to the cost of Zapatista dignity, know that there is not enough money in the entire nation to come close to its price. Don't deceive yourself into thinking that our cry—"Everything for everyone, nothing for ourselves"—is a passing fancy, or a deceit to cover up our ambition for power. The Zapatistas don't have a price, because dignity does not have a price.

In reference to the direct and secret dialogue, in my role as supreme commander of the EZLN, I solemnly reject your invitation to a secret negotiation, behind the back of the nation.

You say that come years of war, thousands of deaths and great destruction, you and I will wind up negotiating; that it is best to do it now; that war should be avoided. But which war is to be avoided? The one that we began against your system by making legitimate use of self-defense and rebellion? Or the one that you have made against us since you have been the power and government in these Mexican lands?

The war that we want to end is the one waged by the political system behind and above you, and against us; the war against any democratizing effort, against any desire for justice, against any aspiration for liberty. This is the war that all Mexicans suffer and that must come to an end. Once it ends, the other war, our war, everyone's war, will extinguish itself. Useless and sterile, it will leave like a nightmare, soothed by the first light of day. This is the peace we want. Any effort in any other direction is a deception.

To prevent the war of the dispossessed by keeping or stepping up the war, which benefits those in power, will only postpone history's judgment: that democracy, liberty, and justice will triumph on the soil and in the skies of Mexico.

If you are a man of honor and dignity, I invite you to resign. You should resign from the shame of heading up that great lie that has betrayed the Mexican people and their hope for a peaceful transition to democracy. But before you do so, bring Carlos Salinas de Gortari to a political trial and help the world avoid another lie, like the one the World Trade Organization prepares: the North American Free Trade Agreement. And before that, as supreme chief of the federal army, let officials, ranks, and troops go, so they can choose the path dictated by their consciences and their patriotic hearts. Don't humiliate them by obliging them to accept foreign intervention, which advises them to kill Mexicans.

I have owned that responsibility, and have released my troops from the commitment to stay, so that they could have a choice: to be able to give up, to choose conformity. Not a one has accepted. Neither a salary nor threats bind them to our ranks, but shame and dignity form chains that are difficult to break. All of them have chosen the same path as yesterday: patriotism and justice.

For my part, I recognize that I have been mistaken about you. In February, I believed that your patriotic interest would be greater than your arrogance, that your intelligence would let you see that you yourselves constitute the major obstacle to the country's development, that you would step aside and open the door to a peaceful transition to democracy.

But it did not happen that way. On August 21, you decided to slam the door shut and to repeat the arrogance of a landslide victory. But history shows that the doors to a peaceful change and to a violent change—to peace and to war—are inversely linked; when one is closed, the other opens. By closing the door to a peaceful transition to democracy, you opened the heavy portal to war.

The stupidity of your behavior in Chiapas suddenly has brought me back to reality; the state-party system is not intelligent. Furthermore, today I see that imbecility is inherent to your decay. Having had the opportunity to ease the knot of the political conflict, you held on to it and tightened it, roping in sectors—once on the margins of the conflict—to the extremes of polarization. The deterioration is irreversible; the middle ground has disappeared, and the extremes confront each other and demand the extermination of each other.

We have grown by tens of thousands. As I pointed out to you, the supreme government has always taken pertinent measures to be rid of us as a problem, and that has made us grow. Facing the risk of eliminating us by political isolation, by creating a vacuum, the government, and its clumsy local and regional politics, has breathed life into the fire, which will ultimately consume it.

You must disappear, not just because you represent a historic aberration, a negation of humanity and a cynical cruelty; you should disappear because you are an insult to intelligence. You made us possible, you made us grow. We are your other, your Siamese opposite. In order for us to disappear, you must disappear as well.

It is very difficult to try to listen to you. One supposes that one is speaking with rational beings, but apparently not. Accustomed to buying, corrupting, imposing, breaking, and assassinating all that is placed in front of you, face to face with dignity you assume the pose of the crafty businessman, seeking the best price for his goods. This has been your systematic attitude during the eleven months of an unstable cease-fire. It is the "intelligent" attitude of a gambler who deposits a coin into a slot machine and waits for the product, which he has chosen and bought—peace—to drop out.

You should know that we have done everything possible to keep the conflict within the political realm, to avoid at all costs the reinitiation of hostilities. We have called upon different national political personalities, inviting them to an initiative that can direct, through political and civil means, the discontent that now overflows toward violence. If these politicians refuse to risk their political capital in what are just demands—the annulment of the elections, a transitional government, and a new electoral process—then there will be no solution, and the inevitable horror will come. Today, Mexico may not have statesmen who are willing to pay the price of their public image in exchange for being responsible to the struggle for democracy. Nevertheless, this does not mean that they will not exist tomorrow, men and women for whom politics is not synonymous with cynicism and a surrender disguised as "gradualism."[8]

Mr. Ernesto Zedillo:

UNTIL TODAY, you were nothing more than a citizen to us. Today, you are the official inheritor of a system without vision, which sacrifices the future and the national sovereignty of the nation. After today, in the unlikely case that you should try to make contact with us, I declare we will make public all communication from your government, while it lasts.

I am sure that in your rise to power you have found men and women ready to sell themselves and compromise, "under reasonable circumstances," which is nothing more than a rationalized surrender. The men and women who have confronted the state-party system since January 1, 1994, are perhaps of a stripe you have not encountered before.

We are men and women for whom "country," "democracy," "liberty," and "justice" should be—besides grand and noble words—a reality for the Mexican nation. For us, it is shameful to live without reaching that goal. To die fighting for it is an honor.

Know that from today, along with the seven elements of the Baton of the Zapatista Command, I carry two original volumes of the *Diary of the Constitutional Congress Debates from November of 1916 to February of 1917.* As long as a new constitution is not created, we will uphold the 1917 Constitution as the true one. We will fight for it.

In historic terms, you and I are of little value; random luck has brought us face to face. You personify all that is reactionary, antidemocratic, and contrary to the sentiments and the interests of the dispossessed. We personify hope: to have, at last, the opportunity to decide our own destiny, that democracy, liberty, and justice be more than just the subject of speeches and textbooks and become a reality for everyone, but above all, for those who have nothing.

You have a face, a name, a past, a present, and a future. With our name comes the curse to carry weapons in our hands, and the honor to rescue a history of dignity; our surname carries our vocation to the nation and to liberty. We are candidates only for a mass grave and immediate oblivion.

But "we" are thousands of Mexicans scattered throughout our national territory. We are men and women, children and old people, who have recuperated, together with the word *dignity,* the conviction that human beings should struggle to be free if they are slaves, and once free, should struggle so that other human beings also can be free. We know that our refusal to a dialogue under the conditions that you propose will make a military solution your first choice in future decisions. We do not fear death nor history's judgment.

If in truth the entire country is willing to give up its desire for liberty and democracy, then the clamor for our annihilation will be gigantic, and you will not have to worry. Important government officials say they will annihilate us all in a few hours, or a few days if the weather is bad. That way, the stock market, foreign trade, and the balance of payments would suffer only a few days of uncertainty.

On the other hand, if the people of Mexico wish to listen to our rebel cry for dignity—and we believe they do—then millions of voices will join us in our demand for the three conditions to a dignified peace: democracy, liberty, and justice.

You are no longer you. You are the personification of an unjust system, antidemocratic and criminal. We, the "illegal," the "transgressors of the law," the "professionals of violence," the "nameless," are everybody's hope, today and always.

This is all, Mr. Zedillo. I have spoken to you with sincerity, in a way in which you have not spoken to me, but I may be mistaken. I reiterate our demands for peace: *democracy, liberty, and justice for ALL Mexicans.* As long as these demands remain unmet, there will be war in Mexico's territory.

Vale. Health to you, and a parachute for that cliff that comes with your tomorrow.

From the mountains of the Mexican Southeast.
SUBCOMANDANTE INSURGENTE MARCOS

NOTES

1. The assassination of Luis Donaldo Colosio, Salinas's hand-picked successor to the presidency, while he was campaigning on the streets of Tijuana on March 23, 1994, remains unsolved. The official story claims the murder was the act of a solitary madman.

2. Sedesol is the Ministry of Social Development.

3. The PRI (Partido Revolucionario Institucional), the ruling party in Mexico, remained in power for seventy-one years.

4. Neoliberalism is a variation on the classical liberalism of the nineteenth century, when Britain and other imperialist powers used the ideology of competition and "free trade" to justify their own colonialisms. Anticolonial revolt ended the empires, and worker revolt in the 1930s ended classical liberalism but was contained by Keynesianism: government management of the wage, the welfare state, and "development." An international cycle of worker, student, peasant, woman, and pro-ecology revolt in the 1960s eroded Keynesian economics, and it was replaced by neoliberalism-designed, pushed, and implemented by some of the biggest, most powerful institutions in the world, such as the International Monetary Fund and the World Bank. Think tanks, university departments, and government agencies house an international army of neoliberal architects, planners, and apologists-backed up by the armed might of the state in all its forms. This history suggests that defeating neoliberalism will not be enough; we must go beyond reformism to defeat all forms of capitalism.

    Neoliberalism is both an ideology and a strategy. Like so many evils, it has many aliases: "Reaganomics," "Thatcherism," "supply-side economics," "monetarism," "new classical economics," and "structural adjustment." Neoliberalism subordinates all economic actors, including government and individuals, to the demands of the market. Its strategy includes privatization, reduced social expenditures, union busting, land enclosure, lower wages, higher profits, free trade, free capital mobility, and the accelerated commodification of natural resources.

5. White Guards, privately funded mini-armies at the disposal of the moneyed ranchers in the Mexican countryside, have been responsible for many indigenous deaths.

6. The North American Free Trade Agreement (NAFTA), which built on the 1989 U.S.-Canada Free Trade Agreement (CFTA), is the most comprehensive regional free trade agreement ever negotiated. It created the world's largest free trade area: 380 million people producing nearly $8 trillion dollars worth of goods and services. Since NAFTA came into force on January 1, 1994, the Clinton administration has worked to ensure that its provisions are swiftly implemented and to eliminate remaining barriers to U.S. exports. Cooperative agreements on labor and the environment are included in the NAFTA package. Mexican opponents feel this has opened the doors for U.S. products to flood Mexican markets and compete with domestic industry, to Mexico's detriment.

7. CCRI stands for Comite Clandestino Revolucionario Indigena (Clandestine Revolutionary Indigenous Committee).

8. Gradualism in Mexican politics is a theory that change must come in increments, not through radical moves.

13

Come, Brothers and Sisters

To the people of Mexico
To the peoples of the world

Brothers and sisters:
WITH OLD PAIN and new death, our heart speaks to you so that your hearts may listen. Just in living we were in pain, just in being we hurt. Being silent, our voice was passing away. Our voice spoke of peace, but not of yesterday's peace, which was dead. Our voice was about tomorrow's peace. The fire tended in days gone by, that spoke for our race when all were deaf to death, had stayed behind. Still lost in the arroyos of the mountains, our tears asked for another way. So our dead spoke. The oldest ones then counseled us to look to where the sun walks, to ask other brothers and sisters of our race, our blood and hope, where our pain should walk, and where to walk our tired step. We did this, brothers and sisters. Then silence arrived to put out the fire, and there was no arrogance in the true men and women's word for those in other lands and other races, who shared the pain and the wish for a tomorrow.

We opened our heart, brothers and sisters. We learned to see and to listen to others, to different brothers and sisters. We listened to their words and saw into their hearts. And we saw in their step the same longing that put the fire in our hands, that broke up our face until it was nothing but a gaze, that hid our name and erased our past: the struggle to rule by obeying, to live free, to free the word and the heart, to give and receive what is deserved—the struggle for democracy, freedom, and justice. Nothing more, nothing less.

These brothers and sisters' words, your word, asked us to try another path, to leave pending and waiting the fire that armed the breast. You said for us to talk, and that through these words would come our destination. And the others were you, who like us are the always forgotten, who like us are the always humiliated. Our brothers and sisters. And so we spoke. Our voice spoke with the powerful lord. Obeying, we sent our word to the great house of money. We spoke, and we listened. We were following that path when treason, once again, put weapons above words. Our voice was silenced all at once by the noise of the machines of war. Terror was unleashed again in the Mexican lands by the one who, from arrogance and power, looks at us with contempt, denies our name, and gives us death in answer to our thought.

It wasn't enough for him to deny us a face and a life. He wanted to humble the dignity of our step, trample our just demands, take truth from our song, bury our flag in oblivion. With the complicity of big money and a foreign vocation, he wanted to humiliate us, even in our speech. Turning back the wheel of history, he wanted to force us with bayonets to deny our history. Our women suffered the harassment and the humiliation of the machines of war. Some of our children—the ones who didn't die—grew with bitterness and impotence between their hands. Hate sharpened in our men's hearts. The eldest grandparents again looked to the earth and asked counsel of the first dead. They spoke, we the always dead. They said:

"Our hand was not raised armed to listen or kneel to insults and humiliations.

"Our step did not rise so that he who is double-faced could humiliate us by filling hope with lies.

"Our hand was armed and our step raised for justice, but not the justice that is the false promise that dresses the powerful.

"Our hand was armed and our step raised for freedom, but not the freedom that is sold for a fistful of coins to a foreign hand.

"Our hand was armed and our step raised for democracy, a democracy that is still absent because of the man who was carried into government by cynicism, crime, and lies.

"Anything, brothers and sisters, but that dignity be trampled again.

"Anything, brothers and sisters, but that lies again fill our table.

"Anything, brothers and sisters, but to forget tomorrow again."

Thus they spoke. Our dead said this, and the war came. Then we saw our brother come in other clothing. He came to kill. To die. Again, we did not want to raise our hand to confront the one sent to kill and to die among the same brothers and sisters. For that reason, our past went to the mountains. We went into the caves of those who came before us. Death cornered us and pursued the lives of those who always passed away in obscurity, shades of death and of the shadow of a forgetful country. Again, Death came to wield its knife-edged oblivion. It came to kill memory. Again, our hand filled with the fire to avenge our own pain, again being animals eating dirt, dying persecuted and forgotten.

Already the drums called to war. Already, the bat men and women prepared their flight of mortal death. Now Pain's night came again to cover the vengeance of the true men and women.

But from where the sun walks, there came another voice that was not of death. It was a big voice that came with the wind. Our hurting heart waited and heard what the voice spoke. War must not walk, it said. Death must wait. That the heart of the true men and women not be a mirror of pain again. This we did. The bitterness was put away in the caves, and our pain waited for that voice to shout. The voice spoke strongly. How could we not hear it? The voice had many parts. Great was the song of its drums. Only the arrogant closed their heart. Without fire, with a name and face, that voice raised again the banner of human dignity. For that voice we were not animals; we were men and women again. The voice came walking from other lands, from far away, from the heart of other lands, from other mountains, from other hopes kin to ours. This voice became strong and great, became the relief to our pain. And by waiting we harvested hope. The voice was a seed in the collective heart that walks in our step.

Brothers and sisters: That voice gives us a name. No longer are we the unmentionables. We the forgotten have a name. Now without hiding, our flag can cover our dead and our history. Now we have a place in the heart of our brothers and sisters—you—and a small corner in the history that really counts: that of the struggle. Having now a collective name, we discovered that death shrinks and becomes small before us. The worst death, that of oblivion, flees so that the memory of our dead will never be buried together with their bones. We have now a collective name and our pain has shelter. Now we are larger than death.

Now that we have a name, we hope that tomorrow, brothers and sisters, you will give us a face, that you will put out the fire that lives in our hands and, instead of the past, give us a future.

Tomorrow's lives smile for those who are the always dead. In the mountains one can hear the bones of the men of wood. The men and women of corn dance. Our heart is joyful, even as our body hurts. A light shines on these shadows that always dance with death, the true men and women of always.

We are named.

Now we will not die.

Come, brothers and sisters, we cannot go. Great is your strength if you make it so. Come, there will be no fire to receive your step, nor will our heart be closed to your word. Come.

We have a name. Now we will not die. Let us dance.

Health to you, brothers! Death to death! Long live the EZLN!

Democracy!

Freedom!

Justice!

From the mountains of the Mexican Southeast
CLANDESTINE INDIGENOUS REVOLUTIONARY COMMITTEE
GENERAL COMMAND OF THE EZLN.

14

The Word and the Silence

To the people of Mexico
To the peoples and governments of the world

Brothers and sisters:

TODAY WE ARE REMEMBERING our oldest elders, those who initiated the long struggle of resistance against the arrogance of Power and the violence of money. They, our ancestors, taught us that a people with pride are a people who do not surrender, who resist, who have dignity. They taught us to be proud of the color of our skin, of our language, of our culture. More than 500 years of exploitation and persecution have not been able to exterminate us. We have resisted since that time because history has been made with our blood. The noble Mexican nation rests on our bones. If they destroy us, the entire country will plummet and begin to wander without direction or roots. A prisoner of the shadows, Mexico would negate its tomorrow by denying its yesterday.

Today we are a fundamental part of a country whose governing officials have a foreign vocation and look with disdain and repugnance at our past. For them we are a bother, an obstacle that must be eliminated, silently. Their cruelty is seen today as a form of charity; death looks for silent paths; it looks for the complicit darkness and the silence that hides. They have already tried to exterminate us. Different doctrines and many different ideas have been used to cover ethnocide with rationality.

Today, the thick mantle with which they try to cover their crime is called neoliberalism, and it represents death and misery for the original people of these lands, and for all of those of a different skin color but with a single indigenous heart that we call Mexicans.

Today, the conquerors continue to persecute the indigenous who are rebellious. Today, the modern invaders of our lands live in the supreme government. They pursue the indigenous people, who cover themselves with the flag of the red five-pointed star, the flag of the Zapatista National Liberation Army. But they pursue not only the Zapatistas: death decreed by Power pursues all the indigenous of Mexico, including those with fair skin. Our brothers and sisters in Guerrero suffer the intolerance of the viceroy who is supported by the central power; our brothers and sisters in Tabasco suffer the imposition of drug trafficking and its dirty money; in Veracruz, Oaxaca, Hidalgo, and San Luis Potosi the blood of the dark ones is pursued by political bosses disguised as government officials; to the north our indigenous brothers pay with death and poverty for the empire of drugs and crime that the bad government has constructed; in the central and western parts of the country, brutality and disdain walk disguised as "progress." Power's servant smiles while he negotiates overseas a price for the motherland. The arrogant one thinks that he has won and that there are no people with dignity left under our Mexican skies. He thinks that death will complete what oblivion and silence have tried to end. They offer a nation of shadows, docile and humiliated. They seek a price for that which cannot be bought: Mexico's dignity. Indigenous blood is nourishment for Mexican blood.

But the color of the skin does not define the indigenous person: dignity and the constant struggle to be better define him. Those who struggle together are brothers and sisters, regardless of the color of our skin or the language that we learned as children.

What matters is the national flag, the one that acknowledges the indigenous foundation of a nation that until now has condemned them to despair. What matters is the national emblem, which prevents Power's serpent from conquering. What matters is the land that sustains us in history and prevents us from abandoning ourselves. What matters is the sky that is carried on our shoulders, the sky that today weighs greatly but that will heal our vision. What matters are Mexicans, and not those who sell us by knocking on foreign doors.

What matters is our eldest elders who received the word and the silence as a gift in order to know themselves and to touch the heart of the other. Speaking and listening is how true men and women learn to walk. It is the word that gives form to that walk that goes on inside us. It is the word that is the bridge to cross to the other side. Silence is what Power offers our pain in order to make us small. When we are silenced, we remain very much alone. Speaking, we heal the pain. Speaking, we accompany one another. Power uses the word to impose his empire of silence. We use the word to renew ourselves. Power uses silence to hide his crimes. We use silence to listen to one another, to touch one another, to know one another.

This is the weapon, brothers and sisters. We say, the word remains. We speak the word. We shout the word. We raise the word and with it break the silence of our people. We kill the silence, by living the word. Let us leave Power alone in what the lie speaks and hushes. Let us join together in the word and the silence which liberate.

Five hundred and three years ago today, October 12, the word and the silence of Power begin to die.

Five hundred and three years ago today, October 12, our word and our silence began to resist, to fight, to live. Today, 503 years later, we are still here. There are more of us and we are better. We are of many colors, and many are the languages that speak our word.

Today there is no shame in our heart because of the color of our skin or our speech.

Today we say we are indigenous, and we say it like giants.

Today, 503 years after death from a foreign land arrived to bring us silence, we resist and we speak.

Today, 503 years later, we live . . .

Long live the indigenous Mexicans!

Democracy!

Liberty!

Justice!

From the mountains of the Mexican Southeast
CLANDESTINE INDIGENOUS REVOLUTIONARY COMMITTEE
GENERAL COMMAND
ZAPATISTA NATIONAL LIBERATION ARMY

15

Fourth Declaration of the Lacandon Jungle

(excerpt)

JANUARY 1, 1996

TODAY WE SAY:
WE ARE HERE,
WE ARE REBEL DIGNITY, THE
FORGOTTEN OF THE HOMELAND.

All those communities, all those who work the land, all whom we invite to stand on our side so that together we may give life to one sole struggle, so that we may walk with your help.

We must continue to struggle and not rest until the land is our own, the property of the people, of our grandfathers, taken from us by those who crush the land with their stone step, beneath the shadow of those who have gone before us, who command us: that with the strength of our heart and our hand held high, we raise, to be seen by all, that beautiful banner of the dignity and freedom of we who work the land; that we must continue to struggle until we defeat those who have crowned themselves, those who have helped to take the land from others, those who make much money with the labor of people like us, those who mock us in their estates. That is our obligation of honor, if we want to be called honest men and good inhabitants of our communities.

Now then, somehow, more than ever, we need to be united, with all our heart, and all our effort in that great task of attaining a marvelous and true unity, commenced by those who preserve purity in their heart, guard their principles, and do not lose faith in a good life.

We beg that those who receive this manifesto pass it on to all the men and women of all communities. Reform, Liberty, Justice, and Law.

—EMILIANO ZAPATA, (original Zapatista manifesto, written in Nahuatl)

To the people of Mexico
To the peoples and governments of the world

Brothers and sisters:

THE FLOWER OF THE WORD will not die. The masked face that today has a name may die, but the word that came from the depth of history and the earth can no longer be cut by power's arrogance. We were born of the night. We live in the night. We will die in her. But tomorrow the light will be for others, for all those who today weep at the night, for those who have been denied the day, for those for whom death is a gift, for those who are denied life. The light will be for all of them. For everyone everything. For us pain and anguish, for us the joy of rebellion, for us a future denied, for us the dignity of insurrection. For us nothing.

Our fight has been to make ourselves heard, and the bad government screams arrogance and closes its ears with its cannons.

Our fight is caused by hunger, and the gifts of the bad government are lead and paper for our children's stomachs.

Our fight is for a worthy roof over our heads, and the bad government destroys our homes and our history.

Our fight is for knowledge, and the bad government distributes ignorance and disdain.

Our fight is for the land, and the bad government gives us cemeteries.

Our fight is for a job that is just and dignified, and the bad government buys and sells our bodies and our shame.

Our fight is for life, and the bad government offers death as our future.

Our fight is for respect, for our right to sovereignty and self-government, and the bad government imposes the laws of the few on the majority of the people.

Our fight is for freedom of thought and movement, and the bad government builds jails and erects graves.

Our fight is for justice, and the bad government is made up of criminals and assassins.

Our fight is for history, and the bad government proposes to erase history.

Our fight is for the homeland, and the bad government dreams with a foreign flag and language.

Our fight is for peace, and the bad government announces war and destruction.

Housing, land, employment, food, education, independence, democracy, liberty, justice, and peace, these were our banners during the dawn of 1994. These were our demands during that 500-years-long night. Today, these are our demands.

Our blood and our word have lit a small fire in the mountain, and we walk a path against the house of money and the powerful. Brothers and sisters of other races and languages, of other colors, but with the same heart, now protect our light, and in it they drink of the same fire.

The powerful came to extinguish us with its violent wind, but our light grew in other lights. The rich still dream about extinguishing the first light. It is useless; there are now too many lights, and they have all become that first one.

The arrogant wish to extinguish a rebellion that they mistakenly believe began in the dawn of 1994. But the rebellion, which now has a dark face and an indigenous language, was not born today. It spoke before with other languages and in other lands. This rebellion against injustice spoke in many mountains and many histories. It has already spoken in Nahuatl, Paipai, Kiliwa, Cucapa, Cochimi, Kumiai, Yuma, Seri, Chontal, Chinanteco, Pame, Chichimeca, Otomi, Mazahua, Matlatzinca, Ocuilteco, Zapoteco, Solteco, Chatino, Papabuco, Mixteco, Cucateco, Triqui, Amuzgo, Mazateco, Chocho, Ixcateco, Huave, Tlapaneco, Totonaca, Tepehua, Populuca, Mixe, Zoque, Huasteco, Lacandon, Mayo, Chol, Tzeltal, Tzotzil, Tojolabal, Mame, Teco, Ixil, Aguacateco, Motocintleco, Chicomucelteco. Castilian was spoken and is still spoken. Rebellion is not a question of language, it is a question of dignity and of being human.

Because we work, they kill us. Because we live, they kill us. There is no place for us in the world of the powerful. Because we fight, they kill; but only by fighting will we make a world where all of us fit, where all of us can live without death in our words. They want to take the land so that our feet have nothing to stand on. They want to take our history so that we and our word will be forgotten and die. They do not want the indigenous. They want us dead.

The powerful want our silence. When we were silent, we died. Without the word, we did not exist. We fight against this loss of memory, against death and for life. We fight the fear of a death because we have ceased to exist in memory.

When the homeland speaks its indigenous heart, it will have dignity and memory.

Brothers and sisters:
MANY WORDS WALK in the world. Many worlds are made. Many worlds make us. There are words and worlds that are lies and injustices. There are words and worlds that are truths and truthful. We make true words. We have been made from true words.

In the world of the powerful there is no space for anyone but themselves and their servants. In the world we want, everyone fits.

We want a world in which many worlds fit. The nation that we construct is one where all communities and languages fit, where all steps may walk, where all may have laughter, where all may live the dawn.

We speak of unity even when we are silent. Softly and gently we speak the words that find the unity that embraces us in history and which will discard the abandonment that confronts and destroys us.

Our word, our song and our cry, is so that the most dead will no longer die. We fight so that they may live. We sing so that they may live.

The word lives.

Enough is enough! lives.

The night that becomes morning lives.

Our step with dignity, which walks besides those who weep, lives.

We fight to stop the powerful's clock of death.

We fight for a time for living.

Word's flower does not die, even though silence walks our steps. The word is seeded in silence. So that it blooms with a shout, it is silent. The word becomes soldier so as not to die in oblivion. In order to live the word dies, forever seeded in the world's belly. By being born and living, we die. We will always live. Only those who give up their history will return to oblivion.

We are here. We do not surrender. Zapata is alive, and in spite of everything, the struggle continues.

From the mountains of the Mexican Southeast
SUBCOMANDANTE INSURGENTE MARCOS
INDIGENOUS CLANDESTINE REVOLUTIONARY COMMITTEE
GENERAL COMMAND OF THE ZAPATISTA ARMY OF NATIONAL LIBERATION

16

Closing Words to the National Indigenous Forum (excerpt)

JANUARY 9, 1996
SAN CRISTOBAL DE LAS CASAS, CHIAPAS

Through my voice speaks the voice of the Zapatista National Liberation Army.

Brothers and sisters:
WE WANT TO SAY a few words to those present at the National Indigenous Forum.

The Counselors

IN MANY OF OUR INDIGENOUS communities in Mexico, there is the custom of looking to the first days of January to see how the months of the year to come will be like. This knowledge helps us know when to prepare the earth, when to plant the seed, and when to harvest. Amongst the most ancient Mayas, this practice was known as *xoc-kin*, the "accounting of the days."

And there were then, as there are today, learned men and women: the *h-men*,[1] "those who know." These *h-men* had great knowledge, which they had learned in their dreams. Through dreams the gods taught the *h-men* the knowledge of the world. In this way they could find things that were lost, they could cure sickness with their medicinal plants and their prayers, and they could read the future in their sacred stones or by counting grains of corn; but their main responsibility and concern was to use their knowledge to ensure a good harvest.

Today we have our *h-men*, those men and women of knowledge who make up the body of counselors of the EZLN in the search for peace with dignity. They are the ones who organized this forum, which will allow us to find one another and construct the bridge to the seventh rainbow. They dreamed together with the great gods, the ones who gave birth to the world, the first ones, and from them learned great words and their best thoughts. They have been able to find things that were lost, like the word, reason, disinterest, and dignity. They have been able to cure that most fatal illness called oblivion. They have been able to read the future by reading what their hearts say, and counting the grains of corn, which in today's world are called hearts.

But, just like our ancient *h-men*, the counselors' principal responsibility and concern is to give us knowledge so that we may have a good harvest. Therefore, we ask you, the participants attending this National Indigenous Forum that concludes today, to join us in this salute to our counselors' knowledge; we ask that it be used to secure a good harvest for the planting of the word and the knowledge of dignity. We ask for an accurate accounting of the *xoc-kin*, so that we may know about the days, and that our harvest may be good, and that the brown chests of the first inhabitants of these lands may always be filled with hope.

There are varying reasons why some of our counselors are not here today to build this bridge; a good number of our *h-men* are not here because they are imprisoned, accused of the crime of belonging to an organization with which the government is holding dialogues sanctioned by law. By keeping them in prison, the government breaks the law that forces it to talk and not to fight. That is why these men and women, who are our counselors on this good road, are not here with us today. We, the Zapatistas, want to ask all of you, together with us, to send a greeting to these prisoners. And we ask you to greet them in the traditional way of indigenous communities, by applauding.

The Participants

IT IS OUR TASK, all of us who are joined here at the National Indigenous Forum, to plant the seed of the words that we have gathered during these days. Here, in the Valley of Jovel, where intolerance, racism, and stupidity of exclusion reign, we have gathered to speak and to know one another. We have gathered up the seed. We must prepare to till the soil. We must prepare tomorrow. Today, we must live in a country that is not like the one of our fathers. Today, we live in a country with a government that wants to sell us to the foreigners, as though we were animals or objects. We, the indigenous people, are not good merchandise, they say. Power's money does not want to buy a merchandise that does not yield good profits. And we, the indigenous people, are not profitable. We are a bad investment. That's why the government's shopkeeper hands us oblivion and repression, because he cannot sell us at a good price. Today, the shopkeeper has to modernize his store and get rid of all the merchandise that is unattractive. And we, with our dark skin and our overwhelming need to stay close to the earth—which makes us short in stature—are not attractive.

They want to forget us, but the indigenous are not the only ones who are threatened by this oblivion; there are many Mexican men and women who are unattractive because they have no dollar value. They, who are not indigenous, and us, who are, have been condemned to oblivion. They sell our house, and with it they sell our history. If we want to save ourselves from oblivion, we must do it together, united. Today, in this motherland in pain, hope has an indigenous heart; with its brown skin, it must save us from oblivion. It is not enough to refuse to die; this we have learned now for five centuries. Now, it is necessary to live, and to live together with the others who are also us.

The past is the key to the future. Our past has wisdom that can help us build a future where we fit without being pressed against each other, the way in which the ones' above us press against us today. The future of the nation must be found by looking toward the past, toward those who were the first inhabitants, to those who first had wisdom, who first made us.

We have to prepare for the planting. We must become rain, we have to be like the *chaacob*[2] gods of rain, who rose from the underground reservoirs, met in the sky, and from there traveled on horseback, each holding a sacred gourd brimming with water, and rained on the earth, from one end to the other, so that all might have water, the giver of life.

If the rain does not come, then we must kneel as our forefathers did and sing the way the frogs sing before the rain, and beat the branches just like the wind from a storm, and someone will represent Kunu-chaac, the great rain god, with his thunderbolt and sacred gourd.

We must know how to sow and how to plant one another. No more are the times when the stones were so soft that they could be moved by whistling, and when it was not necessary to work to plow the field, and when one grain of corn was enough to feed a whole family. Since the chief was defeated by a foreigner at Chichén Itzá, the good times have ended and the bad times have begun. The ancient chief entered a tunnel that ran east from Tulum and went beneath the ocean. Then the foreigner, the *dzul*, took Power. Today, we have to return so that reason can reign in our lands. We will do this by seeding the word.

We are our earth. We understand well how we and the earth are one. In olden times the tilled field, what we call the milpa, was protected by four spirits. There were four more that cared for the village, one for each cross placed at the corners of the village. The Macehuales, our ancient ones, had seven directions; the first four were the corners of the milpa or the village; the fifth was at the center, which in each community was traditionally marked by a cross and, usually, by a ceiba tree.[3] The sixth and seventh directions were above and below. In addition to the four guardians for the field and the four for the village, each person had his own guardian. In order to represent the five points, the four plus the center, our ancestors used a cross. As time passed, the center rose, and the four corners became five. And now this star with five points represents the guardian of men and women and harvests.

The guardian and heart of the people is Votán Zapata, who is also the guardian and heart of the word. He is the man, he is the star with the five points that represents humanity. Because today we have spoken and listened, he is happy; the heart of Votán Zapata is happy.

Brothers and sisters:
EACH ONE HAS HIS own field, his own planting, but we all have the same village, although sometimes we speak different languages and wear different clothes. We invite each of you to plant your own plot and in your own way. We invite you to make of this forum a good tiller and make sure that everyone has seed and that the earth be well prepared.

We have listened to knowledgeable and good planters like our Mixe brothers and sisters, whose position on autonomy has created a bridge between thoughts, between brothers and sisters. The Totonacos and Huichole brothers have also spoken with great truth. From the states of Guerrero, Veracruz, and Oaxaca have come the voices, brown-skinned and dignified, that speak of the word persecuted by power; yet the word of wisdom remains. The Chinanteco brothers and sisters have spoken with the wisdom of the woman representing them. The Mazatecos, Mixtecos, and Zapotecos have opened our eyes and ears, which the heart possesses but which are sometimes forgotten. The Chatinos, the Chochos, the Chontales, Cuicatecos, Mayas, Nahuatl, Nañhu, Otomis, Popoluca, the Tarahumaras, and the Tepehuas are also light and color in their word. Our Zapoteco brothers and sisters from the United States also have given us the benefit of their thought. All of us who are seven, you and us, the brothers and sisters that we are.

All of you have undergone great suffering in order to come here, to speak and be spoken to, to listen and be listened to. We know it, although others may not. You came, even though we did not help you materially; your communities financed you so you could come here. And you always knew that you would not receive any land, money, or promises by coming here. You always knew that you and your community would not have any material reward. You always knew that you were coming to give your word and your example. And in spite of all of this you came. And my superiors, the *comandantes* of the CCRI-CG of the EZLN, have ordered me to thank you in their name and in mine for all that is known and for everything that remains unknown. We thank you for coming all the way here, for speaking and listening, for coming to a good understanding that guides our walk.

We have nothing material to give you; all we have is our greeting, and we ask that you accept it as greetings should be accepted: as a gift.

The Press

FINALLY, WE WANT TO THANK the press, which has also made sacrifices to come and cover this forum. We want to make it clear that we are referring to the real press, and not the policemen who hide behind press credentials. We know that we've been discourteous and rude, and some of you have even said that it is the EZLN's press policy. But today I say again what we said to you almost two years ago, here in San Cristobal, during the first dialogues in the cathedral: The press has had an important role in holding back the war and opening a path for peace.

Like a great mirror, the press helped this country—which is still called Mexico—to see its true image reflected in a war against oblivion. We know that you are doing your job with interest, professionalism, and pride. We also know that what is made public often times is not your work, but that which is convenient for Power and the rich.

Some of you complained yesterday that there were no political declarations that were newsworthy. You complained that the Sup[4] only came to make literature with the stories of Old Don Antonio. So now we want to make a very clear political declaration, like all of the EZLN's political declarations. And, in response to the audiovisual needs of the mass media present, the declaration will be a rough draft for a video clip . . .

P.S . . . DISGUISED AS A VIDEO CLIP.
FIRST, AN UNFOCUSED SHOT and a long, screeching whistle in the sound track. Then an image comes into focus, and in the background you can hear the song "Cartas Marcadas."[5] The images bunch up; Power is laughing calmly, celebrating its historic and definitive triumph in the last minutes of 1993. An army of shadows introduces itself between the damp and the cold. Power looks in the mirror and see itself as eternal and omnipotent. Great wise men predict great triumphs, praise and robust statues scattered throughout the land. A killjoy predicts: "You will rule until the jungle walks toward your palace." The handful of shadows multiplies in the mountains. Power knows that it is impossible for the jungle to walk, and its confidence and euphoria are confirmed. The great wise men are at its side, picking up the party leftovers. The collective shadow approaches with wooden guns in the dawn of the beginning. In the dawn of 1994, the indigenous people come down from the mountains. They go to the palace where Power resides to take Death and Oblivion prisoner. In their wooden guns walk the trees of the jungle. Power trembles and begins to die; a wooden rifle has inflicted a mortal wound. The end and the beginning.

And if this video clip resembles Shakespeare's *Macbeth* too closely, it's not my fault. Perhaps it is the fault of the greatest gods who can't stand still in Chiapas and in these modern times, and get into their heads to go off wandering in other worlds and other times. Because that's how playful and mischievous these gods can be, the greatest ones, the first ones, the ones who gave birth to the world.

Thank you.

From the mountains of the Mexican Southeast
SUBCOMANDANTE INSURGENTE MARCOS

NOTES

1. *H-men* are the *rezadores*, or those who say prayers, in present-day Mayan communities; they are in charge of community rituals, in particular those the earth and the jungle.

2. *Chaacob* are ancient Mayan deities of the milpa (tilled field) and the water. According to a Tomul dictionary, Chaac was a very tall man who taught agriculture. He is considered the god of sustenance, thunder and lightning, and water.

3. The ceiba, or silk-cotton tree, is considered a God-tree by the Mayans.

4. The Sup is a familiar, affectionate play on Sub, which in turn is short for Subcomandante; Marcos uses it of himself whimsically.

5. "Las Cartas Marcadas" ("The Marked Cards") is a Mexican song about deceit in love and life.

17

Today, Eighty-five Years Later, History Repeats Itself

A message from the EZLN at the inaugural ceremony of the American Planning of the Intercontinental Meeting for Humanity and Against Neoliberalism.
La Realidad, America

JAVIER ELORRIAGA BERDEGUÉ, a journalist and video producer who had been covering the Zapatista uprising since January 1994, arrived one day and introduced himself as a volunteer in the effort to find a political and peaceful solution to the conflict. I listened to him as he argued in favor of peace and against war. He seemed to me to be one of those men who believe in what they say. I told him that we would not lose anything by trying. On September 16, 1994, on the anniversary of Mexico's independence, he arrived with the first of a series of letters from Mr. Ernesto Zedillo Ponce de León. After December 1, 1994, Javier came and went with messages from then secretary of the interior, Estéban Moctezuma Barragán.

His work as peace liaison lasted six months. The last time I saw him, on February 8, 1995, I told him that we saw no sign of willingness on the government's part to establish a dialogue. He insisted on looking for a new *encuentro* for peace. As he was leaving the Lacandon Jungle, on the morning of February 9, 1995, Javier Elorriaga was detained and accused of "terrorism." The government began an offensive against the indigenous communities of the Lacandon Jungle and arrested dozens of Mexicans in several parts of the country. It accused them of "terrorism" and exhibited as proof a "threatening" arsenal: paper bombs and some old weapons.

While through the press the government congratulated itself for having recovered its "national sovereignty," in the Lacandon Jungle, Swiss planes bombarded the communities' surroundings, North American helicopters machine-gunned the mountain, French tanks occupied the homes of the indigenous who were fleeing into the jungle, Spanish policemen interrogated suspects, and North American military advisers checked very carefully an artifact that might contain some dangerous military device. This artifact traveled all the way to the Pentagon and was checked by the military's most advanced technological devices. After a few days, the experts turned their findings over to Washington, which, in turn, forwarded them to the offices of the Mexican military, the political police, and the National Palace. The report said that all evidence on the artifact in question, snatched from hands of the transgressors of the law, indicated that the object might be . . . a little toy car, made of metal and plastic. The report also said that they had found a small inscription, probably made with a black ballpoint pen, which read: "This small car belongs to el Heriberto . . . "

Since then, 420 days have elapsed. Mr. Zedillo occupies the Mexican presidential seat, Heriberto lives in the mountains, the army lives in his house, and Javier Elorriaga, along with seventeen other Mexicans, is in jail, accused of "terrorism." One of the seventeen, Joel Martínez, has respiratory problems as a result of having been tortured. Because of his serious condition, he has just been hospitalized. Today, they have him chained hand and foot, like an animal with rabies. Today, 420 days after the facts have revealed who the real terrorist is, we want to dedicate these words:

> To Javier Elorriaga Berdegué, and
> through him,
> to all the incarcerated Zapatistas:

> In the definition of their future
> many more things are defined
> than those imagined by their jailers.

Through my voice speaks the Zapatista National Liberation Army.

American brothers and sisters:
WELCOME TO LA REALIDAD. Our special thanks to the men, women, and children of La Realidad, who have given us permission and have supported us in setting up this planning meeting in their community. I want to ask everyone that together we greet our indigenous brothers and sisters of La Realidad.

We welcome the brothers and sisters from the delegations of Canada, the United States, Mexico, Guatemala, Costa Rica, Venezuela, Puerto Rico, Ecuador, Brazil, Peru, Chile, Uruguay, and Argentina. We welcome the observers from France, Germany, and Spain.

We welcome the Mexican brothers and sisters from the Organizing Commission. We recognize your efforts, which have shaped today, and we thank you. We are grateful to you for having accepted our invitation and having made your way from your countries to the Lacandon Jungle. The Lacandon Jungle—a hideout for transgressors of the law, and a dignified corner of America—has already been visited by diverse representatives from your countries' governments. We have been visited by bomber planes, armed helicopters, war tanks, spy satellites, military advisers, and agents (some secret, some not so secret) from espionage organizations of many countries. All of these visitors have a common objective: assassination and robbery.

The most sophisticated modern war technology is unleashed against the wooden weapons, the broken feet, and the ancestral philosophy of the Zapatistas, which declares—without shame or fear—that the place of knowledge, truth, and speech is in the heart. Modern death versus ancestral life. Neoliberalism against Zapatismo. Why do they fear us? Why so much hate for so few and so small a group? Because we have defied them, and the worst part about defiance is that it establishes a precedent.

On April 3, 1911, two citizens of the Americas, Ricardo and Enrique Flores Magón,[1] wrote: "*Compañeros*, think well, keep on going, and work without wasting time, before your help arrives too late. Try to understand the danger to us, as we confront every government in the world, which sees in this Mexican movement an emerging social revolution, the only kind of revolution that they fear."

Today, eighty-five years later, history repeats itself. In the past, death only came to visit cloaked in illness and misery; today it also comes wearing an olive green uniform, carrying war machines and lead, announcing destruction.

An armed multinational force persecutes us and tries to destroy what we stand for. The powerful of the world are bothered by our existence and honor us with their threats. They are right. The Zapatista defiance is a global defiance. We never assumed it to be so, we never imagined it. But accepting that role, we will be as vocal as possible.

A world system makes it possible to transform crime into government in Mexico. A national system makes it possible for crime to rule in Chiapas. In the mountains of the Mexican Southeast, we struggle for our country, for humanity, and against neoliberalism. That is why the world powers persecute us, jail us, murder us; that is why they want to destroy us.

After visits from the harbingers of death, it is an honor for us to have you visit, you who struggle for life and for humanity in the American continent. We are sure that the trip to La Realidad has not been easy. "Reality" is never easy, but it is well worth getting there. The trip to La Realidad is a journey toward suffering, but also toward hope.

Today, here in La Realidad, are gathered different thoughts from different nations. They are called together, not because of their nationality, not because of their sex or color, not because of their culture or language. Only one thing has summoned us: the struggle for humanity and against neoliberalism.

Eighty years ago, in 1916, General Emiliano Zapata dreamt that life and thought could be free, if they built a new reality. Those in power then dreamt his destruction.

Today, sitting on the desks of Mexican and the U.S. generals, you can find diverse plans, complicated military operations, and seventy-seven different types of death threats, one for each year that has elapsed since Emiliano Zapata's assassination. And all those plans have as their objective the destruction of La Realidad. Why? Because they have discovered that human beings—that is to say, dignified human beings—live in La Realidad, and those in power cannot tolerate that. That is the enemy we are facing, who persecutes us, murders us, jails us, rapes us, humiliates us. Those in power who have the absurd notion of destroying La Realidad.

That is what they want . . . those in power who concentrate crime and wealth and bind them like Siamese twins, using crime's army to hold on to wealth; those in power who monopolize the future, excluding everyone they cannot convert into an accomplice or a victim; those who in the exercise of power forget that by accumulating power they accumulate fear. They hope to destroy La Realidad because there are human beings here, whose very existence is an act of defiance that can set a precedent.

We, who nourish the heart with the bitter bread of hope.

We, who see in the past a lesson to be learned and not an obstacle, who turn toward yesterday to learn, not to repent.

We, who look at the future as something that is built on the present, who hope for a tomorrow for everyone.

We, who balance fear with shame, prudence with courage, indifference with memory.

We, human beings, who exist (who defy power), who want to transform La Realidad and change it into something better, something new, something good.

This is the fight for La Realidad: Some want to build it, others want to destroy it.

They want to destroy it with the absurdity of denying it through oblivion, destruction and death.

We want to build it, with the absurdity of rebuilding it through history, creativity, and life.

This is the dilemma that we have come to think about and begin to speak about, the dilemma of La Realidad. This is a fundamental and definitive theme, for humanity and against neoliberalism. In order to solve this dilemma, we have to face a very powerful enemy, cloaked in neoliberalism. Its crimes recognize no national borders; they represent the globalization of despair. Neoliberalism offers us a new world doctrine: surrender and indifference as the only means of inclusion; death and oblivion as the only future for those excluded; ignorance and arrogance as the only government; crime and impunity as the highest law; robbery and corruption as the main industry; assassination as the source of legitimacy; lying as the supreme god; prisons and graves for those who are not willing to follow.

War always. That is neoliberalism. But its power is also based on our weakness. To our lack of alternative proposals, they offer the continuation of the nightmare. We must go beyond lamentations and propose new possibilities. We did not invite you here to accumulate complaints. We did not call on you to embody our misfortunes or to bring a continental dimension to our nightmare. We invited you to multiply our hopes. We called upon you to lessen our hardships, to give hope a continental dimension. Don't let our enemy's grotesque and terrible image dull the mirror where we seek our own road. Let's not hide arbitrariness and laziness within ourselves, covering them up under the daily crime of a world order that turns history, nations, and individuals into dust. Let's not offer a new nightmare under a different guise. Let not the complicated political geometry, which multiplies centers and extremes ad infinitum, signify impunity for the errors committed. We did not come together today to change the world. We are here today with the most modest of purposes: to make a new world.

We.

Here.

Today.

In America.

A continent of legends, the American continent is a piece of land where all the worlds meet. A people without land, that is to say, a people without a homeland—migrant America—dreams that it can work and live in peace and dignity on any land, regardless of the borders above or below. The migrant finds neither work nor land in the American soil; he finds only war and humiliation in these lands, where he steals nothing and gives everything. The migrant in America is a stranger in America. For an American to enter a xenophobic nightmare, it is not necessary to cross an international border. Sometimes it suffices to cross, even momentarily, one of the many cultural, political, social, religious, and sexual borders that cloud up the American skies, making any notion of collective thought a notion that includes only one. The American migrant is the solitary one, the one made up of millions of beings who search. The American migrant is the endless struggle, the legend . . .

And, among many, the legend becomes a ballad and survives the lack of books, the press, television, radio. The legend of Gregorio Cortéz, being chased by ranchers but never caught, is the legend of history being chased by oblivion, of history always escaping and becoming collective memory. The legend has come to La Realidad to represent all the migrants who venture on American soil, and make a stab at becoming a part of a new culture without losing their own.

Like the legend, Power chases after the migrants for not wanting to be what they are, for trying to build something new but different, which destroys neither the past nor the present. Chases them for trying to build something that might have a place in the future of North America, a dignified future, a future that does not have prison bars or a gravestone on the horizon. Like in the "Ballad of Gregorio Cortéz," the American migrant will always escape and will continue building the collective memory that those in power insist on destroying all over America, especially in . . .

A country that synthesizes, like no other, the great contradictions that express the American continent. A nation built by the labor of migrants from all over the world, the United States of America rises up as a symbol of power and modernity. From its hideaway in North America, the arrogance of Power has managed that the world's rejection—well-deserved for its foreign policy—contaminate, more often than not, the noble North American people. But that arrogance of Power is only possible at a great cost to the people of the United States of America, not just the minorities—Latino, Asian, and black—but also whites. With the crisis raised to the level of the global economy, neoliberalism imposes great suffering north of the Rio Bravo.

According to statistics provided by the Organization for Economic Cooperation and Development, in the United States there is a 5.7 percent rate of unemployment, while in Canada it is 9.5 percent.

The United States of America: its people a complex mixture of European, African, Asiatic, Latin American, and indigenous blood—all American.

The United States of America: its people forgotten at the hour of solidarity, always remembered at the hour of complaints.

The United States of America: its people who, in spite of the government, know when to look below and find there a brother and not a victim.

Today we greet the people of the United States and their noble representatives, not as victims, not as executioners, but as brothers and sisters.

Brothers and sisters of America:
TODAY, HERE IN LA REALIDAD, we must set apart a place for memory, for history, for that mirror which reminds us who we were, shows us what we are and promises what we may become . . .

Thirty years ago, in 1966, after having been nowhere, a man readied memory and hope so that life would return to America. Back then, his *nom de guerre* was Ramón. In one of the many corners of the American reality, this man was remembering, and in his memories he brought to life all the men and women who lived and died for America's life. His name and his memory were buried by history's ever-present gravediggers. For some, his first name was Ernesto, his last name Guevara de la Serna. For us he was and is El Che.

In Punta del Este he denounced the politics of power that, from the offices of the World Bank, proposed the building of latrines as a solution to the grave conditions of misery in the countries of America. Since then, poverty in America has developed at the same rate in which its wealth has been plundered, as always, by the same rich.

The "latrinocracy" also evolved, but only in name. Paradoxically, in one American country it took up the name of "solidarity." Nevertheless, in spite some images to the contrary, the basic functioning of the "latrinocracy" remains the same: today, as yesterday, the poor's place is at the bottom of the latrine, while the rich get to sit on top.

El Che's criticism of power did not translate into an endorsement of one's own deficiencies and an apologia of a system. Criticizing the use of Power's own logic, barely disguised under a new name, to argue against it, he wrote in 1964, "I do not pretend to have exhausted the topic and much less given a papal amen over these and other contradictions. Unfortunately, it is the apologies for a system, rather than a scientific analysis of the system, that most people get to see, myself included."

A citizen of the world, El Che recalls what we have known since the times of Spartacus, and which we often forget: the fight against injustice is a step that elevates humanity, which makes it better, which makes it more human. Some time later, memory and hope held his hand to write in his farewell letter: "One day, they came in asking who should be notified in case of death, and the real possibility of that fact struck us all. Later, we learned that it was true, that in a revolution one triumphs or dies (if it's a true revolution) . . . Other lands in the world call for my modest efforts." And then El Che continued on his journey.

When leaving, El Che would say, "Until victory, always," the way someone would say, "See you later." Thirty years later, during one of those dawns when the moon recovers pieces of light that time's monthly bite snatches from her, and a comet disguised as a flashlight uselessly stands guard at night's entrance, I have looked for some text to carry the opening words to this gathering.

I have gone from Pablo Neruda to Julio Cortázar to Walt Whitman to Juan Rulfo. It was useless; time and again the image of El Che, dreaming in the school at La Higuera, claimed its place between my hands. All the way from Bolivia come those half-closed eyes and that ironical smile, recounting what had happened and promising what was to come.

Did I say "dreaming?" Should I have said "dying?" For some he died, for oth-

ers he fell asleep. Who is wrong? Thirty years ago, El Che was readying the transformation of the American Reality, and those in power prepared for its destruction. Twenty-nine years ago, those in power told us that history was over at the El
Yuro mountain pass. They said that the possibility of a different, better reality,
was destroyed. They said that rebellion was over.

Is it over?

A quick glance at the papers these past few days might help us answer that
question. During the last days of March, several demonstrations against actual
economic and privatizing policies have been reported. Neoliberalism faces resistance and rebelliousness. There are millions who ignore this history, and along
with it deny all dignity.

On March 28, the international news agencies AFP, DPA, EFE, and ANSA
informed us that in Bolivia's La Paz, Cochabamba, and Santa Cruz, thousands
of people marched, demanding a raise in salary and protesting the privatization of the Bolivian oil fields. In Cochabamba, the police detained 250 people,
most of them elderly, who were on a hunger strike, protesting for the same reasons. Rebel elders! Long live America! On the same day in Paraguay, workers
began a general strike demanding a salary increase of 31 percent and called for
a referendum on the privatizations. The democratization of decision making
opposes the imposition of economic measures . . . and of educational measures . . . During those days more than five thousand Brazilian students were
restrained by the police, while protesting against the education policies of
President Fernando Henrique Cardoso.

In Chile, thousands of farmers blocked the southern highways to protest
against Chile's imminent inclusion in the south's common market (Mercosur),[2]
which will result in the unemployment of more than 800,000 farmers.
Impending severe economic adjustment in Venezuela has already unleashed a
"pots and pans" movement and general social discontent. The globalization of
the economy—the modern crime—has met with resistance among its clients to
the death it sells.

Hundreds of street vendors confronted the Peruvian police when it tried to
expel them from Lima's historic center. There were more than twenty wounded.
In order not to become criminals, some of America's poor try out micro businesses. It's useless. For neoliberalism, any earnings that do not come from theft
and pillage are "illegal." America's prisons are filled with the innocent, while the
guilty fill government seats.

Riot police forces held down thousands of Costa Ricans, who were protesting
against the installation of a garbage dump in the city of Santa Ana. Neoliberalism
dumps more than one thousand tons of garbage a day on top of Costa Rica's people; this will not go unpunished.

The bowels of America also protest. The announcement of an increase in the aggregate value tax was accompanied by a quake, measuring 5.7 on the Richter scale, which shook the city of Quito, Ecuador.

All this took place in only two days . . . Thirty years later. Has rebellion stopped?

Thirty years ago, El Che dreamed and dreamed again of a transformed, new, better reality: the dream of rebellion. That dream crossed time and the mountains of the Mexican Southeast. The dream that summons us together today is one of rupture and continuity with Che Guevara's dream, just as his dream was one of rupture and continuity with the dream that kept Simón Bolívar and Manuelita Saenz[3] awake at night. In 1816, Bolívar and Saenz kept alive the dream of a unified America. The history that those in power sell us tell of the fertile insomnia, which liberated Colombia, Venezuela, Ecuador, Perú, and Bolivia, and years later was truncated by borders with walls, fragmenting Bolívar's dream. Was it truncated? In 1826 Bolívar conceived the first hemispheric conference of America, the Panamá Congress. Today, 170 years later and in the American La Realidad, the dream proposed by Bolívar reawakens.

Crystal and mirror, the dream of a better America makes itself comfortable in the best place to dream, La Realidad. And the intellectual madmen, the authors of this delirium, the madmen who dared to dream our dream before us, are: Manuelita Saenz, Simón Bolívar, Ricardo and Enrique Flores Magón, Emiliano Zapata, and Ernesto El Che Guevara.

One hundred-and-eighty years, eighty-five years, eighty years, thirty years later, we are and are not the same.

We are the end, the continuation, and the beginning.

We are the mirror that is a crystal that is a mirror that is a crystal.

We are rebelliousness.

We are the stubborn history that repeats itself in order to no longer repeat itself, the looking back to be able to walk forward.

We are neoliberalism's maximum defiance, the most beautiful absurdity, the most irreverent delirium, the most human madness.

We are human beings doing what must be done in La Realidad; we are—dreaming.

But, it just occurred to me that what is perhaps most important in La Realidad is to know what is ending, what continues, and especially, what is beginning.

One hundred-eighty years after Bolívar and Saenz's sleepless nights, eighty-five years after Flores Magón's prophecy, eighty years after Emiliano Zapata's dream, thirty years after El Che's dream, dreaming the sleeplessness of all true and honest Americans, today, April 4, 1996, in the American La Realidad, in the name of the Zapatista National Liberation Army, I declare the American planning meeting of the Intercontinental Encounter for Humanity and against Neoliberalism has officially started at . . . southeastern time.

Brothers and sisters of America:

THE GREAT WORLD POWER has not yet found the weapon to destroy dreams. Until it does, we will keep on dreaming, that is to say, we will keep on triumphing . . .

Welcome, brothers and sisters of America. Here in La Realidad, we complete, we continue, we begin . . .the dream. And this is our dream . . . for all of America!

Democracy!

Liberty!

Justice!

From the mountains of the Mexican Southeast

SUBCOMANDANTE INSURGENTE MARCOS

NOTES

1. Ricardo and Enrique Flores Magón, anarchist brothers in Mexico at the turn of the century, founded the Partido Revolucionario de Mexico (Mexican Revolutionary Party), which was associated with the Communist organization International Workers of the World. Ricardo was assassinated in a U.S. jail.

2. Mercosur is the common market agreement among Brazil, Argentina, Chile and Uruguay.

3. Simón Bolívar (1783–1830) was one of South America's greatest generals. His victories over the Spaniards won independence for Bolivia, Panama, Colombia, Ecuador, Peru, and Venezuela. He is called El Liberator (The Liberator) and the "George Washington of South America."

   Manuelita Saenz, born in Quito on December 27, 1793, became the loyal adviser, disinterested partisan, and trusted confidante of Simón Bolívar. They separated forever in May 1830, when Bolívar resigned from the presidency of Columbia. Francisco de Paola Santander, who had been vice president under Bolívar, deported Saenz from Columbia. She died of diphtheria on November 23, 1856, at the age of fifty-nine.

18

The Unjust Sentencing of Elorriaga and Entzin

MEXICO, MAY 5, 1996

Through my voice speaks the voice of the EZLN.

ON MAY 3, 1996, through a radio transmission, we found out about the sentence given to Jorge Javier Elorriaga Berdegué and Sebastian Entzin Gómez, declaring them guilty of the crimes of conspiracy, rebellion, and terrorism. Judge Juan Alcántara condemned Jorge Javier Elorriaga Berdegué to thirteen years in jail, a fine equal to seventy-five days' wages, and a four-year suspension of his political rights. Sebastian Entzin Gómez was sentenced to six years in prison, a fine equal to forty days' wages, and a two-year suspension of his political rights.

The Zapatista National Liberation Army views the sentences of these presumed members of EZLN as a clear sign of war. Jorge Javier Elorriaga Berdegué and Sebastian Entzin Gómez were accused of being Zapatistas and were condemned for the felonies of conspiracy, rebellion, and terrorism. This means that for the Mexican government the Zapatistas are terrorists who must be jailed and killed.

The dialogue between the EZLN and the Mexican federal government has received a severe setback as a result of these harsh penalties.

The sentences are aimed beyond these presumed Zapatistas. They are sentences against the Commission of Concordance and Peace (Cocopa)[1] and the group of legislators who, in the main, have maintained a dignified and brave attitude in the peacemaking efforts, who have tried everything to make a success of this search for peace, with the justice and dignity that the Mexican people deserve.

Judge Juan Alcántara's decision wipes out all of the peace efforts of the Cocopa and makes a mockery of the Mexican legislature. For the National Intermediary Commission (CONAI),[2] harassed and held hostage by the government, this is proof of the disregard of those in power.

Another target is the Body of Advisors for Peace with Justice and Dignity. This independent organization, set up to stop the reinitiating of armed violence, joined hands with the EZLN in the dialogue of San Andres Sacamch'en de los Pobres.

Judge Juan Alcántara's decision condemns all Mexican men and women who work for building peace in their country; it categorizes them as terrorists. Prominent Mexicans and organizations beyond suspicion also share the label of terrorist, placed on them by the only terrorist in Mexico: the government.

Also, the sentencing of the presumed Zapatistas aims to intimidate journalists. Mr. Elorriaga has seen his work used as evidence of his guilt and justification for his sentence. In Mexico, today, journalism is synonymous with terrorism.

The national and international civil society, that force without face or name that seeks the transition to democracy through civil and legal means, sees its efforts condemned and its fear confirmed; a peaceful path for change is still not open in Mexico.

Ultimately, the main target of this verdict is the EZLN. By associating our just struggle for a dignified life with terrorism, the government warns that there is no possible way for us to return to public life and peaceful politics. The only future that the government offers us, at the end of the negotiating process, is prison and death.

All efforts for a dialogue and peaceful struggle that the EZLN has undertaken since its public appearance in January 1994 have been condemned along with the presumed Zapatistas.

We want to tell the government that we have received the message and have understood it. At this moment, our brothers from the General Command of the Clandestine Indigenous Revolutionary Committee (CCRI-CG) of the EZLN are meeting to evaluate the situation and review the participation in the Dialogue of San Andres. As military chief of the regular, irregular, and commando forces of the EZLN, in compliance with the instructions of the CCRI-CG of the EZLN, I have sent the relevant orders to all the Zapatista units to be prepared for the decisions of our supreme command.

All this time, the Dialogue of San Andres has been used by the government to gain time and to look for an opportunity to reinitiate the war. What was denounced, again and again, by our Zapatista delegates is now confirmed. At no moment did the government abandon the idea of a military solution to the conflict. The dialogue process was only one more deception, just like those endured every day by our people. War arrives again from where it has always come, from Power.

We want to thank all honest journalists for the interest they have shown throughout these two years of frustrated peace attempts. We would also like to ask them to be the vehicle for us to thank the national and international civil society, for the support they have given us toward a dignified peace and against war.

Thanks for everything to everyone. We expect a decisive effort from Cocopa and the CONAI to forge forward on the path of active dialogue that the government has abandoned.

From the mountains of Southeast Mexico
SUBCOMANDANTE INSURGENTE MARCOS

NOTES

1. Cocopa (*Comisión de Concordia y Pacificación para Chiapas*) was mandated as a legislative branch on March 16, 1995, to serve as a mediating body between the Zapatistas and the Mexican federal government.

2. CONAI (*Comisión Nacional de Intermediación*) was founded by Bishop Samuel Ruiz and civil society.

19

Opening Remarks at the First Intercontinental *Encuentro* for Humanity and against Neoliberalism

JULY 27, 1996
AGUASCALIENTES II, OVENTIC
SAN ANDRES SACAMCH'EN DE LOS POBRES
CHIAPAS, MEXICO

Brothers and sisters of Asia, Africa, Oceania, Europe and America
Welcome to the mountains of the Mexican Southeast.

LET US INTRODUCE OURSELVES.
We are the Zapatista National Liberation Army.
For ten years, we lived in these mountains, preparing to fight a war.
In these mountains, we built an army.
Below, in the cities and plantations, we did not exist.
Our lives were worth less than those of machines or animals.
We were like stones, like weeds in the road.

We were silenced.
We were faceless.
We were nameless.
We had no future.
We did not exist.

For the powers that be, known internationally by the term "neoliberalism,"
we did not count,
we did not produce,
we did not buy,
we did not sell.

We were a cipher in the accounts of big capital.

Then we went to the mountains to find ourselves and see if we could ease the
    pain of being forgotten like stones and weeds.
Here, in the mountains of the Mexican Southeast, our dead live on.

Our dead, who live in the mountains, know many things.
They speak to us of their death, and we hear them.
Coffins speak and tell us another story,
that comes from yesterday and points to tomorrow.
The mountains spoke to us, the Macehualob, we common and ordinary people.
We are simple people, as Power tells us.

Every day and the next night,
Power wants us to dance the *x-tol*
and repeat its brutal conquest.

The *kaz-dzul*, the false man, rules our lands and has giant war machines,
like the *boob*, half puma and half horse,
that spread pain and death among us.
The trickster government sends us the *aluxob*,
the liars who fool our people and make them forgetful.

This is why we became soldiers.
This is why we remain soldiers.
Because we want no more death and trickery for our people,
because we want no more forgetting.

The mountain told us to take up arms so we would have a voice.
It told us to cover our faces so we would have a face.
It told us to forget our names so we could be named.
It told us to protect our past so we would have a future.

In the mountains, the dead live: our dead.

With them live the Votán and the Ikál,[1]
the light and the darkness,
the wet and the dry,
the earth and the wind,
the rain and the fire.

The mountain is the home of the *Halach Uinic*, the real human beings, the
   big chief.
Here we learned and remembered that we are what we are, the real men and women.

So, with our voice strengthening our hands,

with our face reborn,
with our name renamed,
our yesterday at the center of the four points of Chan Santa Cruz in Balam Na,
the star was born who defines humanity
and reminds us that there are five parts that make up the world.

In the season when the *chaacob* ride, spreading the rain,
we came down once more to speak with our own
and prepare the storm that will signal the harvest.

We brought forth the war in the year zero,
and we began to walk this path
that has brought us to your hearts,
and today brings you to ours.

This is who we are.
The Zapatista National Liberation Army.
The voice that arms itself to be heard.
The face that hides itself to be seen.
The name that hides itself to be named.
The red star who calls out to humanity and the world
to be heard, to be seen, to be named.
The tomorrow to be harvested in the past.

Behind our black mask,
Behind our armed voice,
Behind our unnameable name,
Behind us, who you see,
Behind us, we are you.

Behind we are the same simple and ordinary men and women,
who are repeated in all races,
painted in all colors,
speak in all languages
and live in all places.
The same forgotten men and women.

The same excluded,
The same untolerated,
The same persecuted,

We are you.

Behind us, you are us.
Behind our masks is the face of all excluded women,
Of all the forgotten indigenous,
Of all the persecuted homosexuals,
Of all the despised youth,
Of all the beaten migrants,
Of all those imprisoned for their words and thoughts,
Of all the humiliated workers,
Of all those dead from neglect,
Of all the simple and ordinary men and women,
Who don't count,
Who aren't seen,
Who are nameless,
Who have no tomorrow.

Brothers and sisters:
We have invited you to this meeting to seek for and find yourselves and us.

You have all touched our hearts, and you can see we are not special.

You can see we are simple and ordinary men and women.
You can see we are the rebellious mirror that wants to be a pane of glass and
    break.
You can see we are who we are so we can stop being who we are to become the
    you, who we are.

We are the Zapatistas.

We invited you for all of us to hear ourselves and speak to ourselves.
To see all that we are.

Brothers and sisters:
In these mountains, the talking coffins spoke to us and told us ancient stories
    that recall our pains and our rebellions. Our dreams will not end as long as we
    live. We will not give up our banner. Our death will live on forever.
So say the mountains that speak to us.
So says the star that shines in Chan Santa Cruz.
So tells the star that the *cruzob*, the rebels, will not be defeated, and will continue on

their road, alongside everyone in the human constellation, that the red people, the Chachac-mac will always come, the red star that will help the world be free.

So says the star that is the mountain.

That a people who are five peoples.
That a people who are a star of all people.
That the people who are humanity and are all the world's people.
They will come to aid the worlds who become human in their struggle.
So the true man and woman live without pain, and the hearts of stone be softened.

You are all the Chachac-mac,
the people who come to help the man who becomes five throughout the world, among all peoples, in all nations.

You are all the red star who are mirrored in us.
We can continue on the right path if we, the you who are us, walk together.

Brothers and sisters:
Among our peoples, the oldest sages have put a cross that is a star
where the water, the giver of life, is born.

Thus, a star marks the beginning of life in the mountains.
Thus are born the arroyos that come down from the mountain
and carry the voice of the speaking star, of our Chan Santa Cruz.

The voice of the mountain has spoken, and it has said that true men and women
will live free when they commit to the five-pointed star. When the five peoples
become one in the star. When the five parts of humanity, who are the world,
find themselves and find each other. When all five find their place and each
other's places.

Today, thousands of different roads come from the five continents to meet here,
in the mountains of the Mexican Southeast, to join their steps.

Today, thousands of words from the five continents are silent here, in the mountains of the Mexican Southeast, to hear each other and hear themselves.

Today, thousands of struggles from the five continents struggle here, in the
mountains of the Mexican Southeast, for life and against death.

Today, thousands of colors from the five continents are painted here, in the mountains of the Mexican Southeast, to announce a future of inclusion and tolerance.

Today, thousands of hearts from the five continents are alive here, in the mountains of the Mexican Southeast, for humanity and against neoliberalism.

Today, thousands of human beings from the five continents shout, "Enough is enough!" here, in the mountains of the Mexican Southeast. They shout, "Enough is enough!" to conformity, to doing nothing, to cynicism, to egoism, to the modern god.

Today, thousands of small worlds from the five continents are attempting a beginning here, in the mountains of the Mexican Southeast, a beginning to building a new and good world, that is, a world where all worlds fit.

Today, thousands of men and women of the five continents begin here, in the mountains of the Mexican Southeast, the First Intercontinental *Encuentro* for Humanity and against Neoliberalism.

Brothers and sisters of the whole world:
Welcome to the mountains of the Mexican Southeast.
Welcome to this corner of the world where we are all the same because we are different.
Welcome to the search for life and the struggle against death.
Welcome to this First Intercontinental *Encuentro* for Humanity and against Neoliberalism.

Democracy!
Freedom!
Justice!

From the mountains of the Mexican Southeast
THE INDIGENOUS CLANDESTINE REVOLUTIONARY COMMITTEE
GENERAL COMMAND OF THE ZAPATISTA NATIONAL LIBERATION ARMY
PLANET EARTH

NOTE
1.   Ikál is the Mayan god of death, who wanders through the night and attacks humans so he can eat their flesh.

20

Tomorrow Begins Today

(Closing Remarks at the First Intercontinental *Encuentro* for Humanity and against Neoliberalism)

AUGUST 3, 1996

Through my voice speaks the voice of the EZLN.

Brothers and sisters of the whole world
Brothers and sisters of Africa, America, Asia, Europe, and Oceania
Brothers and sisters attending the First Intercontinental Encuentro for Humanity and
   against Neoliberalism:

WELCOME TO THE ZAPATISTA LA REALIDAD.
Welcome to this territory in struggle for humanity.
Welcome to this territory in rebellion against neoliberalism.

The Zapatistas greet all who attended this *encuentro*. Here, in the mountains of the Mexican Southeast, when an assembly greets whoever comes with good words, we applaud. We ask that everyone greet each other and that everyone greet the delegations from: Italy, Brazil, Great Britain, Paraguay, Chile, the Philippines, Germany, Peru, Argentina, Austria, Uruguay, Guatemala, Belgium, Venezuela, Iran, Denmark, Nicaragua, Zaire, France, Haiti, Ecuador, Greece, Japan, Kurdistan, Ireland, Costa Rica, Cuba, Sweden, the Netherlands, South Africa, Switzerland, Spain, Portugal, the United States, the Basque country, Turkey, Canada, Puerto Rico, Bolivia, Australia, Mauritania, Mexico, Norway, and Colombia.

Welcome, all men, women, children, and elders from the five continents who have responded to the invitation of the Zapatista indigenous to search for hope, for humanity, and to struggle against neoliberalism.

Brothers and sisters:
WHEN THIS DREAM that awakens today in La Realidad began to be dreamed by us, we thought it would be a failure. We thought that, maybe, we could gather here a few dozen people from a handful of countries. We were wrong. As always, we were wrong. It wasn't a few dozen, but thousands of human beings, those

who came from the five continents to find themselves in the reality at the close of the twentieth century.

The word born within these mountains, these Zapatista mountains, found the ears of those who could listen, care for and launch it anew, so that it might travel far away and circle the world. The sheer lunacy of calling to the five continents to reflect clearly on our past, our present, and our future, found that it wasn't alone in its delirium. Soon lunacies from the whole planet began to work on bringing the dream to rest in La Realidad,
> to bathe it in the mud,
> to grow it in the rain,
> to moisten it in the sun,
> speak it with each other,
> to bring it forth, giving it shape and substance.

As to what happened in these days, much will be written later.
> Today we can say that we are certain of at least one thing:
> A dream dreamed in the five continents can realize itself in La Realidad.
> Now, who will be able to tell us that dreaming is lovely but futile? Now, who will be able to argue that dreams, however many the dreamers, cannot become a reality?

How is joy dreamed in Africa? What marvels walk in the European dream? How many tomorrows does the dream encompass in Asia? To what music does the American dream dance? How does the heart speak that dreams in Oceania?

To whom does it matter how and what we dream here or in any part of the world?
> Who are they who dare to let their dreams meet with all the dreams of the world? What is happening in the mountains of the Mexican Southeast that finds an echo and a mirror in the streets of Europe, the suburbs of Asia, the countryside of America, the townships of Africa, and the houses of Oceania? What is it that is happening with the peoples of these five continents who, so we are all told, only encounter each other to compete or make war? Wasn't this turn of the century synonymous with despair, bitterness, and cynicism? From where and how did all these dreams come to La Realidad?

May Europe speak and recount the long bridge of its gaze, crossing the Atlantic and history to come to rediscover itself in La Realidad.
> May Asia speak and explain the gigantic leap its heart has taken to come to beat in La Realidad.

May Africa speak and describe the long sailing of its restless image to come to reflect upon itself in La Realidad.

May Oceania speak and tell of the many flights of its thought to come to rest in La Realidad.

May America speak and remember its swelling hope to come to renew itself in La Realidad.

May the five continents speak and everyone listen.

May humanity suspend, for a moment, its silence of shame and anguish.

May humanity speak.

May humanity listen . . .

In the world of those who live and kill for Power, there is no room for human beings. There is no space for hope, no place for tomorrow. Slavery or death is the choice that their world offers all worlds. The world of money, their world, governs from the stock exchanges. Today, speculation is the principal source of enrichment, and at the same time the best demonstration of the atrophy of our capacity to work. Work is no longer necessary in order to produce wealth; now all that is needed is speculation.

Crimes and wars are carried out so that the global stock exchanges may be pillaged by one or the other.

Meanwhile, millions of women, millions of youths, millions of indigenous, millions of homosexuals, millions of human beings of all races and colors, participate in the financial markets only as a devalued currency, always worth less and less, the currency of their blood turning a profit.

The globalization of markets erases borders for speculation and crime and multiplies them for human beings. Countries are obliged to erase their national borders for money to circulate, but to multiply their internal borders.

Neoliberalism doesn't turn many countries into one country; it turns each country into many countries.

The lie of unipolarity and internationalization turns itself into a nightmare of war, a fragmented war, again and again, so many times that nations are pulverized. In this world, Power globalizes to overcome the obstacles to its war of conquest. National governments are turned into the military underlings of a new world war against humanity.

From the stupid course of nuclear armament—destined to annihilate humanity in one blow—it has turned to the absurd militarization of every aspect in the life of national societies—a militarization destined to annihilate humanity in many blows, in many places, and in many ways. What were formerly known as "national armies" are turning into mere units of a greater army, one that neoliberalism arms to lead against humanity. The end of the so-called Cold War didn't stop the global arms race, it only changed the model for the merchandising of mortality: weapons of all kinds and sizes for all kinds of criminal tastes. More and more, not only are the so-called institutional armies armed, but also the armies' drug-trafficking builds up to ensure its reign. More or less rapidly, national societies are being militarized, and armies—supposedly created to protect their borders from foreign enemies—are turning their cannons and rifles around and aiming them inward.

It is not possible for neoliberalism to become the world's reality without the argument of death served up by institutional and private armies, without the gag served up by prisons, without the blows and assassinations served up by the military and the police. National repression is a necessary premise of the globalization neoliberalism imposes.

The more neoliberalism advances as a global system, the more numerous grow the weapons and the ranks of the armies and national police. The numbers of the imprisoned, the disappeared, and the assassinated in different countries also grows.

A world war:
the most brutal,
the most complete,
the most universal,
the most effective.

Each country,
each city,
each countryside,
each house,
each person,
each is a large or small battleground.

On the one side is neoliberalism, with all its repressive power and all its machinery of death; on the other side is the human being.

There are those who resign themselves to being one more number in the huge exchange of Power. There are those who resign themselves to being slaves. He who is himself master to slaves also cynically walks the slave's horizontal ladder. In exchange for the bad life and crumbs that Power hands out, there are those who sell themselves, resign themselves, surrender themselves.

In any part of the world, there are slaves who say they are happy being slaves. In any part of the world, there are men and women who stop being human and take their place in the gigantic market that trades in dignities.

But there are those who do not resign themselves, there are those who decide not to conform, there are those who do not sell themselves, there are those who do not surrender themselves. Around the world, there are those who resist being annihilated in this war. There are those who decide to fight. In any place in the world, anytime, any man or any woman rebels to the point of tearing off the clothes resignation has woven for them and cynicism has dyed gray. Any man or woman, of whatever color, in whatever tongue, speaks and says to himself or to herself: Enough is enough!—¡Ya Basta!

Enough is enough of lies.
Enough is enough of crime.
Enough is enough of death.
Enough is enough of war, says any man or woman.

Any man or woman, in whatever part of any of the five continents, eagerly decides to resist Power and to construct his or her own path that doesn't lead to the loss of dignity and hope.

Any man or woman decides to live and struggle for his or her part in history. No longer does Power dictate his or her steps. No longer does Power administer life and decide death.

Any man or woman responds to death with life, and responds to the nightmare by dreaming and struggling against war, against neoliberalism, for humanity . . .

For struggling for a better world, all of us are fenced in and threatened with death. The fence is reproduced globally. In every continent, every city, every countryside, every house. Power's fence of war closes in on the rebels, for whom humanity is always grateful.

But fences are broken,
in every house,

in every countryside,
in every city,
in every state,
in every country,
on every continent,
the rebels, whom history repeatedly has given us the length of its long trajectory,
     struggle and the fence is broken.

The rebels search each other out. They walk toward one another.
     They find each other and together break other fences.
     In the countryside and cities, in the states, in the nations, on the continents, the rebels begin to recognize each other, to know themselves as equals and different. They continue on their fatiguing walk, walking as it is now necessary to walk, that is to say, struggling . . .

A reality spoke to them then. Rebels from the five continents heard it and set off walking.

To arrive at the intercontinental La Realidad, each one has had to make his or her own path. From the five arms of the star of the world, the step of men and women, whose dignified word searched for a place to be spoken and heard, has come to La Realidad, to this *encuentro*.

Many fences had to be broken to come and break through the fence around reality. There are different fences. In ours, one must get past the police, customs officials, tanks, cannons, trenches, planes, helicopters, rain, mud, insects. Each one of the rebels from the five continents has his or her own fence, struggle, and a broken fence to add to the memory of other rebels.

So it was that this Intercontinental *Encuentro* began. It was initiated on all the continents, in all the countries, in all the places where any man or woman began to speak and say to themselves: "Enough is enough!"

Who can say in what precise locale and at what exact hour and date this Intercontinental *Encuentro* for Humanity and against Neoliberalism began? We don't know. But we do know who initiated it. All the rebels around the world did. Here, we are only a small part of those rebels, it's true. But to all the different fences that all the rebels of the world break every day, you have added one more rupture, that of the fence around the Zapatista reality.

To achieve that, you had to struggle against your respective governments and then confront the fence of papers and procedures with which the Mexican government thought to detain you. You are all fighters, men and women who break through fences of all kinds. That is why you made it to La Realidad. Maybe you can't yet see the greatness of your achievement, but we see it.

. . . Some of the best rebels from the five continents arrived in the mountains of the Mexican Southeast. All of them brought their ideas, their hearts, their worlds. They came to La Realidad to find themselves in others' ideas, in others' reasons, in others' worlds.

A world made of many worlds found itself these days in the mountains of the Mexican Southeast.

A world made of many worlds opened a space and established its right to exist, raised the banner of being necessary, stuck itself in the middle of the earth's reality to announce a better future.

A world of all the worlds that rebel and resist Power.

A world of all the worlds that inhabit this world, opposing cynicism.

A world that struggles for humanity and against neoliberalism.

This was the world that we lived these days.

This is the world that we found here.

This *encuentro* wasn't to end in La Realidad. Now it must search for a place to carry on.

But what next?

A new number in the useless enumeration of the numerous international orders?

A new scheme for calming and easing the anguish of having no solution?

A global program for world revolution?

A utopian theory so that it can maintain a prudent distance from the reality that anguishes us?

A scheme that assures each of us a position, a task, a title, and no work?

The echo goes, a reflected image of the possible and forgotten: the possibility and necessity of speaking and listening; not an echo that fades away, or a force that decreases after reaching its apogee.

Let it be an echo that breaks barriers and re-echoes.

Let it be an echo of our own smallness, of the local and particular, which reverberates in an echo of our own greatness, the intercontinental and galactic.

An echo that recognizes the existence of the other and does not overpower or attempt to silence it.

An echo that takes its place and speaks its own voice, yet speaks the voice of the other.

An echo that reproduces its own sound, yet opens itself to the sound of the other.

An echo of this rebel voice transforming itself and renewing itself in other voices.
An echo that turns itself into many voices, into a network of voices that, before Power's deafness, opts to speak to itself, knowing itself to be one and many, acknowledging itself to be equal in its desire to listen and be listened to, recognizing itself as diverse in the tones and levels of voices forming it.

Let it be a network of voices that resist the war Power wages on them.

A network of voices that not only speak, but also struggle and resist for humanity and against neoliberalism.

A network of voices that are born resisting, reproducing their resistance in other quiet and solitary voices.

A network that covers the five continents and helps to resist the death that Power promises us.

In the great pocket of voices, sounds continue to search for their place, fitting in with others.

The great pocket, ripped, continues to keep the best of itself, yet opens itself to what is better.

The great pocket continues to mirror voices; it is a world in which sounds may be listened to separately, recognizing their specificity; it is a world in which sounds can include themselves in one great sound.

The multiplication of resistances, the "I am not resigned," the "I am a rebel," continues.

The world, with the many worlds that the world needs, continues.

Humanity, recognizing itself to be plural, different, inclusive, tolerant of itself, full of hope, continues.

The human and rebel voice, consulted on the five continents in order to become a network of voices and resistance, continues.

21

Second Declaration of La Realidad for Humanity and against Neoliberalism

AUGUST 1996

Brothers and sisters of Africa, Asia, America, Europe, and Oceania:

Considering that we are:
Against the international order of death, against the globalization of war and armaments.
Against dictatorships, against authoritarianism, against repression.
Against the politics of economic liberalization, against hunger, against poverty, against robbery, against corruption.
Against patriarchy, against xenophobia, against discrimination, against racism, Against crime, against the destruction of the environment.
Against militarism.
Against stupidity, against lies, against ignorance.
Against slavery, against intolerance, against injustice.
Against marginalization, against forgetfulness.
Against neoliberalism.

Considering that we are:
For the international order of hope, for a new, just, and dignified peace.
For a new politics, for democracy, for political liberties.
For justice, for life, and dignified work.
For civil society,
For full rights for women in every regard,
For respect for elders, youth, and children,
For the defense and protection of the environment.
For intelligence, for culture, for education, for truth. For liberty, for tolerance,
For inclusion, for remembrance.
For humanity.

We declare:

First

THAT WE WILL MAKE a collective network of all our particular struggles and resistances, an intercontinental network of resistance against neoliberalism, an intercontinental network of resistance for humanity.

This intercontinental network of resistance, recognizing differences and acknowledging similarities, will strive to find itself in other resistances around the world. This intercontinental network of resistance will be the medium in which distinct resistances may support one another. This intercontinental network of resistance is not an organizing structure; it has no central head or decision maker; it has no central command or hierarchies. We are the network, all of us who resist.

Second

THAT WE WILL MAKE a network of communication among all our struggles and resistances, against neoliberalism, and for humanity.

This network will attempt to create channels so that words may flow to all paths that resist. It will be the medium by which distinct resistances communicate with one another. This network is not an organizing structure, nor does it have a central head or decision maker, nor does it have a central command or hierarchies. We are the network, all of us who speak and listen.

This we declare:
To speak and to listen for humanity and against neoliberalism.
To resist and struggle for humanity and against neoliberalism.
For the whole world:
Democracy!
Liberty!
Justice!
From whatever reality of whichever continent!

Brothers and sisters:
WE DO NOT PROPOSE that those of us who are present here sign this declaration and end this *encuentro* today. We propose that the Intercontinental *Encuentro* for Humanity and against Neoliberalism continues on every continent, in every country, in every countryside and city, in every house, school, or workplace where human beings live who want a better world.

The indigenous communities have taught us that to resolve a problem, no matter how great it may be, it is always good to consult all of the people we are. That is why we propose that this declaration be distributed around the world and that a *consulta* be carried out, at least in all the countries in attendance, regarding the following question:

Do you agree to subscribe to the Second Declaration of La Realidad, for Humanity, and Against Neoliberalism?

We propose that this Intercontinental *Consulta* for Humanity and against Neoliberalism be realized on all five continents, during the first two weeks of December 1996.

We propose that we organize this *consulta* in the same way that this *encuentro* was organized, that all of us who attended and those who couldn't but who followed us from afar, organize and carry out the *consulta*. We propose that we make use of all possible and impossible media in order to consult with the greatest number of human beings on the five continents. The Intercontinental *Consulta* is part of the resistance we are organizing and one way of making contacts and encounters with other resistances. Part of a new way of doing political work in the world—that is what the Intercontinental *Consulta* wants to be.

Not only that. We also propose that we now call people to the Second Intercontinental *Encuentro* for Humanity and against Neoliberalism. We propose that it be carried out in the second half of 1997, and that it be in the European continent. We propose that the exact date and place of the *encuentro* be defined by our European brothers and sisters, in a meeting they will hold after this first *encuentro*.

We all hope that there will be this Second Intercontinental *Encuentro* and that it will be held, of course, on another continent. When this second *encuentro* is held, we want to make it clear that we will find a way to participate directly, wherever it may be held.

Brothers and sisters:
WE CONTINUE to be in the way.
What the theorists of neoliberalism tell us is false:
that everything is under control, including everything that isn't under control.

We are not a safety valve for the rebellion that could destabilize neoliberalism. It is false that our rebel existence legitimizes Power. Power fears us. That is why it pursues us and fences us in. That is why it jails and kills us. In reality, we are the possibility that can defeat it and make it disappear. Maybe there are not so many of us, but we are men and women who struggle for humanity, who struggle against neoliberalism. We are men and women who struggle around the world.

We are men and women who want the five continents to have:
Democracy!
Liberty!
Justice!

From the mountains of the Mexican Southeast
THE INDIGENOUS REVOLUTIONARY CLANDESTINE COMMITTEE
GENERAL COMMAND ZAPATISTA NATIONAL LIBERATION ARMY
PLANET EARTH

22

Civil Society That So Perturbs

To Civil Society, the only force that can save the country
To the people of Mexico
To the people and governments of the world

Brothers and sisters:
AS OF TODAY, September 19, 1996, it's been eleven years since a new political and social force emerged as a result of the government's inability to confront the problems of the earthquake that shook the capital. This new force proved that it could respond to destruction with creativity, to chaos with organization, to death with life.

While the government vacillated between false promises and stealing humanitarian aid, Civil Society organized itself, by itself, to revive and rebuild a city that, amid all the pain, quickly reminded itself that it's nothing without its inhabitants.

Thousands of residents mobilized themselves with nothing more than communal feeling, a feeling that had supposedly been buried in the earthquake of neoliberal modernity. Amid the debris, destruction, and death, these Mexicans rescued self-discovery and dignity.

Eleven years ago thousands of Mexicans didn't invent their strength; they remembered it and put it to work. With the country beside them, they discovered that you can take a direct part in solving problems the government leaders ignore.

There are no historic monuments or government ceremonies for all these men and women who put forth heroic efforts from their unsung places. Without asking for praise or making conditions, they lived and died nameless and faceless.

The anonymous, faceless heroism that illuminated September 1985 was an answer to Power's men in gray, who plotted to sell dignity and forget history.

From the first spontaneous response to that catastrophe, the force that emerged eleven years ago followed its own path, and in many cases, turned itself into a civic organization. The self-discovery of September 1985 was all that was needed to nurture, cultivate, and organize this strength.

This civil force, which has been around for eleven years, organized itself little by little to become proof that you can participate without aspiring to public office, that you can organize politically without being in a political party, that you can keep an eye on the government and pressure it to "lead by obeying," that you can have an effect and remain yourself, give of yourself, be noble and honest and not be selfish. This is how these organizations came to be. They served the people in the city and were compensated with the satisfaction of having done their duty, and having received national and international recognition of their work.

Today, eleven years later, the political forces with the most moral authority, legitimacy, and efficacy aren't the political parties or the government. The community organizations in today's Mexico are the only credible forces.

This new strength, the strength of Civil Society that so perturbs government leaders, today gives us hope that it's possible to rebuild the country despite the destruction the neoliberal project has brought to the Mexican society.

Meanwhile, Power tramples all over itself, administers violence and death, militarizing Mexican life through a state takeover that, although slow, is still authoritarian.

Meanwhile, Power closes its ears, delivers monologues at pointless negotiating tables, and only gives pride and arrogance weight as important issues.

Meanwhile, those who hide behind Power continue to steal the liberty of dissidents and nonconformists and bestow the gift of impunity on the real criminals who, yesterday and today, have made and still make up the government.

Meanwhile, Power enriches itself, decrees death for our national history, and sentences millions of Mexicans to poverty through neoliberalism.

Meanwhile, those who shield themselves behind Power exclude the only ones who can grant them dignity and self-respect through dialogue and a role in history; they persecute and harass everyone who doesn't mouth the message of Power's law and death, and scoff at those who promote agreement through dialogue, instead of armed conflict.

Two national projects, two countries, two Mexicos confronting each other.

On the one hand, there is their nation, their country, their Mexico. A plan for the nation that Power holds up with bloody hands, with law and legitimacy soiled by corruption and crime. A plan for the nation that means destruction, misery, and death, with war everywhere at every level, and the use of force as the sole rationale for Power's monologue before its mirror. Despotism is consecrated as the "rule of law," while sovereignty is squandered. That is the Mexico that belongs to Power, the Mexico that is in agony.

On the other hand, there is the nation of the community organizations, the country of Civil Society, the Mexico of the Mexicans—a plan for the nation bearing the banner of democracy, liberty, and justice. A plan for the nation that means its reconstruction, justice, and life, with peace everywhere for everyone, with dialogue as a way that makes its own way and from which springs hope, with reason and heart as its driving force, with its sovereignty stolen, but this time by the Mexican people. That is the Mexico of Civil Society, the Mexico that lives again.

Two countries struggling between themselves to find a place in the future.

One, belonging to Power, that uses force.

The other, Civil Society's, that uses reason and feeling.

One, belonging to Power, that looks for war.

The other, Civil Society's, that looks for peace.

Yesterday, we Zapatistas were criticized for wanting a dialogue with Civil Society, for addressing her in our initiatives. Today, we are criticized because we don't seek the support of political organizations—armed and unarmed—but reiterate our belief in Civil Society. They tell us that's a poor bet. They tell us we'll lose. They sentence us to defeat. They tell us that you don't speak to or listen to Civil Society; rather, you command it.

The possibility of a new motherland appeared within the debris of a city that, until that moment, had always been seen as synonymous with egoism and inhumanity. Since then, this new motherland walks hand in hand with people like those of September 1985. People, men and women, children and elders. People of no-matter-what faces, that is to say, without faces. People with whatever names, that is to say, without famous names. City people and country people. Workers and farmers, indigenous people and mestizos, teachers and students, housewives and tenant farmers, artists and intellectuals, religious and lay people, professionals and the unemployed, people like every one, but not just like any one.

Civil Society, this discomfiting concept and disturbing reality. The forgotten of always, except at election time. The disposable, except when they are required to fulfill their obligations. The excluded, except at tax time. The disregarded, except at the hour of death.

Civil Society and its proposal for the nation, now not only an intuition but a possibility, is confronting Power and its destruction. While Power militarizes its plan of hopelessness and civil war on Mexican soil, Civil Society insists on holding back war and turning back the militarization of the nation.

While Power delivers a monologue, Civil Society demands a national dialogue, viable and inclusive.

While Power jails its opponents and lets criminals go free, Civil Society questions Power's lack of accountability and the jailing of political prisoners.

While Power brutally imposes a murderous economic model, Civil Society demonstrates for a new political economy.

While Power destroys, Civil Society builds. While Power wages war, Civil Society seeks peace.

While Power belittles mediation, laughs at legislators, and attacks honest intellectual leadership, Civil Society works to create a Commission of Concordance and Peace for the whole nation.

While Power kills, Civil Society lives.

Political parties and organizations—armed and unarmed, legal and illegal, open or secret, regional or national—sooner or later will have to choose between these two plans for the nation.

The EZLN has already chosen.
Long live the Mexican motherland, the new one.

No longer a cardboard motherland of vain, ostentatious military parades that frighten nobody. No longer a motherland full of gray speeches from gray bureaucrats. No longer a motherland up for sale to anyone in the neoliberal marketplace. No longer the dead motherland you can find in books and museums.

May Power and its war die forever.
May the men and women of Civil Society live forever.

Democracy!
Liberty!
Justice!

From the mountains of the Mexican Southeast
BY THE CLANDESTINE REVOLUTIONARY INDIGENOUS COMMITTEE
GENERAL COMMAND OF THE EZLN

23

The Spiral from the End and the Beginning

OCTOBER 23, 1996

ZAPATISTA NATIONAL LIBERATION ARMY

To the International and National Civil Society
Madam:[1]

YES, IT'S US AGAIN. But please don't be upset. Not yet. Today we write to thank you for the troubled joy which took Comandante Ramona, and the rest of us, to the center of power in Mexico. We've seen some of the images of those days during which the whole Mexican political system trembled at the passing of our most powerful weapon.

We also learned about the National Indigenous Congress, and its honest call to join the struggle under the subversive banner of "Never again a Mexico without us!" Yes, that "us" is a difficult invitation to resist. And, well, I think that "Never again a world without us!" will follow. Don't you agree? Yes. Of course, everything turned out fine. And you're right, it was like a party. Of course, it ruined more than one person's breakfast, but these things are inevitable.

Something very strange is happening in this country. When you give no signs of life and wrap yourself up in problems you believe are only yours, Power smiles and leaves everything for later. But the moment you are determined to speak, to hit the streets, to dance, the supreme government gets this strong urge to hold dialogues and show it's serious about resolving the problems. I don't know why this happens, but it's so good that you go out and dance that little rhythm that goes . . . how does it go? Yes, that's the one!

Well, then, today I also write to tell you that we're still participating in the dialogue (I'm writing these lines at dawn). We finished the first encounter they call "tripartite" because you're supposed to split yourself in three and not lose sight of the local, national, and galactic perspectives.

And speaking of galaxies, I'm going back to the ceiba. No, it's not that I'm afraid that Heriberto has eaten all the candy in my absence, or that Eva has organized feminist seminars with that Pedro Infante movie called *What Has That Woman Done to You?* No, madam, she hasn't done anything to me, that's just the name of the movie. And I'm not returning to the ceiba because I want to avoid Olivio's bouncing ball or Yeniperr's questions, and believe me, they're both equally terrible. No. Well, you see . . . Haven't you heard about the moons, that in October the moon . . . etc.? Well, a while back I escaped from my security escort at dawn . . . No, really, the only thing I caught was such a bad cold that every time I sneeze . . . well, forget the blasts on January 1; they were nothing in comparison. Anyway, the thing is, I escaped because whenever I'm here, they keep me inside four white walls where my friends don't come to see me from time to time, two by two, nor from six to seven. I got out, and before my security escort recaptured me, I managed to catch sight of a moon that reminded me of a moon two years ago . . .

And on that dawn, like this one, the moon was a solitary breast disappearing beneath the hand of night's desire. But on this dawn I reread Durito's last letter, and I should warn you that Durito has a penchant for philosophical treatises. So, along with this letter comes what follows and which already begins to explain itself by its title . . .

The Conch of the End and the Beginning

(Neoliberalism and Architecture or The Ethics of the Quest versus the Ethics of Destruction)

IN THE LACANDON JUNGLE, in the southeast Mexican state of Chiapas, there's a deserted village surrounded by well-armed military posts. The name of this abandoned village was Guadalupe Tepeyac. Its inhabitants, indigenous Tojolabales, were expelled by the Mexican government's army in February 1995, as federal troops attempted to assassinate the leadership of the Zapatista National Liberation Army.

But I don't want to talk about the painful exile of these indigenous people, who pay for their rebellion by living in the mountains. I want to tell you about an architectural masterpiece that was born on the skirts of the then-living Guadalupe Tepeyac, in July and August 1994. The Tojolabal architects—for the most part illiterate, their most "educated" having made it to third grade— raised a masterpiece in twenty-eight days, to house what the Zapatistas called the National Democratic Convention. Honoring Mexican history, the Zapatistas called the meeting place Aguascalientes. The place for the gigantic meeting could hold 10,000 seated participants, a stage for 100, a library, a computer room, kitchens, hostels, parking lots. They say it even had "a staging area for assaults."

Anyway, all this is now anecdotal and can be seen through other means (books, reports, photos, videos, and movies from that time). What matters is a detail that went unseen by most of those present at the Aguascalientes of Guadalupe Tepeyac that 1994 (the Aguascalientes was destroyed in February 1995). The detail I refer to was so large that it was hard to see at first glance. This writing is about that gigantic, unnoticed detail.

It seems that the auditorium and the stage were at the center of a giant conch shell coming and going, without end or beginning. Don't get frustrated; let me explain. The indigenous Zapatistas had raised a more or less conventional auditorium; the kind of construction shaped like a boat keel, a flat part in front with seats, and, behind, a gallery with wooden benches rising up the side of a knoll. There was nothing extraordinary except, perhaps, the split-wood benches lashed together with vines. There was no metal in that gallery.

When the time came to deal with the hostels, the library, and the other facilities, the rebel Zapatista Tojolobales—the impromptu architects—began to build structures that sprinkled the immediate surroundings of the gigantic auditorium in what appeared to be great disorder, or so it appeared to the Sup. It wasn't until he was calculating the housing capacity of each structure that the Sup noticed one of the buildings seemed screwy; it had an unaccountable indentation at one end. The Sup didn't give it much importance, until Tojolabal Comandante Tacho asked him:

"What do you think of the conch?"

"What conch?" asked the Sup, in the Zapatista method of answering a question with a question, the eternal game of questioning the mirror.

"The one encircling the auditorium," answered Comandante Tacho in a tone that said, "As the day doth follow the night." The Sup looked blankly at Tacho, and then Tacho understood that the Sup didn't understand what he understood. So he took him to the crooked house and pointed out how the roof had a seemingly capricious indentation.

"That's where the conch curves," he told him.

The Sup then put on a "So?" face (similar to the one you have now). So Comandante Tacho quickly made a sketch in the mud with a stick. Tacho's drawing marked the location of all the buildings, and yes, thanks to the indentation in that crooked house, the whole thing looked like a conch shell. The Sup agreed silently after studying the drawing. Then Comandante Tacho went to see about a tarp to cover the auditorium, in case it rained.

The Sup was left standing there, in front of the crooked house, considering how it really wasn't crooked; it was the curve the conch needed to be complete. He was pondering this when a journalist approached him and, looking for an answer with deep political significance, asked what the Aguascalientes meant to the Zapatistas.

"A conch," was the Sup's laconic reply.

"A conch?" he asked, wondering if the Sup had understood the question.

"Yes," he told him. And the Sup pointed out the curve in the house as he left.

Yes, I agree with you. The conch at the Aguascalientes could be seen only from above, and only from a certain altitude. What I mean to say is that you had to fly very high to discover the Zapatista conch tracing its spiral on these poor rebel lands. At one end of the spiral was a library and at the other was the old "safe house." The history of that safe house is similar to the story of the EZLN in the Mayan indigenous communities. That little house was built far from anyone, so no one would see those first clandestine Tojolabales who joined the EZLN. There they held meetings, they studied, and they stored the tortillas and the beans they would send into the mountains to nourish the insurgents.

So there you have the Mayan conch. A spiral with no beginning or end. Where does a conch shell begin or end? At its innermost point or its outermost point? Does a conch shell wind in or out?

The Mayan rebel leaders' conch began and ended in the "safe house," but it also began and ended in the library. The Aguascalientes conch was the place of the *encuentro*, of the dialogue, of the transition, of the search. From what "architectural" tradition did the indigenous Zapatistas borrow? I don't know, but surely that conch, that spiral, invites entry as well as exit, and really, I would not dare to say where a conch ends or begins.

Months later, in October 1994, a small civilian group arrived at the Aguascalientes to install electricity in the library. They left after a few days' work. That morning, especially cold and misty, the moon was a promise on which to rest your cheek and your desire, and a cello bled a few midnight notes into the half mist. It was cinematic. The Sup watched from a corner, protected by the shadows and his ski mask. A film's beginning or ending? After that group left, no one else returned to Aguascalientes until New Year's Eve. Then they disappeared again. On February 10, 1995, federal troops moved in by air and took Guadalupe Tepeyac. When the government troops entered the Aguascalientes, the first things they did were to destroy the library and the safe house, the beginning and end of the conch. Then they destroyed the rest.

For some strange reason, the indentation in the crooked house remained standing for several months afterward. It is said that it fell apart in December 1995, when other Aguascalientes were born in the mountains of the Mexican Southeast.

All this goes to show that the ethics of Power is identical to the ethics of destruction, and the ethics of the conch are the same as the ethics of the quest. And that's very important for architecture and for understanding neoliberalism. Don't you agree?

So ends Durito's thesis, which, as you can tell, is only for specialists . . .

So what's all this about beetles, sea conches, and tinted moons? Well, the truth is that ten years ago on a morning in October, Old Man Antonio explained that a conch is for looking inside and for leaping out, but I'll tell you about that later.

And so, Madam, I say good-bye. I hope you don't forget that we're still here. Well, I hope you don't forget too often, anyway.

Vale. Health to you, and one remaining question: If you are inside the conch shell, in what direction should you walk? Inward or outward?

From the mountains of the Mexican Southeast
SUBCOMANDANTE INSURGENTE MARCOS

Vale once again. Health to you and, since we're talking about the trap of final options, everyone must agree with me that when it comes to choosing whether to come or go, it's always better to come . . .

THE SUP WITH A BAD COLD, AND, CLEARLY, A TOUCH OF FEVER.

NOTE
1. Marcos refers to civil society as Madam, as a way of giving shape and spirit to the vast, amorphous population that resides outside the political framework.

24

An Urgent Telegram

DECEMBER 8, 1996

To the National and International Civil Society

MADAM:
HEALTH TO YOU, GREETINGS. STOP. I BOW TO YOU MANY TIMES.
STOP. SUPREME GOVERNMENT WITH AMNESIA. STOP. FORGOTTEN
AGREEMENTS. STOP. RENEWED EXCUSES. STOP. PROBABLE NEED FOR
MORE INDIGENOUS BLOOD TO REFRESH MEMORY. STOP. YOUR PRES-
ENCE IS URGENTLY REQUIRED. STOP. AN INTERCONTINENTAL DANCE
MAY SERVE TO REFRESH MEMORY. STOP. THE GRAYS HOPE TO WIN.
STOP. RAINBOW NEEDED URGENTLY. STOP. IF THERE IS DANCE I
WANT ONE. STOP. SIGH. STOP. AFTER YOU. STOP. SIGH. STOP. HAND
IN HAND AND HAND ON WAIST. STOP. SIGH. STOP. 1-2-3. STOP. SIGH.
VALE. STOP. HEALTH TO YOU. STOP. MAY THE DANCE PAINT THE SKY
ON THE GROUND. STOP.

The Sup, thinking telegraphically and naively that the periods and hyphens mark
a beat for dancing and a path for walking.

From the mountains of the Mexican Southeast
SUBCOMANDANTE INSURGENTE MARCOS
CCRI-CG OF THE EZLN

25
Do the Pictures Lie?

JANUARY 5, 1998

To the National and International Civil Society

Dear Madam:

THE GOVERNMENT SAYS THE ZAPATISTAS aren't being persecuted, but here are the pictures. [*See photo section.*] The background's the same as always, an indigenous Zapatista community. There are the people. You can see the soldiers pushing women and children. You can see them pointing their guns. "There's no persecution of Zapatistas," assures the government. See the heavily armed federal soldiers? Do you see the Zapatista women and children armed with sticks and shawls? Are these pictures "irresponsible rumors?"

Do the pictures lie? Have they been retouched? Have the photos been doctored to trick us into believing government soldiers are attacking indigenous people when they're really only offering medicine, haircuts, sex education classes, candy, toys, and electric appliance repairs? Do these pictures lie when they show the look in those Zapatista women's eyes? Do you see submissiveness or shyness in those looks? The government says they're not persecuting Zapatistas, that their army is helping the population. Do you see gratitude in those eyes? Someone's lying. Is it the pictures or the government? In these images of people under attack, we see dignity and rebellion. We see a people who won't allow their blood to relive the ignominy at Acteal. That's what we see. Yet the government says it isn't pursuing Zapatistas. But just look at these photos. You, what do you see?

Vale. Health to you, and I hope you can see the tomorrow living in those eyes, the tomorrow promised in those eyes.

From the mountains of the Mexican Southeast
SUBCOMANDANTE INSURGENTE MARCOS

26

For Those Who Protest with Us after Acteal

JANUARY 21, 1998

PLANET EARTH

Brothers and sisters:

A LITTLE LATE, but the news about the demonstrations in Mexico and all over the world managed to reach us all the way here. According to one count you sent us, from December 22, 1997, through January 13, 1998, there were demonstrations in 130 cities in twenty countries on five continents. Especially on January 12, many actions of many sizes took place both in our country and in different places all over the planet with one identical demand: Stop the war of extermination, punish those responsible for the Acteal massacre,[1] and fulfill the San Andres Accords.[2]

If our answer was a little slow, that isn't true of our feelings. The same day, January 12, in spite of the pain with which we received the news of the murder of our *compañera* Guadalupe López Mendez, the strong echo of your demonstrations in Mexico's capital, in other Mexican cities, and on the five continents reached us and confirmed that we were right in withstanding, resisting, and avoiding those provocations that, yesterday and today, wear olive green uniforms.

They tell me there was a little bit of everything during the protests, and I'm not only talking about the fact that there were men, women, children, and elders, but about the dances, songs, poetry, marches, graffiti, shouts, and pervasive indignation. I also say there was a little bit of everything because there were indigenous people, women, young people, housewives, students, feminists, homosexuals, workers' unions, farmers, workers, solidarity committees, intellectuals, artists, undocumented people, etcetera (which includes everything). In other words, people, people with and without a name. People of the kind who say *¡Ya Basta!* and write meaningful history, the history that counts. People who speak to us, people we listen to, people we are now writing to. People like you, like us.

Their shouts carried far and were heard loud and clear, even though they couldn't reach those in power. Up there, they only hear the noise of money, and their advisers' voices, open or furtive, crying out for our extermination.

But we did listen. That's why we're endorsing the bullfighter's vocation, and here we are, making passes with our capes at assault helicopters, bombers, tanks, and tracking dogs. They say they are trained to sniff out vanilla tobacco (I'm now giving maple a try).

Our interlocutor is not the Mexican government. As we said, it no longer listens. You are our interlocutors, the thousands and thousands of people in Mexico and the world who want and look for an end to an oppressive system that is nothing but a war against humanity—the thousands and thousands who, opposing the war in Chiapas, oppose death in Mexico and the rest of the world, who demand the fulfillment of the San Andres Accords because they embody a new inclusive politics aimed at the poorest, who demand demilitarization and justice instead of bullets and soldiers. Because of you, our hope grows and heals us, because we have heard you, we have listened. As Old Don Antonio used to say, those who know how to listen grow and make out the path that stretches throughout time, stretching far, branching out into many other paths.

From the mountain summit where we perch, you can see very far. Over there, for example, we can see a flag fluttering in the wind as if it were the future. The flag looks very high up and those bearing it aloft are many.

"It's democracy," someone says.

"It's freedom," a woman ventures.

"It's justice," a third affirms.

Perhaps, I think. Perhaps all three. Or perhaps it's dignity, that stubborn walk of life that, in us, becomes addictive.

Around here, things get more difficult all the time. It's clear the new dialogue coordinator, Mr. Emilio Rabasa, is again playing the bait-and-switch ploy that Esteban Moctezuma B. (aka Guajardo) played in 1995. While he talks about a "solution to the conflict" (did you notice that no one in the government speaks of a "peaceful solution to the conflict" anymore?), the soldiers polish up their operational details, compile information, and fine-tune their plans and troop placement.

We expect only a new attack from the government. "The definitive solution," say Power's scribes.

From you, we expect what we always have: an opportunity to live and struggle to become better.

Now, in the midst of these hours of anguish and uncertainty, we are more than sure that we will triumph, that the indigenous peoples will be recognized and included, their differences respected, and that democracy, liberty, and justice will be shared by all. Even then, we may not have the best of all possible worlds, but we shall have an opportunity to build one.

Pictures and stories of the Zocalo[3] on January 12 have reached us down here. Both tell us of the rage and indignation of everyone demanding justice, of the incredulity at the attorney general's office versions of the Acteal massacre, of Mr. Zedillo's loss of prestige. Without any doubt, it was one of the largest, most moving demonstrations in our country's history. There is a greatness to its cause for peace with dignity and justice. And great also are the rage and the refusal to conform, the disagreement, great the resolve not to stand impassive before unjust death.

As for the demonstrations in the twenty-seven other countries, the Mexican government and that racket called the PRI are rather annoyed at the "internationalization" of the conflict these demonstrations signify. It seems what they sneeringly call "an Internet war" has given their embassies and consulates many headaches. Takeovers, protests in central squares and in the streets, and thousands of letters demanding peace and justice are keeping the Mexican government from its sleep and, inexplicably, provoking sudden bursts of "nationalism," rejecting all "foreign interference" (other than foreign capital of course.) The demonstrations for peace, democracy, liberty, and justice that took place on five continents are nothing but "isolated and small attempts at intervention in the internal affairs of the country" to the Mexican government, since the extermination of indigenous people it's carrying out is a "domestic issue." Will the government keep thinking that is so, after the European Parliament's condemnation?

But we agree with you. The struggle for peace and for humanity is an intercontinental issue. As that too-little-credited internationalist Old Don Antonio used to say: Life without those who are different is empty and damns you to stagnation . . .

And I think the most important thing we have to tell you is that we're listening to you, that we recognize you, that we respect you. It might seem a small thing from so far away, but you can see that recognizing the other, respecting him, and listening to him can produce possiblities as enormously transcendent as dancing.

So, to recognize, respect, and listen to each other, and reply to the January 12, 1998 public invitation for us to visit Europe to talk and listen to the world, we reply (as soon as we stop making bullfighting passes at our enemies, which is nothing but a more complicated form of dancing) that we'll look into the possibility of one or several of our *compañeros* and *compañeras* traveling to Europe, or wherever, to recognize, respect, and listen.

About the Observation Commission from the world's civil society that will soon be making a trip to the mountains of the Mexican Southeast to observe human rights violations, we can tell you that the rebel indigenous communities welcome the Observation Commission's initiative and promise to respect their work. We also take this opportunity to respectfully salute the work of the independent Mexican organizations, human rights defenders, who have spared no effort or dedication to care for the needs of the indigenous communities, in spite of the government's hindrance and outright harassment on many occasions.

And since we are talking about the demonstrations in Mexico, the capital's

Zocalo not only dazzled us, it also brought us a certainty and a hope. The certainty is that in this country, the people are infinitely better than those claiming to govern them. The hope is that all those people will attain what has been kept from them up to now, that is, the right to live with democracy, liberty, and justice. That means leaving them in peace.

Well, that's all for now. Always remember that we take it as an honor to see you grow and spread. And that's something that makes us grow and spread, too.

Vale. Health to you, and after the promised flower comes the promised dance (I hope).

SUBCOMANDANTE INSURGENTE MARCOS

P.S . . . WHICH SHOWS CONTEMPT FOR WHAT IS HAPPENING . . .

Look how the government shows its understanding of what's going on. According to the secretary of the interior, Chiapas has reverted once more to the status of a problem confined to four counties. According to the attorney general's office, the Acteal slaughter is the product of the perverse vengeance of a diabolical and resentful old man who alone had the means, time, and knowledge to arm sixty paramilitaries with AK-47s and R-15s, train them in commando techniques, and plan the whole operation with a tactical precision that it's a safe bet he learned while reading about the war of extermination in Guatemala. Or Vietnam? Or Kurdistan?

NOTES

1. On December 22, 1997, in the community of Acteal, municipality of San Pedro of Chenalho, Chiapas, forty-five indigenous civilians—nine men, twenty-one women, and fifteen children—were massacred. About sixty paramilitaries belonging to the PRI (sponsored by the federal and state governments) attacked the indigenous with high-caliber weapons. Among them were refugees of Acteal. According to radio transmissions of the government of Chiapas (intercepted by the EZLN) in the immediate vicinity of Acteal when the massacre was being carried out, public security police of the state of Chiapas backed up the attack and during the afternoon and evening dedicated themselves to picking up cadavers in order to hide its magnitude. Direct responsibility for these bloody events fell upon Ernesto Zedillo Ponce de Leon and the Justice Ministry, who two days prior gave a green light to the counterinsurgency project presented by the federal army.

2. On February 16, 1996, the Zapatista National Liberation Army (EZLN) and the Mexican federal government agreed upon and signed the first phase of the San Andres Accords, thereby agreeing to carry out in their totality the provisions stipulated within this landmark document. Both of these signings were done in the presence of both CONAI and Cocopa. These initial accords were the direct result of the dialogue process between the Mexican government and the EZLN, specifically the talks that began in January 1996 on the subject of indigenous rights and culture. These discussions centered principally around basic respect for the diversity of the indigenous population of Chiapas; conservation of natural resources within the territories used and occupied by indigenous peoples; greater participation of indigenous communities in decisions and control of public expenditures; the participation of indigenous communities in determining their own development plans, as well as having control over their own administrative and judicial affairs; and the autonomy of indigenous communities and their right of free determination in the framework of the State.

3. A *zocalo* is the main square of a Mexican city or town. Here, Marcos refers to Mexico City's Zocalo, where on January 12, 1998—four years to the day after the great March for Peace, announcing "civil society" as a new social and political actor following the Zapatista uprising—Mexico City again burst with urban anger. It was described as one of the largest demonstrations Mexico had seen in decades (and certainly the largest pro-Zapatista demonstration), although no one seemed to be sure of the number of marchers; the figures reported by the press and the organizers ranged up to 300,000 people. "It was a different kind of march," wrote FZLN member Amarela Varela when it was over. "It was different and diverse because within it converged militants of the 'old left,' now grouped under the acronyms of political parties or collectives; entire families which could easily have formed their own contingents; local government bureaucrats; members and sympathizers of the FZLN; campesinos from other regions of the country; students, unions, artists, political parties, and social organizations—all which have rarely marched together to openly manifest their sympathy for the EZLN or their opposition to the federal government."

27

The Sea of My Insomnia

The Table at San Andres

Between the amnesia from above and the memory of below.
For my Mariana, in other words, the sea of my insomnia.

And all this happened to us.
We saw it,
We watched it.
With this lamentable luck,
We were anguished.
On the roads lay broken spines.
Hair is scattered everywhere.
The houses without roofs.
The walls are reddened.
Worms crawl through the streets and plazas,
and brains are splattered on the walls.
The waters are red, they are colored,
and when we drink of them,
it's as though we are drinking brine water.
and our inheritance was a web of holes.
Swords were their defense,
not even the swords could sustain their solitude.

—ANONYMOUS, TLATELOLCO, "Apparition of the Conquered," 1546

I. The Dispute in San Andres: Oblivion against Memory

ON FEBRUARY 16, 1996, the representatives of the federal government and the Zapatista National Liberation Army signed the first agreements of the "Table of San Andres," so named because it took place in the municipality of San Andres Sacamch'en de los Pobres, in the highlands of Chiapas. In those first agreements, a large part of the rights and culture of the indigenous peoples of Mexico are recognized.

Two years have gone by, and the agreement has not been fulfilled—two years during which the true nature of the Table of San Andres has been revealed. The federal government, through its spokesmen (Zedillo, Labastida, and Rabasa)[1] has made it clear that in word and deed THEY WILL NOT fulfill the San Andres Accords.

Why? At the present time there are three interpretations to the possible reasons:

1. It is said that they intend to fulfill them, but they disagree with the "legal interpretation" contained in the initiative developed by the Cocopa.

2. It is said that the government learned, somewhat late, that those agreements constituted an act of "treachery to the nation," since they implied the wounding of national sovereignty, the fragmentation of the country and the creation of a "state within a state."

3. It is said that the government did not sign those agreements in the belief it would fulfill them, but in the pretense of a disposition that is far from reality.

It is not likely that the government's reluctance to honor the agreements it signed almost two years ago—and whose lack of fulfillment has done nothing but aggravate the war in the Mexican Southeast—is due to a "legal interpretation." Since its rejection of the Cocopa initiative, nearly fourteen months ago, the government has been presenting arguments that contradict one another; none of them contain "legal technicalities." Its refusal to fulfill them is not due to a sincere preoccupation with the dangers of "Balkanization" or a threat to the national sovereignty. The San Andres Agreements contain nothing that affect the first or contradict the second, and the government knows it.

Is it the third reason then? Yes, but not solely. The signing of the agreements in themselves does not have major consequences, above all for an illegitimate government with no credibility. To fulfill them presents a grave problem, though; their fulfillment represents a defeat for the government at the Table of San Andres.

Yes, because the Table at San Andres was a place of dialogue and negotiation for the indigenous peoples, while for the government it was a battle site, the scene of a struggle, a struggle between oblivion and memory.

On the side of oblivion are the multiple forces of the market.

On the side of memory is history.

This is the great battle for the Mexican government, the fight of the twentieth century: the market versus history.

II. A Fight of Many Rounds

AT THE END OF THE CENTURY, in the fight that the Mexican government wages against itself, San Andres is only a small boxing ring. The boxers are the same ones who have fought throughout the different eras of humanity.

In one corner is the Market, the new sacred beast—money and its conception of time denying both yesterday and tomorrow. In the other corner is History—the one that Power always forgets. The reaches of memory root and temper humanity in the past, present, and future. In the cult of "modernity," the present serves as both weapon and shield. NOW is the name of the new altar upon which principles, loyalties, convictions, shame, dignity, memory, and truth are sacrificed. The past, a guide to be learned from and upon which to grow, doesn't exist for the technocrats, under whose rule our nation suffers. The future can be nothing more than a lengthening of the present for these professional amnesiacs. In order to defeat history, the past is denied a horizon that goes beyond the neoliberal "here and now." There is no "before" or "after" today. The search for eternity is finally satisfied: the world of money is not only the best of all possible worlds, it is the only one necessary. For the "neo-politicians" the only acceptable attitude toward history is a mixture of nausea and regret. The past should be devalued, ignored, eliminated. The past and all it recalls leads us to regard it with an altered eye.

What better example of this phobia of history is there than the attitude of the Mexican government toward the indigenous peoples? Are not the indigenous demands a worrisome stain on history, dimming the splendor of globalization? Is not the very existence of indigenous people an affront to the global dictatorship of the Market? Fulfilling the San Andres agreements is equivalent to acknowledging that history has a place in the present. And this is unacceptable. To fulfill the San Andres Accords is to admit that the end of the century is not the end of history. And this is intolerable ("not negotiable," says the up-and-coming ex-coordinator of the governmental dialogue, Mr. Emilio Rabasa).

The present is the only acceptable guide. The Mexican federal government will not fulfill the San Andres Accords. It thus believes that the present will defeat history and can proceed to the future. But history, that stubborn and rude teacher of life, will return to pummel a truncated reality, falsified by the masks of power and money. History will return for a rematch when the present will be most vulnerable—in other words, in the future.

Meanwhile, on the clock at San Andres, the hands mark a quarter to twelve. Attention! The fight is about to begin . . . Come on down. It is pointless for you to look for a seat from which to watch the fight. There are no seats outside the ring. The Supreme One, upon transforming the table for a peace dialogue into a boxing ring, has forced everyone to climb into the ring. Silence now, here comes the announcer to introduce the opponents.

III. In This Cornerrrrrr: The Federal Government!
(The strategy of amnesia induced by a knockout blow.)

They put a price on us.
The price for the young man,
for the priest, for the child and the maiden.
Enough: for a poor man the price was
only two handfuls of corn,
only ten loaves filled with flies;
our only price was
twenty loaves of salt-petered pork.

—"Apparition of the Conquered"

POWER, THE BEAST, has made Chiapas into a war for the nation, and in this fight it plays the role of boxer, judge, and adversary. The Hydra of the State-Party system tries to completely fill the small boxing ring at the table of San Andres— not only to capture center stage and display all its trappings, but to keep any rival from stealing the show or winning. In this way Power forces the "others" into the fight, but they are admitted only as losers . . .

"I am waiting for them to get tired," Zedillo informed his true teachers (the North Americans), referring to the more than 10 million indigenous people who are waiting for him to keep his word. Zedillo thus declares that he will wait for the past to get tired of presenting past-due accounts to modernity. The head of the executive branch waits for the indigenous peoples of Mexico to get tired, the ones who already inhabited these lands before it became nation—or an acknowledged nation—the ones who with their blood fought for independence, the ones who with their bodies confronted the successive aggressions of foreign invasions, the ones who with their bones gave a spine to the Mexican Revolution, the ones who shook and awoke the nation from the false dream of modernity.

From the mountains of the Mexican Southeast
SUBCOMANDANTE INSURGENTE MARCOS

P.S. DISGUISED AS ZAPATISTA GRAFFITI:
DEATH WILL DIE a mortal death. From death we shall kill, from life.

P.S. A STORY TOLD ON THE DAY OF THE DEAD.
EVERY YEAR, IT IS THE CUSTOM of our peoples to set out an offering for the

dead during the celebrations from October 31 until the dawn of November 2. In addition to flowers and ornaments made of paper, between two candles some food is gathered—whatever the deceased most liked—and, if he smoked, some tobacco. Some say this offering is to remind the dead person that he still has roots in life, that he walks in others, that he continues in others. Others say this offering is in case the dead person comes and is in need of food and rest. They say the deceased comes because he has not achieved what he wanted in life, and still goes about, seeking. The search can last for a long time, but the dead person is not saddened, because he knows he can return each year to his family to gain strength and to gather heart and so continue on his path. To remind him that he still has roots on this side and that he walks in us and he continues, and in order to help him recover strength and hope in his search, each year the Zapatistas put out an offering for Pedro (fallen in combat in 1974, raised up and fallen again in combat in 1994, raised up again, struggling always). At the dawn of each November 2, thousands of offerings shine for Pedro in many indigenous homes.

Each of the last four years, Don Jacinto offered to watch over the offering that we put out for Pedro, in the general headquarters of the EZLN. Every year, with the arrival of the morning of November 2, the food and the tobacco that we had put out on the little table had disappeared. Early on, we would find Don Jacinto leaving the little room with the offering; we would greet him, and he would respond with: "The deceased came, he ate and drank, and he smoked the tobacco." We all knew it was Don Jacinto who had eaten the little plate with the bread and two oranges, who had drunk the coffee without sugar that Pedro worshiped, and who had smoked the little box of cigarettes (twenty-four stubs were left scattered about). All of us knew. Not now.

Don Jacinto died a few weeks ago, after being brutally beaten in one of those attacks of the "State of Law" against the indigenous autonomous municipalities. Don Jacinto did not die, his son told me; they killed him. And he explains to me that it is not the same to die of death as to die of being killed.

Each year since 1994, Pedro's offering was gone on the morning of November 2. All of us knew that Don Jacinto had watched over it during the night. All of us knew. On the day of October 31, 1998, we put out the offering as was our custom, but now with the added sadness of knowing that Don Jacinto would not be here to watch over the bread, the oranges, the coffee, and the tobacco, as we all knew. The morning of this November 2, we went to clean up the offering, and found the bread plate empty, the orange rinds, the little cup of coffee with grounds, and the stubs on the floor. It was curious . . . the rinds and the stubs were on both sides of the table, in equal parts: twelve stubs on one side and twelve on the other, the rind of one orange on one side, and the rind of the other on the opposite side. We all looked at each other, and we were silent; only the sea said, "Next year you will have to put out a double offering."

All of us knew that Pedro's offering was always gone because Don Jacinto watched over it. All of us knew this. Not now.

All of this occurred at the dawn of the month of November 1998, in the fifteenth year of the armed rebellion, and the fifth year of the war against forgetting, in the mountains of the Mexican Southeast, a dignified corner of the nation, in the America they call "Latin," in the third planet of the solar system, just when, in the worn wheel of history, a century, which some call "Twenty," is about to extinguish itself, all of which I bear witness to, and I affirm that it is destined to remain in the collective memory, which is another way of naming tomorrow.

P.S. FOR THE FEBRUARY THAT IS CONCEALED IN NOVEMBER: NOW WE ARE MORE and stronger. All of our dead will arrive. And they make us great who are so small . . .

THE SUP, ASKING FOR HIS LITTLE SKULL . . .

NOTE

1. Zedillo was president of Mexico from 1994 to 2000; Francisco Labastida, the PRI presidential candidate for the elections in 2000, was defeated by PAN candidate Vicente Fox; and Emilio Rabasa was coordinator for the peace process in Chiapas. The federal government had maintained the official position of CONAI as official mediating body between the government and the EZLN. It was Rabasa who announced to the press that the government had adopted a new strategy between the government and the state of Chiapas, adding that peace in Chiapas was not solely dependent upon the San Andres Accords.

28

Tlatelolco

Thirty Years Later the Struggle Continues

ZAPATISTA NATIONAL LIBERATION ARMY

OCTOBER 2, 1998

To the Generation of Dignity of 1968

Brothers and sisters:

I write you in the name of the men, women, children, and elders of the Zapatista National Liberation Army, to greet you on this date that marks thirty years since the Tlatelolco massacre, as well as thirty years of a movement that struggles for democracy, liberty, and justice for all Mexicans.

Sixty-eight isn't just October 2 and the painful Plaza de las Tres Culturas.[1]

Sixty-eight is not only Tlatelolco and the Chihuahuan building, or the olympic astonishment and shame that beheld the massacre of children, men, women, and elders—unarmed and helpless—before the tanks, rifles, machine guns, and stupidity made government.

Sixty-eight isn't just the plaza that the sum of the blood of three cultures, beneath a death decreed by a political system—still at work today—sustaining itself with mass massacres.

Sixty-eight is also, and above all, the March of Silence,[2] the Poli,[3] the UNAM,[4] the hundreds of students looked down upon by the university institutions, the underground popular autonomy, the assemblies, the graffiti on the walls, the brigades, the lightning meetings, the subversive street dressed in the new clothing of dignity. It is the street as a territory for another politics, the politics of below, a new one, one that struggles, the rebel one. It is the street talking, discussing, displacing cars and traffic lights, asking, reclaiming, demanding a place in history.

Sixty-eight is a window to peer through and learn from the open confrontation between various forms of making politics, between different forms of being human.

The movement of 1968 has definitively marked this country's history. Then, two countries confronted one another: one constructed on the basis of authoritarianism, intolerance, repression, and the most brutal exploitation; and the other that wants to build itself on democracy, inclusion, liberty, and justice.

Up above is the Mexico of the powerful, of those who decide, with force and by force, the direction most convenient to their own interests, those who make monologue, billy clubs, and lies a form of government, those who only hear the voice projected from the trick mirror that Power has made for its servants and worshipers, those who extend their hand and offer direct dialogue while they strike, persecute, jail, rape, assassinate, and lie to those who won't render blind obedience, submission, or lowered heads.

The Mexico of the PRI and the military is the Mexico of violence and lies.

It is the Mexico of those who invent destabilizing fables, foreign conspiracies, welfare for the family, bank bail-outs, a "will" for dialogue, help for the flood victims, roads and bridges.

It is the Mexico of those who simulate government for everyone.

It is the Mexico of those who manage disasters to benefit a few.

It is the Mexico of the criminals who gave the orders to pull the trigger in Tlatelolco, Acteal, Chavajeval, Unión Progreso, Aguas Blancas, El Charco.

This is Mexico, a Mexico in agony.

Below is the Mexico of '68.

The Mexico of those who live and breathe rebellion and the struggle for justice in the only way possible to them, that is, as a lifetime struggle.

The Mexico of those who keep demanding, struggling, organizing, resisting.

The Mexico of those who didn't watch the years go by eaten up with bitterness, but rose up, to fall again, who returned and always will return to rise again.

The Mexico of those who didn't limit rebellion and the demand for justice to mere commemorations on a calendar, to idle recollections stilled by age.

The Mexico of those who didn't define "rebellion" as a fashion statement that goes no further than the length of men's hair and is inversely proportional to the length of women's skirts.

The Mexico of those who aren't content to tune in with a radio dial for an answer blowing in the wind, who don't see rebellion as nothing more than an awkward way to say no, who don't equate the struggle for justice with constantly humming the latest pop hit.

The Mexico of those who don't allow the passage of time to make them surrender the counsel of wisdom.

The Mexico of those who don't sell their dignity short, or let forgetting linger on.

The Mexico of those who don't make '68 out as a past shame, a mere youthful prank, a stepping stone for the bad government.

The Mexico of those who weren't then, are not now, and will never be leaders, but who in their homes, at their jobs—in trucks, in taxis, on horses, at machines, in classrooms, in factories, in churches, on shuttle buses, in wheelchairs, at the plow, in barber shops, in beauty shops, on tractors, on airplanes, in workshops, behind vendors' carts, on motorcycles, at markets, in hospitals, in courtrooms, at stadiums, in waiting rooms, on stages, in laboratories, at bars, in nursing homes, behind desks, in offices, in movie and radio and television studios, in sculptors' studios, down in the metro, in the closet, in press rooms, in shop windows, on bicycles, in every color used to paint the ordinary and silent—raise a hand, an image, a cry, a ticket, a vote, a fist, a thought, a voice to confront the government's lies and say: "Enough is enough! We don't believe you anymore. We want something better. We need something better. We deserve something better."

The Mexico of those who in the unions, in learning institutions, in opposition political parties, in social organizations, in nongovernmental organizations, in neighborhood organizations, in the *ejidos* and the communities, in secrecy, in the streets and the fields and the mountains, everywhere, carry on, persevere, and resist.

The Mexico of those who learned that hope is also built from pain and from taking falls.

The Mexico of those who said "No!" to the false comfort of surrender, of those with short-long-or-no-hair who made their dignity grow, of those who cradled memory and didn't worry whether their skirts covered their knees.

The Mexico of those who lived and died in '68 and began to birth another tomorrow, another country, another memory, another politics, another human being.

The Mexico of those who don't build ladders to climb above others, but who look beside them to find another and make him or her their *compañero* or *compañera*, brother, sister, mate, buddy, friend, colleague, or whatever word is used to describe that long, treacherous, collective path that is the struggle of: everything for everyone.

This is Mexico, the Mexico that will live.

The Mexico of 1968.

The Mexico of 1998.

The Mexico of all those who repeat and renew their struggle for democracy, liberty, and justice, distinctly and differently, without worrying about their age, sex, color, culture, where they came from, where they live now, their language or creed.

The Mexico of those men and women who struggled and continue to struggle to be better in the only way it is possible to be better, that is with everyone.

Those who resist. Those who, even though they died, survived '68, those who we see here beside us, even though we are different and distinct. To all of them. We, the Zapatistas, salute them.

1968. 1998.

It is time to demand that the whole truth be told, that yesterday's and today's crimes no longer go unpunished.

1968. 1998.

Today and tomorrow, the lie from above comes to hide reality.

Today and tomorrow, the truth from below comes to show the truth.

1968. 1998.

The reality of the blood staining the plazas.

The reality of authoritarianism made crime.

1968. 1998.

The reality of the dead and the living remembering and cultivating memory.

The reality of the struggle that continues.

The reality of the tomorrow that announces its coming.

Vale. Health to you, and may we never forget. Thirty years later, the struggle continues.

From the mountains of the Mexican Southeast

BY THE INDIGENOUS REVOLUTIONARY CLANDESTINE COMMITTEE
GENERAL COMMAND OF THE ZAPATISTA NATIONAL LIBERATION ARMY
SUBCOMANDANTE INSURGENTE MARCOS

NOTES

1. Plaza de las Tres Culturas was the site of the 1968 student massacre.

2. March of Silence

3. Poli: the Instituto Politécnico Nacional (Political Science Institute), part of UNAM.

4. UNAM stands for the Autonomous University of Mexico. Here, in 1999, students once again confronted the federal government over its intent to charge admission at the free university. According to the striking students, the move was based on class bias; it would prevent the great majority of the students, who come from humble homes, from getting an education.

29

Under Siege

The Zapatista Community of Amador Hernandez

AUGUST 1999

To the Zapatista compañeras and compañeros of the community of Amador

To the Zapatista compañeras and compañeros of the region supporting the dignified resistance of the Zapatistas of Amador

To the women and men of civil society accompanying the indigenous of the Amador Valley as peace observers

Brothers and sisters:

IN THE NAME OF ALL THE *compañeros* and *compañeras* of the Clandestine Revolutionary Indigenous Committee, I send you our greetings and these words.

The example of dignity and courage you are now giving is reaching not only us, your EZLN *compañeros* and *compañeras*, it's also reaching workers, campesinos, the indigenous, neighbors, housewives, students, teachers, artists and intellectuals, honest religious persons, retired persons, men, women, children, and elders from other parts of Mexico. And it is also reaching further than our country, which is Mexico. The news of the dignified resistance of the indigenous Zapatistas of Amador is reaching other parts of the world.

Those soldiers facing you are defending an unjust, arbitrary, and criminal cause. Those soldiers know the same thing we know, that they're not there to help the people or to bring them a better standard of living. Those soldiers are there so the bad government's war will have a road from which to attack the communities who aren't surrendering. In the radio, television, and press at the service of the lie and of money, they're saying those soldiers are there so a highway can be built that will bring benefits to the indigenous peoples. They, the soldiers and the government, and we know that is not true.

We know well that the highways the government has built haven't brought one single benefit to the indigenous. Doctors haven't come in with the highways, nor have hospitals been built, nor have teachers come, nor have schools been made, nor have materials arrived to improve the housing of the indigenous; the prices of the products the campesinos sell have not improved, nor are the goods that the indigenous must buy less expensive. With Zedillo's highways—we must remind everyone that it's Zedillo who's waging the war against us—have come the war tanks, the cannons, soldiers, prostitution, venereal diseases, alcoholism, rapes of indigenous women and children, death and misery.

Every highway that the government has made has shown that it has brought benefit only to those who enrich themselves at our cost, or who have come to kill us, imprison us, and humiliate us.

Without having to go very far, there are the examples of the highways of San Quintin—the place where the PRIs have come to regret being PRIs—or of Las Tasas or of Taniperlas. With them came the soldiers, as did their vehicles of war; construction materials arrived, not to make schools or houses for the indigenous but to make barracks. Prostitutes and alcohol arrived; more expensive goods came, along with the "coyotes" to buy our products even more cheaply, in addition to thieves and criminals, and those who come to steal our valuable wood and to destroy our forests. Not one single benefit for the indigenous, but much pain and suffering. The women, the mothers, the wives, and the daughters of those indigenous are being used as prostitutes by the soldiers; they pay for them or they take them by force, and the indigenous who protest are threatened with death, taken prisoner, or disappeared.

Ask the PRIs of San Quintin. Let them tell you how they sold their women to the soldiers. Ask the women of San Quintin. Let them tell you how they're used by the soldiers, how they now have venereal diseases that came along with the prostitutes who service the soldiers, how the little that their men make is spent on alcohol and prostitutes, how thefts and assassinations have increased, how fear and anxiety came, hand in hand, with the army and their highway.

Ask them if they ever had any problems with the Zapatistas, and they'll tell you that we always respect them, that we never force them to stop being PRIs or to join the war. Ask the women, and they will tell you that when there was no other army than the EZLN, there was no prostitution, no crimes, no sadness, no anxiety, no fear.

The same can be said by the PRIs of all the communities where highways have entered. Their lives have not improved in any way, and their children keep dying. They're still despised for being indigenous. Now, for them, it no longer means anything to belong to the PRI, because to lend their government support, to help the government break the Zapatistas, they must disguise themselves as Zapatistas.

This is the truth, *compañeros* and *compañeras*. We know it, the PRI's indigenous know it, those cursed with a government highway know it, and the government and their soldiers know it.

Now the government is telling two great lies.

One is that the EZLN opposes the highways because it opposes progress coming into the indigenous communities, because it opposes the indigenous living better. You, *compañeros* and *compañeras*, know well that this isn't so. You know well that the EZLN wants highways that bring true peace, and not war. The EZLN wants highways that bring hospitals, schools, dignified housing, good food, better prices for the products from the countryside, land improvements, and recognition of the democracy the indigenous practice—a much better democracy than that endured by others.

We want the highways to help make the wealth in the Chiapan soil benefit all Mexicans, and not be sold for foreign money. We want the highways to serve Mexico's independence and sovereignty, and not to serve the great and the powerful to order us about as if we were their slaves, or in their buying up this country like so many cheap goods.

When the highways bring peace—not soldiers and war tanks and alcoholism and prostitution and misery and diseases and fear—the Zapatistas will be the first to help make them.

But as long as the highways serve to increase oppression, misery, and death among the indigenous communities, the Zapatistas will oppose them. We will resist. Even though we suffer in resisting, even though they attack us, even though they imprison us, even though they kill us, even though they tell lies about us, we will not permit the government's actions that only cause death, misery, neglect, and fear.

And if we do this, it isn't just for us. We do this for millions of Mexican men and women who are poor like us. They deserve that the nation's wealth benefit them, and not the government and its gang of thieves.

The soldiers in Amador know that I'm speaking the truth. They know we are fighting for liberty, democracy, and justice for all Mexicans, including them and their families, their parents, their spouses, their children. They know well that the day will come in which justice will live in Mexico. The soldiers will know that they are serving injustice, lies, crime, and death, and that we, the Zapatistas, are serving truth, justice, and life.

The soldiers in Amador know we don't fear them, nor the tens of thousands of soldiers all over Chiapas. They know their weapons don't frighten us, nor their war tanks, nor their planes, nor their helicopters, nor the barking of their boss, Albores.[1] They know we're willing to confront them, that we won't allow things to become again what they once were: lands where a hen was worth more than an indigenous life, where contempt and forgetting were the only things an indigenous worker received in exchange for his labor.

The soldiers there know who the Zapatistas are and what we want. If they could speak freely without fear, they would say that we're speaking the truth, that our cause is just, that their families are being manhandled, that they need someone to fight for them. They know that the Zapatistas are needed.

Another lie the government is telling is that the women and men of civil society, accompanying you as peace observers, are agitating for you to oppose the soldiers' presence. The government says that these teachers, students, researchers, and workers came to give you bad advice so that you will rebel.

I know that makes you laugh. You and I know well that many of you were already aware and preparing for the rebellion when these people were barely boys and girls. You and I know well that rebellion and dignity didn't come to us from the city, but rather from the history of resistance and heroism of the indigenous peoples. You know well that you had already rebelled against the presence of the soldiers, when no one from civil society had yet arrived. You know well that the Zapatistas rose up in arms and shouted "*¡Ya basta!*" when everyone was silent and had forgotten. We know all of this very well.

But the government and its media are carrying out a strong campaign against these people, who are good, noble, and generous. They too want a dignified and true peace. That's why they've come to you, to be together with you in opposing the war. They are great Mexican men and women, no matter what their age, whether very young or very old.

We know that it makes us very proud to know there are Mexican men and women like them, willing to face all danger as long as they are defending peace, democracy, liberty, and justice.

That's why I'm asking you, in the name of all the Zapatista peoples, of all the insurgent and militia troops, of all the officials and committees, to look after these people, to treat them well, to protect them and to see that they're always comfortable and healthy and happy. They represent thousands who cannot come to accompany us, but who wish they could.

And so this is my word, *compañeros* and *compañeras*. I tell you that Zapatistas from the Tzotzil, Chol, Tojolabal, Zoque, Mam, and other regions are already mobilizing. We'll be waiting to see how things develop, and, of course, we're not going to surrender.

Thank you for listening to me, *compañeros* and *compañeras*. That's all my heart has to say to you right now.

I send greetings to all those whom I've known for fifteen years, since I first came to these lands.

From the mountains of the Mexican Southeast
FOR THE CCRI-CG OF THE EZLN
SUBCOMANDANTE INSURGENTE MARCOS

NOTE

1. Roberto Albores Guillén is the repressive and corrupt governor of Chiapas. Marcos often refers to him as Croquetas Arbores, croquetas being a type of dog food.

Why We Use the Weapon of Resistance

OCTOBER 1999

I WOULD LIKE TO THANK those who were in charge of the Alicia Multiforum for the invitation they extended to us to participate in this roundtable.[1]

I do not have much experience in roundtables; square tables are more our specialty, like the table, most certainly, where those who are accompanying this act are seated: Zack de la Rocha, Yaotl, Hermann Bellinghausen, Nacho Pineda, a *compa* from the Punk Anarchy collective, and Javier Elorriaga.

What's more, it is quite likely that the participants at this roundtable that is not round are seated on a small platform. Furthermore, perhaps there is not even a table, but only a few chairs. Perhaps the only one who has a table is me, because they have to put the TV on something in order to show you this video.

. . . I am not going to talk to you about underground culture, nor about the culture of resistance, nor about the bridge that most certainly joins them. Besides leaving said topic to those who accompany us at this table—that we are calling it round even though we know that it is square—I will avoid making a fool of myself, and will be able to hide my encyclopedic ignorance on this subject. As the greatest and well-loved Don Durito of the Lacandon[2] would say, "No problem is too big that you can't get around it." I would add to those wise words, which incite to action and to commitment, "Nor is there a roundtable that is not square."

I know that you are all anxious to know what in the hell I'm going to talk about then. More than one of you might be asking if the guitar I have by my side means that I'm going to play a song, one of those that are so honorably played in the Mexico of below, which we all are.

Did you know? We are fighters. We are fighters who are very "other," but fighters nonetheless. And we fighters know a few things. And among the few things that we know, we know about weapons.

So, it is best that I talk to you about weapons. Specifically, I'm going to talk to you about the weapon of resistance.

Besides being fighters, we are indigenous Mexicans. We live in the mountains of the Mexican Southeast, which is turning out to be the most distant corner of this country. We live like the majority of the indigenous in Mexico live, that is, very badly.

Our homes have dirt floors, our walls are made from sticks or mud, and our roofs are tin, cardboard, or grass. A single room serves as kitchen, dining room, bedroom, living room, and chicken coop. Basically, our foods are maize, beans, chili, and the vegetables that grow in the milpa. For medicine we have a popular pharmacy, small and poorly stocked. Doctors? Only in our dreams. When it is not occupied by the government's soldiers, our school is a hall where up to four different groups of students gather at the same time. They are not very numerous, because our children start working when they're very small. Sometime between four and five years of age, the girls start carrying wood, grinding maize, washing clothes, and taking care of their younger brothers and sisters; between the ages of ten and twelve, the boys go to the mountain, to care of the livestock, to carry wood, to work the milpa, the coffee plants, or the pasture. Our lands are poor in two senses: they are poor because they belong to us, who are poor as a matter of course; and they are poor because they yield little in the way of harvest. We have only mud and rocks. The ranchers have the good lands. The livestock and coffee that we sell to make money, we sell to the coyotes, middlemen who pay us as little as ten times less than the price of our products in the market. So, our work, in addition to being hard, is badly paid.

However, even though we live like most of the indigenous population in the country, that is, in poverty, our lives are not the same. Our poverty is the same as the poverty of others, but it is also different; it is an "other" poverty. We are poor because that is what we have chosen. From the beginning of our uprising, they have offered us everything to get us to sell ourselves, to surrender.

If we had done so, if we had surrendered, if we had sold ourselves, we would now have good houses, good schools, hospitals, machinery for working the land, better prices for our products, good food.

We chose not to sell ourselves, we chose not to surrender. Because it so happens that we are indigenous and we are also fighters. And fighters are fighters because they are fighting for something. And we, the Zapatistas, are fighting for good homes, good food, good health, a good price for our work, good lands, good education, respect for the culture, the right to information, liberty, independence, justice, democracy, and peace. Yes, we are fighting for all of that, but for everyone, not just for ourselves. That is why we Zapatistas are fighters, because we want "For everyone, everything, nothing for ourselves."

If we had surrendered, if we had sold ourselves, we would no longer have been poor, but others would have continued to be so.

Good, but you are asking yourselves: Where is the weapon that this handsome, attractive, nice fighter was going to talk to us about? I'll tell you now.

It happened that, when they saw that we were not surrendering, that we were not selling ourselves, the government began attacking us in order to force us to surrender and to sell ourselves. They offered us many things—money, projects, aid—and when we rejected them, they became angry and threatened us. That is how we came to understand that, by refusing to accept government aid, by resisting, we made the powerful angry; and there is nothing a Zapatista fighter likes more than making those in power angry. So with singular joy we dedicated ourselves to resisting, to saying no, to transforming our poverty into a weapon—the weapon of resistance.

Almost six years of war have spoken about the power of this weapon; with it we have resisted more than 60,000 soldiers, war tanks, bomber aircraft, artillery helicopters, cannons, machine guns, bullets, and grenades. With it, we have resisted the lie.

If you would like me to sum it up, I would tell you that in the same way that we became soldiers so that one day soldiers would no longer be necessary, we also remain poor, so that one day there will no longer be poverty. It is for this that we use the weapon of resistance.

Obviously, it is not the only weapon we have, as is clear from the metal that clothes us. We have other arms. For example, we have the arm of the word. We also have the weapon of our culture, of our being what we are. We have the weapon of music, the weapon of dance. We have the weapon of the mountain, that old friend and compañera who fights along with us, with her roads, hiding places, and hillsides, with her trees, with her rains, with her suns, with her dawns, with her moons . . .

We also have the weapons that we carry by nature, but it is not the time to be going around punning, much less now, when you've all become very serious. And in order to chase away your seriousness, I'm going to tell you a joke—no, don't believe it or be frightened, I'm not going to tell you a joke, better that we leave that to Zedillo, who as president is nothing but a bad joke. No, better that I go on to the next issue that I'm going to talk to you about.

. . . It is not just the Zapatistas who are fighters of resistance. There are many groups (and there are several gathered together here) who have also made a weapon of resistance, and they are using it. There are indigenous, there are workers, there are women, there are homosexuals, there are lesbians, there are students, there are young people. Above all there are young people, men and women, who name their own identities: "punk," "ska," "goth," "metal," "trasher," "rapper," "hip-hopper," and "etceteras." If we look at what they all have in common, we will see that they have nothing in common, that they are all "different." They are the "others." And that is exactly what we have in common, that we are "other," and "different." Not only that, we also have in common that we are fighting in order to continue being "other" and "different," and that is why we are resisting. And to those in power, we are "other" and "different"; in other words, we are not like they want us to be, but what we are.

And what we are—far from wanting to impose its being on the "other" or "different"—seeks its own space, and at the same time a space to meet. The "punks" don't go around on a campaign demanding that all young people be "punks," nor do the "ska," the "goths," the "metal," the "trashers," the "rappers," and certainly not the indigenous. Nonetheless, Power does indeed want us to be how it wants us to be, to dress in the style it dictates, to talk the way he says we should talk, to eat what it sells, to consider beautiful and lovely what it considers beautiful and lovely. Power even wants us to love and hate the way it establishes that love and hate should be. And not just that, Power also wants us to do all this on our knees and in silence, without going around jumping, without shouts, without indigenous uprisings. Power wants us to be well mannered. That is why Power has armies and police, to force those who are "other" and "different" to be the same, identical.

But the "other" and "different" are not looking for everyone to be like them. It is as if each one is saying, Everyone should do their own thing (I don't know how that's said these days). And in order for this to be possible, it is not enough just to be; you must be while respecting the other. The "everyone doing his own thing" is two things: it is affirmation of difference, and it is respect for the other difference. When we say we are fighting for respect for our "different" and "other" selves, that includes fighting for respect for those who are also "other" and "different," and who are not like ourselves. And it is here where this entire resistance movement— called "underground" or "subterranean," because it takes place among those of below and underneath institutional movements—meets Zapatismo.

And this meeting is a meeting between men and women fighters, among those who make resistance a weapon, and who fight with it in order to be what they are, in order to exist.

We Zapatistas say: "I am as I am and you are as you are. Let's build a world where I can be, and not have to cease being me, where you can be, and not have to cease being you, and where neither I nor you will force another to be like either me or you." So when we Zapatistas say, "A world where many worlds fit," they are saying, more or less, "Everyone do your own thing."

It turns out that we are the same because we are different. Because we are the same persecuted, the same despised, the same beaten, the same imprisoned, the same disappeared, the same assassinated. And it is not our people who are persecuting, despising, beating, imprisoning, assassinating us. It is not even the "others" from below. It is Power and its names. And our crimes are not stealing, beating, assassinating, insulting. Nor is our crime being "other" and "different." No, our crime is in being who we are, and in being proud of it. Our crime—which in Power's penal code merits the death penalty—is the struggle we are making to continue being "other" and "different." If we were "other" and "different" shamefully, in hiding, guiltily, betrayed by ourselves, trying to be, or to appear to be, what Power wants us to be or to appear to be, then they would give us an indulgent and pitying little pat, and say to us: "These things happen when you are young; you will get over them when you get older." For Power, the cure for rebellion is time.

But Power neglects to say what lies behind the "getting older," that it assumes will cure and do away with youthful rebellion. Hours, months, and years of blows, insults, jails, deaths, rapes, persecutions and neglect. A machinery working to "cure us" if we stop being who we are and turn ourselves into servile beings. A machinery which will eliminate us if we insist on being who we are without regard to a calendar dates on the birth certificate.

And so, we are all transgressors of the law. Because this system has a law that kills and silences those who are "other" and "different." And by living, by shouting—by talking, that is, by being rebels—we are transgressing that law, and automatically we are criminals.

And these criminals that we are, we live in a rebel reality, where resistance is the bridge that allows us to meet, to recognize our differences and our equality. Rock is also like a bridge over which those realities walk in order to meet.

In what way is rock a mirror and crystal for this very "other" and "different" reality? The truth is, I don't know, and I don't understand. I look at and listen to groups like Rage against the Machine and Tijuana NO (to mention just those who are participating in tomorrow's concert, but knowing that there are many others, and that all of them are good musicians and good human beings), and I ask myself why do they do what they do, say what they say, and play what they play? I believe it would be better for them to tell us what goes on with them. Perhaps they too are asking themselves why we Zapatistas do what we do, say what we say, and play what we play (although, when it comes to rock, we are fairly useless. "Useless": How about that? A good name for a group or for a song. "Useless," just like that, with no qualifiers, so that everyone fits: men, women, and those who are neither men nor women, but who are).

Vale. Health to you, and (like it says on the cover of that fanzine that has the good taste to call itself "ZUPterraneo") what with so many things, "Something doesn't smell right." Which means something like: "There are things, and then there are things." *¡Health to you!*

From the mountains of the Mexican Southeast
THE SUP, TUNING UP HIS GUITAR FOR A "SPECIAL APPEARANCE"
MEXICO, "OTHER" AND "DIFFERENT"

NOTES

1. Excerpted from Subcomandante Marcos' Video Message "From the Underground Culture to the Culture of Resistance." at the Roundtable Alicia Multiforum.

2. Don Durito of the Lacandon's stories make up the first part of section 3 of this book.

PART TWO

One World

... **in which Marcos** reaches out to the world, creating moral and political alliances with persons and communities who also struggle for common freedom and justice.

... **in which the struggles** for human rights worldwide become one.

31

Flowers, Like Hope, Are Harvested

SEPTEMBER 1995

To the men and women in solidarity with Chiapas, Mexico, meeting in Brescia, Italy
To the peoples of the world

Brothers and sisters:
IN THE NAME of all the men, women, children, and the elders of the Zapatista National Liberation Army, I greet you and express our hope that your *encuentro* goes well.

We know we have brothers and sisters in other countries and continents.

We are united by a world order that destroys nations and cultures. Today, Money—the great international criminal—has a name that reflects the incapacity of Power to create new things. Today, we suffer a new world war, a war against all peoples, against humanity, against culture, against history. It is an international war, of Money versus Humanity, carried out by a handful of financial centers, without homeland and without shame. Now, this international terror is called neoliberalism—an international economic order that has already caused more death and destruction than the great world wars. We have become brothers with more poor and more dead.

We are united by dissatisfaction, rebellion, the desire to do something, by non-conformity. History written by Power taught us that we had lost, that cynicism and profit were virtues, that honesty and sacrifice were stupid, that individualism was the new god, that hope was devalued money, without currency in the international markets, without buying power, without hope. We did not take in the lesson. We were bad pupils. We did not believe what Power taught us. We skipped class when they taught conformity and idiocy. We failed modernity. Classmates in rebellion, we discovered and found ourselves brothers.

We are united by the imagination, by creativity, by tomorrow. In the past, we not only met defeat but also found a desire for justice and the dream of being better. We left skepticism hanging from the hook of big capital and discovered that we could believe, that it was worth believing, that we should believe—in ourselves. We learned that many solitudes did not make one great solitude but a collective that found itself united beyond nationality, language, culture, race, and gender.

We, the Zapatistas, are still here in the mountains of the Mexican Southeast, still surrounded, still persecuted, with death hanging from our every movement, from each breath, from each step. The government is still in the palace, still circling, still persecuting, still offering death and misery, still lying.

More than a million Mexicans have participated in an unprecedented democratic exercise and made manifest their agreement with our principal demands. Many brothers and sisters in foreign lands have ratified it. The government is still deaf. Tens of thousands of men and women mobilized themselves to support the National *Consulta* for Peace and Democracy. The government is still blind. Hunger and illness drown entire communities. The Federal Army increases its military actions and preparations for murder. Political parties refuse to recognize the indigenous people as citizens. The media make themselves accomplices of the lie and the silence. Desperation and anger become the national heritage. We are ignored, despised, and forgotten.

It's clear, triumph is closer than ever. We are already preparing to form solidarity groups with the struggles in your respective countries. Be assured that we will support you to the end (which may not be in triumph) and will not abandon you. Don't be discouraged by difficulties; you should resist. You should press on and know that in the mountains of Southeast Mexico there is a collective heart that is with you and supports you. Don't feel alone or isolated. We will be watchful and will not forget you.

Vale. Health to you, and don't forget that flowers, like hope, are harvested.

From the mountains of the Mexican Southeast
SUBCOMANDANTE INSURGENTE MARCOS

32

From Vietnam to Chiapas, Twenty Years Before

SEPTEMBER 13, 1995

To the people of the United States:

THE U.S. GOVERNMENT has been wrong, not just a few times, in its foreign policy. When this has occurred, it's because it made a mistake in the man it backed up. History gives us ample examples of this.

In the first half of this decade, the U.S. government made a mistake backing Carlos Salinas de Gortari. It made a mistake signing NAFTA, which lacked the support of the majority of the North American people, and which spelled a summary execution of Mexico's indigenous people.

On the dawn of 1994 we rose up in arms. We rose up not seeking power, not in response to a foreign mandate. We rose up to say: "We are here."

The Mexican government, our government, had forgotten us and was ready to perpetrate a genocide without bullets or bombs; it was ready to annihilate us with the quiet death of sickness, of misery, of oblivion. The U.S. government became the accomplice of the Mexican government in this genocide. With the signing of NAFTA, the U.S. government acted as guarantor of—and gave its blessing to—the murder of millions of Mexicans. Did the people of the United States know this? Did they know that their government was signing accords of massive extermination in Mexico? Did the people of the United States know that their government was backing a criminal?

That man left. We remained. Our demands had not been met, and our weapons kept saying, "We are here," to the new government, to the people of Mexico, to the people and governments of the world. We waited patiently for the new government to listen to us and pay attention to us.

But, within the dark circles of U.S. power, someone decided that we, the insurgent indigenous people of the Mexican Southeast, were the worst threat to the United States of America. From the darkness came the order: Get rid of them! They put a price on our brown skin, on our culture, on our word—but above all they put a price on our uprising. The U.S. government decided, once more, to back a man who continues the politics of deceit of his predecessor, who denies the people of Mexico democracy, freedom, and justice. Millions of dollars were lent to that man and his government. Without the approval of the American people, an enormous loan—without precedent in history—was granted to the Mexican government. Not to improve the living conditions of the people, not for the democratization of the country's political life, not for economic reactivation promoting factories and productive projects—this money was for speculation, for corruption, for simulation, for the annihilation of a group of rebels—indigenous for the most part—poorly armed, poorly nourished, ill equipped, but very dignified, very rebellious, and very human.

So much money to finance deceit can only be explained by fear. But what does the U.S. government fear? The truth? That the North American people realize that their money is helping to back the oldest dictatorship in the modern world? That the North American people realize that their taxes pay for the persecution and death of the Mexican indigenous population?

What are the North American people afraid of? Should they fear our wooden rifles, our bare feet, our exhausted bodies, our language, our culture? Should they fear our shout that demands democracy, liberty, and justice? Aren't these three truths the foundation that inspired the birth of the United States of America? Aren't democracy, liberty, and justice rights that belong to all human beings?

How many millions of dollars can justify that any one human being, in any part of the world, be denied the right to be free to think and to bring about words and actions, free to give and receive that which he justly deserves, free to elect those who govern him and enforce the collective goals?

Shouldn't the North American people instead fear money, modern weapons, the sophisticated technology of drug trafficking? Should the North American people fear the complicity between drug trafficking and governments? Shouldn't they fear the consequences of the single-party dictatorship in Mexico? Shouldn't they fear the violence that the lack of freedom, democracy, and justice irrevocably brings about?

Today the U.S. government—which for decades has prided itself in promoting democracy in the world—is the main support of a dictatorship. Sooner or later, in spite of the support of the U.S. government, in spite of the millions of dollars, in spite of the tons of lies, the dictatorship that darkens the Mexican sky will be erased. The people of Mexico will find the ways to achieve the democracy, liberty, and justice that is their historical right.

Americans

THE ATTACKS AGAINST THE Mexican nation brought about by political U.S. personalities have been big and numerous. In their analysis they point out the awkwardness and corruption of the Mexican government (an awkwardness and corruption that have increased and are maintained under the shadow of the U.S.

government's support), and they identify them with an entire people who take shelter under the Mexican flag. They are wrong.

Mexico is not a government. Mexico is a nation that aspires to be sovereign and independent, and in order to be that, it must liberate itself from a dictatorship and raise on its soil the universal flag of democracy, liberty, and justice. Fomenting racism, fear, and insecurity, the great personalities of U.S. politics offer economic support to the Mexican government so that it controls by violent means the Mexicans' discontent with the economic situation. They offer to multiply the absurd walls with which they pretend to stop the search for life, driving millions of Mexicans to cross the northern border.

The best wall against massive immigration to the U.S. is a free, just, and democratic regime in Mexico. If Mexicans could find in their own land what now is denied them, they would not be forced to look for work in other countries. By supporting the dictatorship of the party-state system in Mexico, whatever the name of the man or the party, the North American people are supporting an uncertain and anguished future. By supporting the people of Mexico in their aspirations for democracy, liberty, and justice, the North American people honor their history—and their human condition.

Today, in 1995, after twenty years and tens of thousands of dead and wounded, the American government recognizes that it made a mistake getting involved in the Vietnam War. By providing war material support—military advisers, undercover actions, electronic espionage, financing, diplomatic support, CIA activities—the U.S. government has begun to get involved in the Mexican government's dirty war against the Zapatista population. Little by little, it is getting involved in an unequal war, condemned to failure for the Mexican government that is carrying it on. Today, in 1995, twenty years before 2015, it is possible to stop; not to not repeat the error of other years. It is not necessary to wait until 2015 for the U.S. government to recognize that it was wrong to get involved in the war against the Mexican people.

It is time for the people of the United States to keep their historical commitment to their neighbor to the south and not make a mistake in the man they support; to support not a man but a people, the Mexican people, who struggle for democracy, liberty, and justice. History will tell, implacably, on which side the people and the government of the United States stood: on the side of dictatorship, of one man, of reactions; or on the side of democracy, of a people, of progress.

Vale. Health to you, and long life to the people of the United States of America.

From the Mexican Southeast
SUBCOMANDANTE INSURGENTE MARCOS

33

A Call to Latin America

MARCH 10, 1996

To Latin America, in the pain-filled South of the American continent, Planet Earth (Seventh planet of the solar system if you're coming from beyond, like from that star that's up there, above . . . no, not that one, the other one . . . and were walking toward the sun, the same way you walk inward, with fear and hope):

SUPPOSE IT ISN'T TRUE that there's no alternative.

Suppose impunity and harm aren't the only future.

Suppose it's possible that the thin line separating war and peace won't grow ever narrower.

Suppose that some madmen and romantics believe that another world, another life, is possible.

Suppose the worst, that these madmen believe there are others, more madmen who think like them.

Suppose the inadmissible, that all these madmen want to get together.

Suppose they suppose that from this meeting of the madmen, some measure of reason will emerge.

Wouldn't you like to attend a such a mad meeting of suppositions?

Yes? No? If you suppose you'd answer no, then get serious, don't bother with the following paragraphs and write "Wrong Address" somewhere on the margin. Don't bother returning it to the sender.

If you suppose you'd answer yes, do something useful with this invitation: start a fire, make a paper plane or a paper doll, something that will make you smile. If beyond supposing that you'd like to go, you suppose you would like to attend this meeting and may even try to get to it, then read on.

If you're not already too dizzy, it may interest you to know that the Pan-American Meeting for Humanity against Neoliberalism will be taking place in La Realidad. Isn't that charming? Now that we have our suspicions, suppositions, and suppositories and you suppose that you are attending, we suppose you'll want to know when and how.

We'd like you to accept our invitation so those April days can witness history being induced to rebel; to shake itself up and wake itself up and change its course so it can accompany us to the Pan-American Meeting for Humanity against Neoliberalism. As the law of these times dictates, we'll be in La Realidad, one of those corners of southeastern Chiapas where pain is transformed into hope thanks to the complicated chemistry of dignity and rebellion.

The days? Yes, they're usually denoted on calendars as 3, 4, 5, 6, 7, and 8 of April of the year we're enduring, 1996.

The "how" has a few details we won't include here so as not to spoil your lunch or ruin your excitement at discovering the existence of the meeting that this invitation to the meeting presupposes. So we'll leave the details to the committee chairwoman, if she can find them.

Good. Now, when someone is supposedly looking for you, you have the option of hiding, or concurring that you're both looking for the same thing, because at this kind of meeting it's better to take the initiative. Just so you know, please pack the necessary pencil (in case you get an opportunity to write something), colored paper of various sizes (so if no one pays attention, you can at least make little paper dolls), a good length of string (so if you stray from the meeting you can find the way back—where?), and patience and discretion.

Around here we're expert at hoping, but will you make it?

Vale. Health to you, and while we're on the subject, here's hoping we make history before history makes it for us.

From the wilds of the Mexican Southeast
SUBCOMANDANTE INSURGENTE MARCOS

P.S.

DID YOU NOTICE this invitation's cold, formal tone? Doesn't this transgressor of the law open this *veeery* important international event with wondrous gravity? Doesn't this invitation at least deserve a simple "yes," "no," or "I don't know" RSVP sent via the only secure conduit, i.e. a paper plane? No, don't worry; the wind knows which way to blow and carry your reply to us, if we can be found at all . . .

34

On Independent Media

A message from Subcomandante Insurgente Marcos to "Free the Media" Teach-In, NYC:

WE'RE IN THE MOUNTAINS of Southeast Mexico in the Lacandon Jungle of Chiapas, and we want to use this medium, with the help of the National Commission for Democracy in Mexico, to send a greeting to the "Free the Media" Conference that is taking place in New York, where there are brothers and sisters of the independent communications media from the United States and Canada.

At the Intercontinental Encuentro for Humanity and against Neoliberalism we said: A global decomposition is taking place—we call it the Fourth World War[1]— through neoliberalism, the global economic process to eliminate that multitude of people who are not useful to Power, the groups called "minorities" in the mathematics of power, but who happen to be the majority population in the world. We find ourselves in a world system of globalization willing to sacrifice millions of human beings.

The giant communication media—the great monsters of the television industry, the communication satellites, magazines, and newspapers—seem determined to present a virtual world, created in the image of what the globalization process requires.

In this sense, the world of contemporary news is a world that exists for the VIPs—the very important people, the major movie stars and big politicians. Their everyday lives are what is important: if they get married, if they divorce, if they eat, what clothes they wear and what clothes they take off. But common people only figure in the news for a moment—when they kill someone, or when they die. For the communication giants and the neoliberal powers, the others, the excluded, only exist when they are dead, or when they are in jail or court. This can't go on. Sooner or later this virtual world clashes with the real world. And that is actually happening: this clash results in rebellion and war throughout the entire world, or what is left of the world to even have war.

We have a choice. We can have a cynical attitude in the face of the media and say that nothing can be done about the dollar power that creates itself in images, words, digital communication, and computer systems that invade not just with an invasion of power but with a way of seeing that world, of how they think the

world should look. We could say, Well, "that's the way it is," and do nothing. Or
we can simply assume incredulity. We can say that any communication by the
media monopolies is a total lie. We can ignore it and go about our lives.

But there is a third option that is neither conformity, nor skepticism, nor distrust. It's the option to construct a different way: to show the world what is really
happening, to have a critical worldview, to become interested in the truth of what
happens to the people who inhabit every corner of this world.

The work of independent media is to tell the history of social struggle in the
world. Here in North America—the United States, Canada, and Mexico—independent media has, on occasion, been able to open spaces even within the mass
media monopolies, to force them to acknowledge news of social movements.

The problem is not only to know what is occurring in the world, but to understand it and to derive lessons from it, just as if we were studying history, not of
the past but of what is happening at any given moment in whatever part of the
world. This is the way to learn who we are, what it is we want, who we can be, and
what we can do or not do.

By not having to answer to the monster media monopolies, the independent
media has a life's work, a political project, and a purpose: to let the truth be
known. This is increasingly more important in the globalization process. Truth
becomes a knot of resistance against the lie. Our only possibility is to save the
truth, to maintain it, and distribute it, little by little, in the same way that the
books were saved in *Fahrenheit 451*; a group of people dedicated themselves to
memorize books, to save them from being destroyed, so that the ideas would not
be lost.

In this same way, independent media tries to save history—today's history—tries to save it and tries to share it so it will not disappear. Moreover, it
tries to distribute it to other places, so that this history is not limited to one
country, to one region, to one city or social group. It is necessary not only for
independent voices to exchange information and to broaden the channels, but
to resist the monopolies' spreading lies. The truth that we build in our groups,
our cities, our regions, our countries, will reach full potential if we join with
other truths and realize that what is occurring in other parts of the world also
is part of human history.

In August 1996 we called for the creation of a network of independent media,
a network of information. We mean a network to resist the power of the lie that
sells us this war that we call World War IV. We need this network not only as a
tool for our social movements but for our lives: this is a project for life, for a
humanity that has a right to critical and truthful information.

We greet all of you, recognizing the work you have done so that the struggle
of indigenous people is known, and that other struggles are known, so that the

great events of this world are seen in a critical form. We hope your meeting is a success and that it results in concrete plans for this network, these exchanges, this mutual support that should exist between cultural workers and independent media makers. We hope that one day we can personally attend your meeting, or perhaps that one day you can have your conference in our territory, so we can listen to your words and you can hear ours in person. For now, well, we take advantage of the help of the National Commission for Democracy in Mexico to use this video to send a greeting. [This section in English] I don't know if my English is okay, but good luck and so long. Cut.

NOTE

1.   The Zapatistas see the Cold War as World War III, and economic globalization, or neoliberalism, as World War IV.

35

Letter to the Indigenous Leadership of the United States

To the leadership of the indigenous peoples of the United States of America

Brother and sisters:

I WRITE THESE WORDS to you in the name of the children, elders, men and women, all of them indigenous, of the Zapatista communities in the Mexican Southeast. We want you to know we recognize your greatness as indigenous peoples and human beings, and we want you to receive this salute sent, through my hands, from all the indigenous rebels of the Zapatista National Liberation Army.s

We have taken up arms against the bad Mexican government because the demands of the indigenous peoples have not been met. For the Mexican government and the great Power that sustains it, the indigenous peoples are nothing more than objects for tourism, producers of arts and crafts, an uncomfortable nuisance for neoliberal modernization. For Power in Mexico, the indigenous are not human beings with rights and legitimate aspirations; they are only museum pieces, legends, and past histories. But our indigenous communities want a life with dignity and justice, a life where they can continue to be indigenous without it signifying misery and death, a life with respect. This is why we declared ourselves rebels and why we say, "Enough is enough," to the oblivion with which they want to annihilate us.

Today we are still waiting for a response from the government of Mexico to our request for peace. It has not arrived. The Mexican government refuses to acknowledge that the indigenous peoples of Mexico have a right to respect, to a life with dignity, to a new peace. Power sees us as small and weak; it believes it can conquer us and make us surrender with its war machines. The great North American government supports the Mexican government with money, war machines, and military advisers; the government of the United States supports the persecution and assassination of Mexico's indigenous blood.

The money, equipment, weapons, and military advisers are not used by the Mexican government to improve the lives of its inhabitants, to combat drug trafficking, and to bring peace to Mexican lands. No, that money, those people, and those weapons are used to asphyxiate, persecute, jail, and assassinate any attempt at indigenous dignity.

But our struggle is not just that of the Zapatistas of the EZLN. Our struggle is that of all the Indian peoples of America: the struggle to recognize our differences and our right to an inclusive autonomy, which makes us members, with full rights, of the great human concert.

That is why we direct our small words to you. You, the leaders of the dignified Indian peoples of North America, have the true word and the path of dignity. Your great wise men have shown you the path for understanding justice in the cries of the first peoples of Mexican lands. You will know how to understand our cries, and we are sure you will know how to extend to us your hearts and your hands in order to achieve the peace that we desire and we deserve.

Your word is heard with attention and respect by the big government of the United States of America; that is why we ask you to support us with your mediation. We do not want war, nor what does not belong to us, nor our destruction or enslavement. We want peace; we want to conquer our right to become better human beings; we want to create our world and be respected inside it. We want liberty.

We ask you, great leaders of the indigenous peoples of North America, to intervene before the powerful one who governs the United States of America and to tell him to stop his support for the war against our people and the persecution of our ideals. We serve no foreign interest; we serve only our history and our desires for dignity, democracy, liberty, and justice.

We ask this of you, great Indian leaders. We ask for your support and your companionship in a struggle that belongs to all human beings in any part of the world, the struggle for liberty.

Vale. Health to you, and may the earth that is mother and root nurture tomorrow.

From the mountains of the Mexican Southeast
SUBCOMANDANTE INSURGENTE MARCOS

36

From Here to There and Back Again

(As the 20th Century hastens to sleep in the place History,
that is, we grant it.)

MARCH 1997

To the committees in solidarity with the Zapatista struggle all over the world, Planet Earth

Brothers and sisters:
GREETINGS AND HEALTH to you. We are still here. We continue to be here. The
night above is a bare gray reflection of the night below. In these mountains, for
some reason, the night below is always a deeper night than the night above. I
don't know whether it's the same in other parts of the world or vice versa. At last,
here's the dawn. Perhaps it's the dark night or the vice versa of its reflection
reminding me of the poem Tweedledee (or was it Tweedledum?) recited to Alice
in *Through the Looking-Glass*. It was called "The Walrus and the Carpenter" and
it begins like this:

> The sun was shining on the sea,
> Shining with all his might:
> He did his very best to make
> The billows smooth and bright—
> And this was odd, because it was
> The middle of the night.
> —LEWIS CARROLL

And like the sea with its insistent force, a kind of urgent desire comes over me to
chat with you and say hello, or maybe this is just an excuse to try building a multiple bridge, a walking octopus that can simultaneously reach to the European continent and the Asian, that can plant one arm on Oceania, another on Australia, and
another on Africa, that can rest its leftover however many arms on whatever
American corner there is where rebellion is a banner. Here, in this shard of the mirror of rebellion in the world, the March Hare wakes up and stretches in the rainfalls
and sunshines that take turns jumbling up the weather and the hours . . .

And speaking of hours, the hour's coming for us to sit down together once
again, we who are so alike in our differences, everyone who we are . . . But, well,

that isn't the substance of this letter (not yet, anyway). What is it, then? Well, strictly speaking, the substance of this letter is paper and ink and the heart that gets dressed in the former and covers itself in the latter to travel a long bridge that gives way to languages, colors, cultures, borders, armies, police, and crosses a considerable number of kilometers by air, sea, and land to reach that other heart that you (and we) carry in our left sides.

So then, assuming the bridge is now spanned and the hearts have found each other, a greeting goes from here to there, to all of you, from the men, women, children, and elders of the Zapatista National Liberation Army.

I.

ON THIS SIDE OF THE greeting and the bridge, on this side with the national power we Mexicans suffer, it's show time, a time for spectacles. Just like a three-ring circus, in Mexico Power photographs itself in tragicomedies, its corruption revealed and exposed, its demagoguery dressed in modernity, a brash, strident, much-touted supermarket of election-time political proposals. There is plenty of time for spectacle, little time for democracy, less time for justice, and no time for liberty. Both the high and low trip over themselves marching to the rhythm Power beats out. Amid the rush to get there, the question, Where are we going? indefinitely postpones its own answer.

Besides this time for lamentable spectacles, the small people's time reflects and looks within itself to find the other small people of Mexico and the world made big by the hope that multiplies itself, which we are given by your walk. We find within ourselves, that is, within you, the breath that dignity needs for food, that hope needs for direction, that patient and tender fury of one who knows his strength lies in the good reason that moves him.

The government's dismissal of the San Andres Accords has served one good purpose. Now it's clear the demands of the EZLN indigenous are not just for Chiapas. They address the aspirations of all the Indian peoples of these lands and, each in their own particular way, reflect the aspirations of the indigenous people of the whole American continent.

A spokesperson for Mexico's power recently said that the government does not need the Internet to demonstrate its willingness for a dialogue with the indigenous Zapatistas. It's obvious that the monologue it proposes doesn't need a thing, with the possible exception of a mirror. But, more than once, Power's bureaucratic tone revealed the frustration and rancor that the ruckus circulating in cyberspace is giving him. Letters and manifestos, addressed to the supposed president of Mexico, bother the government because both ask for the same thing: that the Mexican government keep its word on the San Andres Accords. Some of those letters make it into the Mexican press; others (most) don't. An apparent national indifference tries to cover up the international disquiet, caused by a government incapable of finding a political solution to a situation it provoked with military arguments. The government receives requests to comply with the Accords; they come here from all over the world. The government doesn't heed them, or it seems not to heed them. If only you could see, over here El Supremo only has ears for praise and gratitude . . . and, of course, for the orders coming from the Power of finances.

The Mexican government is bothered. It's not just the protests and demands coming through the Internet, but also the demonstrations in front of the embassies and consulates all over the world.

II.

AND SINCE WE'RE CHATTING, let me tell you something that, I hope you'll understand, is just a timid homage to the efforts you all make to back us up and not let us be forgotten again.

Over here, they're telling a story about the local agent for export sales (the accurate job title of the so-called Mexican secretary of foreign affairs) who, on the eve of a visit abroad, conscientiously prepared himself to explain away the corruption, drug trafficking, and election problems in Mexico, and to pacify the so-called investors with great plans for political and military control and, of course, appetizing merchandise.

But all his preparation didn't do him much good. At the end of the traveling salesman's "brilliant" speech, a foreign spokesperson pressed him with questions about the negotiations with the EZLN and why they're still suspended. The Mexican bureaucrat pulled out a map of Mexico to show the foreigner how the EZLN is only a tiny little problem in a tiny little corner of the tiny little Mexican Southeast—perfectly contained and controlled by the powerful military forces of the federal government. In response, the foreigner showed him a pile of e-mail messages and newspaper clippings about the demonstrations in front of Mexican embassies and consulates in various parts of the world. The Mexican (who someday hopes to acquire full citizenship in Money) argued that subversion has many worldwide ramifications, that these destabilization attempts are bound to fail, and that a few "hackers" (I think that's what they call the pirates of cyberspace) were no reason to interfere with the solid commercial trade with the bountiful Mexican state, and so on . . .

The foreigner interrupted him to clarify: "These demonstrations aren't about subversion, and these messages aren't promoting instability. They're simply asking the Mexican government to keep its word. As to their being few in number, well, millions all over the world use the Internet, and the demonstrations in Europe and the United States represent dozens of thousands. They all say the same thing: 'Keep your word.'"

There was a small respite before the foreigner added: "Tell me something in confidence. Why don't you comply with what you signed? If the Mexican government is afraid of being fragmented, it should look at the example of other countries that have recognized and legislated autonomous zones and not fallen apart. To the contrary, countries that didn't do this have split to pieces. But, in any case, why did you sign something you're unwilling to fulfill? Are we to believe that the agreements you've signed with us won't be kept either? No, Mr. — is Gurria[1] your name? No, there must be more to it. So tell me, what is the Mexican government afraid of?"

The businessman disguised as a Mexican bureaucrat trembled, as did his foreign counterpart, when he answered, "We fear tomorrow—"

III.

"Well, it's no use your talking about waking him," said
Tweedledum, "when you're only one of the things in his dream. You know
very well you're not real."
"I am real!" said Alice, and began to cry.

—Lewis Carroll, *Through the Looking Glass*

FROM THIS SIDE OF THE BRIDGE and the greeting, the middling and small struggles (the large ones are neither here nor there) need your strength and witness. Power practices its magic, juggling tricks, and sound effects of all sorts and sizes so you won't be able to see too clearly. But in spite of them, you've taken the time and trouble to reach out with your support and sympathy, restoring us. While Power has done everything possible to erase us from the map of actual history, you have taken to the word to the streets (media and asphalt) to remind us, and in passing the Mexican government, that we are not alone.

We know little of your struggles. The bridge your generosity has stretched out to us to listen to the word of the indigenous Zapatistas has only just begun its return journey. With surprise and admiration, we're only beginning to recognize your respective histories of rebellion and resistance, your struggles against racism, against patriarchy, against religious intolerance, against xenophobia, against militarization, against ecological destruction, against fascism, against segregation, against moral hypocrisy, against exclusion, against war, against hunger, against poor housing, against big capital, against authoritarianism, against dictatorship, against the politics of economic liberalization, against poverty, against robbery, against corruption, against discrimination, against stupidity , against the lie, against ignorance, against slavery, against injustice, against oblivion, against neoliberalism, for humanity.

For humanity and against neoliberalism is the call for the new *encuentro* of rebellions and resistance coming this year. Up until then and once there, we will have learned more about you and all the still-scattered shards of the mirror that dignity yet keeps whole within humanity's best men and women.

So now, taking advantage of the trip, we want to send you our thanks for having turned to look at us, thanks for the hand that you stretched out to us so we wouldn't fall again back into oblivion. Some time ago, we sent you a flower. Today, we send you one of our little rain clouds so you can water that flower, as you should, by dancing.

Vale. Health to you, and may the joy of rebellion keep filling the streets of all the continents.

From the mountains of the Mexican Southeast
SUBCOMANDANTE INSURGENTE MARCOS

NOTE

1. In 1982, when Mexico defaulted on its foreign debt, José Angel Gurria helped the country renegotiate and reduce its payments to international creditors. As President Salinas's secretary of finance and public credit, he helped formulate the financial aspects of NAFTA and headed Bancomext, the government export bank, and Nafinsa, the national development bank. A lifelong member of the long-ruling Institutional Revolutionary Party (PRI), Gurria served as the party's foreign affairs secretary before joining the Zedillo administration as foreign minister in 1994. He took over as Mexico's secretary of finance and public credit in January 1998.

37

On May Day and Tupac Amaru

APRIL 25, 1997

To the national and international press

Ladies and gentlemen:

. . . SOME DAYS AGO we heard on the radio news of the military assault on the Japanese embassy in Peru. The great international Power decided upon a new crime in Latin American lands and ordered the assassination of the rebels of Tupac Amaru (who, let us not forget, were negotiating a solution to the crisis with the government of Fujimori). You will all recall that an attempt was being made to resolve the problem without violence. But the military went in accompanied by gunfire. "A clean operation," said the news programs, and described Fujimori as smiling and happy. And, way above him, the supranational powers, which had given the order for annihilation, also smiled. For months, the Peruvian government pretended to negotiate in order to find a peaceful solution. In reality it only searched for the precise moment to strike. That is how they are, Power and its neoliberal governments; they pretend to dialogue and negotiate, when in reality they only seek the opportunity to exert their violence.

This new tragic episode for Latin America is an international blow to the path of dialogue and negotiation as a viable means of resolving conflicts.

Fujimori and his bosses hurry to smile. The consent for Zedillo was also hurried. But a lot of history still remains to be written.

And to think they have told us we should wait, not for an attack, but for a compliance to the agreements that were signed by the government.

From the Japanese embassy—oops,
From the mountains of the Mexican southeast
SUBCOMANDANTE INSURGENTE MARCOS

38

This Ocean No Longer Separates Us

SEPTEMBER 14, 1997

Written to be read at the demonstration against racism and the Northern Leagues in Venice on September 13, 1997

To the Zapatista people
To the rebel peoples of Europe

Brothers and sisters:
TODAY, SEPTEMBER 13, 1997, two rebel marches come together.

In the Americas, in a country called Mexico, our brothers and sisters of the Zapatista National Liberation Army march from the mountains of the Southeast to the nation's capital.

In the territories of Europe, in a country called Italy, we Zapatistas walk side by side with you.

Two continents, Europe and America, are once more united in struggle.

Here in Italy and there in Mexico, we struggle against racism and separatism.

Here in Mexico and there in Italy, we struggle for a community of freedom and mutual aid.

Here and there, we clash with a world system making racism a new religion.

There and here, the rich and powerful are the greatest fanatics of intolerance against the different.

Here and there, neoliberalism destroys nations in order to own them.

There and here, it displays its cynicism and cruelty.

Here and there, it persecutes those espousing freedom and mutual aid.

There and here, neoliberalism offers us only dejection.

For this reason, we'll no longer speak of "here" and "there."

For this reason, this ocean no longer separates us or makes us different.

Because lack of freedom makes us the same.

Because we are united in the racism we suffer within and across borders.

Because the war they impose on us makes us *compañeros* and *compañeras*.

In America and in Europe, the oppression we suffer is the same.

Colors, language, and cultures vary, but oppression is a constant.

This is why we Zapatistas are here with you today.

This is why you are here with us today.

Because we no longer want this kind of world.

Because we no longer want crime celebrated.

Because we no longer want falsehood treated as a virtue.

Because we no longer want others to impose their forms of being and thinking on us.

We want to be free.

And the only way to be free is to be so together. This is why we want to be free and in solidarity. We won't enter this world. The rich and powerful want to hunt us down because we are trouble to them.

But we won't go.

We won't remain silent.

We'll stand fast.

We'll struggle.

We'll build another world.

A better one.

Bigger.

Better.

One in which all worlds can fit.

Rebel brothers and sisters, brothers and sisters of Europe,

Italian brothers and sisters, all of you have taught us many things.

We're honored to be with you on today's march.

We thank you for giving space and voice to the Zapatistas.

The bridge you've built with your hearts has spanned this ocean.

Brothers and sisters, crying out is a form of dreaming.

And your dreams are heard far away.

We echo them, all who struggle echo them,

because, throughout the world,

everyone shares them.

Democracy!
Freedom!
Justice!

From the mountains of the Mexican Southeast
COMPAÑERA MARIBEL
SUBCOMANDANTE INSURGENTE MARCOS
COMPAÑERO MESIAS

39
Letter to Mumia Abu-Jamal

To Mumia Abu-Jamal, American Union

Mr. Mumia:

I AM WRITING TO YOU in the name of the men, women, children, and elderly of the Zapatista National Liberation Army in order to congratulate you on April 24, your birthday.

Perhaps you have heard of us. We are Mexican, mostly indigenous, and we took up arms on January 1, 1994, demanding a voice, a face, and a name for the forgotten of the earth.

Since then, the Mexican government has made war on us, pursues and harasses us seeking our death, our disappearance, and our absolute silence. The reason? These lands are rich with oil, uranium, and precious lumber. The government wants them for the great transnational companies. We want them for all Mexicans. The government sees our lands as a business. We see our history written in these lands. In order to defend our right (and that of all Mexicans) to live with liberty, democracy, justice, and dignity we became an army and took on a name, a voice, and a face.

Perhaps you wonder how we know of you, about your birthday, and why it is that we extend this long bridge that goes from the mountains of the Mexican Southeast to the prison of Pennsylvania, where you are unjustly incarcerated. Many good people from many parts of the world have spoken of you; through them we have learned how you were ambushed by the North American police in December 1981, of the lies that they constructed in the procedures against you, and of your death sentence in 1982. We learned about your birthday through the international mobilizations that, under the name of "Millions for Mumia," are being prepared this April 24.

It is harder to explain this bridge that this letter extends, it is more complicated. I could tell you that, for the powerful of Mexico and the government, to be indigenous, or to look indigenous, is reason for disdain, abhorrence, distrust, and hatred. The racism that now floods the palaces of Power in Mexico goes to the extreme of carrying out a war of extermination and genocide against millions of indigenous. I am sure that you will find similarities with what Power in the United States does with the so-called people of color (African Americans, Chicanos, Puerto Ricans, Asians, North American Indians, and any other peoples who do not have the insipid color of money).

We are also "people of color" (the same color as our brothers who have Mexican blood and live and struggle in the American Union). Our color is "brown," the color of the earth, the color from which we take our history, our strength, our wisdom, and our hope. But in order to struggle we add the color black to our brown. We use black ski masks to show our faces. Only then can we be seen and heard. Following the advice of a Mayan elder, who explained to us the meaning of the color black, we chose this color.

Old Don Antonio, this wise elder, died in these rebel Zapatista lands in March 1994, a victim of tuberculosis, which gnawed away at his lungs and his breath. Old Don Antonio used to tell us that from black came light, and from there came the stars that light up the sky around the world. He recounted a story of a long time ago (when time was not yet measured), when the first gods were entrusted to give birth to the world. In one of their gatherings, they understood that the world needed to have life and movement, but in order to have life and movement, light was necessary. Then they thought of making the sun so that the days would move, making day and night, and time for struggling, and time for making love, and the world would go walking with the days and nights. The gods had their gathering and came to this agreement in front of a large fire, and they knew it was necessary that one of them be sacrificed by throwing himself into the fire, and himself become fire and fly into the sky. The gods thought that the sun's work was the most important, so they chose the most beautiful god to step into the fire and become the sun. But he was afraid. The smallest god, the one who was black, said he was not afraid, and he threw himself into the fire and became the sun. Then the world had light and movement, and there was time for struggle and time for love, and while it was day the bodies worked to make the world, and while it was night the bodies made love and sparkles filled the darkness.

This is what Old Don Antonio told us, and that is why we use black ski masks. So we are of the color brown and of the color black. But we are also yellow, because the first people who walked these lands were made of corn so they would be true. And we are also red, because this is the call of blood that has dignity. And we are also blue, because we are the sky in which we fly. And green, for the mountain that is our house and our strength. And we are white, because we are paper so that tomorrow can write its story.

So we are seven colors, because there were seven first gods who birthed the world. This is what Old Don Antonio said long ago, and now I tell you this story so that you may understand the reason for this bridge of paper and ink that I send to you, all the way from the mountains of the Mexican Southeast.

And also so that you may understand that with this bridge go greetings and embraces for Leonard Peltier (who is in Leavenworth prison), and for the more than 100 political prisoners in the United States, who are the victims of injustice, stupidity, and authoritarianism.

Also, on this letter-bridge walks a greeting for the Dine (the Navajo), who fight in Big Mountain, Arizona, against the violations of their traditional Dine religious practices. They struggle against those who favor large businesses and don't respect the religious freedom of the indigenous peoples, against those who want to destroy sacred grounds and ceremonial sites (as is the case with the Peabody Western Coal Company, which, without reason, wants to take the lands, the land rights, and with them the history that belong to the Dine and their future generations).

But this letter-bridge has more than just stories of resistance against North American injustice. In the extreme south of our continent, in Chile, the indigenous Mapuche women in the Pewenche Center of Alto Bio-Bio confront stupidity. Bertha and Nicolasa Quintreman are accused of "mistreating" members of the Chilean government armed forces. There you have it. An armed military unit with rifles, sticks, and tear gas, protected by bullet-proof vests, helmets, and shields, accuses two indigenous women of "mistreatment." But Bertha is seventy-four years old, and Nicolasa is sixty. How is it possible that two elderly people confronted a "heroic" group of heavily armed military? Because they are Mapuche. The story is the same as that of the Dine brothers and sisters of Arizona—it repeats itself throughout the Americas. A company—ENDESA[1]—wants the Mapuches' land, and in spite of the law that protects the indigenous, the government is on the side of the companies. The Mapuche students have pointed out that the government, the company, and the military intelligence have conducted a "study" of the Mapuche communities. Its conclusion? That the Mapuche cannot think, cannot defend themselves, cannot resist. That the Mapuche are incapable of building a better future for themselves. Apparently, the study was wrong.

It now occurs to me . . . perhaps the powerful ones in North America did a similar "military intelligence" study—frankly, this is a contradiction, because those of us who are military are not intelligent; otherwise, we wouldn't be military—on the Dine in Arizona, on Leonard Peltier, on other political prisoners, on you, Mr. Mumia.

Perhaps they made this study and came to the conclusion that they might be able to violate justice and reason, to assault history and lose the truth, and that no one would say anything. The Dine Indians would stand by and watch the destruction of the most sacred of their history, Leonard Peltier would be alone, and you,

Mr. Mumia, would be silenced. (I remember your own words: "They not only want my death, they want my silence.")

But the studies were wrong. Happy mistake? The Dine resist against those who would kill their memory, Leonard Peltier is accompanied by all those who demand his liberty, and you sir, today you speak and shout with all the voices which celebrate your birthday as all birthdays should be celebrated, by struggling.

Mr. Mumia:
WE HAVE NOTHING BIG to give you as a gift for your birthday. It is poor and little, but all of us send you an embrace.

We hope that when you gain your freedom, you will come to visit us. Then we will give you a birthday party, and if it isn't April 24, it will be an unbirthday party. There will be music, dance, and talk, the means by which men and women of all colors understand and know one another, and build bridges over which they walk together, toward history, toward tomorrow.

Happy Birthday!

Vale. We greet you, and may justice and truth find their place.

From the mountains of the Mexican Southeast
SUBCOMANDANTE INSURGENTE MARCOS

P.S.
I READ SOMEWHERE that you are a father and a grandfather. So I am sending you a gift for your children and grandchildren. It is a little wooden car with Zapatistas dressed in black ski masks.

Tell your children and grandchildren that it is a gift the Zapatistas have sent you. You can explain to them that there are people of all colors everywhere, just like you, who want justice, liberty, and democracy for everyone.

NOTE
1. ENDESA: Empresa Nacional de Electricidad Sociedad Anónima, a leading electric utility in South America.

40

Letter to the Supreme Court of Pennsylvania, USA

APRIL 1999

To Mr. Tom Ridge
Governor of Pennsylvania
United States, North America
To the Magistrate and Governor

Dear sirs:
I WRITE TO YOU IN THE NAME of the men, women, children, and elderly of the EZLN. Most of us are indigenous Mexicans, and we struggle for liberty, democracy, and justice.

The purpose of the following letter is to demand justice for Mr. Mumia Abu-Jamal, condemned unjustly to the death penalty in 1982. As you know, the judicial process against Mr. Mumia Abu-Jamal was plagued by lies and irregularities: the police who accuse him lied about a supposed confession; one of the witnesses has changed his testimony and declared that he was forced to lie or face prison; the ballistic evidence has proved it was impossible for Mr. Mumia Abu-Jamal to have fired the weapon that killed the policeman. This should be enough evidence for a new trial, but even this recourse has been denied him. If the judicial system of Pennsylvania and the governor are certain that Mr. Mumia Abu-Jamal is guilty, then they should not fear a new trial that would bring out the truth.

I do not ask clemency, pardon, nor mercy from you for Mr. Mumia Abu-Jamal. I demand justice, something that I believe is within your power to grant him. No one within the Supreme Court of Pennsylvania, nor Governor Tom Ridge, has anything to lose. Justice, supposedly, is all that should matter.

That is all.

From the mountains of the Mexican Southeast
SUBCOMANDANTE INSURGENTE MARCOS

Subcomandante Marcos, First Day of the Uprising, January 1, 1994. © CuartoScuro/IMPACT VISUALS

(top) Checkpoint in La Selva Lacandona, Chiapas. New Year's Eve, 1999. © Greg Ruggiero

Military Caravan. November 1995. © Yuriria Pantoja Millán

(top) Polho: The Burial of a 3-Month Old Infant Who Died of Pneumonia. February, 1998. © Mat Jacob/Tendance Floue

Demonstration Near Polho Protesting the Acteal Massacre. December, 1997. © Mat Jacob/ Tendance Floue

(top) Mexican soldier buying Coca-Cola from machine at PEMEX station near San Cristobal.
© Jack Kurtz/IMPACT VISUALS, 1994

La Guerra. December 1994. © Yuriria Pantoja Millán

Chenalhó, Chiapas. January 1998. © Pedro Valtierra. (See page 139, "Do the Pictures Lie?")

Outside the Kitchen. La Realidad, Chiapas. August 1999. © Maribel Lasuena

Farmer in San Quintin, Lacandon Jungle, 1995. © Mat Jacob/ Tendance Floue

(top) Polho Colorido. February 1998. © Yuriria Pantoja Millán

"We are All Chiapas." Oventic, Chiapas. August 1996. © Celia Escudero-Espadas

Monday, August 16, 1999. Zapatista supporters and the Mexican military clash after the Mexican troops invaded the remote jungle village of Amador Hernandez with paratroopers and special forces. Villagers from Amador Hernandez had been protesting the construction of a highway through their region on the grounds that it would enable the army to have better access to Zapatista support communities. Amador Hernandez, Chiapas. © Associated Press.

Altamirano, Chiapas. January 1998. © Pedro Valterierra

Subcomandante Marcos, 1994. © Antonio Turok

(top) Marcos Signing Entry Passes to Zapatista Territory. March 11, 1994. © Joshua Schwartz/ IMPACT VISUALS

And the Horse. November 1999. © Yuriria Pantoja Millán

To Open A Crack in History. August 1999, La Realidad. © Greg Ruggiero

(top) Los Tres. January 1, 1995. © Yuriria Pantoja Millán

(far right) Saludos. © Yuriria Pantoja Millán

(above and right) Zapatista Embroideries

(top) Miradas de Polho. February 1998. © Yuriria Pantoja Millán

La Realidad Mural. July 2000. © Greg Ruggiero

(top) Zapata Mural. Oventic, Chiapas. January 2000. © Greg Ruggiero

Oventic Mural. January 2000. © Greg Ruggiero

Una Noche en La Realidad. September 1995. © Yuriria Pantoja Millán

La Realidad. January 1, 2000. © Greg Ruggiero

(top) Marcos and the Zapatista Comandancia, Guadalupe Tepeyac. December 5, 1994. © Jack Kurtz/IMPACT VISUALS

Subcomandante Marcos, Comandante Ramona, Camacho Solis, and Bishop Samuel Ruiz. San Cristobal, Chiapas. February 1994. © Pedro Valtierra/CuartoScuro/IMPACT VISUALS

**Female Zapatista Insurgent, San Caralampio (near Ocosingo),
Chiapas, Mexico, January 23, 1994.**© Fred Chase/IMPACT VISUALS

Only Looking. November 1995. © Yuriria Pantoja Millán

"No!" to the War in the Balkans

JUNE 1999

To the peoples in struggle against the war
To civic Europe
To the men and women who are saying "No!"

Brothers and sisters:
GREETINGS TO ALL FROM the Zapatistas in Mexico. Right now, all over the world, different mobilizations and activities are being carried out against the war that Money has sown in the heart of Europe: the war in Kosovo. In this war, Power is bent on making all of us take sides: either we support Milosevic's "ethnic cleansing" war, or we support NATO's "humanitarian" war. This is Money and its great alchemy, which offers us the option of choosing between two wars and not between peace and war. On the counters of the globalized marketplace, Power's only products are different versions of the same war: it comes in all colors, flavors, sizes, and shapes, to satisfy all tastes and all pocketbooks. But the results make them all the same: always destruction, always anguish, always death. And death, anguish, and destruction are always for the other, for the different, for those who are deemed unnecessary, for those who are in the way, for those who are below.

And even within the mercantile logic of the merchants of death, neoliberalism wants to offer us a fraud: a war that will supposedly avoid more deaths has done nothing but multiply them; a war that should be holding the conflict in check has made certain that the conflagration spread beyond the limits of its original geography; the "intelligent" war has done nothing but demonstrate the great destructive capacity of stupidity; the "good-intentioned" war has redefined human life: its loss is now counted as "collateral damage."

It is a lie.
It is not true that we have to take part in this lethal market.
It is not true that the only options are between different kinds of war.
It is not true that we must take sides with one or another stupidity.

It is not true that we must renounce intelligence and humanity.

Nothing can legitimize Milosevic's ethnic war. Nothing can legitimize NATO's "humanitarian" war.

The trap is there, but there are more and more people who are refusing to fall into it, who are saying "No!" to the war in the Balkans.

In Kosovo, it is not just the existence and resistance of civic Europe that is at stake in the face of the Europe of Money; at stake is not just accepting or not accepting the de facto power of the new global police, the new clothing with which the Pentagon is dressing its troops. Also at stake is the possibility of recognizing the other, the different—but not dead, imprisoned, humiliated, subjugated, persecuted, forgotten. We will not fall into the trap. We will not allow human losses to pass into history as "collateral damages." We will not allow cynicism and conformity to be the triumphant generals of the European war.

Despite the power of Money, despite the arms, despite the arbitrary acts, despite the attempts at hegemony and homogenization, despite the traps, we still have the right to say "No!" And that is what we shout today: a world-wide "No!" to the lie that feigns truths in the skies and the grounds of Kosovo; "No!" to the destruction of the different. "No!" to the death of intelligence. "No!" to cynicism. "No!" to indifference. "No!" to the choice between bloodthirsty criminals, who are more perverse or less perverse, more powerful or less powerful.

If we do not say "No!" to Kosovo today, tomorrow we will be saying "Yes!" to the horrors that Money now prepares all over the world.

It *is* possible to have another world, different than what the violent supermarket of neoliberalism is selling us. It *is* possible to have another world where the choice is between war and peace, between memory and forgetting, between hope and resignation, between the gray tones and the rainbow. It *is* possible to have a world where many worlds fit. It *is* possible that from a "No!" will be born an imperfect, unfinished, and incomplete "Yes!" that gives back to humanity the hope of rebuilding, every day, the complex bridge that joins thought and feeling.

This is what we Zapatistas are saying: "No!"
Viva life! Death to death!

From the mountains of the Mexican Southeast
SUBCOMANDANTE INSURGENTE MARCOS

42

For Maurice Najman, Who Keeps Feigning Death

JULY 19, 1999

To Asma Jahangir
UN Special Reporter for Extrajudicial, Summary and Arbitrary Executions

Madame Asma Jahangir:
I AM WRITING TO YOU in the name of the women, men, children, and elders of the Zapatista National Liberation Army. We know we'll get plenty of criticism for what I am about to say, and for wasting a good opportunity to show up the Mexican government in its genocidal policy against its indigenous peoples. But for us, "political opportunity" carries little weight compared to political ethics. And considering our confrontation with the Mexican government, it wouldn't be ethical for us to turn to an international organization that's lost all its credibility and legitimacy, and whose death certificate was signed with the NATO bombings in Kosovo.

With its war in the Balkans, the North American government disguised as NATO—with England, Italy, and France as grotesque pawns—has managed to destroy its prime target: the United Nations. The United States—the global gendarme—with its "intelligent" mega-police actions, has made a fool of what was once the most important international forum. Violating the precepts that gave rise to the UN, NATO has carried out a war of cynical aggression, attacked civilians indiscriminately, and tried to delegate intellectual authority to the satellite countries who, more than ever, demonstrated their insignificance to those who have made the plans and already have made all the decisions.

NATO's bellicose cynicism was only topped by the "brilliance" of their chiefs' and spokespersons' statements. " A humanitarian war," "errors made in good faith," and "collateral damage" weren't the only pearls of war they were selling in Kosovo.

Last Tuesday in Brussels, a NATO military official, with a good number of stars on his chest, made two chilling statements. Out of a total of 35,000 air operations, more than 10,000 were directed at specific targets. And the other 25,000? Could they have been carried out in error? If there are specific targets, does that mean there are nonspecific ones? What kind of target is a person?

The second statement raised as many questions as the first: NATO's objective was never the complete destruction of the Yugoslav army, nor reducing the country to ashes. Thank goodness! But you can't help thinking that before ashes come embers, and before those come coals, and before those come logs. To what size pieces had they been thinking of reducing the country and its army? The postwar banquet is served, and the news, catered by Roger Waters' satellite, fills the media all day long: "The more said, the more you can hide what can't be said" (Jordi Soler, *La Jornada*, June 19, 1999).

The UN's complicity in the war in Europe was obvious. In light of our position on this war, the most minimal consistency forces us to distance ourselves from an organization that for years, it's true, carried out a dignified, independent role in the international arena. It's not so today. From one end of the planet to the other, the UN has turned into a predictable legal support for the wars of aggression the great power of Money repeats, never sated with blood or destruction.

If in its silence the UN was an accomplice to the crime and destruction in Kosovo, it's taken a more active role in the war that the Mexican government is carrying out against its indigenous. In May 1998, at the request of the United Nations High Commissioner for Refugees, the government attacked the community of Amparo Aguatinta, beat up children, and imprisoned men and women while the military occupied what was then the seat of the Tierra y Libertad Autonomous Municipality. The results of the UN's "humanitarian work" in Chiapas are in the Cerro Hueco jail in Tuxtla Gutiérrez.

Just today, July 19, 1999, UN secretary general Kofi Annan is awarding the United Nations Vienna Civil Society Prize to the self-styled Aztec Foundation. The foundation, under the auspices of our native Milosevic, Ricardo Salinas Pliego, spends its time carrying out campaigns against drugs using cocaine addicts, promoting coup attempts, and destroying indigenous schools with helicopters. For all that, for its ties with drug trafficking, for its calls for coups, the Aztec Foundation will receive a medal and a certificate for $25,000 from Mr. Annan.

So, we can't have any confidence in the UN, and not out of xenophobia or a rejection of all things foreign. Risking their lives, liberty, belongings, and prestige, men and women from the five continents have been here as international observers (we shall leave the term "foreigners" to those like Zedillo and his cabinet, who have no other homeland but Money). Going back a little further, in February 1998, the International Civil Commission for Human Rights Observation (CCIODH) was here. Not only is their acronym bigger than the UN's, so is their moral authority, their honesty, their commitment to the truth, and the authenticity of their struggle for peace with justice and dignity.

Men and women from Germany, Argentina, Canada, Denmark, France, Greece, Italy, Nicaragua, Switzerland, Andalusia, Aragon, Cantabria, Catalonia, the Basque country, Galicia, Madrid, Murcia, and Alicante: all defied the Mexican government's most ferocious xenophobic campaign so far this century. They documented everything in a report that they dedicated to the indigenous José Tila López Garcia, assassinated after having presented his community's complaints to the CCIODH. Consult this report. It's inspired not only by the desire for a dignified peace, but also by truth and honesty.

After the CCIODH, another group of Italian observers came in 1998. Things were worse for them than for the CCIODH, because they were summarily expelled by Francisco Labastida—the current aspirant for the Mexican presidency—and by Fernando Solís Camara, the person who's now in charge of international public relations for Labastida's campaign, and who back then was responsible for hundreds of illegal expulsions.

Thousands of men and women from all over the world have come here, all honorable and of good will . . . who are such a bother to the institutionalized left all over the world. They came here, and they saw what the government is denying: a genocidal war. They left—many of them expelled—and they recounted and are still recounting what they saw: an unequal war between those who have all the military power (the government), and those who only have reason, history, truth, and tomorrow on their side (us). It's obvious who's going to win: We are.

And we are not alone. With us, as well, are international organizations, such as Amnesty International, Americas Watch, Global Exchange, Mexico Solidarity Network, the National Commission for Democracy in Mexico—USA, Pastors for Peace, Humanitarian Law Project, Doctors of the World, Bread for the World, Doctors without Borders, and many others whose names escape me now, but not their histories or their commitment to peace.

For us, any one of them (individual or group) has more moral authority and more international legitimacy than the United Nations, which today has been converted into a cocktail party for the end-of-century neoliberal wars.

With good reason, government representatives say they have nothing to fear from your visit. They're not afraid because they know the UN has been an accomplice to, and in the case of the Tierra y Libertad Autonomous Municipality, part of the war of extermination against the indigenous peoples of Mexico.

According to what we've read and heard, you're an honest person. You probably joined the UN during the time when it was preventing wars, supporting different groups who were victims of government injustices, and promoting development for the most needy. Today, the UN promotes and supports wars and helps and rewards those who kill and humiliate the excluded of the world.

It hasn't escaped our notice that various international powers are nursing the idea of using the rich oil and uranium deposits under Zapatista soil for their own benefit. Those up above are making up complex accounts and calculations, entertaining the hope that the Zapatistas will make separatist proposals. It would be easier and cheaper to negotiate purchasing the subsoil with the cooperation of the Banana Republic (Mayan Nation, they call it). After all, it's well known that the indigenous are satisfied with small mirrors and glass beads. That's why they're not giving up their intention to involve themselves in the conflict, so they can manipulate it according to their interests. They certainly have made no headway, because— it just so happens—the Zapatistas take the "National Liberation" part of the EZLN very much to heart and sword. We may be anachronistic, but we still believe in "outmoded" concepts like "national sovereignty" and "national independence."

We haven't accepted, nor will we accept, any foreign interference in our movement. We haven't accepted, nor will we accept, any international force playing a part in the conflict. We will fight it as firmly, or more so, than we have fought against those who decreed death through forgetting for 10 million Mexican indigenous. Only those with moral authority and legitimacy are welcome, those who aren't appendages to armed forces such as NATO or hold military forces at the ready (like the UN, with the unhappily celebrated Blue Helmets), those who want to be part of the PEACEFUL solution to the conflict. We don't need any help to make war. We can manage that on our own. To get peace, we do need help. Many people are needed, but they must be honest, and there aren't many of those.

Don't be too sad, now. The UN is not the only official international body collaborating with the Mexican government's counterinsurgency campaign. You have the International Committee of the Red Cross (IRC), whose delegation in San Cristobal approached sublime servility and stupidity. At a meeting with displaced people from Polhó, the International Red Cross delegates stated, without a blush, that the displaced aren't in their own homes because they're lazy and want to be supported by the Red Cross. For the imbeciles wandering around under the IRC's flag—acclaimed for its neutrality and humanitarian aid—the paramilitaries are an invention, the product of the collective hysteria of more than 7,000 displaced indigenous people; in Acteal the forty-five people executed really died of infections; and in the highlands of Chiapas, peace and tranquillity reign. One can assume that Albores has already congratulated them (and offered them some of his scraps—we're told he isn't very good at sharing), that they're still going about in their modern vehicles, adding accomplishments to the "distinguished" institution's curriculum vitae. How are you feeling, now? The IRC will surely be the next to receive a UN "civil society" service award.

On this dawn in which I write these lines, the moon is a scythe of cold light. It's the hour of the dead, of our dead. And you should know that the Zapatista dead are very restless and talkative. They still speak, despite being dead, and they're shouting history. They're shouting it so it can't go to sleep, so that memory won't die, so that our dead will live, shouting—

Ocosingo, January 3 and 4, 1994. Federal army troops take the municipal seat of Ocosingo—in Zapatista hands since the dawn of January 1—by assault. Following orders from the chief of the Thirtieth Military Zone, Brigadier General Luis Humberto Portillo Leal, Infantry Major Adalberto Perez Nava executed five members of the EZLN. General Portillo Leal had ordered that the Zapatistas—armed or not—were to be executed. The instructions were to take no prisoners, to kill them all. If the press was present, they should only avoid killing prisoners, because that would damage the army's image. Second Infantry Captain Lodegario Salvador Estrada executed other indigenous Zapatistas. Days later, in the Defense Department offices, Infantry Second Lieutenant Jiménez Morales was executed by military personnel so he could be blamed for the assassination of eight indigenous in a hospital in Ocosingo.

We didn't invent any of this information. You can corroborate it in a U.S. Department of Justice act at the Executive Office for Immigration Review, Immigration Court of El Paso, Texas, signed by Bertha A. Zuniga, U.S. Immigration Judge, dated March 19, 1999. Case: Jesus Valles Bahena, A76-804-703. In this file, officer Jesus Valles Bahena narrates how he had to desert from the army after having been threatened with death by Colonel Bocarundo Benavidez for his refusal to carry out summary execution orders. Along with Valles, other officers refused to carry out commands to assassinate. Their fate is unknown.

These, Madame Jahangir, are the noms de guerre and civilian names of those executed in Ocosingo, Chiapas, on January 3 and 4, 1994:

Comandante Hugo (Señor Francisco Gómez Hernández)

Second Lieutenant Insurgente for War Materiel Alvaro (Silverio Gómez Alvarez)

Insurgente for War Materiel Fredy (Bartolo Pérez Cortes)

Infantry Insurgente Calixto (civilian name can't be revealed)

Infantry Insurgente Miguel (Arturo Aguilar Jiménez)

Miliciano Salvador (Eusebio Jiménez González)

Miliciano Ernesto (Santiago Pérez Montes)

Miliciano Venancio (Marcos Pérez Cordoba)

Miliciano Amador (Antonio Guzman González)

Miliciano Agenor (Fernando Ruíz Guzman)

Miliciano Fidelino (Marcos Guzman Pérez)

Miliciano Adan (Doroteo Ruíz Hernández)

Miliciano Arnulfo (Diego Aguilar Hernández)

Miliciano Samuel (Eliseo Hernández Cruz)

Miliciano Horacio (Juan Mendoza Lorenzo)

Miliciano Jeremias (Eliseo Sanchez Hernández)

Miliciano Linares (Leonardo Mendez Sanchez)

Miliciano Dionisio (Carmelo Mendez Mendez)

Miliciano Bonifacio (Javier Hernández Lopez)

Miliciano Heriberto (Filiberto López Pérez)

Miliciano Jeremias (Pedro López Garcia)

Miliciano German (Alfredo Sanchez Pérez)

Miliciano Feliciano (Enrique González Garcia)

Miliciano Horacio (Manuel Sanchez González)

Miliciano Cayetano (Marcelo Perez Jiménez)

Miliciano Cristobal (Nicolas Cortes Hernández)

Miliciano Chuchin (Vicente López Hernández)

Miliciano Adan (Javier López Hernández)

Miliciano Anastacio (Alejandro Santis López)

During those same days, more who weren't executed died in combat.

In addition to execution, there was brazen torture. On January 7, 1994, the army entered the community of Morelia, then the municipality of Altamirano, and kidnapped Severiano Santiz Gomez, aged sixty, Hermelindo Santiz Gomez, sixty-five, and Sebastian Lopez Santiz, forty-five. A little later, their remains were found with signs of fractures and clear evidence of execution. The analyses of the remains were carried out by specialists from the nongovernment organization Physicians for Human Rights.

Torture and execution were also methods used by the "glorious" federal army in the municipal seat of Las Margaritas, Chiapas. There, during the first days of combat, Major Teran (previously tied to regional drug traffic) kidnapped, tortured, and executed Eduardo Gómez Hernández and Jorge Mariano Solis López in the Plan de Agua Prieta neighborhood. The executed men were found with their ears and tongues cut off.

These deaths, our deaths, will not rest. The butchers of Ocosingo and the assassins and torturers of Morelia and Las Margaritas are still free, enjoying health and prosperity. Thousands of shadows pursue them now, vying for the honor of seeing justice done. Last year, contrary to what their propaganda aimed at the international consumer says, the government renewed its armed clashes with Zapatista forces. On June 10, 1998, a military column, heavy with infantry, tanks, planes, and helicopters, attacked the community of Chavajeval, in the municipality of San Juan de la Libertad (to the Zapatistas) or El Bosque (to the government). The Zapatista troops repelled the attack, and a heavy exchange of fire began, which was broadcast by a national television channel. Our troops brought down a helicopter. Frustrated and angry, the soldiers again attacked the community of Unión Progreso that same day. There they took seven Zapatista militia prisoners and summarily executed them. These are their names:

Miliciano Enrique (Adolfo Gómez Diaz)

Miliciano Jeremias (Bartolo López Mendez)

Miliciano Jorge (Lorenzo López Mendez)

Miliciano Marcelino (Andres Goméz Goméz)

Miliciano Gilberto (Antonio Goméz Goméz)

Miliciano Alfredo (Sebastian Goméz Goméz)

Miliciano Pedro (Mario Sanchez Ruiz)

(The television reporter who covered the military attack on Chavajeval received a national prize for journalism earned with rebel indigenous blood. His employers rewarded him by sending him to cover the campaign of one of the two intellectual assassins of *Unión Progreso*, the then secretary of government and now presidential aspirant, Francisco Labastida Ochoa. The other assassin is Zedillo.)

This is the Mexican federal army that now wants to present an image of innocence, and announces the dispatch of almost 7,000 more troops to the Lacandon Jungle with the story that they're going to plant little trees. Everyone is silent. The military chief says that the 7,000 are unarmed, yet the 7,000 who arrive are armed. Everyone is silent. This is the "new" government strategy, promised by the pathetic Rabasa Gamboa (who's paid and paid well for coordinating emptiness). And since we're on the subject, Rabasa's new bray clarifies that Acteal was not an execution.

This time, he's right: Acteal and all the policies his boss Ernesto Zedillo has followed are GENOCIDE.

This is the story: Since Ernesto Zedillo rose to power, with the help of an assassination, the federal army has gained the cover and the money to feed their lust for blood and death.

Seeking to improve the army's impoverished public image, paramilitary squadrons were activated, organized, trained, equipped—protected by soldiers on active duty and, in not a few cases, created by soldiers as well as by PRI members. The objective was and is clear: to turn the conflict around and present it to the international public (the national public doesn't matter in the least to them) as an interethnic war, or as the corrupt PGR tries to present it, as an interfamily war. The names chosen by the soldiers to baptize their new paramilitary units reflect their great imagination:

Red Mask (their greatest "military" success: the Acteal massacre);

Peace and Justice (responsible for the assassinations of dozens of indigenous in the north of the state);

Chinchulines (they act in the north and in the jungle);

Anti-Zapatista Indigenous Revolutionary Movement; (they have training camps in military barracks in the Canadas, and are financed by the state PRI delegation) Los Puñales (they're active in Comitán and Las Margaritas); Albores of Chiapas (they're directly dependent on Croquette Albores Guillén, they wear green caps, and their war cry is "Albores follows through!")

This is the "new" strategy for Chiapas by the federal government, Zedillo's government. There's nothing new about it, nor is it a strategy. It's the same stupid beating down that assumes that the people who've known how to resist for 500 years won't be able to resist a year and a half longer.

As for Ernesto Zedillo Ponce de León, we must say today what everyone will be saying tomorrow: he's not a man of his word, he's a liar and an assassin. When he leaves Los Pinos, everyone (even those who treat him respectfully today) will be saying it, and all his corruption and crimes will come to public light. Persecution, exile, jail, are the probable end points of his future. It doesn't make us unhappy; but then, our dead do not make us unhappy.

I read in the press that you've met with some nongovernmental organizations in Mexico City, and you'll meet others during your visit to Chiapas in a few days. I congratulate you. May you have the good fortune and the honor of personally knowing men and women who, without official and/or institutional paraphernalia, have confronted every kind of threat and persecution for their work defending human rights in Mexico. I won't name any names here, because in Mexico, and especially in Chiapas, the NGOs fighting for human rights are targets for the federal army. But any of these NGOs, from the smallest to the newest, has more moral authority in the Mexico of below than the UN does. Perhaps you're not to blame, and it's only the UN's great leaders who, without protest, accepted the sporadic role of NATO spokespersons and accomplices in the Mexican government's war of extermination against its indigenous peoples.

Nonetheless, we're not pessimistic about the international community's future. The UN's failure isn't humanity's failure. A new international order is possible, a better one, more just and more human. In it, there will have to be a prominent place for international and national NGOs that, unlike the UN, don't have armed forces in their service nor hold themselves at the service of armed forces. In it, there will be a prominent place for men, women, children, and elders who understand that the future of the world is being fought between the choice of exclusion (the war in Kosovo) and a world where many worlds fit (to which Zapatismo in Chiapas begins to hint).

With them, and especially for them, the world will someday be a place where war will be a disgrace and peace a reality, where reporters for the various human rights violations will be rare, their sole activity being to research humanity's prehistory.

Excuse my tone, Madame Asma Jahangir. I don't have a personal issue with you. It's just that the organization you represent no longer represents anything. And that we do not forget Kosovo, nor Amparo Aguatinta, nor Ocosingo, nor Morelia, nor Las Margaritas, nor *Unión Progreso*, nor anything. Whatever's going on, we do not forget. We do not forget.

Vale. Health to you, and may dignity never forget memory. If dignity were to lose memory, it would die.

From the mountains of the Mexican Southeast
SUBCOMANDANTE INSURGENTE MARCOS
CCRI-CG OF THE EZLN

43

Letter to Leonard Peltier

OCTOBER 1999

To Leonard Peltier

Leonard:

THROUGH THE NATIONAL COMMISSION for Democracy in Mexico (NCDM) and Cecilia Rodriguez, we extend greetings from the men, women, children, and elders of the Zapatista National Liberation Army.

Cecilia has told us about the grave injustice the North American judicial system has committed against you. We understand that Power is punishing your spirit of rebellion and your strong fight for the rights of indigenous people in North America.

Stupid as it is, Power believes that through humiliation, arrogance, and isolation, it can break the dignity of those who give thoughts, feelings, life, and guidance to the struggle for recognition and respect for the first inhabitants of the land, over whom the vain United States has risen. The heroic resistance that you have maintained in prison, as well as the broad movement of solidarity that your case and your cause have motivated in the United States and the world, reveal their mistake.

Knowing of your existence and history, no honest or conscientious woman or man can remain silent before such a great injustice. Nor can they remain still in front of a struggle, which like all that is born and grows from below, is necessary, possible, and true.

The Lakota people—who have the honor and fortune to call you their own—have an ethic that recognizes and respects the place of all people and things. They respect Mother Earth's relation to herself and to all living things that live and die within her. They have an ethic that recognizes generosity as a measure of human worth. They recognize the steps of our ancestors along the paths of today and tomorrow. They see women and men as part of the universe, where there is the power of free will to choose paths and seasons, to search for harmony, and to struggle against that which breaks and disorders it. The Lakota people have all of this—and more that still escapes us—to teach the "Western" culture that steers against humanity and against nature, in North America and in the rest of the world.

Probably the determined resistance of Leonard Peltier is incomprehensible to Power in North America, and the world. Power calls it "foolishness" to never give up, to resist. But the foolish are in every corner of the world, and in all of them, resistance flourishes in the fertile ground of the most ancient of histories.

Power fails to understand not only Peltier's resistance, but also that of the entire world. It insists on trying to shape the planet into a coffin, just like the system it represents, with wars, jails, and police officers.

Probably, the Power in North America thinks that in jailing and torturing Leonard Peltier, it is jailing and torturing one man.

It doesn't understand how a prisoner can continue to be free, while in prison.

It doesn't understand how, being imprisoned, he can speak with so many, and so many listen.

It doesn't understand how, in trying to kill him, he has more life.

It doesn't understand how one man, alone, is able to resist so much, to represent so much, to be so large.

"Why?" Power asks itself, and the answer never reaches its ears:

Because Leonard Peltier is a people, the Lakota, and it is impossible to keep a people imprisoned.

Because Leonard Peltier speaks through the Lakota men and women, whose persons and whose nature are the best of Mother Earth.

Because the strength that this man and this people have does not come from modern weapons; rather, it comes from their history, their roots, their dead.

Because the Lakota know that no one is more alive than the dead.

Because the Lakota, and many other North American indigenous people, know that resisting without surrender defends not only their lives and their liberty but also their history and the nature that gives them origin, home, and destiny.

Because the great ones always seem so small to those who cannot see the history that each one keeps inside.

Because the racism that now governs can only imagine the other and the different in jail—or in the trash can, where two Lakota natives were found last month, murdered, in the community of Pine Ridge. This is justice in North America: those who fight for their people are in jail, those who despise and murder walk unpunished.

What is Leonard Peltier accused of?

Not of a crime he didn't commit. No. He is accused of being the other, of being different, of being proud to be the other and different.

For Power, Leonard Peltier's most serious crime is his search to rescue the history of the Lakota, his people, in their past, in their culture, in their roots. For Power, this is a crime, because being rooted in history impedes being tossed around by this absurd machine that is the "system."

If Leonard Peltier is guilty, then we are all guilty, because we seek out history. On its shoulders we fight to have a place in the world, a place of dignity and respect, a place for ourselves exactly as we are, which is also very much how we were.

If the indigenous people of the North, and the indigenous people of Mexico, and all the indigenous people of the entire continent, know that we have our own place (being who we are and not pretending to have another skin color, another tongue, another culture), then the other colors who populate the entire world should know it too. And then, Power must know it. So that it learns the lesson well, so that it doesn't forget it, many more paths and bridges need to be walked from below.

On these paths and bridges, you, Leonard Peltier, have a special place, the best, next to us who are like you.

Leonard Peltier, receive a embrace from one who admires and respects you, and who hopes that one day you will call him "brother."

Vale. Health to you, and the hope that injustice disappears from tomorrow, with yesterday as a weapon and today as a road.

From the mountains of the Mexican Southeast
SUBCOMANDANTE INSURGENTE MARCOS

Beneath the Mask

This section contains the Sup's most philosophical and literary writing. These are texts where the writer sits in deep reflection on the world, where he seeks strength and points of reference in other writers and thinkers. His aloneness, his hopes, his humor, serve as windows to the inner man, as he fashions a selfless self, a person without a face, a personality who, each day, struggles to be better.

44

To Open a Crack in History

SEPTEMBER 1999

For Rodolfo Peña:
Another of death's mistaken embraces

> When I start to write you
> the inkwells stir,
> the cold black inkwells
> blush and tremble,
> and a bright human warmth
> rises from the dark depths.
> When I start to write you
> my bones are ready to write you:
> I write with the indelible
> ink of my love.

—MIGUEL HERNÁNDEZ

NOW THE MOON IS A lacquered nail that strums night's strings and makes a storm in every sense. The frightened moon hides herself, a white girl, a dark light that clothes itself in darkling clouds. Now the storm is the lady of the night, and lightning sketches trees and foolish shadows with short and hurried strokes.

Down below it rains often, as often as war brings pain. It brings pain and remembrances, because memory is made fertile by pain. Without memory, the painful feeling would simply ache and nothing would be born of it, and therefore nothing would grow, while calendars, each one a life, fill up.

The shadow writes or paints. There is a double fifteen, second two of seven, that's an anniversary and fiesta and remembrance and pain and joy and memory.

Barely was the first letter gone, the messenger of death, when the shadow that fills us starts sharpening the point of the second letter. If the first was for the person who left, the second is for the one who trails the absent one. August's long and humid passage reaches September and touches dates for celebrations and remembrances.

Like dissatisfied memory, the rain taps her impatience on the little roof, and, more than once, the mocking wind turns out the lights, sending papers and ink into the mud. The shadow toils between opening sails and lifting papers, as if for the sailor sailing was only about the winds.

One sheet of paper has been left in a corner of the little hut. Between the lightning winks one can see something is written. Just a moment. I'll try to get closer.

Right, the mud. And this fog falls in just like that. It is hard. Good! There it is. This is what I manage to read:

Letter Two

I propose to you, with the gravity of life's final words, that we embrace in a commitment: let's go out into open spaces, let's take risks for another, and with him wait with outstretched arms for a new swell in history to lift us. Perhaps it is already doing so, in a silent and subterranean way, like buds which beat beneath a winter's ground.

—ERNESTO SABATO, *Before the End*

P.S.

WHICH, AS YOU WILL SEE below, explains the why of the fifteen double, as this is the second of the seven.

Fifteen Years Ago

EVERY AUGUST, year after year, the mountains of the Mexican Southeast manage to give birth to a particularly luminous dawn. I don't know the scientific causes, but during this dawn, this one single dawn in the whole of a disconcerting August, the moon is a hammock of swaying iridescence, the stars marshal themselves to encircle and center, and the Milky Way proudly lights up its thousand wounds of clotted light. In this August of the end of the millennium, the calendar pointed to the sixth day when this dawn appeared. And with the swaying moon came back a memory of another August and another sixth, fifteen years ago, when I began my entry into these mountains that were and are, like it or not, home, school, road, and door. I began my entry in August, and I didn't complete it until September.

I should confess something to you. When I laboriously climbed the first of the steep hills that abound in these parts, I was sure it would be my last. I wasn't thinking of revolution, of high human ideals or a shining future for the dispossessed and forgotten of always.

No, I was thinking I'd made the worst decision in my life, that the pain that squeezed my chest, more and more, would end up totally closing off my increasingly skimpy airway, that the best thing for me would be to go back and let the revolution manage itself without me, along with similar rationalizations. If I didn't go back, it was only because I didn't know the way back. All I knew was that I had to follow the *compañero* preceding me who, judging by the cigarette he was smoking while effortlessly negotiating the mud, seemed to be merely out for a stroll. I didn't think that one day I'd be able to climb a hill while smoking and not feel as if I was dying with each step, or that a time would come when I'd be able to manage the mud that was as abundant underfoot as the stars are overhead. No, I wasn't thinking at all then. I was concentrating on every breath I was trying to take.

What finally happened is that at some point we reached the highest crest of the hill, and the man in charge of the meager column (we were three) said we would rest there. I let myself fall in the mud that seemed closest and told myself that perhaps it wouldn't be so hard to find the way back, that all I would have to do would be to walk down for another eternity, and that someday I would have to reach the point where the truck had dropped us off. I was making my calculations, including the excuses I would give them and give myself for abandoning the beginning of my career as a guerrilla, when the *compañero* approached me and offered me a cigarette. I refused with a shake of my head, not because I didn't want to talk but because I'd tried saying, "No thanks," and only a groan had come out.

After a bit, taking advantage of the fact that the man in charge had gone off some distance to satisfy what is referred to as a basic biological need, I used the .20-caliber rifle that I was carrying more like a walking stick than a combat weapon, and pulled myself up as best I could. That was how I was able to see something from the top of that mountain that had a profound impact on me.

No, I didn't look down. I didn't look toward the twisted scribble of the river, nor to the weak lights of the bonfires that dimly illuminated a distant hamlet, nor to the neighboring mountains that painted the ravine, sprinkled with small villages, fields, and pastures.

I looked upward. I saw a sky that was a gift and a relief—no, more like a promise. The moon was like a smiling nocturnal swing, the stars sprinkling blue lights, and the ancient serpent of luminous wounds that you call the Milky Way seemed to be resting its head there, very far away.

I stayed looking for a time, knowing I'd have to climb up that wretched hill to see this dawn, that the mud, the slips, the stones that hurt my flesh inside and out, the tired lungs incapable of pulling in the necessary air, the cramped legs, the anguished clinging to the rifle walking stick to free my boots from the imprisoning mud, the feeling of loneliness and desolation, the weight I was carrying on my back (which I came to know later, was only a token, since in reality there would always be three times that or more; anyway, that "token" weighed tons to me), that all of that—and much more that would come later—is what had made it possible for that moon, those stars, and the Milky Way to be there and no other place.

When I heard, from behind, the orders to renew the march, up in the sky a star, surely fed up by its subjugation to the black roof, managed to break away, and by falling to leave a brief and fugitive trace on the nocturnal blackboard. "That's what we are," I said to myself, "fallen stars that barely scratch the sky of history with a scrawl." As far as I knew, I had only thought this, but apparently I had thought it aloud, because the *compañero* asked: "What did he say?" "I don't know," replied the man in charge. "Could be he's already got a fever. We have to hurry."

What I'm telling you happened fifteen years ago. Thirty years ago, a few people scratched history, and knowing this, they began calling to many others so that, by dint of scribbling, scratching, and scrawling, they would end up rending the veil of history, so that the light would finally be seen. That, and nothing else, is the struggle we are making. And so if you ask us what we want, we will unashamedly answer: "To open a crack in history."

Perhaps you are asking what happened to my intention to turn back and abandon the guerrilla life, and you might suppose that the vision of that first dawn in the mountains made me abandon my idea of fleeing, lifted my morale and firmed my revolutionary conscience. Well, you are wrong. I put my plan into operation and went down the hill. What happened is I mistook which side to go down. Instead of going down the slope that would take me back to the road and from there to "civilization," I went down the side that took me deeper into the rain forest and that led me to another hill, and another and another . . .

That was fifteen years ago. Since then, I have kept climbing hills and I have kept mistaking which side to go down, and every August 6 keeps giving birth to a special dawn, and all of us keep being falling stars barely scratching our history.

Vale with nuts on top, health to you, and . . . wait a minute! Wait. What is that shining so bright in the distance? It looks like a crack . . .

THE SUP, ON TOP OF THE HILL,

TOSSING A COIN TO SEE ON WHICH SIDE OF THE HILL TO GO DOWN

NOTES

1. Rodolfo Peña, a writer of progressive tendencies and a member of the SME, the electricians' union, was the director of *La Jornada*, the second largest daily paper in Mexico.

2. Miguel Hernández, a twentieth-century Spanish poet and shepherd, was born in Horijuela, Murcia. Active in the Spanish Civil War, he was imprisoned by Franco and died in jail.

45

We Know What We're Doing; It Is Worth It

DECEMBER 1994

To whom it may concern:

> *I am a fugitive,*
> *Once I was born*
> *They locked me up inside of me*
> *But I left.*
> *My soul searches for me*
> *Through hills and valleys,*
> *I hope my soul*
> *Never finds me.*

—FERNANDO PESSOA

WHILE I WRITE THIS, from one side reports arrive from our *compañeros* about preparations for the advance of our units, and on the other side the last stack of unanswered letters burn. That is why I write to you now. I always said to myself I would respond to each and every letter we received. It seemed to me that it was the least we could do, to answer the many people who had bothered to write a few lines and risked sending their names and addresses, hoping for a response.

Again, war is imminent. I definitely cannot save these letters. I should destroy them. Should they fall into the hands of the government, they could cause problems for many good people and a few bad people. Now the flames are high and their colors change. Sometimes they are an iridescent blue that never fails to surprise this night of crickets and faraway lightning, which approaches a cold December of prophecies and pending accounts. There were quite a few letters. I managed to answer a good part of them, but I would barely deplete a pile when another would arrive. "Sisyphus," I said to myself. "Or the vulture eating Prometheus's entrails," my other self adds, never missing a beat with his skepticism.

I should be sincere and confess that, lately, the little pile that arrives habitually was growing smaller. At first I attributed it to the nosy government agents. Then

I realized that good people get tired . . . and they stop writing . . . and, sometimes, they stop fighting.

Yes, I know that writing a letter isn't exactly an assault on the Winter Palace. But the letters made us travel so far. One day we would be in Tijuana, the next in Merida, sometimes in Michoacan, or in Guerrero, Veracruz, or Guanajuato, Chihuahua, Nayarit, Queretaro or Mexico City. Sometimes we would travel farther on, to Chile, Paraguay, Spain, Italy, Japan. So now they are over, those trips that brought to our lips more than one smile, that warmed cold sleepless nights or refreshed the days of tired heat.

Anyway, as I said, I had decided to respond to all the letters, and we, the knights-errant, know how to keep our promises (as long as they're not about love). So I have thought of your generosity and how it would alleviate my heavy guilt if all of you accepted one single and overwhelming missive in which each of you would feel uniquely addressed.

Vale, since you cannot protest or express disagreement (you could but I won't hear about it, given the mail and etceteras). I will proceed, then, to give free reign to the insane dictatorship that rules my agile hand when it comes to writing a letter. What better way to begin than with a few lines from Pessoa which are curse and prophesy, and that say, I think . . .

> The gaze, which is looking
> where it cannot see, turns:
> We both speak of
> What was not retained.
> Does this begin or end?

ON SUCH AND SUCH A MONTH, OF THE INEFFABLE YEAR OF 1994.
To whom it may concern:
I WANT TO SAY A FEW THINGS about what has happened since January. Many of you wrote to say thank you. Imagine our surprise when we read in your letter that you are grateful that we exist. I, for example, whose most affectionate gesture from my troops has been one of resignation when I arrive at one of our posts, was surprised to find myself surprised. And when I am surprised, unusual things happen. For example, I might bite down too hard on my pipe and break the stem. For example, as I look for another pipe I might find some candy and commit the grave error of crackling it, a sound that only cellophane-wrapped candy makes and which that plague called "children" can hear from dozens of meters away, even kilometers, if the wind is in their favor. And if this happens, for example, I might raise the volume on the little tape player to drown out the noise from the wrapper with a song that goes—

He who has a song
will have a storm,
he who has company,
will have solitude.
He who follows a good road
will have dangerous points
which will invite him to stop.
But the song is worth
a good storm
and the company
is worth the solitude.
The agony of haste
is always worth it
though the points
are filled with truth.

—Heriberto appears in the little room (all these things invariably happen in a little room with a roof of tin or cardboard or grass or nylon) with a face on him that
says, "I found you." I pretend not to see him and whistle a tune from a movie whose
name I can't remember. Anyway, in the movie the whistle works for the hero
because a girl—a very good-looking girl—smiles and comes up to him. But, I realize that it is not a girl but Heriberto who approaches. Next to him comes Toñita with
her corncob doll. Toñita—who gripes about giving me a kiss because "it itches,"
who has pointy little teeth, who will be five years old and then will be six—is the
Sup's favorite. Heriberto—the biggest crybaby in the Lacandon Jungle, who draws
the Anti-Sup-marine ducks, who is the terror of the large red ants and the
Christmas chocolate, who is Ana María's favorite—is the punishment that some
vengeful god has sent the Sup for being a transgressor from violence and a professional of the law. What, wasn't that it? Well, don't worry about it . . .

So, pay attention! Listen to what I have to tell you! Heriberto arrives and tells me
that Eva is crying because she wants to see the singing horse and the major does not
let her because he is watching *Decameron* by Passolini. Of course, Heriberto does-
n't refer to the movie by title, but I can guess by his description: "The major is
watching old women naked." For Heriberto all women who wear a skirt above the
knee are "naked," and any woman above the age of four, like Eva, is a "*vieja*."[2] I
know that this is one of Heriberto's sneaky schemes to take the cellophane-wrapped
candy that called like a siren on the Titanic in the middle of the fog. Heriberto and
his ducks are coming to the rescue, because there is nothing sadder in this world
than a candy without a child to rescue it from the prison of its cellophane.

Toñita, on the other hand, discovers a "mudproof" rabbit; in other words, it's black. She decides to submerge it in a puddle that, in her estimation, has all the necessary characteristics to test its mudproof quality.

Faced with this invasion of the "general command of the e-ze-el-en,"[3] I play dumb and pretend I'm *veeery* caught up in my writing. Realizing this, Heriberto draws a duck. Irreverently, he calls it the "Sup." I pretend to be offended because Heriberto argues that my nose is just like the duck's bill. Toñita, meanwhile, puts the muddy bunny on a rock next to her corncob and looks and analyzes them with a critical eye. It occurs to me that the results don't satisfy her because she shakes her head with the same obstinacy she does when she refuses to give me a kiss. Heriberto, confronted by my indifference, seems to give up and walks away, and I am satisfied with my unquestioned victory. Then I realize that the candy is gone, and I remember that Heriberto made a strange movement as I gazed at the drawing. He took it from under my very nose! And with this nose, that says a lot! I am depressed, and more so when I learn that Salinas is packing to go off to the World Trade Organization. It seems to me that it was unjust when he called us "transgressors of the law." If he knew Heriberto, he would know that compared to Heriberto we are even more law-abiding than the leadership of the PRI.

Anyway, I was talking about my surprise when I read those thankyous in your letters. Sometimes they were addressed to Ana María, to Ramona, or to Tacho, el Moy, Mario, la Laura, or to any of the men and women who cover their faces to make themselves present to others or who uncover their faces to hide.

I adopt my most reverent tone to give thanks for so many thank yous, when Ana María appears in the doorway. Heriberto is crying and holding her hand. She asks me why I won't give Heriberto any candy. "Not give him candy?" and I look at his face, all evidence of the candy now hidden beneath the snot and tears, which have won over Ana María. "That's right," she says. "Heriberto says he gave you a drawing in exchange for candy, and you didn't keep your word." I feel the victim of an unjust accusation and put on the look of an ex-president of the PRI who is preparing to take over a powerful government agency and climbs the podium to give his best speech. Ana María, without a word, takes the bag of candy—let's see where that candy is—and gives it all to Heriberto! "Here," she says, "the Zapatistas always keep their word."

They both leave. I am *really* sad because that candy was for Eva's birthday. And I don't quite know how old she is, because when I asked her mother, she said six. "But the other day you told me she was going to be four," I complained. "Yes, when she turns four, she begins to be five. In other words, she's around six," she explained firmly. And I am left counting my fingers and doubting the entire educational system that teaches that 1+1=2, 6x8=48, and other transcendent things.

In the southeast mountains of Mexico, obviously, these precepts do not hold true. There is another mathematical logic at work here.

"We Zapatistas are very 'other,'" el Monarca once observed, and told me that when he ran out of brake fluid, he would use his urine instead. The other day, for example, there was a birthday party. The "youth committee" got together and organized the "Zapatista Olympics." The master of ceremonies declared that the long jump competition was about to start, which really meant who jumps highest. Next was the high jump, which really meant who jumps the farthest. I was counting on my fingers again, when Lieutenant Ricardo arrived and told me that they had gone to sing Happy Birthday at dawn. "Where was the serenade?" I asked. I was happy that everything was returning to normal, since it was logical that "*Las Mañanitas*"4 be sung at dawn. "In the cemetery," answered Ricardo. "The cemetery?" I began to count on my fingers again. "Yes, well, it was the birthday of a *compa*5 who died in combat in January," Ricardo says on his way out (the drag races were next). "Good," I said to myself. "A birthday party for a dead person. Perfectly logical . . . in the mountains of Southeast Mexico." I sighed.

I am sighing with nostalgia, remembering the good old times when the bad guys were the bad guys and the good guys were the good guys. When Newton's apple followed its irresistible trajectory from the tree toward some childish hand. When the world smelled like a schoolroom on the first day of class: of fear, of mystery, of newness. I'm sighing emphatically when, without warning, Beto comes in to ask if there are any balloons. Without waiting for my answer, he starts to look among maps, operative orders, war communiqués, pipe tobacco ashes, dried tears, red flowers colored with pen, cartridge belts, and a smelly ski mask. Somewhere Beto finds a bag of balloons and a photograph of a playmate, pretty old (the picture, not the playmate). Beto stops for a minute to decide between the bag of balloons and the picture, and he decides what all children do: he takes both of them.

I've always said that this is not an army headquarters but a kindergarten. Yesterday I told el Moy he should put in some antipersonnel mines. "You think the soldiers will come all the way here?" he asks me, worried. I answer, trembling, "I don't know about the soldiers, but what about the kids?" El Moy nods agreeably and begins to tell me about his complicated design for a booby trap: a fake hole, with stakes and poison. I like the idea, but since the kids aren't boobies, I recommend that we electrify everything and place machine guns at the entrance. El Moy thinks a while, says he has a better idea, and leaves me.

What was I saying? Oh, yes! About the candy for Eva that Heriberto took. So there I am, calling every camp over the radio in search of candy so I can replace the bag of candy for Eva, when Eva shows up with a little pot of tamales. "My mother sends these because today is my birthday," she says to me with a look that in ten years or so will provoke more than one war.

I thank her profusely and—what else could I do?—say I have a present for her.

"Whereizit?" she says·asks-demand and I begin to sweat because there is nothing more terrible than a look of dark anger. Eva's face begins to transform itself like in that movie *El Santo Meets the Wolfman*, and all I can do is stutter. To make things worse, Heriberto arrives to see "if the Sup is still mad" at him. I begin to smile to give me time and figure out how I can give Heriberto a good kick, when Eva notices that Heriberto has an almost-empty bag of candy. She asks him where he got it, and he says, in a sugary and slurry voice, "the Chup." I don't realize that he means the "Sup" until Eva turns and reminds me, "and my present?" Heriberto's eyes pop out when he hears the word "present." He drops the bag of candy, which by now is empty, and, sidling up to Eva, says with a sticky cynicism, "Yeah, what about our present?" "Our?" I repeat, once again thinking about that kick, when I notice that Ana María is close by. Right away I say, "It's hidden." "Where?" asks Eva, already tired of the mystery. But Heriberto views this as a challenge and opens up my backpack. He tosses out my blanket, altimeter, compass, tobacco, a box of bullets, a sock. He stops when I shout, "It's not there!" Heriberto then starts on el Moy's backpack and he is about to open it when I say, "You have to answer a riddle to know where the present is."

By now Heriberto is fed up with the tight straps of el Moy's backpack and he comes to sit by my side. Eva does too. Beto and Toñita come near, and I light my pipe to give me time to measure the size of the riddle problem I have gotten myself into . . . I take out the photo of Zapata from my backpack and show it to them.

"Is he climbing up or down?" asks Beto.

"Is he standing still or is he walking?" asks Eva.

"Is he taking out or putting away his sword?" asks Toñita.

"Has he just fired his pistol or is he going to fire?" asks Heriberto.

I'm always surprised by that eighty-four-year-old photograph that Old Don Antonio gave me in 1984 and how many questions it elicits. I look at it one last time, before I decide to give it to Ana María, and the picture raises one more question: Is it our yesterday or our tomorrow?

In this climate of curiosity and with a surprising coherence for her four-years-almost-five-or-six, Eva asks, "What about my present?" The word "present" provokes identical reactions in Beto, Toñita, and Heriberto. They all start yelling, "Where's my present?" I'm trapped and on the point of being sacrificed. But in walks Ana María, who saves my life, as she did in San Cristobal almost one year ago (under very different circumstances). Ana María has an enormous bag of candy with her. "Here's the present the Sup has for you," she says, while giving me that I-don't-know-what-you-men-would-do-without-women look.

While the children decide, or fight over how they will divide the candy, Ana María salutes me and says:

"Reporting, sir. The troops are ready to leave."

"Good," I say as I strap on the pistol. "As always, we will leave at dawn."

Ana María leaves.

"Wait!" I call to her and give her the picture.

"What's this for?" she asks peering at the photograph.

"We'll need it," I reply.

"For what?" she persists in asking.

"So we'll know where we're going," I reply while inspecting my gun.

Above us a military airplane negotiates the sky. Well, don't get fed up. I am almost done with this "letter of letters." First, though, I need to get the kids out of here . . .

To conclude, I will answer some questions you are surely asking:

Do we know where we're going? *Yes.*

Do we know what awaits us? *Yes.*

Is it worth it? *Yes.*

Who can answer the previous three questions with a *yes* and remain still and do nothing, without feeling that something deep inside is tearing apart?

Vale. Health to you, and a flower for this tender fury. I think it deserves one.

From the mountains of the Mexican Southeast
SUBCOMANDANTE INSURGENTE MARCOS
ZAPATISTA NATIONAL LIBERATION ARMY

P.S.

FOR WRITERS, ANALYSTS, and the general public. Brilliant writers have found some valuable parts in the Zapatista movement. Nevertheless, they have denied us our fundamental essence: the national struggle. For them we continue to be provincial citizens, capable of a consciousness of our own origins and everything relative to it, but incapable—without "external" help—of understanding and making *ours* concepts like "nation," "motherland," and "Mexico." They will chime-in during this gray hour with minuscule letters. For them it is all right that we struggle for material needs, but to struggle for spiritual needs is an excess. It is understandable that these pens now turn against us, and that is too bad. Someone has to be responsible; someone has to say, "No!" Someone has to say, "Enough!" Someone has to leave prudence to one side, and value dignity and shame above life. Someone has to . . . Well, to these magnificent pens: we understand the condemnation that will flow from your hands. All

I can argue in our defense is that nothing we ever did was for your pleasure. What we have said and done has been to please ourselves with the joy of the struggle, of life, of speech, of walking . . . Good people of all social classes, of all races and generations, helped us. Some helped to unburden their conscience, and others to be fashionable. The majority helped because of their convictions, because of their certainty that they had found something good and new.

We are good people; that is why we are letting everyone know what we are about to do. You should prepare yourselves. You should not be taken by surprise. This warning is a disadvantage for us, but not as great a disadvantage as a surprise would be.

To those good people I want to say: I hope you continue to be good, that you continue to believe, that you not allow skepticism to bind you to the sweet prison of conformity, that you continue to search, to seek out something in which to believe, something for which to fight.

We have also had some brilliant enemies—writers who have not been satisfied with easy condemnation, who have sought out strong, firm, coherent arguments with which to attack us. I've read some brilliant texts that attack the Zapatistas and defend a regime that must pay dearly, for the sake of appearances, for someone to defend it. It's a shame that, in the long run, you wound up defending a vain and childish cause. It is a shame that you will end up falling along with that edifice that is crumbling . . .

P.P.S

. . . WHICH ON HORSEBACK, accompanied by a *mariachi*, sings beneath an old woman's window that Pedro Infante song that's called, "They Say I Am a Womanizer" and ends with—

> Among my sweet loves
> One is worth more than others
> one who has loved me without rancor
> of my tarariraran[6] . . .
> A beautiful old woman
> Who I don't deserve
> Who with all her heart
> Offers me love divine.

In front of a grandmother one is always a child, and it hurts to leave . . . Good-bye, grandmother, I am coming. I've finished, I'm beginning . . .

NOTES

1. Portuguese poet Fernando Pessoa (1888–1935), author of *The Book of Disquiet*.

2. *Vieja* means "old lady"; it has the same idiomatic connotations in Spanish as in English.

3. E-ze-el-en is a whimsical spelling of EZLN, the Zapatista National Liberation Army.

4. "Las Mañanitas" ("Early Mornings") is a song usually sung on someone's birthday.

5. *Compa* is short for *compañero*, "buddy, companion."

6. *Tarariraran* is onomatopoeic for "singsong"; it also has the connotation of emotional or sexual wandering.

46

The Library of Aguascalientes

To the weekly magazine Proceso
To the national newspaper El Financiero
To the national newspaper La Jornada
To the local newspaper of San Cristobal de Las Casas, Tiempo

Sirs:

COMMUNIQUÉS ARE FLYING about, indicating that the winds have changed direction. Again, you are threatening us with unemployment, and I hope this time it's true. They tell me that Mr. Robledo Rincón[1] has sequestered himself and his armed guards, the self-named "state public security police," somewhere in the governor's palace. Even though the upheaval of those who oppose the popular will in Chiapas is limited to four neighborhoods in its old capital, Tuxtla Gutierrez, they could be offered a dignified out. Let them explain where the money came from to arm the White Guards who assassinate indigenous people in the Chiapas countryside. Perhaps it comes from the "peace agreements" of San Cristobal, money that never reached the poor of this state of the Mexican Southeast (because we're still called "Mexico"? No?).

Vale. Good health to you, and a bit of hope to foretell tomorrow.

From the mountains of the Mexican Southeast
SUBCOMANDANTE INSURGENTE MARCOS

P.S.

WHICH REMEMBERS A PREVIOUS dawn and a cold within. One night of tanks, planes, and helicopters, I was in the library of Aguascalientes. I was alone, surrounded by books and a cold rain that forced the use of the ski mask, not to hide from others' eyes but to hide from the cold. I sat in one of the few chairs that were not broken, and contemplated the languid abandonment of the place.

Like other dawns, this one was empty of people, while the library began the complicated ceremony of its unveiling. The heavy bookcases began a movement much like a disordered dance. The books exchanged places and pages, and in the back and forth a book fell, silent, unhurt, exposed by a single page. I did not pick it up; avoiding the dancing shelves, I got near enough to read . . .

> The Library exists ab aeterno. It is a truth whose immediate corollary is the eternal future of the world, that no one can reasonably doubt. Humanity, the imperfect librarian, can be a work of luck or of malevolent demiurge; the universe with its elegant dosage of shelves full of enigmatic tomes, indefatigable ladders for the traveler and latrine for the sedentary user, can only be a work of a god . . .
>
> The imps affirm that the babble is normal in the Library and that the reasonable (even a humble and pure coherence) is almost a miraculous exception.
>
> The Library is limitless and temporary. If an eternal voyager traverses it in any direction, he would prove that at the end of the centuries the same volumes are repeated in the same disorder (which, once repeated, would be an order: an Order). My loneliness becomes joyful with that elegant hope.
>
> Leticia Alvarez de Toledo has observed that the vast Library is useless; rigorously, one would only need one volume, of common format, printed in nine or ten editions, which would consist of an infinite number of infinitely thin pages . . . The handling of this silky portfolio will not be comfortable; each page attempts to unfold in other analogies; the inconceivable central page would not have an opposite side.
>
> —JORGE LUIS BORGES, *The Library of Babel*

"My loneliness becomes joyful with that elegant hope," I repeat as I slip away from the library. Aguascalientes is deserted. I am tempted to say "abandoned," when a fox bounds past me toward the kitchen. I walk to the cemented clearing and sit next to the palm of "hope that the flowers that die in other lands may live in this one." The library continues its metamorphosis. Noises, creaks, and something that I imagine to be laments escape through doors and windows. Did I say doors? I lie. The library has no doors. It has two holes that are impossible to define. There are those who insist that they are there to allow one to enter, and some who say they allow one to exit, while others argue that they allow the Library to breathe; only a few suspect that they are for gorging on people, animals, and hopes . . .

The library of Aguascalientes is the beginning and the end of a spiral; it has no defined entrance nor exit. I mean to say that in the gigantic spiral that Tacho described in order to explain the architectural intent of Aguascalientes, the library is its inception and conclusion. The safe house that "keeps the organization's greatest secrets" is at the other end and beginning of a whirlwind. I run my eyes over the gigantic volute to which all constructions are aligned, and I imagine that only from a special satellite can one appreciate the spiral that "beckons from the jungle."

My gaze runs from the safe house to the library, which now gives out a phosphorescent blue and a continuous, hoarse noise. The library, even if unimaginable, by day is inhabited by children. They come not because of the books, Eva tells me; the children believe there are multicolored balloons hidden there. Apparently no one ever finds them, because the children end up making color drawings. Lately, there are many helicopters and planes, I mean not just in the skies of Aguascalientes, but also flat in the children's drawings. The purples, reds, and greens in the drawings repeat themselves too much for my liking, and yellow seems to limit itself to the sun which these days is extinguished by the gray of the sky. At night, the library shelters and agitates transgressors of the law and professionals of violence (like the one who writes this.) They gaze at the shelves filled with books, looking for something that is missing, and which they're sure was once there ... The library was the only thing, in all of Aguascalientes, that the Democratic National Convention considered their property, and it sometimes has books. The caravans made efforts to put in electricity, bookshelves, books, tables, chairs, and an old computer that has the virtue of never being used. The rest of Aguascalientes has remained abandoned since that ninth day of August 1994. Every once in a while, el Mister, el Bruce, y el Saqueo² will make an effort to patch up the tent for the less-and-less-frequent parties.

Now the library remains in silence, and the phosphorescence, concentrated to a single point at the center of the room, turns emerald green. I moved carefully to one of the windows. The green light was blinding, and it took some time for me to get used to it. In it I saw—

—all of a sudden, that the blue sails of *Aguascalientes* caught a favorable wind. I turned toward the captain's quarters, but it was empty. The sea thrust its waves against the keel, and the creaking of the anchor chains could be heard above the wind. I climbed starboard and took the rudder in order to free it from the spiral's labyrinth. Was it leaving or arriving?

The emerald of the library ceased to glow.

P.S.

WHICH REPEATS WHAT was told to him from the lands of Zapata: *Cruelty in Uaymil-Chetumal* ...

Ten years after Alonso Davila was flung out from Villa Real de Chetumal, the rash Francisco de Montejo again considered the conquest of the province of Uaymil-Chetumal (1543—1545). He commissioned Gaspar Pacheco, Melchor, his son, and 30 soldiers for this action. Thus they began the desolate war of Uaymil-Chetumal. A report of the era stated "Mayan men and women, in equal measure, were killed with clubs, or thrown into the lakes with weights tied to their feet so they would drown. Wild dogs used in the war tore to pieces these defenseless indians. The Spanish considered them animals and they dragged and beat them like vile beasts. It is said that the Pachecos cut off many hands, ears and noses from many indians.

As you can see, the bad government started many years ago, and its methods are somewhat passé . . .

Meanwhile, I look worriedly at the "prominent nose," now red and cold, because of that "cutting off noses . . . "

Greetings to the pipe of Popocatepetl, and always remember that . . .

In Popocatepetl aic ixpolihuiz, in mexicayotl aic ixpolihuiz, Zapata nemi iyihtic tepetl, iyihtic macehuiltin.[3]

(Look: it is Nahuatl.)
Vale once again.

THE SUPMARINE FROM THE HIGH SEAS

NOTES

1. Robledo Rincón was elected governor of Chiapas on November 1, 1994; his election was openly recognized as won through fraud. He was in office during the Zapatista uprising on December 19, 1994, when thirty-eight municipalities were taken over peacefully.

2. El Mister, el Bruce (Lee), and el Saqueo are noms de guerre of three indigenous leaders of Guadelupe Tepeyac who on May 15, 1994, appeared to speak before presidential hopeful Cuauhtémoc Cardenas.

3. "The mountain that smokes will never be lost, the origins of Mexico will never be lost, Zapata is alive in the mountains, the people, dignified and deserving, are in the mountains."

47

The Retreat Is Making Us Almost Scratch the Sky

To the national weekly magazine Proceso
To the national newspaper El Financiero
To the national newspaper La Jornada
To the local newspaper in San Cristobal de las Casas, Chiapas, Tiempo
To the national and international press

Dear sirs:
HERE ARE THE COMMUNIQUÉS. Everything looks so dire, we are on the verge . .
. It is amazing the cynicism with which they deny what is evident: the decision to seek
a military solution. Us? Well, the heavens hang so low over our heads, we can almost
scratch the sky. It's the first time that something falls up into the sky. I fell.

Vale. Health to you and a well-sharpened knife to tear through so much darkness.

From The Mountains Of Southeastern Mexico
SUBCOMANDANTE INSURGENT MARCOS

P.S.
. . . WHICH NARRATES THE fifteenth of February 1995, sixth day of the retreat (we
recommend that it be read before each meal; it is an excellent dieting regime.) At dawn
on the fifteenth we were going to drink our urine. I say, "We were going to," because
we didn't do it; we all began to vomit after the first swallow. Previously there had been
a discussion. Although we all agreed that each person should drink his or her own
urine, Camilo suggested we wait until dawn and let the night cool the urine in the can-
teens so we could drink it imagining it to be soda.

In defense of his suggestion, Camilo argued that he had heard on the radio
that imagination made anything possible. I opposed the idea, suggesting that
time would only make the odor stronger, and that the radio had not been too
objective lately. My other self argued that letting it rest could help the ammonia
settle to the bottom. "It must be the adrenaline," I said, surprised that the skep-

ticism was my own and not my other self's. Finally, we decided to take a sip, all at the same time, to see what would happen.

I don't know who began the "concert," but almost immediately we all began to vomit what we had ingested, and also what we hadn't. We were left even more dehydrated, prostrate on the ground, like dunces, stinking of urine. I think that our image was hardly soldier-like. Hours before sun up, a sudden rain washed over us, alleviating our thirst and our spirits. With the first light of the sixth day we continued walking. In the afternoon, we reached the outskirts of a small village. Camilo went to ask for something to eat.

He returned with a little fried pork, hard and cold. We ate it right there without any modesty. In a few minutes the cramps began. The diarrhea was memorable. We were strewn at the foot of a small wooded hill. A federal troops patrol passed us by a mere 500 meters away. They didn't find us because God is grand. The smell of shit and urine could be smelled kilometers away.

P.S

... WHICH REITERATES ITS REBELLION. They can do it again. They can do in all of the villages what they did in Guadalupe Tepeyac.[1] For each resident, child or adult, they brought in ten soldiers; for each horse, a war tank; for each chicken, an armored vehicle. In total 5,000 soldiers patrol a deserted village and "protect" a slew of dogs and animals belonging to no one. Let them do that in all the autonomous communities, everywhere, in all of the ranches. Let them fill the whole state of Chiapas with soldiers ...

Despite everything and everyone, the mountains of southeastern Mexico will continue to be territory in rebellion against a bad government. This will continue being Zapatista territory. It will be forever ...

P.S.

WHICH CLARIFIES AND RECTIFIES. It was not the ezln who broke off the dialogue and reinstated the war. It was the government.

It was not the EZLN who feigned political willingness while preparing a military attack and betrayal. It was the government.

It was not the EZLN who detained and tortured civilians. It was the government.

It was not the EZLN who murdered. It was the government.

It was not the EZLN who bombed and razed communities. It was the government.

It was not the EZLN who raped indigenous women. It was the government.

It was not the EZLN who robbed and plundered the *campesinos*. It was the government.

It was not the EZLN who betrayed the will of an entire nation to find a political solution to the conflict. It was the government.

P.S.

. . . WHICH POINTS OUT incongruencies in the investigations of the attorney general.If the Sup had received political and military training from the Sandinistas, he would have already organized a *piñata*[2] with the recovered properties, and he would have expelled all those who have criticized it from the organization. If the Sup had received training from the Salvadorans, he would have already made a gift of his weapon to Cristiani.[3] If the Sup had received aid from the Russians, he would have already bombed Chechnya—excuse me, Guadalupe Tepeyac.

Besides, what other guerrilla army, "of the millennium," "fundamentalist," and headed by "whites from the university," has carried out military actions like the EZLN did in January 1994 and again in December 1994, breaking through the military blockade? What other guerrilla force has agreed to sit down and dialogue only fifty days after having taken up arms? What other guerrilla force has appealed, not to the proletariat as the historical vanguard, but to the civic society that struggles for democracy? What other guerrilla force has stepped aside in order not to interfere in the electoral process? What other guerrilla force has convened a national democratic movement, civic and peaceful, so that armed struggle becomes useless? What other guerrilla force asks its bases of support about what it should do before doing it? What other guerrilla force has struggled to achieve a democratic space and not take power? What other guerrilla force has relied more on words than on bullets?

P.S.

Please send the responses to the, supposedly disappeared, CISEN (National Center for Investigation and Security),[4] so that it can help think in a "modern" way. Yes, to the CISEN. The attorney general is only a pimp paying the ruling class.

P.S.

. . .WHICH APPOINTS ITSELF "special investigator on the Sup's case," and invites the national and international civic society to be the jury and to pronounce the sentence. Being such and such hour, on such and such day, of such and such month, in the current year, standing before this P.S. is a man of indefinite age, between five and sixty-five years old, his face covered with one of those garments that appears to be a sock with holes in it (and which the gringos call a ski mask, and Latin Americans call pasamontañas). There are two visible features on the face, one which, after several sneezes, we deduce is the nose. The other, judging by the emanations of smoke and the smell of tobacco, could be a pipe, like the ones used by sailors, intellectuals, pirates, and fugitives from justice. Sworn to say the truth and nothing but the truth, the individual in question says his name is "Marcos Montes de la Selva," son of Old Don Antonio and Doña Juanita, brother to young Antonio, Ramona, and Susana, uncle to Toñita, Beto, Eva, and Heriberto. Speaking before me, he declares himself to be in full use of his physical and mental faculties, and without any pressure (other than the 60,000 federal soldiers who are looking for him dead or alive) states and confesses the following:

First. That he was born in the guerrilla camp called Agua Fria,[5] in the Lacandon Jungle, Chiapas, early one morning in August 1984, and that he was reborn January 1, 1994, and reborn, successively, on June 10, 1994, on August 8, 1994, the nineteenth of December 1994, the tenth of February 1995, and each day and each hour and each minute and each second since that day up to this moment, in which I am making this statement.

Second. That, in addition to his name, he has the following aliases: "Sub," "Subcomandante," "Sup," "Supco," "Marquitos," "Pinche Sup," "Sup, son of a—," and others that the modesty of this P.S. Public Prosecutor prevents it from writing.

Third. The owner of the voice confesses that, since having been born, he has conspired against the shadows that darken the Mexican sky.

Fourth. The owner of the voice confesses that, before being born, being able to possess everything in order to have nothing, he decided to possess nothing in order to have everything.

Fifth. The owner of the voice confesses that, in the company of other Mexicans, the great majority of them Mayan Indians, they decided to make a certain piece of paper live up its words, a piece of paper that they teach about in school, which lists the rights of the Mexican citizens and which is called "The Political Constitution of the United Mexican States." The owner of the voice points out that, in Article 39 of this paper, it is written that the people have the right to change the government. At this point, the P.S., anxious to defend his own right, orders that subversive paper to be confiscated and burned, without giving it a glance. Having done this, he continues to take the statement from the individual with the prominent nose and the polluting pipe. The owner of the voice confesses that, not being able to exercise this right by peaceful and legal means, he decided, together with his accomplices (the owner of the voice refers to them as "brothers") to take up arms against the supreme government and to shout "Enough!" to the lie that, says the owner of the voice, rules our destinies. The P.S. could not help but be terrified in the face of such unusual blasphemy, and was shaken with the mere thought of being left without a handout.

Sixth. The owner of the voice confesses that, facing the choice between comfort and responsibility, he always chose responsibility. This statement evinced the disapproval of the people present at this preliminary hearing and an instinctive reflex that brought the P.S.'s hand to cover his wallet protectively.

Seventh. The owner of the voice confesses that he has always been irreverent concerning all supreme truths, except with those that originate from being human. The owner of the voice declared them to be dignity, democracy, liberty, and justice. A murmur of disagreement ran through the Holy Inquisition—excuse me, the office of the special investigator.

Eighth. The owner of the voice confesses that they had tried to threaten him, to buy him off, to corrupt him, to put him in jail, and to murder him, and that they have failed to intimidate him, buy him off, jail him, or kill him ("Up until now," the investigating P.S. points out threateningly).

Ninth. The owner of the voice confesses that, since he was born, he decided that he prefers to die before turning over his dignity to those who have made lies and crime a modern religion. Such an impractical thought earned a cynical look from the people present.

Tenth. The owner of the voice confesses that, since then, he had decided to be humble with the humble, and to be arrogant with the powerful. The P.S. added "irreverent" to the charges that were being made against the owner of the voice.

Eleventh. The owner of the voice confesses that he has believed and still believes in human beings, in their capacity to try indefatigably to be a little better each day. He confesses that, among the human race, he has a special affection for the Mexican race, and that he has believed, still believes, and will always believe that Mexico is something more than six letters and an underpriced product on the international market.

Twelfth. The owner of the voice confesses that he believes, firmly, that the bad government everywhere has to be brought down by all means. He confesses that he believes that a new political, economic, and social relation has to be created among all Mexicans, and later on, among all human beings. These promiscuous intentions make the P.S. investigator shiver.

Thirteenth. The owner of the voice confesses that, to his dying day, he will dedicate himself to fight for his beliefs.

Fourteenth. The owner of the voice confesses that, in a small and egotistical act, he will dedicate the last second of his life to killing himself.

Fifteenth. The owner of the voice confesses that he was completely bored with this interrogation. This earned him a severe reprimand from the P.S. interrogator, who explained to him that the case will continue until the supreme government finds another tale with which to entertain itself.

After these confessions, the owner of the voice was exhorted to spontaneously declare himself innocent or guilty of the following series of accusations. To each accusation, the owner of the voice responded:

The whites accuse him of being dark. Guilty.
The dark ones accuse him of being white. Guilty.
The authentic accuse him of being indigenous. Guilty.
The treasonous indigenous accuse him of being *mestizo*. Guilty.
The machos accuse him of being feminine. Guilty.
The feminists accuse him of being macho. Guilty.
The communists accuse him of being anarchist. Guilty.
The anarchists accuse him of being orthodox. Guilty.
The Anglos accuse him of being Chicano. Guilty.
The anti-Semites accuse him of being pro-Jews. Guilty.
The Jews accuse him of being pro-Arab. Guilty.
The Europeans accuse him of being Asiatic. Guilty.
The government officials accuses him of being an oppositionist. Guilty.
The reformists accuse him of being an extremist, a radical. Guilty.
The radicals accuse him of being reformist. Guilty.
The "historical vanguard" accuse him of appealing to the civic society and not to
    the proletariat. Guilty.
The civic society accuses him of disturbing their tranquillity. Guilty.
The Stock Exchange accuses him of ruining their breakfast. Guilty.
The government accuses him of increasing the consumption of antacids by gov-
    ernment agencies. Guilty.
The serious ones accuse of being a jokester. Guilty.
The adults accuse him of being a child. Guilty.
The children accuse him of being an adult. Guilty.
The orthodox leftists accuse him of not condemning the homosexuals and les-
    bians. Guilty.
The theoreticians accuse him of being a practitioner. Guilty.
The practitioners accuse of being a theorist. Guilty.
Everyone accuses him of everything bad that has happened. Guilty.

Not having anything else to declare in this preliminary hearing, the P.S. investigator ends the session and smiles, imagining the congratulations and the check that he will receive from his bosses.

P.S.

WHICH TALKS ABOUT what was heard on February 16, 1995, on the afternoon of the seventh day of the retreat. "And why don't we attack instead of retreating?" Camilo throws my way halfway up a hill, precisely when I am concentrating intensely on breathing and on not falling into the ravine at our sides. I don't respond immediately, and make signs that he should continue climbing. At the top of the hill the three of us sit down. Night comes to the mountain before it reaches the sky, and in the semidarkness of this indecisive hour in which light isn't the same, and the shadows waver, we hear something in the distance . . .

I tell Camilo to listen carefully. "What do you hear?"

"Crickets, leaves, the wind," responds my other self.

"No. Pay attention," I insist.

Now it is Camilo who responds: "I hear voices . . . very far away . . . a boom-boom-boom . . . like a drum . . . from over there— " Camilo points to the west.

"Yes. Exactly," I tell him.

"And?" intervenes my other self.

"It is civic society calling out that there can't be war, that there must be dialogue, that words, not weapons, should do the talking, " I explain.

"And the boom-boom-boom?" insists Camilo.

"Those are their drums that call for peace. There are thousands, many thousands, hundreds of thousands of them beating and the government is not listening, even though it sits before them. We, all the way from here, we have to listen to them. We have to answer their call. We cannot turn a deaf ear like the government is doing. We have to listen. We have to avoid the war until there is no other choice . . . "

"And then?" muses my other self.

"Then we fight," I tell Camilo.

"When?" he insists.

"When they cease to call, when they tire. That will be the black hour in which we will have to talk. "

"Fight," says my other self.

I insist: "Everything we do is for them. If we fight, it is for them. If we stop fighting, it is for them. In the end they will win. If we are annihilated, they will have the satisfaction of having done everything possible to avoid our demise, to avoid war. For this reason they rose up, and now they will not be held back. What's more, they are the custodians of the flag that they hold in their hands. If we live, they will have the satisfaction of having saved us, of having avoided the war and having shown us that they are better and that they can take care of the flag. Whether we live or die, they live and will become stronger. Everything for them, nothing for us."

Camilo said that he prefers his version: "For them nothing, for us everything."

P.S.

IN WHICH IT RESUMES its nocturnal delirium. Oblivion, that distant lark, is the reason for our faceless wandering. To kill oblivion with a little memory, we cover our chests with lead and hope. If in some improbable flight, the wind joins our paths, I will strip you of so much covering and of the mask of sweet deceit, and with lips and skin make the memory, that of tomorrow, better. For this reason, a message goes from the earth to the concrete. Listen well!

As an unperfect actor on the stage,
Who with his fear is put besides his part,
Or some fierce thing replete with too much rage
Whose strength's abundance weakens his own heart;
So I, for fear of trust, forget to say
The perfect ceremony of love's rite,
And in my own love's strength seem to decay,
O'ercharg'd with burden of mine own love's might.
O, let my books be then the eloquence
And dumb presagers of my speaking breast,
Who plead for love, and look for recompense
More than that tongue that more hath more express'd.
O, learn to read what silent love hath writ;
To hear with eyes belong to love's fine wit.
—WILLIAM SHAKESPEARE, Sonnet XXIII

Vale, amber lark; don't look for us beneath your flight, but up above, yes, where our pain has lifted us, to the sun where hope rains.

P.S.

WHICH CAN MAKE A GIFT of nothing on this birthday. Heriberto's birthday is on the fifth of March. They say he will be four years old and enter his fifth year. Heriberto walks the mountains, while soldiers live in his home, and a tank sits in his patio.

The toys that an "Operation Toys" brought him on the feast of Three Wise Men are now in the hands of some general, or being analyzed by the attorney general in search of some secret strategy. Despite all of Heriberto's preparation for the events of February 10 (the invasion of the federal soldiers), at zero hour he left behind his favorite toy: a little car; sitting on top, Heriberto rode around the cement patio where the coffee beans were put to dry and made believe he was a driver. They tell me that Heriberto consoles himself, saying that his little car wouldn't work in the mountain. Heriberto asks his mom if he can ever have his car again, and if the Sup is ever again going to give him chocolates. Heriberto asks his mom why the war from last year returned, why his car was left behind.

"Why?" asks Heriberto.

His mom does not respond, and continues to walk with the boy and the pain weighing on her shoulders . . .

P.S.

WHICH REMEMBERS AND recites from memory verses from Antonio Machado[6] that refer to different things, but which are fitting now.

I

In my heart I had
a passion's thorn.
One day I pulled it out,
now I cannot feel my heart.
Sharp golden thorn,
who will feel it
pierce the heart again . . .

II

Last night I dreamed I heard
God shout to me: Watch out!
then it was God who slept
and I who yelled: Wake up!

P.S.

WHICH BLEEDS unendingly.

A wound I carry in my chest
It bleeds wheat

and there is no bread
to alleviate the hunger . . .

THE SUP, FROM THE TOP OF A HILL, SEEING TO THE WEST HOW THE SUN
BRINGS DOWN A FADING BEAM . . .

NOTES

1. Guadelupe Tepeyac was the host site for the first *encuentro* in the Lacandon Jungle in August 1994. It was razed by the federal army shortly thereafter, and a military barracks has been set up in the now-deserted village.

2. Piñata here refers to the parceling out of properties, likening the process to the practice of smashing piñatas to get at the candy inside.

3. Alfredo Cristiani Burkard, president of El Salvador, made peace with the FMLN (Fuerzas Armadas de Liberación Nacional; Armed Forces for National Liberation) in 1992.

4. Centro de Investigación y Seguridad Nacional (Center for Investigation and National Security), political police equivalent to the FBI.

5. Marcos is making a play on words to contrast the rebel Aguascalientes ("hot springs"), where he was reborn, with his pre-guerrilla home and birthplace, calling it Agua Fria ("cold springs").

6. A member of the Generation of 1898 and a popular poet in Spain. Antonio Machado was born in Seville in 1875. His early poetry, including *Soledades* (1903) and *Galerías y otros poemas*, reflected the beliefs of the Generation of 1898. His poem "Los Ojos" is dedicated to another member of this illustrious group, Miguel de Unamuno. Antonio was yet another victim of the Spanish Civil War. In February, 1939, he fled across the Pyrenees with his mother and a brother, but became ill during the trip and died shortly thereafter in Collioure. Machado's *Obras completas (Complete Works)* was published in 1947.

48

Death Has Paid a Visit

FEBRUARY 25, 1995

To the national weekly magazine Proceso
To the national daily newspaper La Jornada
To the national daily newspaper El Financiero
To the local daily newspaper in San Cristobal de las Casas, Chiapas, Tiempo
To the national and international press

Sirs:

DIVERSE COMMUNIQUÉS are on the way. Let's see for when and how. Here the cold and the military blockade bears down. The tobacco now smells and hurts of death. What's going on outside? Are you happy with the $20 billion?[1] And who's going to pay it back?

Vale. Health to you, and one of those piggy banks to save hopes, the size of an old cent (one is as scarce as the other.)

From the mountains of Southeastern Mexico
SUBCOMANDANTE INSURGENT MARCOS

And Now To Continue Our Favorite Section:
"The Recurring Postscript of Transgression and Illegality"

P.S.

WHICH TELLS WHAT IT read in the Sup's notebook on February 14, day of love and friendship. Here I go, breaking myself to pieces, and patching body and spirit. Today I broke a piece off my shoulder. It broke just like that and sounded like a dry branch under a boot. Hardly a "crack," just a dull light thud on the floor. I picked it up, and I replaced it to the best of my knowledge of guerrilla anatomy. I tied it up with a reed and continued walking. Yesterday it was a piece off my right thigh that broke and fell. I'm not losing hope that a good piece of this impertinent nose will fall off and leave me with a profile perhaps less aerodynamic but more manageable, not because I want to contradict the attorney general and the story of the man from Tampico,[2] but because it wouldn't deform the ski masks so much.

Yesterday, the thirteenth, death, dressed in olive green, came within ten or fifteen meters of where we were. I told Camilo that it was twenty meters, but when the soldiers left, we went down and measured exactly ten meters to where the patrol of federal soldiers had passed. Now, like a year ago, every second is a flight between life and death. Heads or tails, life comes up or death comes up. Heads or tails like in the Cantinflas[3] movie with Medel, where he sings that song that goes, "What are you missing, woman, what are you missing . . . ," and Marcelo explains to Cantinflas that it means "Woman, from our mother Eve on . . . because in the first global conflagration . . . ," and Cantinflas responds with, "A woman is like a flower and a flower has to be watered, when one waters it, well, one waters it . . . "

And, despite Cantinflas, the coin makes circles in the air, and we, advancing slowly, drag ourselves along, without water or food but with mud and with enough thorns to pay the total sum of the Mexican external debt, if a price were set on them in the stock market. "But they don't have any value," Camilo says to me. "Neither does our blood," adds my other self, who instead of a suitcase carries skepticism everywhere and does not appear to tire.

I noticed that my senses begin to dull. On that day, ten meters from death, I was leaning against a rock. Bit by bit, I lowered myself, and without making a sound, I cocked my gun and pointed it towards the sound. I wasn't thinking; the only sound was of time standing still at my fingertip, on the trigger—with neither fear nor courage, as if I were seeing everything from outside, as if I was very tired, as if I had seen this scene many times before, in a movie, in history, in life, in death. Dulled, I say. "Like a machine," says my other self.

Camilo doesn't say a thing, and only murmurs that there were thirty soldiers only ten meters away,and that we were three and that, according to higher mathematics, each of us had to take on 10 to come out alive. Camilo said that he made that calculation. I didn't calculate anything. All I saw was me with my finger on the trigger, immobile, like a single still repeated to excess in an endless movie. Camilo didn't study at Oxford or in Massachusetts. (Is that how it's spelled?) He barely got through second grade in a village in the jungle, and learned mathematics in the mountains. Myself, I was thinking about a wonderful pun with my finger on the trigger . . . but my other self told me that this wasn't the time for sexual fantasies . . .

Did I say "a year ago"? I lie, it was more than a year ago. It was last January. A year ago, in February, we were in the Cathedral in San Cristobal de las Casas talking of peace. Today we are in the jungle talking of war. Why? Has someone asked that man why? Why did he trick us? Why did he feign a commitment to coming to a just political agreement and then unleash a terror that now escapes his hands?

Well, then, I talked to him, but really I talked with Camilo and to this page in my notebook about how the body parts are falling and I don't understand why, and Camilo is not going to answer because he has fallen asleep beneath the sunflowers. The helicopters above, and the *chac-chac-chac-chac* of the blades are all around us, and I remember that *chac* in Tzotzil means "ass," and from the "ass-ass-ass" of the helicopters I return again to my notebook. My other self says to me, biting my pipe, "It's no use, no one is going to read it." And the notebook, for a change, doesn't say anything, and lets me tell how a small crack first appears on my body, and how it deepens, and then a piece breaks off and falls. I try to put it back again, and tie it with a reed, and it doesn't hurt. I'm not worried about that, but what if I happen to put it on the wrong side? What if it belongs on the right side and I put it on the left side, or vice versa? What political implications would this error have? Clearly, until now it has not been a problem, because the two sides have not fallen off at the same time . . . My other self approaches to read the last lines and murmurs, "No one is going to read it," and feigns sleep when the helicopters surrender their place to the crickets.

Today is the day of love and friendship. Here there is no woman other than death, and no other love than her mortal kiss . . .

P.S.

. . . WHICH FORESEES a reproach. Anyway, I prefer to die here, rather than have to confront Eva someday and try to explain why I couldn't rescue her videocassettes of *Bambi*, *The Jungle Book*, and *The School of Vagabonds* with (somebody doubts it?) Pedro Infante and Miroslava.[4] Eva says that Bambi is a she, Heriberto says that it's a he. Eva argued that you could tell it was a she by the eyes. Heriberto said that it is a he because of the horns. "Besides, at the end he leaves with a girlfriend," argues Heriberto, who, as one can see, is not a child but a dwarf.

P.S.

. . . THAT, WITH A BROKEN heart, remembers a scornful gesture. Toñita also left fleeing for the mountains. She had a pair of new white shoes that some good person from somewhere had sent her. Toñita carried the shoes in her hands. "Why don't you put them on?" I asked her after having been rejected for the nth time from getting a kiss. "Well, because they will get dirty," she replied with the inexplicable logic of a 6-year-old girl in the Lacandon Jungle. I have not seen her again . . .

. . . THAT OFFERS ITSELF AS adviser to the supreme government.

I, the recurring postscript, recommend that the government withdraw the arrest order against the Sup. The result has been that, since he has known that he was pursued, the Sup has been insufferable. And I don't just refer to his obsession with death. As it turns out, he now believes he is John the Devil and is always telling us not to worry, that the Twisted One is going to come to save us . . . But that's not the worst of it. Now he keeps us up all night telling us what he plans to do when he meets up with a certain Monica or such and such Aimée. What does he plan to do? Nothing decorous, believe me. My discretion prevents me from jotting down the details. I tried to dissuade him by telling him this soap opera on TV had ended a long time ago, so then he said he was going to look for *Marimar*.[5] I reminded him of the boycott against Televisa,[6] and he responded that then he was going to go with the kittens of Purrr-cell.[7] Arguing against that, telling him that TV Azteca also had asked for his head (the Sup's), he murmured something like "Some day there will be objective television in this country." He left, sleepy and murmuring: "What are we supposed to do, this is where we are supposed to die, in the most transparent region in the air . . . " I told him that we are supposed "to live," but he no longer was listening. Overhead the sound of a military plane, and Orion were the only cover for his sleeplessness . . .

Vale, once again. Health to you, and a small tonal keepsake for that J. M. Serrat song that ends:

> It is not that I haven't returned
> because I have forgotten,
> It is that I have lost
> the road to my return . . .

THE SUPDELINQUENT TRANSGRESSOR OF THE LAW,

FLEEING THROUGH THE HILLS.

SUB MARCOS

NOTES

1. On December 20, 1994, a financial package organized by President Clinton and the IMF was set in place, in which the United States loaned Mexico $20 billion to pull itself out of short-term debt.

2. Marcos had been identified by the attorney general as Rafael Guillén, born in Tampico, Mexico.

3. Cantinflas, born Mario Moreno in 1891 in Mexico City, became perhaps the best-known Latin American comedian ever. He made several films, the most popular, internationally, being *Around the World in Eighty Days.* He died on April 20, 1993.

4. Pedro Infante (1917–1957), born in Mazatlan, Sinaloa, is undoubtedly one of Mexico's biggest idols. His

movies, records, and public appearances in Mexico and Latin America made him a beloved star whose fame has been unrivaled by any other actor in Mexico since his death in a plane crash. Miroslava Stern, or Miroslava Sternova (1926–1955), born in Prague, was a beautiful actress who appeared in thirty-two films; she worked with the Mexican-born director, Luis Buñuel. At the height of her glory in the 1950s, she killed herself after being disappointed in love by a bullfighter.

5. *Marimar* is a popular television soap opera starring Thalia, a Mexican household name.

6. Henry Purcell (1659–1695) was considered the greatest English Baroque composer.

7. Joan Manuel Serrat was born in 1943 in Spain. His songs, which are highly political, revolve around the Spanish people.

49

A Year of the Zapatista Government

MARCH 17, 1995

To the men and women who,
in different tongues and roads,
believe in a more humane future
and struggle to achieve it today

Brothers and sisters:

THERE EXISTS ON THIS PLANET called Earth, and in the continent called America, a country whose shape appears to have had a big bite taken out of its east side, and on the west an arm thrown out, deep into the Pacific Ocean so that the hurricanes don't blow it far away from its history. This country is known by both natives and foreigners by the name of Mexico. Its history is a long battle between its own desire to be itself and foreign desires to have it exist under another flag. This is our country.

We, our blood already in the voices of our oldest grandparents, walked this land when it was not yet known by this name. But later in this eternal struggle, between being and not being, between staying and leaving, between yesterday and tomorrow, it came into the thinking of our ancestors, with the blood of two branches, that this piece of land and water and sky and dreams, a land which we had because it had been a gift from our earlier ancestors, would be called Mexico. Then we became that other and had more, and then the history of the way that we all got the name was good and thus all who were born had a name. And we were called Mexicans, and they called us Mexicans.

Later history continued delivering blows, giving pain. We were born between blood and gunpowder; and between blood and gunpowder we were raised. Every so often the powerful from other lands came to rob us of tomorrow. For this reason it was written in a war song that unites us: "If a foreigner with his step ever dares profane your land, think, Oh beloved motherland, that heaven gave you a soldier in each son." For this reason we fought. With flags and different languages the foreigner came to conquer us. He came and he went. We continued to be Mexicans because we weren't happy with any other name nor to walk

241

beneath a flag without the eagle devouring a snake, without a white background flanked by green and red. And that's what happened to us.

We, the first inhabitants of these lands, the indigenous, were left forgotten in a corner, while the rest began to grow and become stronger. We only had our history with which to defend ourselves, and we held it tightly so we would not die. And that's how this part of history arrived, and it seems like a joke because a single country, the country of money, put itself above all flags. When they uttered, "Globalization," we knew that this was how the absurd order was going to be called, an order in which money is the only country served and the borders are erased, not out of brotherhood but because of the bleeding that fattens the powerful without nationality. The lie became the universal coin, and for a few in our country it wove a dream of prosperity above everyone else's nightmare.

Corruption and falsehoods were our motherland's principal exports. Being poor, we dressed in the wealth of our scarcities, and because the lie was so deep and so broad, we ended up mistaking it for truth. We prepared for the great international forums and, by the will of the government, poverty was declared an illusion that faded before the development proclaimed by economic statistics. Us? We became even more forgotten, and until our history wasn't enough to keep us from dying just like that, forgotten and humiliated. Because death does not hurt; what hurts is to be forgotten. We discovered then that we no longer existed, that those who govern had forgotten about us in their euphoria of statistics and growth rates.

A country that forgets itself is a sad country. A country that forgets its past cannot have a future. And so we took up arms and went into the cities, where we were considered animals. We went and told the powerful, "We are here!" And to the whole country we shouted: "We are here!" And to all of the world we yelled, "We are here!" And they saw how things were because, in order for them to see us, we covered our faces; so that they would call us by name, we gave up our names; we bet the present to have a future; and to live . . . we died. And then came the planes and the bombs and bullets and death. And we went back to our mountains, and even there death pursued us. And many people from many places said, "Talk." And the powerful said: "Let's talk." And we said, "Okay, let's talk." And we talked. And we told them what we wanted, and they did not understand very well, and we repeated that we wanted democracy, liberty, and justice. And they made a face like they didn't understand. And they reviewed their macroeconomic plans and all their neoliberal points, and they could not find these words anywhere. And they said to us, "We don't understand." And they offered us a prettier corner in history's museum, and a long-term death, and a chain of gold with which to tie our dignity. And we, so that they would understand our demands, began to organize ourselves according to the wishes of the majority, and so that we too could see what it was like to live with democracy, with liberty, and with justice. And this is what happened:

For a year the law of the Zapatistas governed the mountains of Southeastern Mexico. We the Zapatistas, who have no face, no name, no past, governed ourselves. (For the most part we are indigenous, although lately more brothers and sisters of other lands and races have joined us.) All of us are Mexicans. When we governed these lands, we did the following:

We lowered to zero the rate of alcoholism. The women here became very angry and said that alcohol was only good to make the men beat their women and children; therefore, they gave the order that no drinking was allowed. The people who most benefited were the children and women, and the ones most suffered were the businessmen and the government. With support of nongovernmental organizations, both national and international, health campaigns were carried out, lifting the hope of life for the civilian population, even though the challenge from the government reduced the hope for life for us combatants. The women are a full third of our fighting force. They are fierce and they are armed. And so they "convinced" us to accept their laws, and that they participate in the civilian and military direction of our struggle. We say nothing, what can we say?

The cutting down of trees also was prohibited, and laws were made to protect the forests. It was forbidden to hunt wild animals, even if they belonged to the government. The cultivation, consumption, and trafficking of drugs were also prohibited. These laws were all upheld. The rate of infant mortality became very small, as small as the children. And the Zapatista laws were applied uniformly, without regard for social position or income level. And we made all of the major decisions, the "strategic" ones, of our struggle, by means of a method called "referendum" and "plebiscite." We got rid of prostitution. Unemployment disappeared and with it ended begging. The children came to know sweets and toys. We made many errors and had many failures, but we also accomplished what no other government in the world, regardless of its political affiliation, is capable of doing honestly, recognizing its errors and taking steps to remedy them.

We were doing this, learning, when the tanks and the helicopters and the planes and the thousands of soldiers arrived, and they said that they came to defend the national sovereignty. We told them that where sovereignty was being violated was at the IUESAY[1] and not in Chiapas, that the national sovereignty cannot be defended by trampling the rebel dignity of indigenous Chiapas. They did not listen because the noise of their war machines made them deaf, and they came in the name of the government. As for the government, betrayal is the ladder by which one climbs to power, and for us loyalty is the level playing field that we desire for everyone. The legality of the government came mounted on bayonets, and our legality was based on consensus and reason. We wanted to convince, the government wanted to conquer. We said that no law that had to resort to arms to be carried out could be called a law, that it is arbitrary regardless of its legalese trappings. He who orders that a law be carried out and enforced with weapons is a dictator, even if he says that the majority elected him. And we were run out of our lands. With the war-tanks came the law of the government, and the law of the Zapatistas left. And once again, prostitution, drinking, theft, drugs, destruction, death, corruption, sickness, poverty, came following the government's war tanks.

People from the government came and said that they had now restored law in Chiapas, and they came with bulletproof vests and with war tanks, and they stayed there just long enough to make their statements in front of the chickens and roosters and pigs and dogs and cows and horses and a cat that had gotten lost. And that's what the government did, and maybe you all know this because it's true that many reporters saw this and publicized it. This is the "legality" that rules in our lands now. And this is how the government conducted its war for "legality" and for "national sovereignty" against the indigenous people of Chiapas. The government also waged war against all other Mexicans, but instead of tanks and planes, they launched an economic program that is also going to kill them, just more slowly . . .

I am writing this on March 17, which is Saint Patrick's Day, and now I remember that is when Mexico of a century ago was fighting against the empire of the stripes and crooked stars. There was a group of soldiers of different nationalities who fought alongside the Mexicans who called themselves the "Saint Patrick Battalion."[2] And for this reason the *compañeros* said to me, "Go on, take this opportunity to write to the brothers from other countries and thank them because they stopped the war." I believe that this is their way of getting to go dance, and so that I don't yell at them because the government plane is wandering around up there. And so I am writing you in the name of all of my *compañeros* and *compañeras*, because just like the Saint Patrick Battalion, we now see clearly that there are foreigners who love Mexico more than some natives who are now in the government, and tomorrow will be in jail or in physical exile, because their heart now belongs to other lands, because they love another flag that is not theirs and another thinking that is not of their people. We learned that there were marches and songs and movies and other things to prevent war in Chiapas, which is the part of Mexico where it is our lot to live and die. And we learned that these things happened, and that "No to war!" was said in Spain, France, Italy, Germany, Russia, England, Japan, Korea, Canada, the United States, Argentina, Uruguay, Chile, Venezuela, and Brazil, as well as other parts where it wasn't said but it was thought. And so we saw that there are good people in many parts of the world and that these people live closer to Mexico than those who live in "Los Pinos," which is what the house where the government lives is called.

Books, medicine, laughter, sweets, and toys flourished under our law. Theirs, the law of the powerful, came without any argument other than that of force, and destroyed libraries, clinics, and hospitals. It brought sadness and paved a bitter road for our people. And we thought that a "legality" that destroys knowledge, health, and happiness is a very small legality for such grand women and men, and that our law is better, infinitely better, than the law of these gentlemen, who with foreign vocations say that they govern us.

So we want to give you all our thanks. And that if we had a flower we would give one to each of you. But since we don't have enough flowers for each man or woman, then one will have to do. And let each person save a little piece of it, and when they are old, they can talk with the children and young people of their country and say, "I struggled for Mexico at the end of the twentieth century, and from over here I was there with them, and I only know that what they wanted is what all human beings want, who have not forgotten that they are human beings, and what democracy, liberty, and justice are. And I did not know their faces but I did know their hearts, and they were the same as ours." And when Mexico is free (which is not to say happy or perfect, but only free; that is, free to choose its road, its errors, and its successes), then that part of you that lies at chest level and—despite, or precisely because of, the political implications—it is situated a little to the left, will also be a part of Mexico.

And now it occurs to me that with this letter you can make a paper flower and put it in a buttonhole or in your hair, and you could go dancing with this enchanting adornment on. And now I'm going to go because here comes again the plane of wakefulness and for surveillance, and I have to blow out the candle, but not the hope . . . Never—over my dead body.

Vale. Health to you, and the promised flower: a green stem, white petals, red leaves, and don't worry about the serpent, that which flaps its wings is an eagle; it will take care of the snake, you will see . . .

From the mountains of the Mexican Southeast
SUBCOMANDANTE INSURGENTE MARCOS

NOTES

1   IUESAY is a phonetic play on U.S.A.

2   During the U.S. intervention in Mexico in 1857, an Irish group joined the Mexican army to battle against the United States, as Catholics helping other Catholics.

50

Zapatistas, Guadalupanos, and the Virgin of Guadalupe

MARCH 24, 1995

To the national weekly Proceso
To the national newspaper El Financiero
To the national newspaper La Jornada
To the local newspaper of San Cristobal de las Casas, Chiapas, Tiempo

Sirs:

HERE GOES A COMMUNIQUÉ-REPORT on the progress of the never-ending dialogue. Please take into account how many days it takes for things to reach us and for things to get out, so don't be anxious.

Here spring is disguised as autumn, and the leaves tend to don brown uniforms, with horseflies by day and with glowworms by night. The forest is swathed with cloths and surprises.

Vale. Health to you, and a fresh wind that relieves the tedium of desperation.

From the mountains of the Mexican Southeast
SUBCOMANDANTE INSURGENTE MARCOS

P.S.

WHICH SHOWS HOW MUCH the e-ze-el-en has "imposed" itself on the needs and customs of the communities, and explains how interests "foreign" to the indigenous people camp out among the ranks of the "neocriminals."

A few days ago, in the now transient town of Guadalupe Tepeyac, there was an argument. A gift came to them from the city. Among the little humanitarian aid they receive, the Zapatistas Guadalupanos (as they call themselves) found a statuette of the Virgin of Guadalupe. From what I am told, it measures some thirty centimeters, has a few golden cords, and colored votive candles. "It's pretty," says the one who's describing it to me. The gift has given rise to different opinions: first a controversy, then an argument, and finally a general assembly of people who, far from their homes, traveling uphill and down refuse to surrender, and call themselves with pride Guadalupe Tepeyac. The yellow laces that adorn the image were the first topic. "They're painted gold," said a man when he looked at them from a distance. "No, they're made of gold," said a lady. Rapidly, the community began to take sides.

The argument takes place by the church, in a little field that serves as playground, dance floor, or, like now, as a debating hall. The inhabitants of the settlement, which today serves as temporary refuge for the Guadalupanos, keep out of it; this concerns the people from Guadalupe Tepeyac, and no one else. Even the militia, there to safeguard their people, don't intervene. They smoke quietly by the houses, their weapons at rest across their laps, and their backpacks ready.

At some point—the one who tells me all this can't say how it happened and describes the scene from different angles at the same time—the argument moves to the topic of whether the statuette will be left in the town now sheltering them, or if it will go with the Guadalupanos when they return home. The sides become radicalized, and a confrontation begins to emerge between the men and the women. Some men are in favor of leaving the statue as a gift to thank the people who received them; the women, who begin to gather in greater numbers, say that the image is a gift, and that a gift should not be given again, because then it is no longer a gift. The one who tells me all this says everything at full speed. I gather that the argument is more complicated and that he is sparing himself the trouble of dealing with something that is hard to understand and even harder to explain.

Clearly, some are thinking of the weight and bulk when their improbable move comes, but the women don't give in. Each side gives rise to reasons and spontaneous orators. The man in charge of the town is found on one side of the playground, seated and silent, listening. At a certain point, he gets up and proposes that the matter be resolved in a general assembly. In Guadalupe Tepeyac they have assemblies and votes even to see how long a dance should go on, so his proposal is welcomed. The agreement on this is unanimous, since after all, the gift is for the whole village, and there are still men burning cornfields and women washing clothes in the river. The assembly will be held in the evening, when the heat abates and the cool air caresses and relieves the dark skins of these men and women who in August 1994 and in January 1995 housed the Zapatistas' will for peace. In return, dozens of tanks and helicopters and thousands of soldiers came and now occupy their lands. (Yes, I know I'm continually changing the tense of the verbs, but that's how they're telling me the story.)

When the meeting starts, the day has already dropped its sun coin into the mountain's money chest, yet enough light remains to make candles and lighters useless. Over the past hours, each side has worked at convincing those who were not there. After this "conferring" (which between some couples sounds like threats), the assembly repeats the arguments: the image of the Guadalupana stays in the town that gave them shelter, or the Virgin goes when the people of Guadalupe Tepeyac go.

Doña Herminia—or "Ermiña," as the one who's telling me the story says—clears her throat, a sign that the founder of Guadalupe Tepeyac is about to speak. All fall silent. With the weight of a hundred years on her, Doña Herminia begins to speak slowly and quietly. She demands special attention, out of respect, and in order to hear her speak. She says that the Virgin of Guadalupe came again from the city, came to find her sons and daughters, the Zapatistas Guadalupanos, and because she couldn't find them, she searched for them up the mountain, and finally reached their hands after much traveling, from place to place.

The *doña* says that the Virgin must be tired of so much going up and down hills, especially with this heat that parches saints and sinners alike. And that a little rest would do her no harm at all. And now that she is with them, it is good that the Virgin rest a while with her own. But Mother Lupita didn't come from so far away to stay behind, she didn't travel from one place to another seeking us to end up staying somewhere while the Guadalupanos went off to another.

The *doña* thinks—and now the women, and a man here and there, nod their heads in agreement with the *doña*—that the Guadalupana will want to be with her sons and daughters wherever they are, that her tiredness will be lighter if she rests together with her family, that her sadness will be lessened if she hurts together with them, and that her joy will be brighter if it shines on all of them. The *doña* says—now there are more who agree—that the Virgin will want to go wherever the people of Guadalupe Tepeyac go, that if the war chases them into the mountains, the Virgin will go to the mountains, turned soldier like them, to defend her dark-skinned dignity, that if peace brings them back to their homes, the Guadalupana will return to the village to rebuild what was destroyed. "So, I ask you, Madrecita, if you agree to go wherever we go, with all of us you have given yourself to," the *doña* asks the image that sits in front of the assembly. The dark-skinned Virgin doesn't answer, her downward gaze unaltered. After a moment of silence, the *doña* concludes: "Those are all my words, brothers and sisters."

The one who is leading the assembly asks if anyone else wants to speak. A unanimous silence is the answer. "There will be a vote," he says, and he takes the vote. The women win. The Virgin of Guadalupe will go wherever the Guadalupanos go. After the assembly there is a dance. A marimba and the dark-skinned Virgin preside over the festivity. Some continue to argue whether the little cords are made of gold or only painted yellow. A *cumbia* starts up and grabs those still arguing by the feet and carries them out to what is now the dance floor.

"So the women won again?" I ask.

"Sure!" says the one who is telling me the story. You never contradict a woman, and much less when spring is already warming the nights in the mountains of the Mexican Southeast . . .

WHICH REFLECTS ON A LUNATIC theme and hopes, ingenuously, to appear in the scientific columns of the important dailies and magazines.

Mounted on a spiral of the smoke rising from my pipe, I climb to the highest branch of the *ceiba* tree. It is night, and a sorrow is gaining on the moon, now darkening a good bit of her figure. The Sup reflects:

The Moon is a satellite of Earth. That is, the Moon spends her life turning around Earth, with the same tedium with which a merry-go-round turns, empty, in a town fair. Faced with this punishment, the Moon says nothing. What can she say, when, in any case, there is a long and invisible chain that ties her to Earth and keeps her from leaving to take a turn around so many other stars and planets. Nevertheless, as far as one can see, the Moon is not vengeful. It doesn't occur to her, for example, to let herself fall onto Earth with the same wavering spin of a coin, falling to shed light on that initial mystery: heads or tails?

No, the Moon doesn't let herself fall. This can only mean that the Moon has hope. And until now, this fact has gone unnoticed by astronomers, astrophysicists, astrologers, astronauts, and the Houston Astros. Up until now, I say, because I intend to unveil this technical and scientific datum that will revolutionize all modern science and, above all, the daily and nightly gathering of lovers. "The Moon has hope," I have said, and in there lies an epistemological breakthrough and the birth of a new scientific paradigm. By the way, speaking of T. Kuhn and of *The Scientific Revolutions*,[1] I once wrote a letter to Güilly[2] in which I explained the futility for scientists and the police of speculating over who is behind the criminal nose and the ski mask. Time and the pathetic PGR[3] have proven me right, (and served me with an arrest warrant).

Well, let's say it again: "The Moon has hope." The simpleminded will go away burdened by the question: "What does the Moon hope for?" But the problem will have no solution unless we first answer the following question: "What makes it possible for the Moon to have hope?" Clearly it isn't the same, but the question is as momentous as if we referred to "The Moon is sleepy," something that of course is nonsense, because being a nocturnal animal, the Moon obviously suffers from insomnia. A statement such as, "The Moon is feverish," sounds hot and sensual, and perhaps may help melt away another person's resistance to a more intimate touch and to the inevitable contagion, but nothing more. The pragmatic will discard such a claim immediately, since, they will argue, there is no thermometer capable of gauging such temperature, nor any known fire extinguisher to deal with such hot flame.

An utterance like "The Moon has desires" is as ambiguous as "The Moon has hope," and leads one to ask: "What does the Moon desire?" By the way, I'll be right back ...

(With admirable balance, the Sup approaches the upper edge of the *ceiba*, and after emitting the characteristic sound that betrays the way in which mammals empty their bladders, returns with a face that reads, Mission accomplished.) All right, let's return to science, now that the prosaic requests of the body, with its ebbs and flows, have been satisfied. Where were we? Oh yes, with "The Moon has desires." No, we had already dealt with that (in more than one sense). Let's go back to the rash statement that "The Moon has hope." It's elementary. Can you imagine someone circling and circling the same old thing, always seeing the same landscape, repeating always the same routine? What? The special assistant attorney for the murder cases of LDC, JFRM, and Cardinal Posadas?[4] For God's sake! We're talking about science, not comic strips! Back we go.

All right, isn't it logical to suppose that this "someone" would be bored and wish to be freed of such a circular punishment? Yes, I know that in the case of the Moon there is that silly chain called "gravity." But—why then not let herself drop? You still have doubts! Okay, it's not important . . . We geniuses have always been misunderstood—at first. All right, all right, be kind (remember that it's spring). Humor me and say it is so, that the Moon is a prisoner and that, even so, she seeks no vengeance on her jailer. Who is it that keeps her prisoner? Human beings! If they hadn't invented the "law of gravity," the Moon would have been long gone, romping about Jupiter or Saturn or perhaps beyond . . .

Thus the Moon undoubtedly has hope, hope of seeing herself free and able to go wherever her lunacy desires. What would be one of the main effects of this event? Well, if the Moon escapes—whether it's because the silly chain of gravity breaks, or because her jailer forgets to tether her—lovers will no longer be able to use her as a reference to convince or to deny. Then, how could they say, "In the double moon of your breast, hands, kisses, and gazes surrender"; or that other one: "With the complicity of the Moon I discovered the pleasure you had hidden in your womb"; or "Don't bring your breath any closer, the Moon will flee, frightened to see that we are one"? So, these are only some examples, but you can see what kind of problems would arise on the night the Moon abandons her usual route and simply leaves to ride off into the stars . . . .

P.S. TO THE LUNATIC P.S.

ONE MUST ALSO BE CAREFUL with the Moon. Many years ago, a certain Knight of the White Moon defeated me on the beaches of Barcino and made me—ungrateful one—put away for a good while all weapons and warlike desires. Now I have freed myself, but that's another story I will tell you . . . beneath some other moon.

P.S.

WHICH, UNDERSTANDING, offers an alternative. All right, if you don't want to publish it in the science column, at least do me the favor of tying that postscript with a little string to the UNAM-SAT-1[5] and tell them to let it go when it passes by the Moon. It will do her good to know that someone understands her . . . .
Vale, once again. Health to you, and may hands and moons find each other.

THE SUP, A LITTLE EMBARRASSED BECAUSE NOW HE DOESN'T KNOW HOW TO GET DOWN FROM THE *CEIBA*. HOW ABOUT SLIDING DOWN THAT SIL-VER RAIL THAT SPIRALS TO THE GROUND?

NOTES

1. Thomas S. Kuhn, one of the most influential scientists of the twentieth century, insisted on society's influence on science.

2. Güilly is a germanized version of Mexican writer Adolfo Gilly's name. He is the author of *A Revolution Interrupted*.

3. PGR stands for *Procuraduria General de la Republica* (General Attorney of Mexico), Mexican equivalent of the U.S. Justice Department.

4. LDC stands for Luis Donald Colosio, whose assassination while campaigning for the presidency of March 23, 1994, remains unsolved. JFRM stands for José Francisco Ruiz Massieu, secretary general of the PRI and a former governor of Guerrero.

5. Marcos is playfully suggesting that the Autonomous University of Mexico (UNAM) has a communications satellite.

51

A Land to Harvest a Future

FOR THE DIALOGUE OF THE CIVIC SOCIETY

AGUASCALIENTES, CHIAPAS, MEXICO

MARCH 25, 1995

Brothers and sisters:

WELCOME TO ZAPATISTA TERRITORY, which is to say, "a territory in rebellion against the evil government." That is how things are, even though these lands are filled with war, even though they want to trample dignity with war tanks, even though they want to shut up reason with the noise of planes and helicopters.

We wanted to participate personally in this dialogue, but there are approximately 60,000 olive green reasons that prevent us from doing so. It doesn't matter. We hope that you accept this letter as the means by which our voice, our thinking, and our hearts can reach all of you, who, after detaining the government's war, came to our lands to reaffirm the search for civic and peaceful ways to resolve the problems that we—nationals and foreigners—suffer from in this last part of the twentieth century.

We hope that this will not be the last time that you visit us, and that many of you will be able to stay in the "Peace Camps" located in various villages in the state of Chiapas, and which have made it possible for our civilian brothers and sisters to return to their homes.

We hope, also, that on another occasion we can be present to receive you as it is the custom to receive brothers and sisters: with flowers and the music of marimbas. We owe you those two things, in addition to everything that we owe you.

In continuation, we present to you our proposal for a "Complementary Protocol" to be incorporated into the "Universal Social Convention" which is to be approved by you. We are clear that our proposal is equal to all the others, that it is subject to discussion, and that we will respect from here whatever decision that you make.

Complementary Protocol for the Universal Social Convention

WE, THE PERSONS PRESENT HERE today, demand:

1. That reason always win over force.

2. That the will of the majority be imposed on the minority, without the minority disappearing or having its right to become the majority restricted.

3. That any man can give any woman any flower in any part of any world, and that this woman give thanks for the flower not with just any smile, but with the best and only one.

4. That the morning no longer be a great question or a disaster waiting to happen; that the morning be just that: the morning.

5. That the night not be a cave of fear; that the night be a bed of desire.

6. That sadness be surprised with a simple look of disdain; and that happiness and laughter be free and never lacking.

7. That for everyone there be, always, bread to illuminate the table, education to feed ignorance, health to surprise death, land to harvest a future, a roof to shelter hope, and work to make hands dignified.

8. That the words and hearts of men and women no longer be prisoners of jails, tombs, or threats.

9. That war be part of a long ago and foreign past, and that neither armies nor soldiers be any longer necessary.

10. That those who govern command by obeying. That those who do not fulfill this, be changed for others.

11. That there always exist someone who is willing to struggle so that all that came before becomes not a demand, but a reality.

Respectfully,

From the mountains of the Mexican Southeastern
SUBCOMANDANTE INSURGENTE MARCOS

52

Letter to Eduardo Galeano

MAY 11, 1995
MONTEVIDEO, URUGUAY

Mr. Galeano:

I'M WRITING YOU BECAUSE . . . because I feel like writing you. Because Children's Day just ended, and it occurs to me that I might talk to you about what happens in a child's day in the middle of a secret war here in Mexico. I'm writing you because I have no reason for doing so, which means I can tell you things as they occur to me, without worrying that I stray from the purpose of this letter. I'm also writing you because I have lost the book you gave me, because Destiny's sleight of hand has replaced it with another, because a passage in your book *Las Palabras Andantes (Walking Words)* keeps dancing around in my head. Because it says:

> Do words know to fall silent when they can't find the time or place for which they're called?
> And the mouth does it know how to die?
> —Walking Words VIII P. 262

And so I have sat down to smoke and think. It's dawn. For a pillow I have a rifle. (Okay, it's not really a rifle; it's a police carbine that until January 1994 was used to kill the indigenous. Now, it serves to protect them.) With my boots on and a pistol within easy reach, I think and smoke. Outside the ring of smoke and thoughts, May lies to herself and pretends she's June, and now a rainstorm's thunder and lightning have managed the seemingly impossible feat of silencing the crickets.

But I'm not thinking of the rain. No. I'm not trying to guess which of the lightning bolts that rip the fabric of the night spells death. No. I'm not worrying that the nylon tarp is too small to cover my dwelling and that the side of my bed is getting soaked. (Ah! Because it just so happens that I made my bed out of boughs and poles fastened with vines. It is a desk, a storage space and sometimes a bed. I can't get comfortable in the hammock, or rather, I get too comfortable. I sleep very soundly, and deep sleep is a luxury that you can pay for very dearly around here. This bed of sticks is uncomfortable enough that a wink could be called sleep.)

No, I am not worried about the night, the rain or the thunder. What worries me is that business of "Do words know to fall silent when they can't find the time or place for which they're called? And the mouth, does it know how to die?"

Ana María, an indigenous Tzotzil who is an infantry major in our army, sent me the book. Someone sent it to her, and she sent it to me, not knowing that I had lost your book, and that this one is replacing the lost one, which is almost the same but not quite; this one is full of little drawings in black ink. That's how books and words should be, I think, with little drawings that pop out of the head or the mouth or the hands, dancing on the page each time the book is opened, dancing in the heart each time the book is read. The book is the greatest gift man has given to himself. But let's get back to your book, the one I have now. I read it by the light of a little candle stub I found in my backpack. The wick gave up on the last passage on page 262 (A palindrome, no? A sign?). So, I remembered the Perón[1] quote you relayed to me and my awkward response, and, later, the book you sent me. And now I am embarrassed to tell you I abandoned the book in February's "lucky escape." Now I have received this book and those words about knowing to be silent. I had been turning this matter over for some nights, even before the book returned to me, and I ask myself whether the time has come to fall silent, if the moment has passed and this isn't the place, if this isn't the hour for the mouth to die.

I'm writing you this in the dark of a May dawn; April 30, 1995, Children's Day here in Mexico, is now past. We Mexican children celebrate the day, more often than not, despite the adults. For example, thanks to the supreme government, many indigenous Mexican children celebrate their day in the mountains far from home, in unhygienic conditions. There is no party, but there is great poverty: they have no place to relieve their hunger and despair. The supreme government claims it hasn't expelled these children from their homes; it's only deployed thousands of soldiers in their lands. But with the soldiers came drink, prostitution, robbery, torture, and hostilities. The supreme government says the soldiers have come to defend our "national sovereignty." They're "defending" Mexico against Mexicans. These children haven't been expelled, says the government, and they have no reason to be alarmed by the planes, the tanks and helicopters and the thousands of soldiers. They need not be frightened even though the soldiers have orders to arrest and kill their fathers. No, these children haven't been expelled from their homes. They share the mountain's uneven floor out of a desire to be close to their roots. They share mange and malnutrition for the simple pleasure of scratching and showing off their slim figures.

The children of the masters of the government spend the day at parties surrounded by gifts. Zapatista children, masters of nothing if not their own dignity, spend the day at play; they play at war, they play at being soldiers who take back the

land the government has stolen from them, of being farmers who sow their cornfields and gather wood, of being the sick whom no one cures, of being the hungry
who must fill their mouths with song instead of food. At night, when the rain and
fog press in, they especially like to sing a song that goes more or less like this:

> Now we can see the horizon,
> Zapatista combatant.
> The path will be marked
> for those who come behind.

And so, for example, Heriberto appears marching in step in the horizon. And
coming behind Heriberto, for example, is Oscar's little son, Osmar. The two of
them march along, armed with two sticks they've scavenged on a hill nearby.
("They're not sticks," says Heriberto. He assures us that they're carrying powerful weapons capable of destroying the red ant nest near the stream. They bit him
and action had to be taken.) Heriberto and Osmar march in line. On the opposite
front, Eva advances, armed with a stick that turns into a doll in a less warlike
atmosphere. Behind her comes Chelita, whose two years of life raise her a meager few centimeters off the ground, and whose eyes—like those of a frightened
deer caught in the light—are sure to haunt that Heriberto some night in years to
come, or whomever lets himself be blinded by their dark gleam. Following
Chelita is a puppy so skinny it looks like a tiny marimba.

I'm being told all of this, but just as if I were watching Wellington pitted
against Napoleon in the movie Waterloo, (I think with Orson Welles), and
Napoleon is defeated because he has a bellyache. But there is no Orson here, or
infantry or artillery support, or defensive formations against cavalry charges.
Dispensing with preliminary feints or skirmishes, both Heriberto and Eva have
opted for a full frontal attack.

I'm just about to give my opinion that it looks like a battle of the sexes, but
Heriberto has already flung himself at Chelita, evading Eva's direct charge, so
that she suddenly runs up against an unsuspecting Osmar, who's much less prepared for face-to-face combat, since he's off to one side in the bushes pooping.
Eva declares that he's been scared shitless, but Osmar doesn't say a thing back
because he wants to ride the puppy that has been drawn over by the smell.
Meanwhile, Chelita has been crying ever since she saw Heriberto coming at her,
and now he doesn't know how to quiet her down, so he offers her a stone as a
prize ("It's not just a stone," says Heriberto, assuring her she's looking at pure
gold). While Chelita keeps on screaming, I'm thinking that they give Heriberto
a dose of his own medicine, when Eva arrives in a maneuver known as "shifting
the enemy position." She falls on Heriberto from behind. Heriberto has just

offered Chelita his anti-red-ant weapon, which Chelita is considering in between sobs . . .

Eva's doll weapon crashes down on Heriberto's head—Take that!—and the screaming goes stereo (because Chelita, excited by Heriberto's screams, doesn't want to fall behind). And now there's blood and already someone's mother—I don't know whose—is on the way with a belt in hand, and both armies disband and desert the field. In the infirmary, they announce that since Heriberto has a lump the size of an egg and Eva is unscathed, the women have won this battle of the sexes. Heriberto complains of referee bias and prepares his counterattack, but it will have to wait for tomorrow because right now there are beans to eat that don't quite fill the plate or his belly . . .

And that's how they spent Children's Day, say the children of a settlement called Guadalupe Tepeyac. They spent it in the mountains because in their town there are several thousand soldiers defending the "national sovereignty." And Heriberto says that when he grows up, he's going to be a truck driver and not an airplane pilot, because if you blow a tire on the truck, you just climb down and go on walking, but if you blow a tire on the airplane, there's nowhere to go. And I tell myself that when I grow up I'm going to be an Uruguayan-Argentine and a writer, in that order, and don't think its going to be easy, because I can't stand that stuff they call *maté*.

But that's not what I wanted to tell you. What I wanted to tell you is a story for you to recount . . .

Old Don Antonio taught me that you are as big as the enemies you choose to fight, and as small as the fear is big. "Choose a big enemy, and it will make you grow so you can confront him. Lessen your fear because if it grows, it will make you small," Old Don Antonio told me one rainy May afternoon, in the hour when tobacco and words reign. The government fears the Mexican people; that's why it needs so many soldiers and police. Its fear is very big. Consequently, it is very small. We're afraid of oblivion, which we have made smaller with our pain and blood. Consequently, we are big.

Put this in one of your writings. Say that Old Don Antonio told you all this.

We've all had an Old Don Antonio at some point. But if you never had one, you may borrow mine this time.

Tell them how the indigenous of the Mexican Southeast lessen their fear to make themselves big, and choose colossal enemies to make themselves grow and get stronger.

That's the idea. I'm sure you'll find better words to convey this. Pick a rainy night with lightning and wind, and you'll see how the story will slip out just like a little drawing that begins to dance and stirs the heart. That's why there are dances and hearts.

Vale. Health to you, and a little smiling face, like the ones with which you sign your letters.

From the mountains of the Mexican Southeast
SUBCOMANDANTE INSURGENTE MARCOS

P.S. . . . POSING AS A POLICE NOTICE.
IT IS MY DUTY TO INFORM you that I'm a criminal according to the supreme government of Mexico. Therefore, my correspondence can incriminate you. I beg you to memorize the damming contents of this letter—that is, the appeal of the indigenous villages—and destroy the evidence immediately. If paper was chewing gum, I'd advise you to chew it up and make one of those little bubbles that so outrage a good conscience and show a decided lack of breeding and education among those who make them. Although some blow them hoping one of those little bubbles will be big enough to carry us to that path shining there above us, stretching in pain and hope across the sky of our America.

P.P.S. . . . WHICH IS UNLIKELY.
IF YOU SHOULD SEE Benedetti,[2] please give him my regards. Please tell him I whispered words of his into a woman's ear and they took her breath away. Words like that move all humanity . . .

NOTES

1. Juan Domingo Perón (1895–1974), twice president of Argentina, was a populist dictator who vowed to raise the living standard of the working man. His first wife, Evita, helped him tremendously with many grand acts of charity. She is a living legend. His second wife, Isabelita, became president of Argentina after Perón's death. There continue to be many Peronistas today, and his tomb is guarded twenty-four hours a day.

2. Mario Benedetti (1920–), a world-renowned Argentinian author, has written more than seventy works of literature, including *Andamios, The Neighboring Shore,* and *Blood Pact and Other Stories.*

53

Letter to John Berger

HAUTE SAVOY, FRANCE
MAY 12, 1995

To John Berger
Haute Savoy, France:

A reader could ask himself: What is the relationship between the writer and the place and peoples
about whom he writes?

—JOHN BERGER, *Boar Land*

AGREED, BUT HE COULD also ask himself: What is the relationship between a letter written in the jungle of Chiapas, Mexico, and the response that it receives from the French countryside? Or, even better, what is the relationship between the slow beating of the heron's wings and the eagle's hovering over a serpent?

For example, in Guadalupe Tepeyac (now a village empty of civilians and filled with soldiers), the herons took over a night sky in December. There were hundreds. "Thousands," claimed Lieutenant Ricardo, a Tzeltal insurgent who sometimes has a propensity to exaggerate. "Millions," said Gladys, who, despite being twelve years old (or precisely because of it), does not want to be left out. "They come every year," says the grandfather, while small flashes of white hover above the village and disappear, maybe bound for—the east?

Are they coming or going? Are they your herons, Mr. Berger? Perhaps a winged reminder? Or a greeting filled with premonition? A fluttering of wings of something that resists death?

Because, as it turns out, months later I read your letter (in a dog-eared clipping from a newspaper, the date hidden under a mud stain). And in it (your letter) the wings of dawn again are circling the sky, and the people of Guadalupe Tepeyac now live on the mountain and not in the little valley whose lights, I imagine, are of some significance on the navigation maps of the herons.

Yes, I know now that the herons about which you wrote me fly during the winter to North Africa, and that it is improbable that they have anything to do with those that arrived in December 1994 in the Lacandon Jungle. What's more, grandfather says that every year the disconcerting tour above Guadalupe Tepeyac is repeated. Perhaps southeastern Mexico is an obligatory layover, a necessity, a commitment. Perhaps they were not herons, but fragments of an exploded moon, pulverized in the jungle's December.

I. December 1994

MONTHS LATER, THE INDIGENOUS of southeastern Mexico again reiterated their rebellion, their unwillingness to disappear, to die . . . The reason? The supreme government decides to carry out the organized crime—essential to neoliberalism—that the god of modernity has planned: money. Many thousands of soldiers, hundreds of tons of war materials, millions of lies. The objective? The destruction of libraries and hospitals, of homes and fields seeded with corn and beans, the annihilation of every sign of rebellion. The indigenous Zapatistas resisted, they retreated to the mountains, and they began an exodus that today, even as I write these lines, has not ended. Neoliberalism disguises itself as the defense of a sovereignty that has been sold in dollars on the international market.

Neoliberalism, the doctrine that makes it possible for stupidity and cynicism to govern in diverse parts of the earth, does not allow participation other than to hold on by disappearing. "Die as a social group, as a culture, and above all as a resistance. Then you can be part of modernity," say the great capitalists, from their seats of government, to the indigenous campesinos. These indigenous people with their rebellion, their defiance, and their resistance irritate the modernizing logic of neomercantilism. It's irritated by the anachronism of their existence within the economic and political project of globalization, a project that soon discovers that poor people, that people in opposition—which is to say, the majority of the population—are obstacles. The Zapatista indigenous people's character, armed with, "We are here!" does not matter much to them; they lose no sleep over them. (A little fire and lead will be enough to end such "imprudent" defiance.) What matters to them, what bothers them, is their mere existence, and that the moment they speak out and are heard it becomes a reminder of an embarrassing omission by the "neoliberal modernity": "These Indians should not exist today; we should have put an end to them BEFORE. Now, annihilating them will be more difficult, which is to say, more expensive." This is the burden that weighs upon the born again neoliberal government in Mexico.

"Let's resolve the causes of the uprising," say the government's negotiators (the leftists of yesterday, the shamed of today), as if they were saying, "All of you should not exist; all of this is an unfortunate error of modern history." "Let's solve the problems" is an elegant synonym for "we will eliminate them." The campesinos, the indigenous, do not fit in the plans and projects of this system, which concentrates wealth and power and distributes death and poverty. They have to be gotten rid of, just like we have to get rid of the herons . . . and the eagles.

> *Mystery is not what can be hidden deliberately, but rather, as I have already shown, the fact that the gamut of the possible can always surprise us. And this is hardly ever represented. The campesinos do not present papers as do urban personalities. This is not because they are "simple" or more sincere or less astute; simply the space between that which is unknown of a person and what all the world knows of him—and this is the space of all representation—it is extremely small.*

—BERGER, *Boar Land*

II.

A COLD DAWN DRAGS itself between the fog and the thatched roofs of the village. It is morning. The dawn leaves, the cold remains. The little streets of mud begin to fill with people and animals. The cold and a small bench accompany me in the reading of *Boar Land*. Heriberto and Eva (five and six years old respectively) come and snatch the book. They look at the picture on the front cover (it is a Madrid edition from 1989). It is a copy of a painting by John Constable, an image of an English countryside. The drawing, Mr. Berger, elicits from them a quick connection between image and reality. For Heriberto, for example, there is no doubt that the horse in the painting is La Muñeca [The Doll]—a mare that accompanied us in the long year when the indigenous rebellion governed southeastern Mexico, which no one could mount except Manuel, a playmate who was twice the age, size, and weight of Heriberto, Chelita's brother and consequently also his future brother-in-law. And what Constable called "a river" is really a stream that passes through "La Realidad." ("La Realidad" is the name of the reality of the village of La Realidad, which is the outer reaches of Heriberto's horizons.) The most distant place that Heriberto's trips and running around have taken him is "La Realidad."

Constable's painting does not transport Heriberto and Eva to the English countryside. It does not take them outside the Lacandon Jungle. It leaves them here, or it brings them back. It brings them back to their land, their place, to their being children, to their being campesinos, to their being indigenous, to their being Mexicans and rebels. For Heriberto and Eva, Constable's painting is a colored drawing of La Muñeca and its title, *Scene on a Navigable River*, is not a valid argument: the river is the stream in "La Realidad," the horse is the mare La Muñeca, Manuel is riding it, and his hat has fallen off. That's it. On to another book. This time it is Van Gogh's turn, and for Eva and Heriberto, the Dutch man's paintings are scenes from their land, of their being indigenous and campesinos. After this, Heriberto tells his mother that he spent the morning with the Sup. "Reading grown-up books," says Heriberto, and believes that this earned him a free hand with a box of chocolate cookies. Eva is more farsighted, and asks me if I have a book about her doll with the little red bandanna.

III.

The act of writing is nothing more than the act of approximating the experience of what is being written about; in the same manner, it is hoped that the act of reading the written text is another act of similar approximation.

—BERGER, *Boar Land*

OR OF DISTANCING ONESELF, Mr. Berger. The writing and, above all, the reading of the written text could be an act of distancing. "The written word and the image," says my other self, who to make more problems imagines himself alone. I do think it's so, that the "reading" of the written word and the image could approximate the experience or create a distance. And so returns the photographic image of Alvaro, one of the dead in the battles at Ocosingo in January 1994. Alvaro returns in the photo; Alvaro speaks in the photograph with his death. He says, he writes, he shows: "I am Alvaro, I am indigenous, I am a soldier, I took up arms against being forgotten. Look. Listen. Something is happening in the dusk of the 20th century that is forcing us to die so we can have a voice, so we can be seen, so we can live." And through the photo of Alvaro dead, a reader, far away, from a distance, can come closer to the indigenous situation in modern Mexico, from NAFTA, from the international forums, from the economic bonanza, the first world.

"Pay attention! Something is wrong with macroeconomics plans, something is not working out in the complicated mathematical calculations that sing the praises of neoliberalism," says Alvaro with his death. His photo says more, his death speaks, his shoeless body on Chiapas soil calls out, his head resting in a pool of blood: "Look! This is what the numbers and the speeches hide. Blood, flesh, bones, lives and hopes crushed, squeezed dry, eliminated in order to be incorporated into the indexes of economic growth and profit. Come!" says Alvaro. "Come close! Listen!"

But Alvaro's photo also can "be read" as a distance, seen as a vehicle that serves to create more space in order to stay on the other side of the photo, like "reading" it in a newspaper in another part of the world. "This does not happen here," is the reader's take of the photo. "That is Chiapas, Mexico, it's a historical accident that can be fixed, can be forgotten, . . . is far away." There are, in addition, other readings that confirm it: public announcements, economic figures, stability, peace. That's what the indigenous war at the end of the century is good for, to give value to "peace," like a stain does the white cloth that suffers its blemish. "I am here, and this photo happened over there, far away, small," says the "reading" that creates distance.

And I imagine, Mr. Berger, that the end result of the relationship between the writer and the reader, through the text ("or from the image," insists my other self again), escapes both. Something is imposed on them, gives meaning to the text, provokes an approach or a distancing. And that "pause" has everything to do with the new division of the world, with the democratization of death and misery, with the dictatorship of power and money, with the regionalization of pain and despair, with the internationalization of arrogance and trade. But it also has to do with Alvaro's decision (and that of thousands of indigenous along with him) to take up arms, to fight, to resist, to seize the voice denied to them before, not to devalue the cost of blood that this implies.

And this too has to do with the ear and eye that are open to Alvaro's message, that see and hear it, that understand it, that draw near to him, to his death, to his blood that pools in the streets of a city that always ignored him, always . . . until this past January 1. And the eagle and the heron also have to do with this, and the European campesino who resists being subsumed, and the indigenous Latin American who rebels against being murdered. It also has to do with the powerful and the panic, the trembling, that is growing in their guts, no matter how strong and powerful they appear, when, without knowing, they prepare to fall . . . .

And, I reiterate and greet you this way, so do the letters that come from you to us, and those that with these lines and words reach you: the eagle received the message and understood the hesitant approach of the heron's flight. And there below, the serpent trembles and fears the morning . . . .

Vale, Mr. Berger. Health to you, and look closely; the heron up above can appear to be a small and mischievous cloud, a flower rising . . .

From the mountains of the Mexican Southeast
SUBCOMANDANTE INSURGENTE MARCOS

54

Dignity Cannot Be Studied; You Live It or It Dies

JULY 5, 1995

To Eric Jauffret,
France:

I have seen Siqueiros mask the children and incite the walls to rebellion, and Rivera free the enigmatic and anonymous and tender accomplice . . . .[1]

——ERIC JAUFFRET

ON THE OTHER HAND, I have seen our own cover their faces to show themselves to the world, and take off their ski masks to hide from the enemy. Take the recent arrival of additional government troops. One of the officials said good-bye to the townspeople and sent greetings to the Zapatistas. I will return in four months, he said. During those five months he looked for the Zapatistas and did not find them. "They have left the mountain and have come into the towns. We'll never be able to find them," says the official, explaining in his own way that he is involved in an absurd war where the enemy shows himself by hiding and hides by showing himself.

I've also seen that Beto (ten years old, going on eleven and a half and a quarter to twelve) has turned the world on its head. As proof, he sends me a drawing made with worn-out colored pencils where the ocean is the sky and the sky is the ocean. Beto is, in terms of work in the community, old now. He carries his share of firewood and has already complicated the life of one of the women in the peace camps. "What is the ocean about?" Beto asks, and has to seek his answer in a pile of books full of photos, drawings, and letters. The explanation begins answering the question that, according to the volunteer teacher, appears important: Is it a "he" or a "she"? Beto only wants to know if helicopters and planes can fly in the ocean. "No, they can't," the teacher answers and continues a complicated explanation about density, the laws of physics, aerodynamics, the chemical composition of H_2O, and other rules of grammar.

Beto sends a message with his uncle that among the demands of the EZLN there be one about raising the ocean to the sky and lowering the sky to the ocean. That way, Beto thinks, the ocean will be more democratic because everyone will be able to see it. And he, Beto, won't have to suffer through another long explanation just to learn that the ocean, like hope, is of the female gender.

Beto also says that he has a friend called Nabor. Nabor's father died on February 10, 1995, when the government sent its troops to recover the "national sovereignty." Mortally wounded, he was separated from his unit, which retreated in order not to confront the federal troops. Days later, hovering vultures pointed out where he lay. Beto has adopted Nabor and has shown him all he needs to know to survive in the Lacandon Jungle. Nabor is a fortunate student; we assume he has already kissed a *compañera*. "Hmm, delicious!" says Nabor as he brings his hand to his lips and gives it a mock kiss.

Nabor agrees with Beto that the sky should be below and the ocean above. A military helicopter overhead confirms it. Beto thinks the change will not be too complicated. They're both blue, right? Both big? Anyway, Nabor says it's simpler to change the world than for us to learn how to walk on our heads. For Beto and Nabor happiness would be stooping in order to see the sky.

Oh, I forgot. Nabor is three years old, and, as is obvious, over here each year is a decade and the classes for "responsible sex" should begin at age two . . .

But Mr. Jauffret, I am not writing to tell you about Beto's drawing or about his friend Nabor and his plans to turn the world upside down. I am writing to thank you for your letter and to tell you about our actual situation.

The indigenous peoples who support our just cause have decided to resist without surrender, without accepting the alms with which the supreme government hopes to buy them. And they have decided this because they have made theirs a word that is not understood with the head, that cannot be studied or memorized. It is a word that is lived with the heart, a word that is felt deep inside your chest and that makes men and women proud of belonging to the human race. This word is DIGNITY. Respect for ourselves, for our right to be better, for our right to struggle for what we believe in, for our right to live and die according to our ideals. Dignity cannot be studied; you live it, or it dies. It aches inside and teaches you how to walk. Dignity is that motherland that has no borders and that we often forget.

Our ideals are simple, and for that reason quite grand: we want, for all the men and women of this country, and of the entire world, three things that are fundamental for any human being: democracy, liberty, and justice. It can appear, and a powerful media certainly helps to perpetuate this image, that these three things are not the same thing for an indigenous person of the Mexican Southeast as for a European. But it is about the same thing: the right to have a good government, the right to think and act with a freedom that does not imply the slavery of others, the right to give and receive what is just.

For these three values—for democracy, liberty, and justice—we rose up in arms on January 1, 1994. For these three values, we resist today without surrender. Both things, the war and resistance, mean that these three values represent everything for us, represent a cause worth fighting for, worth dying for—so that life is worth living. We believe this cause is not only ours. It belongs to any honest man or woman in any part of the world. And for this reason we hope our voice will be heard throughout the world, so that our struggle will be understood by everyone. Our cause is not the cause of war, or the cause of destruction, or the cause of death. Our cause is that of peace, but peace with justice; it is the cause to build, but with equity and reason; it is the cause of life, but with dignity—always new and better.

Today, our situation is difficult. The war is dressed in its terrible suit of hunger, and entire communities suffer in conditions below the minimum level for survival. We willingly accept this not because we like martyrdom or sterile sacrifice. We accept it because we know that brothers and sisters the world over will know how to extend their hand to help us triumph in a cause that is theirs as well.

Like yesterday, when we covered our faces in order to show the world the true face of the Mexico of the basement and after washing with our blood the mirror in which Mexicans can see their own dignity, today we hide our faces to escape treachery and death which follow the steps of those who say they govern the country. We are not fighting with our weapons. Our example and our dignity now fight for us.

During the peace talks the government delegates have confessed that they have studied hard to learn about dignity and have been unable to understand it. They ask the Zapatista delegates to explain what is dignity. The Zapatistas laugh— after months of pain, they laugh. Their laughter echoes and escapes behind the high wall behind which arrogance hides its fear. The Zapatista delegates laugh even when the dialogue ends, and when they report what has happened. Everyone who hears them laughs, and the laughter recomposes faces that have been hardened by hunger and betrayal. The Zapatistas laugh in the mountains of the Mexican Southeast, and the sky cannot avoid the contagion of that laughter, and the peals of laughter resound. The laughter is so great that tears well up and it begins to rain, as though the laughter were a gift for the dry land . . . .

With so much laughter raining, who can lose? Who deserves to lose?

Vale, Mr. Jauffret. Health to you, and remember that "*Le monde est bleu comme une orange*" (The world is blue like an orange).

From the mountains of the Mexican Southeast,
SUBCOMANDANTE INSURGENTE MARCOS

NOTE

1. David Alfaro Siqueiros and Diego Rivera, together with Orozco, are considered Mexico's most illustrious twentieth-century muralists. Their work represents and glorifies the struggle for freedom of the Mexican people.

55

Letter to the Eureka Committee[1]

AUGUST 28, 1997
MEXICO

Canek says:

Boy, my son, it's a good thing the Pujuy bird is coming with us. We have to keep on moving, over-come our weariness, our fear and our yearning. Fatigue sneaks up on you. Weariness makes trav-elers sleepy, easily distracted, hopeless. Keep your eyes wide open, son, and follow the Pujuy bird. It will never steer you wrong. Its destiny is like ours: to walk so others won't get lost.

—EMILIO ABREU GOMEZ, *Canek: Historia y Leyenda de un Heroe Maya*

To the mothers and relatives of all the disappheared and political prisoners that we are

Ladies:
I WRITE TO YOU ON BEHALF of all the men, women, children and elders of the Zapatista National Liberation Army. The occasion for this bridge building to the history and dignity you represent is Eureka's twentieth anniversary.

The blood that's been terror's prisoner has found in you the hope that justice may someday correct the page of lies Power has written about the dead, disap-peared, and political prisoners in Mexico. A democracy of lies and cover-ups, of misery and repression for all of us below, has turned hypocrisy into Mexico's main instrument of foreign policy. The country that once took in with open arms the victims who'd managed to escape from their respective Latin American terrors now turns repression and authoritarianism into its favorite form of domestic policy.

Twenty years ago, not only was there impotence before the domestic terrorism against dissidents, not only was there farce and servitude as a means of political ascent, not only was there the impossibility of peaceful change, not only was there dignity trying to form a collective on the complicated roads of clandestine and armed revolutionary struggle, not only was there the strangled hope of jus-tice for all . . .

267

Twenty years ago, there was already rebelliousness,
there was the third dignity of the nonconformists,
there was the result in thoughts and words,
there was life as struggle,
there was prison, or death as the only other possibility,
there was victory as a reality for all.

Twenty years ago, there was also the dirty war,
there was the untouchable Power of the military and the police,
there was law as a useless ornament and justice as a papier-maché decoration,
there was the White Brigade as an argument for rebels,
there was Military Camp Number 1^2 as a destination for the noncompliant,
there was the vanished future for those who refused to surrender, to sell them-
    selves, to betray themselves, and were caught in the claws of Power.

Twenty years ago there was silence, the motherland stilling its pain for the torture
and death of the men and women—some of the best in our national history—
who were erased from life when Power answered their demands for democracy,
liberty, and justice.

Twenty years ago and today, the nightmare continues. To win, Power kills not
only life, but memory. Power offers oblivion to sanction its crimes.

Twenty years ago there was, as the Mayan hero Canek used to say, weariness,
fear, and fatigue.

Twenty years ago, there was hopelessness.

But you showed up. The new, tenacious Pujuy bird, now in skirts, has returned
to help us all overcome weariness, compliance and oblivion.

Because in the midst of oblivion, you remembered.
Because in the midst of immobility, you started to walk.
Because in the midst of silence, you screamed.
Because in the midst of despair, you hoped.

"They took them away alive! We want them back alive!" was and is your song that
began softly and soon grew loud, reaching all the way to the palaces of Power.
That amazing mixture of blood, dignity, rebelliousness, and history—all ordinary—began a movement that knows that resignation, forgiveness, and oblivion

are not limits. Men, women, children, young and old, began to make history into their strength, dignity into their road, hope into their blood, and reason into their rebelliousness.

Twenty years ago they began walking, gathering, meeting each other, recognizing each other, talking to each other, knowing each other as equals, building a collective.

Twenty years ago they began to shout, to demand, and to struggle, which were only other ways of having memory.

Twenty years ago they began to work together, and with everyone's pain and impotence, they made as one.

Twenty years ago, and hope goes on.

You struggled and continue to struggle so that the "Eureka!" of "We found them!" of "We liberated them!" may relieve the families who are not whole, because Power bit them in the most tender and deeply loved place: in their own blood, in their history, in their future.

Mothers and relatives of the disappeared and political prisoners:

> In the plain of Sibac, the henchmen caught Canek and his friends. One of the henchmen, named Malafacha, tied his hands.
> "Captain," said Canek. "You're going to run out of rope."
> Malafacha tightened his knot.
> "It's useless, Captain," added Canek. "You'll never have enough rope to tie up everyone's hands."
> Canek smiled. Blood trickled from his wrists like a docile flame.
> —GOMEZ, CANEK: *Historia y Leyenda de un Heroe Maya*

We too are a part of you; we too are your blood; we too are mothers and relatives of all the disappeared men and women, of all the political prisoners.

History has not ended. It journeys on, and its anonymous makers journey on— all of us below—forcing History to dawn once and for all.

Now and forever, together with you, we are the rebellious (not docile) flame that will help light the way to the future.

To your health, ladies of Eureka. Long live the dignified blood that gives you voice and memory!

Farewell. To your health, and may your voice and your light never be extinguished . . . so that others won't get lost . . . .

From the mountains of the Mexican Southeast
SUBCOMANDANTE INSURGENTE MARCOS

NOTES

1. The Eureka Committee, formed in 1978 by Rosario Ibarra to demand information about family members hauled into prison to disappear, never to be seen again, is similar in its function to Las Madres de la Plaza de Mayo in Buenos Aires, Argentina. It was the first Mexican human rights group.

2. Military Camp Number 1 in Mexico City was used as a prison during the student uprising of 1968. Many students, political prisoners, and urban guerrillas were incarcerated there, and some disappeared.

56

It Continues Raining Here

SEPTEMBER 8, 1998

To whom it may concern

Ladies and gentlemen:
THE RESPONSE TO THE INVITATION has already gone out. It continues raining here. The government only remembers Chiapas when it needs to make demagoguery or to improve its public image. Certainly Zedillo will come to the southeastern coast to hide the dead, to promise aid, to have photos taken, to repair croquettes, and to cover up omissions and negligence. For the rest, the rains have been here several days now, but Albores[1] is too busy in the boudoir to even think about an emergency plan. Here the government knows how to kill indigenous, but never how to keep them from dying. Meanwhile the army's planes and helicopters are making their flights over Zapatista communities . . . when they are freed up they will go to attend to the victims.

The rivers seem to be angry; with ferocity they are destroying weak bridges and roads that the government reports call "important infrastructure works" in the social spending in Chiapas. Why don't they go take a look at those works, whose inauguration they broadcasted so widely? Regardless, the rains do not watch television, nor do they respect the set design for operettas. As always, not until the deaths reach national and international news is there any sense of urgency to those forgetful ones whom we suffer as the government. This is how it is now with the indigenous in Mexico: they only exist and are named when they are dead.

Vale. Good health to you, and when will Chiapas exist on government maps not only when there are rebellions, deaths, or catastrophes?

From the mountains of Southeastern Mexico
SUBCOMANDANTE INSURGENTE MARCOS

P.S.

DESPITE INSIGNIFICANT AND irrelevant government reports, and as part of the great festivities, here is . . . the recurring postscript section!

271

P.S.

... WHERE IT RAINS AND GETS WET. Marshal "croquettas" albores[1] and his little soldiers are rubbing their hands together about the catastrophic rains battering the Chiapas coast. Millions of pesos will be sent to help the victims. Little or nothing will reach the hands of the needy ... But you can be sure you will now see Zedillo on the front page in photos and reports, trying to look serious, announcing rescue plans, declaring "calm-everything-is-under-control, children." Ah, poor Chiapas! The government wanting to forget about you, and the rains, which do not listen to government reports, come to beat down paths and memories ....

P.S.

WHICH SAYS WHAT IT SAYS. I was with pedrito one afternoon, both of us smoking (he a chocolate cigarette, and I a pipe), when I wanted to be like Old Don Antonio, and so I began to lecture Pedrito (a Tojolabal and two years old) about life and other painful treasures. And I began to tell him:

"Look, Pedrito, there are things you need to know about when you grow up. Important things like tying your boots, doing up your shirt without missing any buttons, getting comfortable in the hammock, lighting the pipe with the pot mouth down, and other etceteras that you will be learning about. But now we are going to talk about when a man loves a woman."

Pedrito was looking at me seriously, and he continued sucking on his chocolate cigarette. I suppose that I had then, as they say, "captured" his imagination, fand I continued: "Look, Pedrito, when a man loves a woman ... because it's not the same as when a woman loves a man, or when a man loves another man, or when a woman loves another woman, because there is a bit of everything, and it's necessary to know and to understand it. Well, when a man loves a woman ... well, it's not that easy to explain as, say, what you need to do so you have no extra buttons when you've buttoned up your shirt, which can be a complicated thing if you don't pay attention and do it with care. For example, I use a 'from the bottom up' technique, which, in addition to being a concept of political science, is very good for buttoning up. Look, you put on the shirt and look down to the bottom end of the shirt, seriously and with concentration."

Pedrito frowned and looked at me seriously.

"Like that! Good, then you line up the lower edges of the shirt, the right at the same level as the left, which is not as simple as the 'centrists' in politics make it appear. Here, if you aren't careful, the left side could be higher, which wouldn't be an issue, however, the right side could be higher, in which case it would be *very* regrettable indeed. The balance is very important; they must be even. Then you have to look for the bottom button on the shirt, but the bottom button isn't always the last one. You should know this, Pedrito, there are some evil shirt manufacturers who put on an extra button (to replace a button if you lose one, they say) for the obvious purpose of making this indispensable garment difficult to button. Good, now that you've found the last button, keep on looking for the corresponding buttonhole (*double-entendre* fanciers, refrain), something that is more difficult to find than any reference to Chiapas in a Zedillo report. As you will learn later on, *you'll never lack a ripped seam for a buttonhole.* That could be, but what is certain is that there are more buttons than buttonholes, as you will see when you skip buttons.

"Certainly there are other techniques for not missing buttons. There is, for example, the Sea's method, who puts on shirts as if they were T-shirts. That is, she does not undo the buttons. Ergo, there are no missing buttons. However, I do not recommend that technique because . . . Well, because the Sea and etceteras, and I was explaining to you that when a man loves a woman . . . So, you see now, Pedrito, that it is very difficult to explain how it is when a man loves a woman, but, nonetheless, it's very important to understand it, because . . ."

While I was explaining, Pedrito ate his cigarette. "Cocate," he said to me, stretching out his hand, asking me in his dialect for more chocolates. "There aren't any," I told him. He turned around and left. It's obvious that today's youth has no interest in important issues (sigh). Where was I? Ah, yes! When a man loves a woman . . .

Vale again. Health to you, and wishes that it stops raining in history.

SUP THE ARCHER, LEADER OF THE GORGONITES

P.S.

DECEMBER 23, 1995

WHICH SPEAKS OF LOVE, OF NO LOVE, AND OTHER NUISANCES. La toñita arrives to show off her new teacup. Without warning, she comes out with—

"Love is like a teacup that every day falls to the ground and breaks to pieces. In the morning the pieces are gathered, and with a little wet and a little warmth, the pieces are glued together, and again there is a little teacup. He who is in love spends life fearing that the terrible day will come when the teacup is so broken that it can no longer be mended."

She leaves just as she arrived, reiterating her refusal to give me a kiss, that now more than ever "really prickles."

NOTE

1. Marcos often refers to Roberto Albores Guillén, the repressive governor of Chiapas, as Croquetas Arbores; croquetas are a type of dog food.

57

Democratic Teachers and the Zapatista Dream

This is the tree of the emancipated.
The earth tree, the cloud tree.
The bread tree, the arrow tree,
the fist tree, the fire tree.
The stormy water of our nocturnal
epoch floods it,
but its mast balances
the arena of its might.

—Pablo Neruda, *"The Liberators," Canto General*

THE OLDEST OF THE OLD ones say the world holds itself over the abyss of oblivion by the grace of the ceiba tree. The first gods, the greatest gods, set the world above the mother tree. With colors, words, and songs, the first gods made the world. When it was finished, the gods didn't know where to leave the world so they could then go off to sing and dance, because these gods were very musical and quite the dancers, those gods who gave birth to the world, the very first. And the first gods could find no place to put the world.

Then the gods held an assembly to reach an agreement, and yes, it took some time, but no one noticed because the world had just been born and the time for time hadn't yet come. The gods of the beginning reached their accord and called on the mother ceiba so that she could keep the world over her head, and they hung it over her highest boughs, and she kept quiet so the world wouldn't be frightened.

What I am telling you happened long ago, so long ago that it came to pass that men and women forgot and, afraid of being unable to explain the location of the world in the schools, invented stories of black holes, "big bangs," solar systems, galaxies, universes, and other absurdities that fill the geography books we put up with in all the schools.

Everyone forgot, but not quite everyone.

The first gods were knowing, and they saw clearly that everyone would forget how the world had been born and where it was. That is why they wrote down the entire history of how the world was made and even made a map so that it would be clear where the world was. The greatest gods—those who gave birth to the world, the very first—wrote everything in their school notebooks.

And then the gods searched for someplace to put the notebook where the story of how the world was made was written and the map of where the world was drawn.

The gods argued a lot over where to put the notebook, and then they held another assembly to reach an accord.

And then they called on the men and women of maize, the true ones, and they told them the story of how the world was born, and they explained to them the place where it was; and so that they could remember it even if it was forgotten, they put some notes down on a little piece of paper and folded it with many creases like an accordion, and tucked it away in one of the scars that cover the bark of the ceiba.

The first gods went off to their dancing and their singing. And—long after the echo of marimbas, guitars, and *zapateados* had faded away—the mother ceiba stood firm supporting the world so it wouldn't fall and so it would stay in its place.

Ever since then, the world has been where it is. The ceiba keeps it far from the night of the worst death, the most terrible, that of oblivion.

The world is above the mother ceiba. But winds from above have assaulted it time and again throughout history, trying to make it fall into the obscurity of despair.

Not few have been the times the world has been at the point of being lost. From all sides, the winds of Power have hurled wars, catastrophes, crises, dictators, neoliberal fashions, promanagement teachers' leaders, corrupt governments, assassins in government posts, criminals disguised as presidential aspirants, institutional revolutionary parties, NATOs, and private television stations. Thousands and thousands of nightmares blowing their terrors on all sides, trying to bring down the world from the lofty grace of the mother ceiba.

But the world has resisted, and it hasn't fallen. True men and women from all the worlds that make up the world have become trunk and branches and leaves and roots next to the mother ceiba so the world will not fall, to resist, to be created anew, to make themselves new.

Terrible have been the struggles between those of above and those of below, between the powerful and the dispossessed. Much has been written of the reasons and causes for these clashes. The truth is, they all have the same foundation: the powerful want to bring down the world the ceiba holds up; those of below want to keep the world and memory, because that is where the dawn comes from.

The powerful fight against humanity.

The dispossessed fight and dream for humanity.

This is the true history. And if it does not appear in primary school textbooks, that is because history is still being written by those above, even though it is made by those below.

But even though it's not part of the official curricula, the story of the birth of the world and the map that explains where it is, is still held in the scars of the mother ceiba.

The eldest of the elders of the communities entrusted the secret to the Zapatistas. In the mountain, they spoke with them and told them where the note was left by the first gods, those who gave birth to the world, so memory wouldn't be lost.

Ever since, because they were born without faces, without names, and without individual pasts, the Zapatistas have been students of the story taught by the land. One dawn in the year 1994, the Zapatistas became teachers; consulting the old note of memory, they could teach how the world was born and show where it is to be found.

That is why the Zapatistas are students and teachers. That is why teachers are Zapatistas, even though the reason is hidden behind the thousand centuries in which dignity has existed.

In one of the corners of the Aguascalientes of La Realidad, the ceiba presides, watches over, encourages, and shelters the dizzy coming and going of men and women.

There are days when no one walks on this ground, but on other mornings it is covered with men and women of all colors, sizes, and tastes, who speak and laugh and worry and dance and sing and talk and make accords, although not always, and yes, they always meet each other.

In the solitary dawns of La Realidad, when some cloud is given itself to weeping at wet-length, when it is raining hardest above and below, you can see someone left behind among the shadows, always faceless, who approaches the mother ceiba and looks for a little piece of paper among the damp scars of history. Trembling he finds it, trembling he opens it, trembling he reads it, and trembling he returns it to its place.

That something written on the little piece of paper is an enormous burden, which frees the person who carries it. It is a work, a mission, a task, something to do, a path to walk, a tree to plant and nurture, a dream to look after.

Perhaps the little piece of paper speaks of a world where all worlds fit and grow, where the differences of color, culture, size, language, sex, and history don't serve to exclude, persecute, or classify, where the variety may once and for all break the grayness now stifling us.

Who knows?

There is something about that little piece of paper—I don't know if it's an optical illusion or one of those hallucinations that abound in the mountains of the Mexican Southeast—but you could swear that the shadow is smiling now, yes, a smile like a glow . . .

Brothers and sisters, democratic teachers:

WELCOME TO THE FIRST "Democratic Teachers and the Zapatista Dream" *encuentro.*

Welcome to La Realidad, to that which suffers and dreams, to that which patiently waits for something good, more just, more free, more democratic. To Mexico's La Realidad, which dreams not of the best of all possible worlds, but dreams and deserves a tomorrow.

This is our dream—the Zapatista paradox—one that takes away sleep. The only dream that is dreamed awake, sleepless. The history that is born and nurtured from below.

Democratic teachers:

WELCOME TO SLEEPLESS La Realidad, sleepless because it stays awake for the Zapatista dream.

Democracy!

Liberty!

Justice!

From the mountains of the Mexican Southeast

SUBCOMANDANTE INSURGENTE MARCOS

P.S. . . . REGARDING REDUNDANCY.

IN REALITY, SINCE WE are in La Realidad, "Democratic Teachers" is an unnecessary redundancy. To be a teacher is to be democratic. Those who aren't democratic aren't teachers; they scarcely attain the rank of dog-riding cowboys.

58

Closing Words at the National *Encuentro*
in Defense of the Cultural Heritage

I scatter flowers of war, I of the smiling face
For I come with war.
I am the quetzal and I come flying,
Through strait ways, I come with war.
I am the beautiful black bird with the red neck,
I come flying: I come to turn into a flower,
I, into the bloodstained rabbit.
Look at me, I'm serious now; gird your sides.
I, whose eyes wink, who goes smiling.
I come from within the flowered courtyard.
Look at me, I mean it; gird your sides.
I m going to turn into a flower,
I, into the bloodstained rabbit.

—NAHUATL POEM

Being what they were, eves and charged memories are more real than the intangible present. The
eve of a voyage is a precious part of the trip.

—JORGES LUIS BORGES

AUGUST ONCE AGAIN, and once again dawn. The sea is asleep, and a small wisp of cloud, its white weariness reposing above the mountain, once again begins its flight; its flutter disturbs but does not awaken the stars. Up above, the great serpent bleeds blue pearls of light. The Moon, a lady, has just finished washing her face, and she appears at her balcony and is uncertain whether the cloud is taking flight flying, or staying standing. Below, beside a candle, a shadow guards the night and memory. Another shadow approaches him, and a flame momentarily illuminates two faceless faces; shadows, then, of shadows.

The cloud that was rising in flight hesitates a bit, the illuminated drip from the serpent of light ceases, the midnight sun becomes a far-off torch, the moon stands still at her window, and even a falling star neither falls nor rises. Everything is quiet, still.

Attention! Listen! Now the word reigns . . . .

Brothers and sisters, participants in the National Encuentro in Defense of the Cultural Heritage:

WE ACKNOWLEDGE THE END of this first meeting in defense of memory. We know others will follow, and that this has just been the first of many more *encuentros* and accords that will have to be built among those who are resisting the buying and selling of Mexico's cultural heritage.

These have been difficult and beautiful days. Perhaps that is just how it is. The government—all of you know this now—is still attacking the indigenous Zapatista communities, and it is still going forward with its war. In attacking us, the government knows it is attacking memory. That is the reason for its stubbornness, cruelty, and arrogance. What is at stake in these lands isn't negligible; it is what saw you throughout these days and nights, speaking, discussing, agreeing, disagreeing, singing, and dancing, which is how true *encuentros* are made.

It has been a great honor for us to have met you, and it has been an honor for us to see you sharing the pain and suffering, the indignation and outrage over this new military attack against the Zapatista peoples. What the government did was remind everyone that there is a war going on here, that there is an entire rebel people resisting, and that there is an occupation army—the federal army—trying to guarantee the merchandise that those who govern and command have already sold. The merchandise has a name; it's called "national sovereignty."

It is not the first time blows have sought to make us silent. It is not the first time they have failed. Now, as well as our silence, the blows seek to sever us from the main resistance movements in the country: the UNAM university students, who are defending the right to a free education; the Mexican Electricians Union, who are defending the electric industry; and yours, the communities from the National School of Anthropology and History and from the National Institute of Anthropology and History, as well as all the persons and organizations who make up the National Front in Defense of the Cultural Heritage. All these movements and ours have something in common: the defense of history. Because of that, every attack against one of these movements is an attack against all the others.

At least, that is how we understand it. That is why we feel that the repression against the UNAM students last August 5 was also against us. That is why we have supported the mobilizations and calls of the SME.[1] That is why we have joined you in defense of memory and against attempts to privatize the cultural heritage.

Over the last few days, we have received some notes and letters. The *compañeros* have been collecting them in a little cardboard box. We read everything they had to say. That is why, I believe, they say there are little talking boxes here. There are requests for interviews, for meetings, doubts, requests for meetings to exchange experiences, questions. The intense, difficult nature of these days has kept us from dealing with them by giving each and every one of them the response they require. We hope you will forgive us and accept our promise to answer them when and where we can.

Among these papers, there is one that asks what the Zapatistas want. It maintains that a lot of information has been manipulated by the media, distorting what is happening here and the path that moves and inspires us.

This is the month of August, and for us it is also the month of memory. So I will try to respond a bit to the question: "What do the Zapatistas want?"

Now, it is not going to be easy for the media to understand us. For some strange reason, the Zapatistas speak to the future. I mean our words don't fit in the present, but are made to fit into the puzzle that is yet to be finished. Therefore, patience is a guerrilla virtue.

It was fifteen years ago that I first came to these mountains. It was then, in one of the guerrilla camps, that I was told a story at dawn—as was mandated—of fifteen years before. In this August that soaks us, thirty years will have gone by. Now, I will tell it to you just as it comes back to me. Perhaps it won't be in exactly the same words, but I'm sure it will be in the same spirit as that of the man who related it to me—between jokes about my pathetic appearance and the clown pants I was wearing—when he welcomed me to the Zapatista National Liberation Army.

To Plant the Tree of Tomorrow

THERE IS A STORY TOLD that, in a certain town, men and women toiled away at their work to survive. Every day the men and women went out to their respective jobs: the men to the corn and bean fields, the women to fetch firewood and water. Sometimes, there was work that brought them together as equals. For example, men and women would join together to harvest the coffee when its time had come. And so things went.

But there was one man who didn't live like that. He worked all right, but not in the corn and bean fields, or on the coffee plantations when the beans reddened among their branches. No, this man worked planting trees on the mountain. The trees this man planted would not grow fast; each one took entire decades to grow and send out all its branches and leaves. The other men laughed at this man and found no little fault with him.

"Why work for things you will never see finished? It is better to work in the fields that give you a crop in a few months instead of planting trees that will only be grown after you are already dead. You are a fool or crazy, because you work for nothing."

The man defended himself, saying, "Yes, it is true I won't see these trees full grown, full of branches, leaves and birds, nor will my eyes see children playing under their shade. But if all of us work for just the present day and the day after that, who will plant the trees our descendants are going to need to have shelter, comfort, and joy?"

No one understood him. The crazy man, or fool, kept planting trees he would never see full grown, and sensible men and women kept planting and working for the present. Time passed, and they all died, and their children carried on their work, and they were followed by the children of their children.

One morning, a group of boys and girls went out for a walk and found a place filled with huge trees, with a thousand birds living in them and their great branches giving shade from the heat and shelter from the rain. Indeed, they found an entire mountainside dense with trees. The boys and girls went back to their town, speaking of this marvelous place.

The men and women gathered together and went there and were filled with wonder. "Who planted this?" they asked. Nobody knew. They asked their elders and they didn't know either. Only one old one, the oldest in that community, could give them the information, and he told them the story of the crazy man and fool.

The men and women assembled and had a discussion. They saw and understood the man who their ancestors had dealt with so harshly, and they admired that man very much and were fond of him. They knew that memory can travel very far and arrive where no one can guess. The men and women of that day went to the place of the great trees. They made a circle around one great tree in the middle of the grove, and put a sign on it in colored letters. There, they held a fiesta. Dawn was already approaching when the last dancers were leaving to go to sleep. The great forest was left alone in silence. It rained. When the sky cleared the Moon came out, and the Milky Way reshaped its twisting body one more time. Suddenly a ray of moonlight insinuated itself among the great branches and leaves of the tree in the middle, and by its faint light you could read the sign of colors that had been left there:

To the first ones
Those who came later understood.
Health to you.

What I am recounting to you was told to me fifteen years ago, and fifteen years had gone by when what they told me had come to pass. And yes, perhaps it is pointless to say it in words because we say it with deeds; but still, those who came later did understand.

And if I am telling you this story, it is not just to give our regards to the first ones, nor is it just to make you a gift of a little piece of that memory that seems lost and forgotten. No, not just for those things, but also to try to answer the question of what the Zapatistas want.

To plant the tree of tomorrow, that is what we want. We know that in these frenetic times of "realistic" politics, of fallen banners, of polls substituting for democracy, of neoliberal criminals who call for crusades against what they are hiding and what feeds them, of chameleon-like metamorphoses, saying we want to plant the tree of tomorrow sounds foolish and crazy; but nevertheless, to us it is not a phrase born of drama or obsolete utopianism.

We know all that, and nevertheless, that is what we want. And that is what we are doing. How many people in the worlds that make up the world can say as we do, that they are doing what they want to? We think there are many, that the worlds of the world are filled with crazy and foolish people each planting their trees for each of their tomorrows, and that the day will come when this mountainside of the universe that some call Planet Earth will be filled with trees of all colors, and there will be so many birds and comforts that . . . yes, it is likely no one will remember the first ones, because all the yesterdays which vex us today will be no more than an old page in the old book of the old history.

The tree of tomorrow is a space where everyone is, where the other knows and respects the other others, and where the false light loses its last battle. If you press me to be precise, I would tell you it is a place with democracy, liberty, and justice: that is the tree of tomorrow.

This is what the Zapatistas want. It might seem I've been vague in my answer, but I haven't. I have never spoken so clearly before. In any case, times will come in which these words will fit, and together their embrace will expand, and they'll be heard and guarded, and they'll grow. That is what the words are for, and yes, also those who go speak them.

Memory Has Its Own Reality

Brothers and sisters:

IT MIGHT SEEM ODD THAT I'm bringing together a Nahuatl poet, the Popul Vuh, and Jorge Luis Borges for this closing. Especially Borges. And although I could say that this month is the one hundredth anniversary of his birth, that is not the reason why he is sharing space with our most ancient wise ones and storytellers. No, it so happens that a book reached my beat-up desk. The wind had played with it and opened it to the page headed "August 22, 1983." I don't know if August was insinuating itself into my memory in this way, but the fact is that nature was imitating art, and the words at the top of this piece of writing with the Nahuatl poem, jumped out from that page. Perhaps Borges came so we can remember that our cultural heritage is not just one thing and that everything has something of the universal. Or perhaps he only came to tell us in his own way that memory has its own reality, like the memory of La Realidad that today joins us together. Or perhaps he only came so that he might tell us all that, in effect, this is just the eve of a long voyage, and that therefore the voyage has already begun.

In the end, we know—and that is why we are here—that the fangs of the false light will fall, and, with stones and grains of maize, a tree will grow in any place in any world. And, even if no one then will have memory, the tree will know that the first ones were necessary and kept their word.

Meanwhile, the soil will still have to be readied. We will have to learn to let time take its time and, despite the stupid olive drab, continue the struggle so that the word becomes bridge and stone and maize and tree and the hope of tomorrow. All that and more is what the Zapatistas are and what they want.

Vale. Health to you, and although it looks like we are defending the past, in reality, in La Realidad, we have agreed to defend tomorrow.

Democracy!

Liberty!

Justice!

From the mountains of the Mexican Southeast
BY THE CLANDESTINE REVOLUTIONARY INDIGENOUS COMMITTEE
GENERAL COMMAND OF THE ZAPATISTA ARMY OF NATIONAL LIBERATION
SUBCOMANDANTE INSURGENTE MARCOS

La Realidad, awake.

NOTE

1. SME (Sociedad Mexicana de Electricistas) is an electrician's union.

SECTION III
Creating Memory

...includes the writings that most express Marcos´ sense of playfulness, personal reflection, and humor—but also tales that assert age-old community beliefs, perspectives, and orientations as active and living currents in the fabric of present-day Mexico, and humanity as a whole. Through the characters of the beetle Durito, Old Don Antonio, the Sea, and the ancient gods of indigenous lore, Marcos fashions tales from the deeper forces that shape and inform the Zapatistas´ revolutionary project—the human frailty, tenderness, inventiveness, indomitable sense of dignity, longing to connect, and demand for freedom that centers their resistance and advances their movement for democratic "otherness," openness, and autonomy.

PART ONE

TALES FOR A SLEEPLESS SOLITUDE—
The Stories of Don Durito

59

Ten Years Later: Durito Found Us Again

DECEMBER 25, 1995

IN THE BREATHLESS SOLITUDE of the first years of the Zapatista uprising, a peculiar fellow appeared at our camp; a little smoking beetle, very well read and an even better talker, who gave himself the task of giving his company to a soldier, el Sup.

Legally named Nebuchadnezzar, this beetle, traveling incognito, goes under the *nom de guerre* Durito, because of his hard shell. Durito, like all children, has a thick skin, and it's for that very reason that he chose the child we all have inside—whom we've completely forgotten because it shames us—as his primary interlocutor.

Early one morning ten years later, toward the end of our retreat from February's military treachery, Durito found us again, and again touched the best in us: our astounding capacity for human tenderness, and our hope of growing better together with others.

Sometimes a detective, sometimes a political analyst, sometimes a knight-errant as well as a writer of epistles, Durito addresses us, holding up for us a mirror to the future, showing us what might be.

In the still darkness, help comes to breasts gone tight with fear of the unknown. Durito opens a wound in our breast—a painful wound—that lets us draw our breath.

The self-dubbed knight-errant has returned with a new title: Don Durito of the Lacandon. This little beetle has traveled the roads of the world, righting wrongs, rescuing damsels in distress, healing the sick, aiding the weak, instructing the ignorant, humbling the mighty, and exalting the humble. The greatest knight-errant the world has ever seen, Don Durito of the Lacandon lives, still amazing the stars that find him back in the jungle's night. News of his deeds has circled the world. Millions of women sigh for him, thousands of men speak his name with respect, and hundreds of thousands of children worship him.

Don Durito shares some of his thoughts with us, recounting his adventures—a thousand and one nights of harrowing tales—that teach and lighten the endless, breathless nights of the Mexican Southeast.

Durito will be ten years old this month, December 1995. He's anxious for the results of the intergalactic convention that met to determine whether he would keep dazzling us with his wonders, or would be lost among the countless footpaths of the mountains of the Mexican Southeast.

Today, December 25, 1995, we salute the best and greatest practitioner of knight-errantry: Don Durito.

From the mountains of the Mexican Southeast
SUBCOMANDANTE INSURGENTE MARCOS

60

To Mariana Moguel (age ten)

APRIL 10, 1994

Subcomandanta Mariana Moguel:

I GREET YOU WITH RESPECT and congratulate you for the new rank you have acquired with your drawing. Permit me to tell you a story that, perhaps, you will understand someday. It is the story of . . . Durito . . .

I AM GOING TO TELL YOU a story that came to me a little while back. It is the story of a small beetle who wears glasses and smokes a pipe. I met him one day as I was looking for my tobacco and I couldn't find it. Suddenly, on one side of my hammock, I saw that a bit of tobacco had fallen to the ground and formed a small trail. I followed to see where the tobacco thread was going, and to see who the hell had taken it and spilled it. A few meters away, behind a rock, I found a beetle sitting at a little desk, reading some papers and smoking a tiny pipe.

"Ahem, ahem," I said, so that the beetle would notice my presence, but he paid no attention to me. Then I said: "Listen, that tobacco is mine."

The beetle took off his glasses, looked me up and down, and told me angrily: "Please, Captain, I beseech you. Do not interrupt me. Don't you realize that I am studying?"

I was a bit surprised and was going to give him a good kick, but I calmed myself and sat down to one side to wait for him to finish studying. In a little while, he gathered up his papers, put them away in the desk, and chewing on his pipe, said to me: "Well, now, what may I do for you, Captain?"

"My tobacco," I replied.

"Your tobacco?" he asked. "You want me to give you a little?"

I was beginning to get pissed off, but the little beetle passed me the bag of tobacco with his little foot and added: "Don't be angry, Captain. Please understand that you can't get tobacco around here, so I had to take some of yours."

I calmed down. The beetle was growing on me and I told him, "Don't worry about it. I've got more around somewhere."

"Hmm," he answered.

"And you, what is your name?" I asked him.

"Nebuchadnezzar," he said, and continued, "but my friends call me Durito. You can call me Durito, Captain."

I thanked him for the courtesy and asked him what he was studying.

"I'm studying neoliberalism and its strategy of domination for Latin America," he answered.

"And what good is that to a beetle?" I asked him.

He replied, very annoyed, "What good is it?! I have to know how long your struggle is going to last, and whether or not you are going to win. Besides, a beetle should care enough to study the situation of the world in which he lives, don't you think, Captain?"

"I don't know," I said. "But why do you want to know how long our struggle will last, and whether or not we are going to win?"

"Well, you haven't understood a thing," he told me, putting on his glasses and lighting his pipe. After letting out a puff of smoke, he continued: "We beetles need to know how long we are going to have to make sure that you do not squash us with your big boots."

"Ah!" I said.

"Hmm," he said.

"And what conclusion have you come to in your study?" I asked him.

He took out the papers from his desk and began to leaf through them. "Hmm . . . hmm," he said, every so often, as he reviewed them. After having finished, he looked me in the eye and said, "You are going to win."

"I already knew that," I told him. "But how long will it take?"

"A long time," he said, sighing with resignation.

"I already knew that, too . . . Don't you know exactly how long?" I asked.

"It's uncertain. Many things must be taken into account: the objective conditions, the ripeness of the subjective conditions, the correlation of forces, the crisis of imperialism, the crisis of socialism, etcetera, etcetera."

"Hmm," I said.

"What are you thinking about, Captain?"

"Nothing," I answered. "Well, Mr. Durito, I have to go. It was a pleasure to have met you. And you may take all the tobacco you want, whenever you like."

"Thank you, Captain. You can be informal with me if you like."

"Thank you, Durito. Now I'm going to give orders to my *compañeros* that it is forbidden to step on beetles. I hope that is of some help."

"Thank you, Captain. Your order will be very useful to us."

"But regardless, be very careful, because my boys are very distracted, and they don't always watch where they are going."

"I'll see to that, Captain."

"See you later."

"See you later. Come whenever you like, and we'll talk."

"I'll do that," I told him, and went back to headquarters.

That's all, Mariana. I hope to meet you personally someday, and to be able to trade ski masks and drawings.

Vale. Health to you, and more color pens, because the ones you used surely must have run out of ink.

From the mountains of the Mexican Southeast
SUBCOMANDANTE INSURGENTE MARCOS

61

The Glass to See to the Other Side

FEBRUARY-MAY 1995

CUT FROM THE INVERSE side, a mirror ceases to be a mirror and becomes a glass. Mirrors are for looking on this side, and glass is made to look to the other side.
Mirrors are made to be etched.
A glass is made to be broken . . . to cross to the other side . . .

From The Mountains of southeast Mexico
SUBCOMANDANTE INSURGENTE MARCOS

P.S.
. . . THE IMAGE OF THE REAL or the unreal, which searches among so many mirrors, for a glass to break.

Durito

DAWN. MEXICO CITY. Durito wanders through the streets adjoining the Zocalo. Sporting a small trench coat and a hat angled like Humphrey Bogart in *Casablanca*, Durito pretends to pass unnoticed. His outfit and slow crawl are unnecessary, as he sticks to the shadows that escape the bright display windows. Shadow of the shadow, silent walk, angled hat, a dragging trench coat, Durito walks at dawn through Mexico City. No one notices him. They do not see him, not because he is well disguised or because of that tiny, quixotic detective outfit from the 1950s, or because he is barely distinguishable from the mounds of garbage. Durito walks amid papers being dragged here and there by a whisk of the unpredictable winds that populate the dawns of Mexico City. No one sees Durito, for the simple reason that in this city no one sees anyone.

"This city is sick," Durito writes to me; "It is sick from loneliness and fear. It is a great collective of solitudes. It is a collection of cities, one for each resident. It's not about sums of anguish (do you know of a loneliness without anguish?), but about a potency; each loneliness is multiplied by the number of lonely people that surround it. It is as though each person's solitude entered a House of Mirrors, like those you see in the country fairs. Each solitude is a mirror that reflects another solitude, and like a mirror, bounces off more solitudes."

Durito has begun to discover that he is in foreign territory, that the city is not his place. In his heart and in this dawn, Durito packs his bag. He walks this road as though taking inventory, a last caress, like a lover who knows this is good-bye. At certain moments, the sound of footsteps diminishes and the cry of the sirens, which frightens outsiders, increases. And Durito is one of those outsiders, so he stops on the corner each time the red-and-blue blinking lights crisscross the street. Durito takes advantage of the complicity of a doorway in order to light a pipe guerrilla-style: a tiny spark, a deep breath, and the smoke engulfing his gaze and face. Durito stops. He looks and sees. In front of him, a display window catches his eye. Durito comes near and looks through the great glass pane to what exists beyond it. Mirrors of all shapes and sizes, porcelain and glass figurines, cut crystal, tiny music boxes. "There are no talking boxes," Durito says to himself, without forgetting the long years spent in the jungle of the Mexican Southeast.

Durito has come to say good-bye to Mexico City and has decided to give a gift to this city, about which everyone complains and no one abandons. A gift. This is Durito, a beetle of the Lacandon Jungle in the center of Mexico City.

Durito says good-bye with a gift.

He makes an elegant magician's gesture. Everything stops. The lights go out like a candle extinguished by a gentle wind-lick on its face. Another gesture and a reflecting light illuminates a music box in the display window. A ballerina in a fine lilac costume holds an endless stillness, hands crossed overhead, legs held together, balanced on tiptoes. Durito tries to imitate the position, but promptly gets his many arms entangled. Another magic gesture, and a piano, the size of a cigarette box, appears. Durito sits in front of the piano and puts a jug of beer on top—who knows where he got it from, but it's already half empty. He cracks and flexes his fingers, doing digital gymnastics just like the pianists in the movies. Then he turns toward the ballerina and nods his head. The ballerina begins to stir and makes a bow. Durito hums an unknown tune, beats a rhythm with his little legs, closes his eyes, and begins to sway.

The first notes begin. Durito plays the piano with four hands. On the other side of the glass pane, the ballerina begins to twirl and gently lifts her right thigh. Durito leans on the keyboard and plays furiously. The ballerina performs her best steps within the prison of the little music box. The city disappears. There is nothing but Durito at his piano and the ballerina in her music box. Durito plays, and the ballerina dances. The city is surprised; its cheeks blush as when one receives an unexpected gift, a pleasant surprise, good news. Durito gives his best gift: an unbreakable and eternal mirror, a good-bye that is harmless, that heals, that cleanses. The spectacle lasts only a few instants. The last notes fade as the cities that populate this city take shape again. The ballerina returns to her uncomfortable immobility; Durito turns up the collar of his trench coat and makes a slight bow toward the display window.

"Will you always be behind the glass pane?" Durito asks her and asks himself. "Will you always be on the other side of my over here, and will I always be on this side of your over there?"

Health to you and until always, my beloved malcontent. Happiness is like a gift; it lasts for a moment, and it is worth it.

Durito crosses the street, arranges his hat and continues to walk. Before going around the corner, he turns toward the display window. A star-shaped hole adorns the glass. The alarms are ringing uselessly. Behind the window, the ballerina is no longer in the music box . . . .

"This city is sick. When its illness becomes a crisis, it will be cured. This collective loneliness, multiplied by millions and empowered, will end by finding itself and finding the reason for its powerlessness. Then, and only then, will this city shed its gray dress and adorn itself with brightly colored ribbons, which are so abundant in the provinces.

"This city lives a cruel game of mirrors, but the game of the mirrors is useless and sterile if finding the transparency of glass is not a goal. It is enough to understand this and, as who-knows-who said, struggle and begin to be happy . . . .

"I'm coming back. Prepare the tobacco and the insomnia. I have a lot to tell you, Sancho." Durito signs off.

It is morning. A few piano notes accompany the day that comes and Durito, who leaves. To the west, the sun is like a rock, shattering the glass pane of the morning . . . .

Vale once again. Health to you, and leave surrender to the empty mirrors.

EL SUP, GETTING UP FROM THE PIANO AND, CONFUSED BY SO MANY MIRRORS, LOOKING FOR THE EXIT DOOR . . . OR IS IT THE ENTRANCE?

62

Deep Inside the Cave of Desire

MARCH 17, 1995

I WAS LISTENING ON THE little tape player to that tune by Stephen Stills, from the album *Four Way Street*, that goes—

Find the cost of freedom,
buried in the ground.
Mother Earth will swallow you,
lay your body down . . . .

—when my other self comes running and tells me:

"It looks like you got what you deserved . . . "

"Could it be the PRI has already fallen?" I ask with hope.

"No, man! . . . They killed you," says my other self.

"Me! When? Where?" I ask, while I search my memory for where I've been and what I've done.

"Today, in a confrontation . . . but they don't say exactly where," he responds.

"Oh, good! . . . And did I end up badly hurt or really dead?" I insist.

"Really dead . . . that's what it says in the news," explains my other self and then leaves.

A narcissistic sob competes with the crickets.

"Why are you crying?" asks Durito, as he lights his pipe.

"Because I can't attend my funeral. I, who loved me so much . . ."

. . . and so, this what happened to El Sup and Durito on the twelfth day of the withdrawal, which speaks of the mysteries of the Cave of Desire, and of other unfortunate events that today make us laugh, but at the time took away even our hunger.

"What if they bomb us?" asked Durito in the early morning of the twelfth day of our withdrawal. ("That was no withdrawal! It was pure flight!" says Durito.) It's cold, and in the dark a gray wind licks the trees and the earth with its icy tongue. I'm not sleeping; solitude makes the cold hurts twice as much. Nevertheless, I keep quiet. Durito comes out from beneath the leaf he's been using as a blanket and climbs up on top of me. To wake me up, he starts tickling my nose. I sneeze so soundly that Durito ends up tumbling over himself onto my boots. He recovers and makes his way back to my face.

"What's up?" I ask him, before he tickles me again.

"What if they bomb us?" he persists.

"Yes . . . well . . . well . . . we'll look for a cave, or somewhere like that to hide ourselves . . . or we'll crawl into a hole . . . we'll see what to do," I say with annoyance and a look at my watch to insinuate that it is no hour to be worrying about bombings.

"I won't have any problems. I can fit anywhere. But you, with those big boots and that nose . . . I doubt that you'll find a safe place," says Durito, as he covers himself again with a little *huapac* leaf.

The psychology of terror, I think, with respect to Durito's apparent indifference to our fate . . . Our fate? He's right! He won't have problems, but me . . . I think. I get up and speak to Durito:

"Psst . . . Psst . . . Durito!"

"I'm sleeping," he says from under his leaf.

I ignore his sleep and begin talking to him: "Yesterday I heard Camilo and my other self saying that there are a lot of caves around here. Camilo says he knows most of them. There are small ones, where an armadillo would barely fit. And there are some as big as churches. But he says there is one that no one dares to enter. He says there is an ugly story about that cave which they call the Cave of Desire."

Durito seems to get interested; his passion for detective novels is his ruin.

"And what is the story of that cave?"

"Well . . . it's a very long story. I've heard it myself, but that was years ago now . . . I don't remember it well," I say, making it interesting.

"Fine, go on, tell me the story," says Durito, more and more interested.

I light my pipe. From within the aromatic smoke comes the memory, and with it . . .

The Cave of Desire

"IT HAPPENED MANY years ago. It is a story of a love that was not, that was left unfulfilled. It is a sad story . . . and terrible," says El Sup, sitting to the side, with his pipe in his lips. He lights it, and looking at the mountain, continues:

"A man came from far away. He came, or he already was here. No one knows. It was back in times long past, and however that may be, in these lands people lived and died just the same, without hope and forgotten. No one knows if that man was young or old. At first, only a few people had seen him. They say that was because this man was extremely ugly. Just to see him produced dread in men and revulsion in women. What was it that made him so unpleasant? I don't know—the concepts of beauty and ugliness change so much from one age to another and from one culture to another . . . In this case, the people native to these lands avoided him, as did the foreigners, who owned the land, the men, and their destinies. The indigenous people called him the Jolmash, or Monkey-face; the foreigners called him The Animal."

The man went into the mountains, far from the gaze of all, and set to work there. He made himself a little house, next to one of the many caves that were found there. He made the land produce, planted corn and wheat, and hunted animals in the forest. This gave him enough to get by. Every so often, he went down to a stream near the settlements. There, he had arranged with one of the older members of the community to get salt, sugar, and whatever else he, the Jolmash, couldn't get in the mountains, in exchange for corn and animal skins. The Jolmash would arrive at the stream at the hour when the afternoon began to darken, and the shadows of the trees brought forth night onto the earth. The old man had an illness in his eyes and couldn't see well, so that, with the dusk and his illness, he couldn't make out the face of the man who caused so much revulsion in the daylight.

One evening the old man didn't arrive. The Jolmash thought that he had mistaken the hour and arrived when the old man had already gone home. In order not to miss him, the next time he made sure to arrive earlier. The sun still had a few finger-lengths to go before it covered itself with the mountains when the Jolmash came near the stream. A murmur of laughter and voices grew as he approached. The Jolmash slowed his steps and, silently, got closer. Among the branches and vines he made out a pool formed by the waters of the stream. A group of women were bathing and washing clothes. They were laughing. The Jolmash looked on quietly. His heart became all eyes, his voice turned into a gaze. Long after the women had gone, the Jolmash stayed on, looking . . . The stars rained down on the fields as he returned to the mountains.

I don't know if it came from what he saw, or from what he thought he saw, whether the image that was engraved on his retina corresponded to reality, or if it existed only in his desire, but the Jolmash fell in love, or thought that he had fallen in love. And his love was not something idealized or platonic. No, it was quite earthy. The feelings that he bore were like the call of a war drum, like lightning that becomes fierce rain. Passion took his hand, and the Jolmash began to write letters, love letters, the lettered delirium that filled his hands. And he wrote such things as:

"Oh, lady, glimmering, moist! My desire becomes a proud leaping colt. My hunger, sword of a thousand mirrors, yearns for thy body; in vain, this double-edged yearning rips the thousand gasps that ride the wind. One grace, long sleeplessness! I ask of thee for one grace, lady, failed repose of my gray existence! Let me rest on thy shoulder. Let thine ears listen to my clumsy longing. Let my desire tell thee, gently, very gently, that which my breast silences. Do not look, lady so not-mine, at the pitiful mess that adorns my face! Let thine ears become thy gaze; give up thine eyes to see the murmurs that walk within me, longing for thee. Yes, I wish to enter you and, with sighs, walk the path that hands and lips and sex desire. You with thy wet mouth, and I thirsting to enter with a kiss. On the double hill of thine breasts I long to run my lips and fingers, to awaken the cluster of moans that hide within. I long to march southward and imprison thy waist in warm embrace, burning now the belly's skin, a brilliant sun announcing the night born from below. Diligently and skillfully, to rise and fall on the see-saw on which thy grace rides, and whose fulcrum promises and denies. To give thee a tremor, cold and hot, and arrive, whole, to the moist stirring of desire. To fasten the warmth of my palms in the double warmth of flesh and movement. At first, one slow step, a light trot next. Next, the runaway gallop of bodies and desire to reach the sky to then collapse. One grace, promised tiredness! One grace I ask thee, lady of the quiet sigh! Let my head rest on thy shoulder, for there, I am saved, and far away, I die."

One stormy night, like the passion that burned his hands, a bolt of lightning burned down the Jolmash's little house. Wet and shivering, he took refuge in a neighboring cave. With a torch he lit his way in and found there little figures of couples giving and receiving, the pleasure worked in stone and clay. There was a spring, and little boxes that when opened, spoke of terrors and marvels that had passed, and that would come to be. The Jolmash now could not or would not leave the cave. There, he felt the desire fill his hands once more and wrote, weaving bridges to nowhere . . .

And now, dear lady, I am a pirate longing for port. Tomorrow, a soldier at war. Today, a pirate lost among trees, aground. The ship of desire unfolds its sails. A continual moaning, all tremor and wanting, leads the ship between monsters and storms. Lightning illuminates the flickering sea of desperation. In command, a saline moisture takes the helm. Pure wind, word alone, I navigate, seeking thee among sighs and panting, seeking the precise place the body sends thee. Desire, lady of storms to come, is a knot hidden somewhere beneath thy skin. I must find it and, muttering spells, untie it. Then thy longings, thy feminine swaying, shall be free, and they will fill thine eyes and mouth, thy womb and belly. But free for just one moment, for my hands already have come to make them prisoners, to lead them out to sea in my embrace and with my body. I shall be ship and restless sea, so that I may enter thy body. And there shall be no rest in so much storm, capricious waves will toss our bodies about. And one last and ferocious slap of salty desire will hurl us to a beach where sleep arrives. Now I am a pirate, lady of tender storm. Don't await my assault; come to it! Let the sea, the wind, and this stone turned ship be witnesses! The cave of desire! The horizon clouds over with black wine; now we are arriving, now we go . . . .

So it happened, they say. And they say that the Jolmash never again left the cave. No one knows whether the woman to whom he wrote the letters existed in truth or was a product of the cave, the Cave of Desire. What they say is that the Jolmash still lives in it, and whoever comes close becomes afflicted with the same desire . . . .

Durito has followed the whole story attentively. When he sees I have finished, he simply says:

"We have to go."

63

Durito and Pegasus

THE MOON IS A PALE almond. Silver sheets reshape trees and plants. On the tree trunks, panicky crickets pierce white leaves, as irregularly as the shadows of the night below. Gusts of gray wind agitate trees and anxieties. Durito makes a bed in my beard. The sneeze he provokes makes the armed gentleman roll on the floor. Durito gathers himself deliberately. To his already imposing body armor, Durito puts on his head half a cololte shell (a species of hazelnut native to the Lacandon Jungle), in addition to holding a medicine cap like a shield. Excalibur is sheathed, and a lance (which looks suspiciously similar to a stretched-out paper clip) completes his attire.

"Now what?" I say as I try, somewhat pointlessly, to help Durito with my finger. Durito rearranges his body, I mean, his armor. He unsheathes Excalibur, clears his throat twice, and says in a deep voice:

"It is dawn, my battered shield bearer! It is the hour in which the night arranges its garments to go, and the day sharpens Apollo's spiky mane so he can peer at the world! It is the hour when knights-errant ride in search of adventure to raise their prestige before the absent eyes of the maiden, who prevents them, even for an instant, from closing their eyes to seek oblivion or rest!"

I yawn and let my eyelids lower to bring me oblivion and rest. This irritates Durito, and he raises his voice:

"We must be off to wrong maidens, straighten out widows, give refuge to bandits, and jail the destitute."

"Sounds to me like a government program," I say to him with my eyes closed. Durito appears to have no intention of leaving without waking me fully.

"Wake up, scoundrel! You must remember to follow your Master wherever misfortune or adventure may take him!"

At last I open my eyes and stare at him. Durito looks more like a broken-up army tank than an knight-errant. I wanted to clear up my doubt so I asked him, "And who are you exactly?"

Durito answers, assuming, according to him, his most gallant pose. "I am a knight-errant, but not one of those whom fame forgot to immortalize in history. I am one of those who, in spite of envy, of all Persia's magicians, of India's brahmans, of Ethiopia's sophists, will put his name in the temple of immortality so it may serve as an example, in the coming centuries, so that other knights-errant may see what steps to follow, if they wish to reach the peak and high honor of arms."[1]

"Sounds to me like . . . like . . ." I begin to say but Durito interrupts me. "Silence, insensitive commoner! You pretend to slander, me saying that the Ingenious and Noble Don Quixote of La Mancha has plagiarized my speeches. And certainly, since we are on this subject, I should say there are those who say that you are wasting space in your epistles. Bibliographical notes, huh! If you continue you will end up like Galio,[2] citing six or seven authors in order to cover up his own cynicism."

I felt profoundly wounded by the harsh comments, and I decided to change the subject. "That thing on your head looks like a *cololte* shell."

"It is a helmet, ignorant one," Durito says.

"Helmet? It looks like a shell with holes," I insist.

"*Cololte*, helmet, and halo. In that order, Sancho," Durito says as he arranges the helmet.

"Sancho?" I stutter-say-ask-protest.

"Look, stop this nuisance and get ready so we can leave. Many are the injustices that my indefatigable sword must right, and its blade is anxious to feel the necks of independent unions." As Durito says this, he brandishes his sword like a regent from a capital city.

"I think you've read too many newspapers recently. Be careful, or they will lead you to suicide," I say to him, while I attempt to delay getting up. Durito abandons his sixteenth-century language for a moment, and proudly explains that he has secured a mount. He says it is as swift as lightning in August, silent as the wind in March, docile as the rain in September, and many more marvels that I don't remember, but there was one quality per month. I appear incredulous, so Durito announces solemnly that he will do me the honor of showing me his mount. I agree, thinking that in this way I can sleep a little longer. Durito leaves and is so long in returning that I actually do fall asleep.

A voice awakens me: "Here I am!"

It's Durito, and he is mounted on the logical reason for his delay: a turtle!

At a pace that Durito insists on calling an "elegant trot" and which to me appears more prudent and slow, he approaches me. Mounted on his turtle (they call it *coc* in Tzeltal), Durito turns to look at me and asks, "So, how do I look?"

I gaze at this knight-errant, who for some unknown reason has been brought to the solitude of the Lacandon Jungle, and keep a respectful silence. His appearance is peculiar. Durito has baptized his turtle—excuse me, his horse—with a name that seems pure madness: *Pegasus*. So that there is no doubt, Durito has written on the turtle's shell, in large and decisive letters: "PEGASUS. Copyright Reserved," and below that, "Please, fasten your seat belts." I can hardly resist the temptation of making a comparison with the economic recuperation program, when Durito turns his mount so I can see the other side. Even though Durito has announced a "vertiginous turn of his horse," Pegasus takes his time, making a slow turn. The turtle does it so carefully one might think he fears dizziness. After a few minutes, one can read on Pegasus' left flank: "Smokers' Section," "Union cowboys not allowed," "Free advertising space. For information call Durito's Publishing Company." I can't make out much free space; the advertising covers Pegasus's entire left flank and rear.

After praising Durito's ultra-mini-micro entrepreneurial vision—the only way to survive the failures of neoliberalism and NAFTA—I ask him, "So, where does your fortune lead you?"

"Don't be a clown. That language belongs only to noblemen and lords, not to vagabonds and commoners who, were it not for my infinite compassion, would continue with their empty lives and never be able to dream about the secrets and marvels of knight-erranthood," Durito answers, while trying to hold Pegasus, who for some strange reason acts impatient to leave, back.

"It seems to me that, for 2 A.M., I've had enough scoldings," I say to Durito, "Wherever you go, you'll go alone. I don't plan to go out tonight. Yesterday, Camilo found tiger tracks close by. "

Apparently I've found a vulnerable flank on our brave knight, because his voice shakes when he asks, after swallowing saliva with great difficulty, "So what do those tigers eat?"

"Everything. Guerrillas, soldiers, beetles . . . and turtles!" I watch Pegasus's reaction, but he must really believe he is a horse, because he does not seem to be alarmed. I think I even hear a soft whinny.

"Bah! You just want to frighten me. If you must know, this armed knight has defeated giants disguised as windmills, which in turn disguised themselves as artillery helicopters; he has conquered the most impenetrable kingdoms, melted the resistance of the most demure princesses, he has—"

I interrupt Durito. It's evident he can use up pages and pages talking, and I'm the one who gets criticized by the editors, especially when the communiqués arrive so late at night.

"Fine, fine. But tell me, where are you going?"

"To Mexico City," Durito says, brandishing his sword. This final destination surprises Pegasus, because he gives a slight jump, which for a turtle is like a discreet sigh.

"Mexico City?" I ask, incredulous.

"Sure! Do you think that just because Cocopa didn't let you go there, that it would deter me?" I wanted to warn Durito about speaking badly about Cocopa—the legislators are so sensitive, they might get mad—but Durito continues:

"You should know I am an knight-errant, and more Mexican than the failure of the neoliberal economy. I have a right, therefore, to go to the 'city of palaces.' What do they want palaces for in Mexico City if not so that knights-errant like myself, the most famous, the most gallant, and the most respected by men, loved by women, and revered by children, should honor them with my footsteps?

"With your many feet," I tell him. "Let me remind you that besides being an knight-errant and a Mexican, you are a beetle, too."

"With my foot or my feet, but a palace without a knight-errant is like a child without a present on April 30,[3] like a pipe without tobacco, like a book without words, a song without music, or an knight-errant without a shield . . . ." Durito gazes at me steadily and asks: "Are you sure you won't come with me on this intriguing adventure?"

"It depends," I say, pretending to be interested. "It depends on what you mean by 'intriguing adventure.'"

"I'm going to the May Day parade," Durito says, almost as though he were announcing a walk to the corner for cigarettes.

"To the May Day parade! But there will be none! Fidel Velazquez, who has always cared about workers' well-being, says there is no money for the parade. Some rumormongers are insinuating that he is afraid that the workers will get out of control, and instead of being grateful, they will curse him with words useless for the cartoonists. But it's a lie, the labor secretary is quick to point out, it is not due to fear. It is a *veeery* respectable decision made by the workers, and—"

"Stop, stop your allegorical chatter. I'm going to the May Day parade to challenge Fidel Velazquez—who, as we all know, is a fierce ogre who oppresses the poor—to a duel. I will challenge him to fight in the Aztec stadium, maybe that will sell more tickets. Ever since they let Beenhaker[4] go (don't criticize me if I didn't spell it right, not even the American directors could spell the name, and they were the ones who wrote him checks), not even the eagles can see the vultures."[5] Durito is silent for a moment and looks pensively at Pegasus, who must have gone to sleep, since he hasn't moved in a while. Then Durito asks me:

"Do you think Fidel Velazquez has a horse?"

I sort of doubt that.

"Well, he's a *charro*[6] —so it's likely he has a horse."

"Wonderful," says Durito, and digs his spurs into Pegasus.

Pegasus may think he's a horse, but he still has a turtle's body, and his hard shell proves it. He doesn't even notice Durito's cowboy maneuvers, as he eggs him on. After struggling a bit, Durito discovers that by hitting his clip, excuse me, his lance on Pegasus's nose, he can make him go into a gallop. For a turtle, this is about ten centimeters per hour, so it will take Durito a while before he arrives in Mexico City.

"At that rate, by the time you get there Fidel Velasquez will be dead," I offer as a parting thought.

I should never have said anything. Durito tosses the reins and pulls his horse back, like when Pancho Villa took Torreon. Oh well, it's a good literary image. In reality Pegasus stopped, which, at his rate, was almost imperceptible. In contrast to Pegasus's calm, Durito was furious:

"The same thing is happening to you that has been happening to the advisers of the labor movement in the last few decades! They recommend patience to the workers, and sit and wait for the *charro* to fall off his horse, but do nothing to make him fall."

"Well, not all of them have sat down to wait. Some have really struggled to make a truly independent labor movement," I tell him.

"I'm going to see those folks. I'm going to join them so I can show them that workers, too, have dignity," Durito says, and I recall that once he told me he was a miner in the state of Hidalgo and an oil worker in Tabasco.

Durito leaves. He takes a few hours to disappear behind the bush a few meters from my plastic cover. I get up and notice that my right boot is loose. I turn on the flashlight—the lace is missing! No wonder Pegasus's reins looked familiar. Now I have to wait until Durito returns from Mexico City. While looking for a reed with which to tie my boot, I remember that I forgot to recommend that Durito visit that restaurant with the tiles.[7] I lie down, and dawn arrives . . . .

Above me the sky clears and with reddish-blue eyes is surprised to see that Mexico is still there, where it was yesterday. I light my pipe, watch the last slashes of night leave the trees, and say to myself that the struggle is long and it is worth it . . .

P.S.

. . . IN WHICH WITH A full moon for a face, he looks toward the jungle and asks . . . who is that man who gallops over a squalid shadow? Why does he not seek relief? Why does he seek new pain? Why so many journeys when standing still? Who is he? Where is he going? Why does he say good-bye with such a noisy silence?

NOTES

1. Quoted from *Don Quixote*, chapter 1: "About the strange way in which Don Quixote de la Mancha was enchanted, and other Events."

2. Galio is a character from Hector Aguilar Camín's novel *La Guerra de Galio* (Galio's War), which dealt with the guerrillas in Mexico during the 1970s.

3. April 30 is Children's Day in Mexico.

4. Leo Beenhacker, the Dutch soccer coach.

5. "Not even the eagles can see the vultures" makes a play on eagles as U.S. interests, who don't care who the individuals are who sell off Mexican wealth.

6. *Charro* means "cowboy," which has a connotation of being very macho; but it also refers to a labor union head in Mexican slang.

7. Samborn's Restaurant in Mexico City, where Emiliano Zapata came to breakfast before going on to take the presidential seat.

64

The Story of the Tiny Mouse and the Tiny Cat

AUGUST 7, 1995

DON DURITO OF THE LACANDON, knight-errant, the undoer of wrongs, the ladies' restless dream, the young men's aspiration, the last and grandest of that exemplary race that made humanity great with such colossal and selfless feats, the beetle and warrior of the moon, writes to you.

I have commanded my loyal squire, the one you call "Sup Marcos," to send you a greeting in writing, with all the requirements fit for today's diplomacy, excluding the rapid-intervention forces, the economic programs, and the flight of capital. Nevertheless, I want to write you some lines with the sole intent the spirit, to fill your minds with good and noble thoughts. That is why I send you the following tale, full of rich and varying feats. The story forms part of the collection *Stories for a Night of Asphyxiation* (which will probably not be published in the near future).

The Story of the Tiny Mouse and the Tiny Cat

THERE ONCE WAS A TINY mouse who was very hungry and wanted to eat a tiny bit of cheese, which was in the tiny kitchen of a tiny house. Very decidedly, the tiny mouse went to the tiny kitchen to grab the tiny bit of cheese. But, it so happened that a tiny cat crossed his path, and the tiny mouse became very frightened and ran away and was not able to get the tiny bit of cheese from the tiny kitchen. Then the tiny mouse was thinking of what to do to get the tiny bit of cheese from the tiny kitchen and he thought and he said:

"I know. I am going to put out a small plate with a little milk and the tiny cat is going to start drinking the milk because tiny cats like very much a little milk. And then, when the tiny cat is drinking the little milk and is not paying attention, I am going to the tiny kitchen to grab the tiny bit of cheese and I am going to eat it. That's a *veeery* good idea," said the tiny mouse to himself.

And then he went to look for the milk, but it turns out that the milk was in the tiny kitchen, and when the tiny mouse wanted to go to the tiny kitchen, the tiny cat crossed his path and the tiny mouse was very frightened and ran and could not get the milk. Then the tiny mouse was thinking of what to do to get the milk in the tiny kitchen and he thought and he said:

"I know. I am going to toss a tiny fish very far away and then the tiny cat is going to run to go eat the tiny fish, because tiny cats like very much tiny fish. And then, when the tiny cat is eating the tiny fish and is not paying attention, I am going to go to the tiny kitchen to grab the tiny bit of cheese and I am going to eat it. That's a *veeery* good idea," said the tiny mouse.

Then he went to look for the tiny fish, but it happened that the tiny fish was in the tiny kitchen, and when the tiny mouse wanted to go to the tiny kitchen, the tiny cat crossed his path and the tiny mouse became very frightened and ran away and could not go to get the tiny fish.

And then the tiny mouse saw that the tiny bit of cheese, the milk, and the tiny fish, everything that he wanted, was in the tiny kitchen, and he could not get there because the tiny cat would not allow it. And then the tiny mouse said; "Enough!" and he grabbed a machine gun and shot the tiny cat, and he went to the tiny kitchen and he saw that the tiny fish, the milk, and the tiny bit cheese had gone bad and could not be eaten. So he returned to where the tiny cat was, cut it in pieces, and made a great roast. Then, he invited all his friends, and they partied and ate the roasted tiny cat, and they sang and danced and lived very happily. And once there was . . .

This is the end of the story and the end of this missive. I want to remind you that the divisions between countries only serve to illustrate the crime of "contraband" and to give sense to war. Clearly, there exist at least two things greater than borders: one is the crime disguised as modernity, which distributes misery on a world scale; the other is the hope that shame exists only when one fumbles a dance step, and not every time we look in the mirror. To end the first and to make the second one flourish, we need only to struggle to be better. The rest follows of its own accord, and is what usually fills libraries and museums.

It is not necessary to conquer the world, it is sufficient to make it anew . . .

Vale. Health to you, and know that a bed is only a pretext for love; that a tune is only an adornment to dance; and that nationalism is merely a circumstantial accident for struggle.

From the mountains of the Mexican Southeast
DON DURITO OF THE LACANDON

P.S.

PLEASE EXCUSE THE BREVITY of these letters. It so happens that I must press ahead with my expedition to invade Europe this winter. How do you feel about a landing for the next January 1?

65

The Story of the Cold Foot and the Hot Foot

OCTOBER 27, 1995

DAWN BARELY BEGINS to trace itself. The cold and darkness cover the wake of a gallant knight-errant and the sorrow of his wretched squire. No one can find the moon, and the lightning is followed by thunder. The mud renews itself with rain, and the wheat with a kiss. Durito reviews the newspaper, bites his pipe, and looks at me with reproach. "So you have caused a scandal like those who make history!" he says while putting down the newspaper.

"Me?" I say, pretending to be *veeery* busy with my torn boot.

"Definitely! Who else? Once again, you have demonstrated that when you talk, you have the same finesse as a stampede of elephants inside a china shop. And not just that. Your clumsiness has allowed an avalanche of mediocre minds to declare one-and-a-half idiocies about the half-idiocy that you uttered—"

"I . . . What happened is that they didn't understand me! I didn't want to say what I said, but to say what I did not say, and that is why I did not say what I wanted to say, and said what I did not want to say . . . " I try to defend myself while hiding my shame in the hole—does anybody doubt it?—of my left boot.

"Rubbish! This reasoning has the same logic as that of a PRI congressman explaining his vote against the reduction of IVA."[1]

I remain quiet and start to draw spirals and little circles on the ground with a short stick. Durito feels sorry for me and pats my shoulder. To do this, Durito must climb on my arm and loosen the bullet straps. He sits next to the collar seam, and says:

"Oh my dear and clumsy squire, speaking is a slippery and problematic thing. In reality, one should only speak with women, the only beings with whom it is gratifying to be slippery and get into trouble. To speak to a woman one should do it up close to her ear. That way, what you say won't matter as much as the warm closeness of her neck. In politics, words hide many traps and tangles, and not just the words spoken to us, but those we speak. And now that we are speaking of politics, a story comes to mind that might be useful for the book that you are preparing, which is entitled, if I remember well, *Stories for a Night of Asphyxia*."

I sigh, resigned to tolerating another of Durito's stories, but he thinks that it is because I am saddened by the statements made against Don Porfirio, so he continues. He clears his throat and orders me to take pen and pencil. While he dictates, I write the story that he calls . . .

The Story of the Cold Foot and the Hot Foot

ONCE THERE WERE TWO feet that were together. They were together, but not united. The one was cold, and the other was hot. The cold foot said to the hot foot, "You are very hot." And the hot foot said to the cold foot, "You are very cold." They were fighting each other like that when Hernán Cortés[2] arrived and burned them both.

"Is it over?" I ask, unbelieving.

"Of course! It is a story, not one of your press conferences," he answers me.

I look at him with reproach. He says:

"Enough. It's fine. Let me think . . . mmmh, mmmh, I know! At the end write: 'And Hernán Cortés lived happily ever after . . . and that's not the end of the story.'"

"It isn't?" I ask him, while I put the paper in my pocket.

"Of course not! There are still many cold and hot feet, so Hernán Cortés might end up having a *very* disagreeable surprise."

"Speaking of disagreeable things," I interrupt, "they are complaining about you in some newspaper."

"About me? Who dares complain about the knight-errant who is the longing of damsels young and old, who is in the dreams of children big and small, and who is respected and admired by all the noblemen of all times?"

"Well, they don't precisely complain about you. They only say that enough of Durito being everywhere. Anyway, they suggest that I leave you out of my epistles and that . . . "

Durito does not allow me to continue and shouts in my ear:

"Shut up, you insolent coward! Only a ragamuffin like you could think that respectable people would not enjoy the stories of my great feats, of my undeniable sympathy, and the profound and ample wisdom of my discourse."

"But Durito! It's not me who has thought of such absurdity! Consider that some person could exist—it's a hypothesis—who does not respond with the same enthusiasm as . . . "

Durito interrupts again.

"Well, I concede that it is possible some being could exist who might not be interested in me or my feats. So we can do something to compare your ranking, you insolent ruffian, with mine, a tall knight-errant.

"I agree with the 'errant,' but allow me to doubt about that 'tall.' "

"I am talking of the stature of my ideals, you cretin."

"Well, what do you propose?"

"A *consulta*."

"A *consulta*? But Durito . . . they are going to say this is a joke . . . "

"Not another word! A *consulta* it shall be. National, international, and interplanetary. And the questions shall be:

"First: Should El Sup eliminate the Durito stories in his letters?

"Second: Should the despicable being who dares to demand the disappearance of the Durito stories die in an inferno that would make Dante's[3] look like a freezer?

"These are two questions to be answered with: 'yes,' 'no,' or 'I don't know.'"

"And where should the ones who want to respond send their answers?" I ask skeptically.

"To my office: Don Durito of the Lacandon, Hoyito of Huapac number 69. Mountains of the Mexican Southeast, Chiapas, Mexico."

I see that Durito is very determined, so it's better for him to clarify some matters.

"What are the minimum and maximum ages to participate in this *consulta*?"

"Minimum is six months. Maximum is a minute before breathing one's last breath."

"But Durito, do you think that a six-month-old person could answer these questions?"

"Of course! When I was six months old, I was already writing those sonnets that make a woman's moist belly provoke storms and, paradoxically, also bring calm."

"But you are a beetle!"

"Even more in my favor! No more discussion! Write up the convocation and add that all females may attach to their ballot their best sigh . . . Although, on second thought . . . No, better leave out the sighs . . . For sure, with so many sighs here, they could turn into a hurricane which would make "Roxana" seem like an inopportune breeze.[4] Better still, let them send red carnations. Maybe we can set up a flower export business with them . . . Well, what do you think?"

"I think you are delirious. You have gone mad," I say to him.

"My dear, skinny squire! The morning can become dawn only if there are doses of delirium and madness," Durito says while he goes back to his place and covers himself again with the little *huapac* leaf, but not before drawing a great and rotound "69" on the top.

"Let me know when the replies start arriving. Hell! I won't be able to get to sleep because of this sweet wait," Durito says seconds before starting to snore as if he were a power saw with no exhaust valve.

I remain quiet. I light up my pipe and slowly inhale some memory. The dawn above me dilutes its last dark grays, far away the day takes a bite of the horizon, and the cold turns lukewarm, here . . . in the mountains of the Mexican Southeast . . .

Vale again. Health to you, and may the madness and the delirium multiply.

EL SUP, YEARNING FOR THE FLOWER WITH WHICH OCTOBER DECORATES THE CEIBA.

NOTES

1. IVA stands for *impuesto valor agregado*, "value-added tax."

2. Hernán Cortés (1485–1547), Spanish conquistador of Mexico, the Aztec empire of Monteczuma. He founded the city of Vera Cruz, burned his ships to prevent his forces from turning back, and enlisted the help of the defeated Tlaxcalans. He extended his conquest to most of Mexico and North Central America. Though Charles V of Spain made Cortés a marquée, he refused to make him governor of Mexico. Cortés returned to Spain in 1540, where he died, frustrated and neglected by the court.

3. Dante Alighieri (1265-1321). His most famous work, *The Divine Comedy*, describes Dante's journey through the three otherworld kingdoms of hell (*Inferno*), purgatory (*Purgatorio*), and heaven (*Paradiso*).

4. An allusion to Hurricane Roxanne of October 11, 1995, which centered on the Gulf of Mexico and moved inland at Campeche after sinking a barge and several boats.

66

The Story of the Bean-brown Horse

JANUARY 9, 1996

PRESENT AT THIS NATIONAL INDIGENOUS Forum is a personality who, because he is so shy, is now hurrying out of the room. I am referring, of course, to the very great and beloved Don Durito of the Lacandon, wandering knight and nobleman, who gallops through the mountains of the Mexican Southeast. The most exalted and most dignified representative of the most honorable profession of knight-erranthood, the always lively Don Durito of the Lacandon has asked me—since I am his shield bearer and companion—to say a few words to you in his name. Due to one of those promises made and carried out by knight-errants, Durito has had to remain silent for some time, awaiting the results of the inter-galactic *consulta* that he requested. I have to say—taking advantage of his absence—that his silence was pretty strident, and that he never gave me a morning's rest, which, I believe, all good shield bearers deserve.

So today at dawn I was smoking and thinking about how to thank you for having come, when suddenly I see something that looks strangely like a beetle, scurrying underneath the door. It was . . . Durito!

He was dressed in an old torn coat, and a rather large hat—to my thinking it was too big for him—and with a cane in hand. Durito quickly informed me that he was under-cover to avoid his many female admirers. He also made it clear that he was not carrying a cane but Excalibur, his justice-seeking sword disguised as a cane.

"The ones you need to avoid are the national security agents, the PGR, the military intelligence, the CIA, the FBI, and the other etceteras who like to attend events of this kind," I said, while watching with alarm how he sacked a bag of tobacco.

"Quickly!" he said to me. "Write down what I'm about to tell you, because I have to go!"

And without giving me a chance to ask why the hurry, Durito dictated . . .

The Story of the Bean-brown Horse

THERE ONCE WAS A BROWN horse that was brown like a bean, and he lived in the home of a very poor farmer. And the poor farmer had a very poor wife, and they had a very thin chicken and a lame little pig. And so, one day the very poor farmer's wife said:

"We have nothing more to eat because we are very poor, so we must eat the very thin chicken." So they killed the very thin chicken and made a thin soup and ate it. And so, for a while, they were fine; but the hunger returned and the very poor farmer told his very poor wife:

"We have nothing more to eat because we are so poor, so we must eat the lame little pig." And so the lame little pig's turn came and they killed it and they made a lame soup and ate it. And then it was the bean-brown horse's turn. But the bean-brown horse did not wait for the story to end; it just ran away and went to another story.

"Is that the end of the story?" I asked Durito, unable to hide my bewilderment.

"Of course not. Didn't you hear me say that the bean-brown horse fled to another story?" he said as he prepared to leave.

"And so?" I ask exasperated.

"And so nothing—you have to look for the bean-brown horse in another story!" he said, adjusting his hat.

"But, Durito!" I said, protesting uselessly.

"Not one more word! You tell the story like it is. I can't do it because I'm on a secret mission."

"Secret? And what's it about?" I asked in a whisper.

"Insolent knave! Don't you understand that if I tell you, it won't be a secret anymore," Durito manages to say while he slips beneath the door.

Durito already knows the results of the intergalactic *consulta* that ended in 1995. He knows that he had a resounding and indisputable victory, which condemns me to narrating his great feats and adventures. That is why Don Durito of the Lacandon is off already to straighten out injustices and astound the entire world with his achievements. The greatest thief of feminine sighs, the role model for young men, the children's hero, the great Don Durito of the Lacandon, has returned. I know that many of you are happy that he is back, but for me it's no huge favor to have to be the scribbler of such absurd and marvelous stories like this one . . . *Stories for a Night of Asphyxia.*

67

Love and the Calendar

A bottle came floating in on the crest of a cloud and got stuck on the branches of the ceiba. I approached it carefully—a fall from these heights would make as much of an uproar as the economic crash in 1988—and grabbed it. As you would expect, the bottle had a message inside. I took it out and found the following letter from Durito:

My dear decadent Cyrano:[1]
I JUST LEARNED THAT, once again, you are a prisoner on the crown of the ceiba. These things happen because you allow yourself to be led around by your nonsense about mirrors and falling upward. I simply cannot rescue you right now. I'm very busy writing the second part of *Stories for a Night of Asphyxia*, which I have renamed *Stories for a Sleepless Solitude*. Here's a sample so you can find me an editor.

Love and the Calendar

THERE WAS ONCE A MAN who always came late to everything. And it wasn't because he was lazy or slow, or that his watch was behind, or that it was a bad habit. It happened because the man lived in another time before time. Not exactly true, but close enough. For example, when the calendar said it was September, this man walked in on an April morning. That's why his spring never coincided with its improbability. Death, on the other hand, remained obedient to time's passage and went around spreading absences as each person's numbered days and nights were up. But since this man was never on time, he would always arrive late for the hour of his death and not find her, since Death had to follow the calendar. Death knew he was only living in a state of suspension, that this man, who should already be dead, was still alive due only to his chronic tardiness. This man grew tired of living and walking, which are really the same thing, and began to look for Death so he could die. And so, time and untimeliness passed each other, Death waiting for the man to arrive so she could take him, and the man waiting for Death to arrive so he could die. There is no day on the calendar in which these two times can find one another.

Tan-tan.[2]

What do you think? No, leave the praise for another time. OK, I'm leaving. I'll write you later, my decadent, big-nosed shield bearer.

DON DURITO OF THE LACANDON

P.S.

DON'T FORGET TO KEEP a tight hold on the tiller. They say fierce storms approach.

End of the letter from Durito. No comment.

NOTES

1. Cyrano de Bergerac, the protagonist in what is considered the greatest work of Edmond Rostand (1868–1918), a French dramatist whose plays represent the final flowering of the nineteenth-century romantic tradition. *Cyrano de Bergerac* was a dazzling popular success and remains a worldwide favorite to this day. Its hero, marred by an enormous nose, rises heroically above his bodily defect in scenes of unparalleled verve, wit, and pathos.

2. The two final notes in a song, which the author here uses to indicate the end of the story.

68

Another Cloud, Another Bottle, and Another Letter from Durito

SEPTEMBER 30, 1996

My beloved, persecuted and harassed Cyrano:
IT'S MY DUTY TO TELL YOU that your time is running out. That ceiba makes an excellent target for mortars, grenade launchers, snipers, cannons, and machine guns, and I won't even mention satellites. At the end of this letter you'll find an infallible recipe for climbing down from ceiba. Follow it to the letter, and you'll get down quickly.

Assuming you won't be staying up there much longer, and that you're not, shall we say, an attractive client for a life insurance company, I recommend that you get moving on the contacts for the publication of my next book, *Stories for a Sleepless Solitude.* Since time's running out, I now send you another story, part of a special section called "Stories for Getting Pregnant." It's perfectly self-explanatory; you only have to read it. Here goes, then:

The Story of the Magic Chocolate Bunnies
(Neoliberalism, a Rabbit's Libido, and the Children)

(Durito's Homage to the Westerns by do you remember *The Good, the Bad, and the Ugly?*)

ONCE UPON A TIME there were three children. One was good, one was bad, and the other was El Sup. Coming from different directions, they arrived at a house and went in. Inside the house there was only a table. On that table there was a plastic container, like the kind used for ice cream or slushies, one for each child. Inside each white plastic container (take note: they had no brand name or logo), there were two chocolate bunnies and a slip of paper. The slip of paper said:

Instructions for Using the Two Chocolate Bunnies
After 24 hours, this pair of chocolate bunnies will reproduce and make a new pair of bun-

nies. Every twenty-four hours thereafter, the pairs of chocolate bunnies inside this white plastic container will multiply into other pairs. In this way, the owner of this magic plastic container will always have chocolate bunnies to eat. The only condition is that there must always be one pair of chocolate bunnies inside this plastic container, like the kind used for ice cream or slushies.

Each child took his white plastic container.

The bad child couldn't wait twenty-four hours and ate his two chocolate bunnies. He enjoyed the moment, but he no longer had chocolate bunnies. Now he has none to eat, but he is left with the memory of and nostalgia for the chocolate bunnies.

The good child waited the twenty-four hours and was rewarded with four chocolate bunnies. After another twenty-four hours, he had eight chocolate bunnies. As the months passed, the good child opened a chain of chocolate bunny stores. After a year, he had branches all over the country. He was financed with foreign capital and began to export. He was eventually named "Man of the Year" and became immensely rich and powerful. He eventually sold his shares in the chocolate bunny industry to foreign investors, and became a mere executive in the company. In order not to cut into the profits, he never tasted the chocolate bunnies. He no longer owns the magic white plastic container, nor does he know what chocolate bunnies taste like.

The child Sup, instead of chocolate bunnies, put walnut ice cream in the white plastic container, like the kind used for ice cream or slushies. Changing the whole premise of the story, he packed a half-liter of walnut ice cream between his chest and back, and ruined the moral of the story of the chocolate bunnies, deducing that all final options are a trap.

Neo-moral: Walnut ice cream has dangerous implications for neoliberalism.

Questions for understanding the story:

1. Which of these children will become president of the republic?

2. Which of these children will belong to an opposition party?

3. Which of these children should be killed for violating the Law for Dialogue, Reconciliation, and a Peace with Dignity in Chiapas?

4. If you're a woman, would you like to give birth to one of these children?

Send your answers to Huapac Leaf #69, with copies to the Ministry of the Interior and the Cocopa.

Tan-tan.

SO, WHAT DO YOU *think of the story? Come now, don't be shy to say it's grand! I hope you find a really good editor, like the ones who work with Carlos Monsivais,*[1] *etcetera.* Vale.

DON DURITO OF THE LACANDON

P.S.

I ALMOST FORGOT THE instructions on how to get down from the ceiba. They are very simple, just follow the . . . *Instructions on How to Get Down from the Ceiba.* Are you sure you don't want to come down? With your eyes shut, walk to the end of the branches. Don't be afraid (although I'm not denying that a good parachute would come in handy). Soon you will reach your destination (?).

NOTE

1. Carlos Monsivais (1935–) one of Mexico's most important contemporary writers, has been an observer of Mexican culture and politics from comics to the student massacres of 1968 and the Zapatista presence.

69

P.S. . . . that Fulfills Its Editorial Duty

OCTOBER 23, 1996

Oh, I forgot. In Durito's letter, there's a story I guess I should add to his book, Stories for a Sleepless Solitude, *in the section called "Stories for Deciding." Here goes then:*

The Story of the Live Person and the Dead Person

ONCE THERE WAS A LIVE person and a dead person. And the dead person said to the live person:

"My, I envy your restlessness."

And then the live person said to the dead person:

"My, I envy your tranquillity."

And there they were, envying each other, when suddenly, a bean-brown horse went by at full gallop.

Tan-tan.

THE MORAL OF THE story, I repeat, is that all final options are a trap. It's imperative to find the bean-brown horse.

DON DURITO OF THE LACANDON

(Please send fan letters, requests for interviews, carnations, and signatures of support for the Anti-Big-Boots Beetle Society to Huapac Leaf #69, Mountains of the Mexican Southeast [on the side where the Sup lives]. Phone callers, please note: don't worry if the answering machine isn't on. I don't have one.)

70

Durito the Pirate

"NO, NO AND NO!" I tell Durito for the umpteenth time.

Yes, Durito has returned. But before explaining my repeated "No," I should tell you the whole story.

The other day at dawn, when the rain cut a river right through the middle of the hut, Durito arrived aboard a sardine can with a pen stuck in the middle, and a handkerchief or some such thing attached to it, that I would later realize was a sail. Atop the main mast—excuse me, the pen—flew a black flag with a fierce skull resting on a pair of crossbones. This was no proper ship making its way quickly to the edge of the table, and doing so with such a bump that Durito came vaulting through the air and landed right on my boot. Durito gathered himself up as best he could and exclaimed:

"Today?! Today?!" He turned around to look at me and said, "Ahoy, you! Carrot Nose! Tell me the date right now!

I wavered, one small part of me wanting to hug Durito on his return, and another small part wanting to kick him for the "Carrot Nose" bit, and another bigger part for . . . for . . . the date? I looked at my watch and said:

"October 12, 1999."

"October 12? By my faith, how nature imitates art! Good. Today, October 12, 1999, I declare the discovery, conquest and liberation of this beautiful Caribbean island answering to the name of . . . of . . . Quick, the name of the isle!"

"What island?" I asked, still taken aback.

"What do you mean, 'What island,' fool? This one! What other island would it be? There is no pirate worthy of the name who doesn't have an island where to bury his treasure and sorrows."

"An island? I always thought it was a tree, a ceiba, to be more precise," I said, leaning over the edge of the dense branches.

"Then you're fooled again. It is an island. Who ever heard of a pirate landing in a ceiba? So either tell me the name of this island, or your fate will be to be served to the sharks for lunch!" threatened Durito.

"Sharks?" I said, swallowing. And I hesitantly ventured, "It has no name."

"Ithasnoname. Mmh. By my faith, 'tis a right worthy name for a pirate's island. Good. Today, October 12, 1999, I declare that the island of Ithasnoname has been discovered, conquered, and liberated, and I name this man with the conspicuous nose my first mate, cabin boy, and lookout."

I tried to ignore the insult, as well as the multitude of positions conferred on me, and I said:

"So . . . Now, you're a pirate!"

" 'A pirate!' Blast your eyes! I am THE PIRATE!"

All this while I had been observing Durito's appearance. A black patch adorned his right eye; a red bandanna covered his head; a piece of wire had been twisted into a hook on one of his many arms; and another held the shining wand that was once Excalibur. I was not quite sure what it had become now, but it must be the kind of sword, cutlass, whatever it is, that pirates use. In addition, there was a little twig tied to one of his little legs just like, just like . . . a pegleg!

"So! What do you think?" asked Durito, making a half turn to show off all the finery he has concocted for his pirate's costume. I carefully asked him:

"So now you're called . . .?"

"Black Shield!" Durito announced pompously, adding, "But for someone who is not cosmopolitan, you can call me 'Escudo[1] Negro.'"

" 'Black Shield'? But— "

"Certainly! Wasn't there a Barbarossa and a Blackbeard?"

"Well, yes, but—"

"But no buts! I am Black Shield! Next to me, Blackbeard was a graybeard, and that was only when he was trying, and Barbarossa was as washed out as your old neckerchief." Durito said all this while simultaneously brandishing both his sword and his hook. Finished now, in the bow of his sardine ca—, pardon me, his vessel, he began reciting the "Pirate's Song":

With ten cannons at each side . . .

"Durito." I try to bring him back to his senses.

The wind astern, and in full sail . . .

"Durito . . . "

It doesn't sail the seas, it soars.

"Durito!"

What? A royal galleon within reach? Quick! Unfurl the sails! Prepare to board!

"Duritooo!" I shout, desperate now.

"Pipe down. Stop yelling, or I will make you look like an unemployed buccaneer. What's going on?"

"Could you tell me where you've been, where you came from, and what has brought you to this land, pardon me, this island?" I asked more calmly now.

"I have been in Italy, in England, in Denmark, in Germany, in France, in Greece, in Holland, in Belgium, in Sweden, in the Iberian Peninsula, in the Canary Islands, all over Europe," Durito said, all the while bowing right and left. "While I was in Venice with Dario, I ate one of those pastas that the Italians are so crazy about that leave me i-m-m-o-b-i-l-i-z-e-d."

"Just a minute! Which Dario? You don't mean you were eating with Dario . . . ?"

"Yes, Dario Fo.[2] Right, eating or rather, not eating. He ate, and I watched him eat. Because mind you, that spaghetti gives me a stomachache, and all the more when they put pasto[3] on it."

"Pesto," I corrected him.

"Pasto, pesto . . . it's all grass. As I was telling you, I arrived in Venice from Rome, after having escaped from one of those 'temporary' detention centers for immigrants. They are a kind of concentration camp where Italian officials isolate everyone who comes from other countries—therefore, who are 'different'— before deporting them. Getting out wasn't easy. I had to lead a sit-in. Clearly, the support of the Italian men and women who oppose institutionalized racism was vital. The fact is, Dario wanted me to help him with some ideas for a theater piece, and I just didn't have the heart to say no."

"Durito . . ."

"Afterwards, I marched against the UN because of the war in Kosovo."

"You mean against NATO."

"Same thing. Then, after a series of adventures, I set sail for the island of Lanzarote."

"Just a minute! The island of Lanzarote? Isn't that where José Saramago[4] lives?"

"That is right; I call him Pepe. What happened is that Pepe invited me for coffee so I could discuss my experiences in the Europe of the Euro. It was great—"

"Yes, I imagine it would be great to chat with Saramago."

"No, I'm talking about the coffee that Pilarica made for us. She truly makes a magnificent cup of coffee."

"You're referring to Pilar del Rio?[5]"

"The very one."

"So, one day you're eating with Dario Fo, and the next you're having coffee with José Saramago."

"Yes, I was hanging out with nothing but Nobel Prize winners. But let me tell you, I had some sharp words with Pepe."

"Whatever for?"

"The prologue, the one he wrote for my book. It seemed to me in poor taste that I, the great and even-tempered Don Durito of the Lacandon, should be reduced to the world of Coleopterous Lamellicorn."[6]

"And what did you have words about?"

"Well, I challenged him to a duel, in the manner demanded by the laws for a knight-errant."

"And . . . ?"

"And nothing. I saw that Pilarica's heart was breaking, since it was obvious I'd win. So, I forgave him . . . "

"You forgave José Saramago?"

"Well, not completely. For me to truly forget the affront, he'll have to come to these lands and, at the top of his voice, declare the following speech: 'Hear ye, hear ye! Tyrants, tremble. Damsels, sigh. Children, be of good cheer. Let the sad and needy rejoice. Hear ye all. Once again over these lands, walks the ever-grand, the magnificent, the incomparable, the much-loved, the eagerly awaited, the onomatopoeic, the greatest of knights-errant, Don Durito of the Lacandon.'"

"You forced José Saramago to come here to say those . . . those . . . those things?"

"Yes. It seemed light punishment to me, too. But, after all, he is a Nobel Prize winner, and maybe I'll need someone to do the prologue for my next book."

"Durito!" I chided him, adding, "That is all very well, but just how did you happen to turn into a pirate, excuse me, into THE PIRATE?"

"It was Sabina's fault," Durito said, as if he were talking about a *compañero* at a party.

"You visited Joaquín Sabina[7] too?"

"Of course! He wanted me to help him with the musical arrangement for his next record. But don't interrupt me. It so happened that Sabina and I were hopping bars and women in Madrid, when we reached Las Ramblas."

"But that's in Barcelona!"

"Yes, it's quite a mystery, because only a few minutes before we'd been in a bar in Madrid, captivated by an olive-skinned beauty, an Andalusian from Jaén to be more precise, and then I had to go satisfy what is referred to as a 'basic' biological need. That's when I mistook the door, and instead of entering the water closet, I stepped into the street. And it turned out that the street was in La Ramblas. Yes, there was no more Madrid or Sabina or bar or olive-skined beauty, but I still needed a water closet because a knight can't just relieve himself at any corner. Ergo, I tried to find a bar I recalled from when I had been hanging out with Manolo—"

"I guess you are referring to Manuel Vázquez Montalbán?"[8] I asked, no longer capable of being astonished by anything.

"Yes, but his name is too long, so I just call him Manolo. Anyway, I was desperately, frantically, looking for someplace with a water closet, when there before me, in a dark alley, appeared three gigantic shadows—"

"Muggers!" I interrupted, startled.

"Negative. They were three trash dumpsters, in whose shadow I calculated I'd be able to privately and discreetly do what I'd planned doing in the water closet. And that's what I did. And, with the satisfaction of a job well done, I lit my pipe and heard distinctly Big Ben chiming two o'clock."

"But, Durito, that's in London, England—"

"Yes, it seemed strange to me, too, but what wasn't strange that night? I walked until I came to a sign that read: 'Pirates Wanted. No Experience Necessary. Beetles and Knights-Errant Preferred. Inquire at the Black Spot.'" Durito lights his pipe and continues, "I kept walking, looking for a sign of the Black Spot. I had to feel my way along, scarcely able to make out the street corners and walls for a thick fog was falling over the alleys of Copenhagen that night—"

"Copenhagen? But weren't you in London?"

"Look, if you keep interrupting me over what is perfectly obvious, I'll make you walk the plank and from there to the sharks. I already told you everything was strange, and even if I did read the sign recruiting pirates in London, afterward I was looking for the sign of The Black Spot in Copenhagen, Denmark. I got lost for a few minutes in the Tivoli Gardens, but I kept looking. Suddenly, I found it. A weak light was emanating from a solitary street lamp, barely scratching through the fog, illuminating a sign that read: 'The Black Spot, Bar and Table Dancing. Special Rates for Beetles and Knights-Errant.' I hadn't realized before in what high esteem they hold beetles and knights-errant in Europe."

"It could be because they don't have to suffer them," I barely whispered.

"Don't think your ironic mutterings escape me," Durito said. "But, for the benefit of your readers, I'll continue my narrative. There will be time enough later to settle accounts with you. As I was saying, after remarking the Europeans' grand intelligence in recognizing and admiring the greatness that some of us creatures possess, I entered the bar in Montmartre close to the Sacre Coeur . . ." Durito fell silent for a moment, waiting for me to interrupt him, to state that the Sacre Coeur is in Paris, France, but I said nothing. Durito nodded, satisfied, and continued:

"Once inside, an amethyst mist crept through the atmosphere. I sat down at a table in the darkest corner. Not a second went by before a waiter said to me in perfect German: 'Welcome to East Berlin,' and, without saying another word, left what I took to be *la carte* or menu. I opened it, and it contained just one line: 'Would-be pirates, second floor.' I went up a staircase right behind me. I reached a long corridor flanked by windows. Through one of them, I could see the canals and 400 bridges that lift Amsterdam above its ninety islands. In the distance, I could see the White Tower that reminds the Greeks of Salonica of the extremes of intolerance. Farther along the corridor, through another window, the curved peak of the Swiss Matterhorn came into view. Going on, I could make out the miraculous stone in the Irish Blarney Castle that gives the gift of gab to those who kiss it. To the left rose up the belltower of Bruges's main square in Belgium. Where the passageway finally led to a dilapidated door, a window looked out on the Piazza Miracoli, and if you just stretched your hand out a little, you could feel the slight tilt of the Leaning Tower of Pisa. Yes, that corridor looked out on half of Europe, and I wouldn't have been surprised if there had been a sign on the door reading 'Welcome to the Maastricht Treaty. But, no, the door didn't have a single word on it. What's more, it didn't even have a knob. I knocked . . . nothing happened. I pushed the heavy wooden slab and it gave way without difficulty. The door opened with a mournful creak . . . I then entered a room half in shadow . . . Inside, on a table full of papers, I could see, by a poorly lit oil lamp, the face of a man of uncertain age, with a patch over his right eye and a handmade hook tugging his long beard. The man's gaze was fixed on the table. I heard nothing, and the silence was so heavy it clung to your skin like dust." Durito brushed dust off his pirate outfit.

"'I see a Pirate here,' I said to myself, moving toward the table. The man didn't move an inch. I gave a little cough, something we educated knights do to gain someone's attention. The pirate didn't lift his gaze. Instead, the parrot I'd spied on his left shoulder, in such an excellent voice that even Don José de Espronceda[9] would have applauded, began intoning the song that goes: 'With ten cannons to each side, the wind astern, in full sail, she doesn't sail the seas, she soars . . . '

"'Sit down,' I was told—I don't know whether it was the man or the parrot who spoke—then, without a word, the pirate, or the person I surmised was a pirate, handed me a piece of paper. I read it. I won't bore your readers or you, I'll just summarize by telling you it was an application to join the Great Brotherhood of Pirates, Buccaneers, and Terrors of the Sea, the A.C. of C.V. of R.O. I filled it out without hesitation. I handed the paper back to the man—not before underlining my beetle and knight-errant status—and he read it in silence.

"When he finished, he looked at me slowly with his one eye and said to me:

"'I've been waiting for you, Don Durito. Know that you're one of the last true pirates in existence. I say true because there is an infinite number of "pirates" now, stealing, killing, destroying and looting from inside financial centers and great government palaces, without ever touching water except in their bathtubs. Here is your mission.' He hands me a dossier of old parchments.

"'Find the treasure and stow it in a safe place. And now, if you'll excuse me, I must die.' And as he spoke these words, his head fell to the table. Yes, he was dead. The parrot rose up in flight and went out a window, crying, 'I go to the exile of Mitilene, I go to the bastard son of Lesbos, I go to the pride of the Aegean Sea.

Open your nine doors, fearsome hell, the great Barbarossa goes to his rest there. He has found the one who will follow in his footsteps. He who once reckoned the ocean but a tear sleeps at last. The pride of all true Pirates now sails with the Black Shield, "beneath the window, the Swedish port of Goteborg was spread out, and in the distance, a mermaid was weeping."

"So what did you do?" I asked, now completely immersed in the story (although a bit seasick from hearing the names of so many places and locales).

"Without even opening the dossier of parchments, I retraced my steps. I went back down the corridor and down to the Table Dance Bar. I opened the door and went out into the night, right onto the Paseo de Pereda in Santander on the Cantabrian Sea. I set off toward Bilbao, entering Euskal Herria. I saw young people dancing Eurresku and Ezpatadantza to the rhythm of the *txistu* and the tabor close to Donostia-San Sebastian. I climbed the Pyrenees and picked up the Ebro River between Huesca and Zaragoza. There, they managed to make me a ship, and I carried on to the delta where the Mediterranean receives the Ebro amid the roar of the Vent de Dalt. I climbed Tarragonia by foot, and from there to Barcelona, passing the site of the famous Battle of Montjuic." Durito paused, as if to gather speed.

"In Barcelona, I set off in a freighter that carried me to Palma de Mallorca. We headed southwest, skirting Valencia and, farther south, past Alicante. We sighted Almeria, and, farther along, Granada. Throughout Andalusia, a flamenco song spread across palms, guitars, and heels. A huge gypsy fiesta accompanied us until, after doubling back by way of Algeciras, we crossed Cadiz, and at the mouth of the Guadalquivir, voices of death sounded·from Cordoba and Seville. A flamenco song called out: 'Sleep now. Durito, beloved son of the world, cease your aimless wandering, and may your path be beautiful.'

"We had just managed to sight Huelva, and then we headed to the seven main islands of the Canaries. We put in there, and joined up with a bit of sap from the 'Dragon' tree—it is said to cure the ills of body and soul. That's how I came to the island of Lanzarote and had the altercation with Don Pepe that I mentioned before."

"You've traveled far," I said, weary of hearing about Durito's long journey.

"And what I've left out!" he said, proudly.

"Then you are not a knight-errant anymore?" I asked.

"Of course I am! This pirate thing is just temporary. It's only for as long as it takes me to carry out the mission the dying Barbarossa entrusted me with." Durito was staring at me.

I was thinking: Whenever Durito stares at me like that, it's because . . . because . . .

"No!" I told him.

"No what? I haven't said a thing," says Durito, feigning surprise.

"No, you haven't said a thing, but I know that look and it bodes no good. Whatever you were going to say, my answer is no. I have enough problems as a guerrilla without getting involved in being a buccaneer. And I'm not crazy enough to set sail in a sardine can!"

"Pirate, not buccaneer. They're not at all the same, my dear large-nosed cabin boy. And it's not a sardine can. She's a frigate, and she's called *Learn from Mistakes.*"

I ignored the personal insult and replied, *"Learn from Mistakes?* Hmm, strange name. But buccaneer or pirate or whatever, what it all comes down to is trouble."

"Whatever you like, but you should carry out your duty before all other things," Durito says solemnly.

"My duty?" I ask, letting my guard down.

"Yes, you should communicate the good news to the whole world."

"What good news?"

"Why, that I'm back. And you don't have to make it one of those long, dense, boring communiqués you torture your readers with. Besides, to avoid any chance of that, I have the text written out here." Having said that, Durito takes a paper from one of his bags.

I read and reread it. I turn around to look at Durito and exclaim the "No, no and no!" where we began this tale.

NOTES

1. *Escudo,* "shield, carapace," describes Durito's black beetle shell. Here it is referring to Durito's "rank" as a knight-errant.

2. A popular and controversial Italian playwright, actor, and director, Dario Fo (1926–) has earned international acclaim for his political satires and farces. Often considered the rightful heir of Aristophanes, Fo has led the field in political satire in Europe for over thirty years. The main targets of his ideologically inspired attacks have been capitalism, imperialism, and corruption in the Italian government. For performances outside Italy, his comedies are frequently adapted to reflect local political conditions. His best known plays include *Accidental Death of an Anarchist, We Won't Pay! We Won't Pay!* and *Orgasmo Adulto Escapes from the Zoo.* He was awarded the Nobel Prize for Literature in 1997 for "emulating the jesters of the Middle Ages in scourging authority and upholding the dignity of the downtrodden."

3. Pasto, which means "grass" in Spanish, is compared to the green color of the Italian "pesto" sauce.

4. José Saramago is a writer from Portugal who was awarded the Nobel Prize in Literature in 1999. He has been very interested in the situation in Chiapas.

5. Pilar del Rio, a Spanish writer and translator, is married to José Saramago.

6. Coleopterous Lamellicorn is a beetle whose antennae end in flat disklike forms called *lamellae*.

7. Joaquin Sabina (1949–) is a Spanish composer whose songs are political. He is very much influenced by Bob Dylan, with themes revolving around human misery. He has been a great influence in promoting Spanish pop.

8. Manuel Vázquez Montalbán (1939–) is a world-famous Spanish writer, thanks mainly to his series of Pepe Carvalho detective novels.

9. Don José de Espronceda (1808–1842) is the author of many songs, including "Song of the Pirate," "Song of the Cassock," and "Song of the Beggar." His characters express their alienation from society, which views them as victims.

71

The Hour of the Little Ones

I. Those Below

For all those who are little and different:

> soon will come those crazed with power
> refined/disloyal/a bit cannibalistic
> owners of the mountains and the valleys
> of the floods and the earthquakes
> those standard-bearers sans standard
> charitable and mean
> clothing letters favors demands
> sheathed in the letter box of time

——MARIO BENEDETTI

THE STORM IS CLEARING a little now. The crickets take advantage of the short let-up to go back to chirping at dawn. But a great black cowl covers most of the sky. More rain is in store, even though the puddles down below report they are already full. The night gets to have its own word now, pulling out apparently forgotten stories. This is the hour of the story of those from below, the hour of the little ones.

Down below, the long wail of a conch calls. Shadows answer it in silence, clutching weapons and hastily covering their faces in black. The guards exchange passwords; to: "Who goes there?" hope invariably answers: "The motherland." Night watches over the world of the forgotten. To do so, she has made soldiers out of their recollections and armed them with memory to relieve the smallest ones' pain.

Raining or not, down below the faceless shadow pursues his vigil. He certainly keeps at his writing or reading, but always smoking that increasingly shorter pipe. Well, since there is nothing to do up here, let's visit the little hut again. Then if it rains again, we'll be under cover. Here we are. ¡Vaya! The mess is even more spread out now. Papers, books, pens, old lighters. The shadow toils away at his writing. He's filling page after page. He goes back over them. He takes some out, adds others. From the little tape player comes a very *other* sound, like music from a faraway land, in a faraway language.

"Very other," I said. Yes, at the hour of the small ones, the other, the different, have their place too. And that is what the shadow we are visiting must be thinking about, since I have just managed to read "The Other" heading one of the pages.

But let's give him time to finish, to more fully craft the bridge between what he thinks and feels and that elusive coquette, the word. Good, he seems to be done. He gets up slowly, and leisurely goes over to the corner that is his bed. We are in luck; he has left the candle lit. Yes, here are a few pages conveniently left on the table. The one on top reads . . .

II. The Undocumented Others

For the "café" men and women in the United States:

> we are the emigrants
> the pale anonymous ones
> with the heathen and carnal century
> on our backs
> where we accumulate the legacy
> of questions and perplexities
>
> —MARIO BENEDETTI

DURITO RECOUNTS THAT, once he got over the border, a wave of terror struck out and pursued him. It's not just the threat from the *Migra*[1] or the KKK. It is also the racism that fills each and every corner of the reality of the country of the clouded stars and stripes. In fields, on the street, in businesses, in school, in cultural centers, on television, and in publications, even in bathrooms, everything pursues you to renounce your color, which is the best way of renouncing your culture, land, and history, to surrender the dignity of being other that is inherent in the café color of the Latinos in North America.

"Those 'little brown people,' " say those who hide behind the classification of human beings by the color of their skin, those in a criminal system that classifies people by purchasing power, always in direct proportion to the sales price: the more you sell, the more you can buy. If the *cafecitos* have survived the bleach and detergent campaign of the American Union's powers, it has been because the Latino communities (Mexican, Puerto Rican, Salvadoran, Honduran, Nicaraguan,

Guatemalan, Panamanian, Cuban, Dominican—to mention just some of the shades that Latin America's café color is painted in North America) have known how to build a network of resistance, without a name, without a hegemonic organization, and without becoming a product with a sponsor. Without ceasing to be "the other" in a white nation, Latinos carry one of the most heroic and unknown stories of our time: that of their color, their hurt and work-until-it-becomes-hope that café will be one more color in the rainbow of the races of the world, and no longer the color of humiliation, of contempt, of forgetting.

And it is not just the "café" who suffers and is persecuted. Durito recounts that, on top of his Mexican status, he must add the black color of his shell. Thus this courageous beetle was both "brown and black," and doubly persecuted. And he was doubly helped and supported, since the best of the Latino and black communities protected him. That is how he was able to travel through the main North American cities, as they call those urban nightmares. He didn't walk along the tourist routes, through the glamour and the marquees. Durito walked the streets below, where blacks and Latinos are building the resistance that will let them be, without ceasing to be the other. But Durito says that is a story for another page.

And now Durito Black Shield, or "Durito Escudo Negro" (if you're not globalized), is insisting on the importance of my announcing, with grand fanfare, his new book, which he calls *Insomniac Tales in Full Sail.* Now, he's given me a story that he says he wrote in remembrance of his days as a wetback, or *mojado,* in the United States.

III. Above and Below are Relative to the Struggle Waged to Subvert Them

"That's a very long title," I tell Durito.

"Stop whining and include the story or you'll get no treasure," Durito threatens with his hook. So, let's go, then.

ONCE UPON A TIME, there was a little floor who was very sad because everything happened above him.

"What are you complaining about?" the other floors asked him. "What else can a floor expect?"

So the little floor never spoke of his dream that, suddenly light, he could fly up into the sky where the little cloud would fall in love with him, the little cloud who showed up, from time to time, and never paid any attention to him. The little floor just grew more and more unhappy, until his sorrow was so great he started to weep. To weep and weep and weep and weep.

"How many times are you going to put 'and weep'? Two or three are plenty," I interrupted Durito.

"No one censors the great Durito Black Shield, much less a big-nosed cabin boy, and a runny-nosed one at that," Durito said pointing a threatening finger to the fearsome plank on which wretches walk directly into the sharks' bellies. I desisted without comment, not because I'm afraid of sharks, but because a dip in the water would be fatal with my perennial flu.

And weep and weep and weep. The little floor wept so much that all the things sitting on top and people walking above him began to slip off. The next thing you knew, there was nothing and no one above him, and the little floor had wept so much that he became very light. Now that nothing was on him, the little floor started to float upward and flew very high up. He finally got his own way, for now he is called Sky. And the cloud in question became rain and fell to the ground, from where she writes him letters, in vain, saying: "*Cielito lindo*, pretty little sky."

The moral of this story: Don't look at what is down below you, for when you least expect it, it could fall on your head.

Tan-tan.

"*TAN-TAN?* IS THE STORY OVER?" I asked uselessly. Durito was no longer listening to me. Remembering the old days when he worked as a mariachi in the East End of Los Angeles, California, he had put on a cowboy hat and was singing off-key, the song that goes: "Ay, ay, ay, ay, sing and do not weep, because when you sing, oh pretty little sky, you make all hearts grow happy." And afterward, he let go an out-of-tune cry: "Ay, Jalisco, no te rajes!²

Vale. Health to you, and I believe we'll be late weighing anchor. Durito is determined to modify the sardine ca—excuse me, the frigate—so it will look like a low rider.

EL SUP, *ORALE.*

NOTES

1. *The Migra*, the Mexican immigration department, sets up road blocks in Chiapas.

2. "Ay, Jalisco, no te rajes!" means "Jalisco, don't fall apart!"

72

The True Story of Mary Read and Anne Bonny

So they loved, as love in twain
Had the essence but in one
Two distincts, division none;
Number there in love was slain.

—WILLIAM SHAKESPEARE, "The Phoenix and Turtle," ll.25-28

For lesbians, homosexuals, transsexuals, and transvestites, with admiration and respect

While reviewing the parchments, I discovered a story Durito had asked me to include in his new book, Insomniac Tales in Full Sail. *It is about a letter whose sender is unknown, (the signature is illegible). The addressee is also an enigma, although it is clear that it is not apparent whether it is a he or a she. Oh, you'd better see it for yourselves. Upon my soul, the absence of a distinction between masculine and feminine is explained completely in the letter itself. The date is smudged, and we don't have the technology here to determine when it was written, but it seems to me that it could just as easily have been written centuries as weeks ago. You'll see what I mean. Let's go, then.*

Dear You:
PIRATES' STORIES RECOUNT that there were two women, Mary Read and Anne Bonny, who dressed up as men and, as such, sailed the seas in the company of other buccaneers, taking towns and vessels, hoisting the standard of the skull and crossbones. The year was 1720, and different stories have one or the other living and fighting the eventful sailing life of those times. They met each other on the pirate ship commanded by Captain John Rackam. Legend has it that as each one thought the other was a man, a love blossomed between them, but on learning the truth, everything returned to normal and each went her own way.

However, the story wasn't like that at all. What I'm writing you is the real story—the one that will not appear in books—of Mary Read and Anne Bonny. It was entrusted to me because people still persist in spinning yarns only from the conventions and common sense they all share, while the conventions of the "other" get no further than disapproving silence, condemnation, and neglect. This is part of the story that walks across underground bridges that the "others" extend, so that they can exist and be recognized.

The story of Mary Read and Anne Bonny is a love story, and as such it has its visible parts, but the greatest parts are always hidden in the depths. In the visible part, there is a ship (a sloop, to be more precise), and a pirate, Captain John Rackam. Both, ship and pirate, were protectors and accomplices of that love that was so very "other" and "different" that the story above was used to cover it up so it could be heard by later generations.

Mary Read and Anne Bonny loved each other knowing they shared the same essence. Some stories relate that the two were women who, although dressed as men, met knowing each other to be women, and as women, loved each other beneath the affectionate gaze of Lesbos. Others say the two were men who hid behind pirates' clothing, that they were attracted to the same sex, and that they hid their homosexual love and their passionate meetings behind the complicated story of women pirates disguised as men.

In either case, their bodies met in the mirror that discerns what is forgotten by being obvious: those hidden places of the flesh entwined in knots that when undone inspire sighs and torments, places sometimes only known to those who are the same. With lips, flesh, and hands, they extended the bridges that joined those who were the same, making them different.

Yes, whatever the case, Mary Read and Anne Bonny were transvestites who discovered each other and met in masquerade. Both the same, they revealed themselves as different, and lost all separateness and became one. To the unconventionality of their being pirates, Mary Read and Anne Bonny added that of their "abnormal" and marvelous love.

Homosexuals or lesbians, transvestites always, Mary and Anne courageously overcame being castouts, those whom "normality" would put in chains. While the men surrendered without putting up any resistance, Mary and Anne fought to the end before being taken prisoners. In this way they honored Mary Read's words:

> Asked whether she feared dying, she replied that, as to dying on the gallows, she did not think it so cruel, because, if it were not for that, all cowards would become pirates and would infest the seas to such an extent that the men of courage would die of hunger; that if the punishment were left up to the pirates, they would have none other than death, because their fear of that fate kept some cowardly criminals honorable; that many of those who today were swindling widows and orphans and oppressing their poor neighbors would go out onto the seas to rob, and the ocean would become full of thieves in the same way that the land is.
>
> —DANIEL DEFOE, General History of the Robberies and Murders of the Most Notorious Pirates

Homosexuals or lesbians? I don't know. The truth that has come down to us follows John Rackam to his grave, hung in Port Royal on November 17, 1720; it follows the sloop that served them as bed and accomplice to the shipwreck that rent it asunder. Their love was very "other" and great for being different, because, it just so happens, love follows its own path and is always a transgressor of the law . . .

I have done my duty and told you this story.

Good-bye.

(an illegible signature follows)

There ends the story . . . or does it go on?

Durito says that those who are different in their sexual preferences are doubly "other," since they are "other" within those who themselves are "other."

I, a little seasick from so much "other," ask him, "Can you explain that a bit more?"

"Yes," says Durito. "When we are struggling to change things, we often forget that the struggle also includes changing ourselves."

Above, the dawn is changing itself, making itself "other" and different. The rains follow suit, as well as the struggle . . .

VALE, ONCE MORE, with pleasure. Health to you, and don't tell anyone, but I haven't been able to figure out how the hell I'll fit in the sardine can (sigh).

THE SUP, BAILING WATER OUT OF THE FRIGATE BECAUSE, AS YOU CAN WELL IMAGINE, IT HAS STARTED RAINING AGAIN, AND DURITO SAYS THAT BAILING IS ONE OF MY "PRIVILEGES" . . .

PART TWO

Tales of Many Others

73

The Tale of the Ever Never

DECEMBER 8, 1996

ONCE THERE WAS A HE of the night. Shadow of shadows, solitary step, He walked many nights to find Her.

Once there was a She of the day. Twinkle of wheat, dance of light, She walked many days to find Him.

They were always looking for each other, He and She. The night was always pursuing the day. They both knew, She and He, the quest for what can never be found. It seemed as if it would never happen; it seemed impossible; it seemed never ever . . .

And then the dawn came, for Him and for Her. Always, forever . . .

Tan-tan.

74

The Parrot's Victory

(UPDATING A 174-YEAR-OLD STORY)

Once there was a parrot who knew only one word: "victory." Yes, sir, the days came and went, and on one of those days when our poor parrot was sitting on his perch without a care in the world, a hawk set his eye on him and swept him away through God's air. The poor green thing clutched in the hawk's claws began to complain, but he couldn't say a thing except the one word he knew by heart. Each peck the hawk gave drew forth a cry of "victory." A peck, a "victory," another peck, another "victoryds." The whole while he was being pecked to pieces, he kept saying "victory."

—JOSÉ JOAQUIN FERNANDEZ DE LIZARDI, "The Parrot's Victory," El Pensador Mexicano, October. 11, 1823

TODAY, YOU CAN REPLACE "victory" with "democracy," "independence," or "justice." The role of the parrot can be played by the bureaucrat of your choice.

75

Tales of the Seahorse

Beads and Accounts of Numbers

AUGUST 25, 1997

Roman Numeral One Tale: The 600s

THE NUMBERS IN THE 600s are very envious. For example, one afternoon I just happened to overhear a discussion between 609, 665, and 637. The subject, as usual, was 616.

"He's so spoiled!" 609 said angrily, who can't forgive 616 because he always follows him about.

"He's hateful!" 637 almost screamed, who's jealous of 616 because he's always in front of him.

"Intolerable!" argued 665, who finds 616's symmetrical proportions hard to endure.

"We must get rid of him!" brayed 687, who can't stand the fact that 616 totals up to the mysterious 13 when you add his digits together.

These particular 600s conspired against 616 (the other 600s were too busy keeping their places in the tale of the sea to participate in this tale), and they took number 616 prisoner and banished him to the land of the 700s.

That's why when the sea counts seahorses to fall asleep, when she gets to 615, she becomes confused and can't go on. Then she falls quickly to sleep.

And number 616? He was detected almost immediately by the repressive forces of the 700s. He was accused of being a destabilizing, incompatible force and condemned to divide himself 88 times until he reached his 7 of origin.

Tan-tan.

Roman Numeral Two Tale: The 100

NO ONE WOULD THINK IT, but the 100s are the most complex of all the numbers. According to them, they reflect good taste and exclusivity. "To be one of the 100s," they say, "is a sign of superior taste and lineage."

This arrogance is reflected in the 100s' daily behavior. Number 101, for example, believes he is unique and original, seeing himself as alpha and omega. The rest share his sentiment.

343

"After us, there are only commoners," goes the slogan of the 100 Club, which, as its number indicates, has only 100 members.

Tan-tan.

Roman Numeral Three Tale: The 1

THE NUMBER ONE IS well known as the most elusive of numbers, and rightly so. I mean, it's enough to know that when one has one, one wants two.

Tan-tan.

Roman Numeral Four Tale: The 200s

FRANKLY, THE 200S ARE numbers with aquatic tendencies. Their undeniable duck shapes, right from their opening number, makes their floating on the sea's dreams a common sight.

Tan-tan.

The Tale of the Little Seamstress

SEPTEMBER 3, 1997

ONCE UPON A TIME, there was a little seamstress who sewed mightily on his sewing machine. The other machines in his neighborhood laughed at him, and shouted:

"Fairy! Only old women are seamstresses!"

So the little seamstress sewed shut the mouths of everyone who made fun of him. That's why, to this day, we don't know how the story ended, because no one could tell it.

Tan-tan.

The Tale of the Little Newsboy

SEPTEMBER 3, 1997

ONCE UPON A TIME there was a little newsboy who was very, very poor and he only sold old newspapers because he didn't have enough money for new ones. People didn't buy his newspapers because they were all so out of date, and they wanted new newspapers. So the little newsboy never sold any, and every day he accumulated more and more old newspapers. What the little newsboy did was put up a paper recycling plant, and he became a millionaire, bought out all the newspaper businesses and the news agencies, prohibited publishing current news, and thus obliged people to read only news of the past. In the papers on sale today, for example, you'd read that the Zapatistas are about to arrive in Mexico City and that they'll meet with the Villistas there. You can't quite make out the date, but it seems to be either 1914 or 1997.

Tan-tan.

78

The Tale of the Little Wisp of a Cloud

NOVEMBER 7, 1997

ONCE UPON A TIME, there was a cloud who was very tiny and very lonely and used to stray far from the big clouds. She was very little, barely a wisp of a cloud. And whenever the big clouds made themselves rain so as to paint the mountains green, the little cloud would come flying to offer her services. But they scorned her because she was so small.

"You have nothing to give," the big clouds used to tell her. "You're so little."

They made terrible fun of her. Then, very sad, the little cloud would try to go off somewhere else to make herself rain, but wherever she went, the big clouds would push her aside. So the little cloud went even farther off until she came to a very dry place, so dry there wasn't a single branch growing, and the little cloud told her mirror (I forgot to tell you this little cloud carried a mirror so she could talk to herself when she was alone):

"This is the perfect spot to make myself rain because nobody ever comes here."

The little cloud made a great effort to make herself rain, and finally let out one little drop. That is, the little cloud disappeared and turned herself into a little rain-drop. Little by little, the little cloud, now a little raindrop, came falling down. All on her lonesome, she fell and she fell, but there was nothing waiting for her down below. At last, the little raindrop splashed down all by herself. Since that desert was so very quiet, the little raindrop made a lot of noise when she splashed down, right on a stone. It woke up the Earth, who asked:

"What's that noise?"

"It was a raindrop falling," the stone answered.

"A raindrop? That means it's going to rain! Quick! Get up! It's going to rain!" she warned the plants hiding underground from the sun.

And the plants got right up and took a peek, and for a moment the whole desert was covered in green, and then the big clouds saw all that green from afar and said:

"Look. There's a lot of green over there. Let's make ourselves rain on that place. We didn't know it was so green."

And they went to make themselves rain on the place that had been desert.

They rained and rained and the plants grew and everything seemed to turn green at once.

"It's a lucky thing we're around," said the big clouds. "Without us, there'd be no green."

And nobody remembered then the little wisp of a cloud who let out one raindrop whose splash woke up the sleeping ones.

Nobody remembered, but the stone kept the little raindrop's secret. Time passed, and those first big clouds disappeared and those first plants died. And the stone, who never dies, told the new plants who were born and the new clouds who arrived the tale of the little wisp of a cloud who let out a little raindrop.

Tan-tan.

79

The Story of the Schizophrenic Pig

SO, I'LL JUST TAKE A MOMENT TO tell you that I've drawn a mule for Andulio. Andulio is five years old and was born without hands. Two small stumps and the genetic cost of so many decades of misery mark the ends of his arms. Nevertheless, Andulio ingeniously grips colored pencils between his stumps to color the drawings I make for him. Every once in a while, he comes to demand a drawing and, secretly hoping for a candy reward, shows me what he's colored. Here comes the mule now. Andulio has chosen to paint it blue.

"So, now there are blue mules?" I ask him.

"There are," he says slowly.

Since it's impossible to show him that mules with blue heads don't exist (and Andulio knows this, so he can brazen it out), I opt for telling him one of those stories the seahorse whispers to the sea, during the long dawns of the mountains of the Mexican Southeast. And so, even as he looks at me skeptically, I recount . . .

Once there was a little piglet (*puerquito* or "porky" in Chiapan dialect) who thought he was a chick. From the time when he was just a baby, he played, ate, and slept with all the little chicks. But he had a problem that grew bigger just as fast he did. He had trouble climbing onto the roost where the other chicks slept. As he grew larger, he began to break the roost and fall down. But these setbacks didn't change his belief that he was a chick—well, a rooster—now. He was learning how to crow cock-a-doodle-doo.

Tan-tan.

Andulio stared at me. Finally he said: "There are blue mules," and went off with his notebook.

I LOOK TO THE SEA for a bit of understanding. She consoles me with: "That was a very stupid story."

I keep to myself what I want to answer: "I thought we were all Marcos." What else can I do?

Vale again.

THE SUP, LOOKING FOR CHICKEN THAT TASTES LIKE PORK.

The Tale of the Lime with an Identity Crisis

JANUARY 9, 1998

ONCE UPON A TIME, there was a lime who was in torment.

"I'm neither a lemon nor an orange," it told itself, worrying a great deal as it hung from its tree. It looked and looked at the oranges on their tree and the lemons, too, and grew even more tormented because it didn't belong anyplace. Then Saul and Andulio came along, cut the lime down from its tree, and began playing soccer with it, using it for a ball.

"I'm cured!" shouted the ex-lime, as Andulio dribbled to Saul and kicked it toward the opposing goal, which was, of course, a chicken coop. The yell—G-o-o-o-o-a-l—woke up a little piglet who, thinking he was a chick, had been sleeping on a roost in the chicken coop.

Tan-tan.

Moral: The closet has more than one door.

The Tale of the Nonconformist Little Toad

FEBRUARY 24, 1998

ONCE UPON A TIME, there was a little toad who wouldn't conform to being a toad. He wanted to be a crocodile. So, he went down to the swamp looking for a crocodile, and told him; "I want to be a crocodile."

The crocodile answered, "You can't be crocodile, because the way things are, you're a little toad."

"Yes," said the little toad. "But, I still want to be a crocodile. What do I have to do to be a crocodile?"

The crocodile said, "There's nothing you can do. You have to be born a crocodile. That's just how things are. A crocodile is a crocodile. A little toad is . . ."

The little toad said, "But I don't want to be a little toad. I want to be a crocodile. Do you know anyplace I can go or anyone I could talk to about my not wanting to be a toad so they can let me be a crocodile?"

"I don't know. Maybe the owl knows," the crocodile answered.

So the little toad went into the woods to look for the owl. There he met another little toad and asked him where he could find the owl.

"He only works at night," the other little toad answered. "But, be careful when you talk to him, because owls eat little toads."

The little toad waited for nightfall, and while he waited, he built himself a fort to protect himself if the owl attacked. He piled one stone on top of another until he had himself a little cave, and he went inside it. When night came, so did the owl. From inside the cave, the little toad asked, "Mr. Owl, do you know anyplace I can go or anyone I can talk to about my not wanting to be a toad, so they can let me be a crocodile? That's what I really want to be."

"Who-o-o-o's that? Where are you?" the owl asked in turn.

"It's me, and I'm right here," answered the little toad.

The owl swooped down on the little toad to grab him in his claws, but since the little toad was inside his cave, the owl only grabbed one of the stones and ate it, thinking it was the toad. Then the stone's weight made the owl drop right down to the ground, and his belly began to ache.

"Ow! Ow!" howled the owl. "Help me get this stone out of my belly, or else I won't be able to fly."

The little toad said he would help him only if he would answer his question.

"First help me, and then I'll answer you," the owl told him.

"Oranges and lemons!" said the little toad. "Tell me the answer first. If I help you get rid of the stone first, you'll eat me, and I'll never get my answer."

"OK," said the owl. "I'll answer, but the one you should tell about your not wanting to be a little toad is the lion. He's the king of all beasts and he knows why everyone is who everyone is. Now help me get rid of this stone."

"Lemons and limes," said the little toad. "If I take the stone out of your belly, you'll just keep on eating little toads."

"There, you see!" said the owl. "You won't conform to being a toad for no reason at all! You still worry about the other little toads, even while you say you don't want to be one."

But the little toad paid him no mind and went to look for the lion.

The lion lived in a cave, and the little toad thought that perhaps lions might eat little toads too, so he had an idea. He soaked himself in a puddle and rolled himself in the dirt, and he came out disguised as a rock. When the lion came out of his cave, the little toad said, "Mr. Lion, I've come to tell you how I don't want to be a toad, because I want to be a crocodile."

"Who ar-r-re you?" asked the lion.

And the little toad answered, "It's me, and I'm right here."

"But you're a little rock. What's all this about little toads and crocodiles?" asked the lion.

"Well, I've come to tell you how I don't want to be a toad, because I'm not what I want to be but only what I already am," said the little toad.

"That's the way things usually are," said the lion. "You a-r-r-re what you a-r-r-re, and you can't be something else. All you can do is be good at being what you a-r-r-re." The lion yawned philosophically.

Just then it began to rain, and the rain washed away all the mud covering the little toad so you could see that he was a little toad and not a rock. The little toad still didn't know whether lions eat little toads, so he left, hopping all the way back to his pond.

The little toad hopped along very sadly, hopping and hopping, because he was what he was and he couldn't be anything else, and all that he could do was be good at being what he was. With these sad thoughts, the little toad arrived at his pond and he hurried to look for the crocodile.

But, when he arrived at the swamp, he didn't see the crocodile. He looked and looked, but he couldn't find him anywhere. He asked the other animals, who said, "Didn't you hear? A hunter caught the crocodile, and now he's a purse and a pair of crocodile shoes."

The little toad sat and thought. Everyone was sure that now he would be very happy not to be a crocodile and very content to be a little toad, but he exclaimed, "He didn't come to a bad end! Don't you see? He transcended being a crocodile!"

So the little toad began to study and practice being a good crocodile. And he must have done a fairly good job, because one day he succeeded in deceiving a hunter. They say the little toad is now a very swanky change purse.

"It's made from the hide of a very rare crocodile," boasts the wealthy matron who bought it.

The moral of the story is, you always get your just desserts.

Tan-tan.

82

The Tale of the Pink Shoelaces

SEPTEMBER 7, 1998

ONCE UPON A TIME there was a pair of shoes. Like all the other shoes, he had dark shoelaces, black or brown. By day, this pair of shoes went around like all the other shoes, that is, shuffling along the ground. But it just so happened that this pair of shoes had pink shoelaces hidden in his closet, and at night he put them on and cut loose. And so things went for this pair of shoes until one day he got tired of hiding his happiness in the closet, and he put on his pink shoelaces. All the other shoes regarded him with grave disapproval and made a cordon of brown and black shoelaces around him to quarantine him, so he couldn't contaminate all the other shoes. The pair of shoes with pink shoelaces protested, and every day he marched with a sign saying: "Respect and Dignity for Pink Shoelaces!" But the other shoes ignored him, tying their black and brown knots even tighter to cut the pair of shoes with pink shoelaces off. And they organized a counterprotest with signs saying: "End the Pink Shoelace Plague."

And that is what they were doing when someone saw the pair of shoes with the pink shoelaces, and they put a big ugly hat on him, and the hat had pastel blue feathers, and they made a song about him, and the pair of shoes with pink shoelaces became very famous, and everyone danced to the song, and no one put a hat or feathers on the shoes with brown and black shoelaces, and no one ever made a song for them. Poor things, what will they do now?

Tan-tan.

83

The Tale of Always and Never

SEPTEMBER 12, 1998

ONCE UPON A TIME, there were two times: one was called One Time, and the other was called Another Time. One Time and Another Time made up the At Times family, who lived and ate from time to time. There were two ruling empires, Always and Never, who for obvious reasons hated to death the At Times family—they couldn't tolerate their existence. They could never let One Time live in their kingdom, because Always would then cease to be, since if it's One Time now, then it can't be Always. Nor could they let Another Time show up even once in their kingdom because Never cannot live with One Time, and even less if that One Time is Another Time.

But time and again, One Time and Another Time bothered Always and Never. And they kept it up until they were finally left in peace, when Always and Never never bothered them again. And time and again, One Time and Another Time played.

"Do you see me?" asked One Time.

"Don't you see?" Another Time answered.

And so, from time to time, they were quite happy, you see. So, there was always One Time and Another Time, and they never stopped being the At Times family.

Tan-tan.

Moral 1: At times, it's very difficult to distinguish one time from another.

Moral 2: Never say always. (Well, okay, sometimes.)

Moral 3: The "always" and "never" are imposed from above. But below, time and again, you find "nuisances," which at times is another way of saying "different," or from time to time "rebels."

Moral 4: I'll never write a story like this again, and I always do what I say. (Well, okay. Sometimes not.)

84

The Little Tree and the Others

FEBRUARY 1999

One of these early, early mornings, the sea was very tired, so I lit my pipe and turned to my copy of Tales of the Seahorse and read aloud the story about . . .

THERE WAS ONCE A little tree who was very lonesome and wished with all its heart to grace another's orchard with its singing. But the little tree stayed right where it was, until one day another came to look it over and take it away. Well, it turned out that the other was not an other but others.

These others wanted to take the little tree away each to his own orchard, but there was only one little tree, and the others were many . And the little tree wished it could plant itself in all the orchards, but it was only one little tree, and the others were many.

Then the others began to argue about who would get the little tree to take to his orchard. One other said he would take it because he was a greater other than the others. And another other said no to that; he would take the little tree because his orchard was prettier and so on, and yet another other said that he should be the one because he was a real gardener, he should be the one because he could take proper care of the little tree, and so the arguing went on for quite a while. They couldn't come to an agreement with each other because, even though they were others themselves, each didn't respect any other of the others other than himself. Finally they stopped fighting when they said that each one of them should take a piece of the little tree.

Then the little tree spoke up: "I don't agree! Aside from the fact that you can't go around cutting up trees because it's bad for the environment, nobody will win anything. If one of you takes my branches, and another takes my trunk, and another my roots and each takes his piece to his orchard, well, nobody's going to come out ahead. The one who takes my branches and plants them won't have anything because they're missing the trunk to hold them up and the roots to feed them. The one who takes the trunk won't have anything either because without the branches or roots, the trunk won't be able to breathe or drink. The one who takes the roots will end up in the same way because without the trunk or the branches, the roots won't be able to grow or breathe.

"Instead, if we can all be reasonable, I can plant myself for a while in one's orchard and then for another while in another's orchard and so on. This way, you'll all have fruits and seeds in each and every one of the orchards."

The others were left thinking.

Tan-tan.

"THAT'S IT?" asks the sea.

"Well, yes," I say, closing the book.

The sea insists: "But, what happens? Do they split the little tree up, or do they take turns, or what?"

"I don't know. We'll just have to wait and see," I answer, dodging the pen the sea throws at me.

EL SUP, HUMMING THE SONG THAT GOES: "MY FATHER AND I PLANTED THEM AT THE EDGE OF THE PATIO JUST WHERE THE HOUSE ENDS . . . " AND SO ON.

85

A Light, a Flower, and a Dawn

NOVEMBER 1, 1999

Canek thought it but he didn't say it. The Indians who were near him were aware of it. At the moment of attack the Indians in front had to wait until the enemy opened fire. Then the Indians who were behind would advance over the bodies of their dead.

—ERMILO ABREU GÓMEZ, *Canek: History and Legend of a Mayan Hero*

ON THIS DAY IN ALL of our villages, in our mountains, the dead are walking, returning to us, and they are once again talking and listening to us. In all the huts, in all the camps, an offering in some small place greets our dead and invites them to eat, laugh, smoke, have some coffee, dance. Yes, dance, because our dead are true dancers. They are dancers, and they also love to talk, our dead. They tell us stories, because it was by telling stories that our very first ones taught and learned to walk. So our dead take the same way, as do we, too, the dead whom we are. The Days of the Flowers are the days of the dead in our mountain. Today's story is . . .

The Light, a Flower and Dawn

THE ELDEST OF THE ELDERS of our communities say that our very first ones were living in rebel struggle even then, because the powerful had already been subjugating and killing them for a long time. The powerful becomes so because he drinks the blood of the weak. And so the weak become weaker and the powerful more powerful. But there are weak ones who say, "Enough is enough! ¡Ya Basta!" and who rebel against the powerful and give their blood, not to fatten the great but to feed the little ones.

And that is how it's been for a long, long time. And if there has been rebellion ever since, there has also been punishment ever since, with which the powerful punishes the rebel. Today there are jails and graves to punish the rebel; before, there were houses of punishment. And seven were the houses of punishment that existed before to punish the rebel, just as there are seven today, bearing different names.

The seven of our first ones were:

The House of Darkness had no light inside it. Total darkness and emptiness was the House of Darkness. Whoever entered it went astray and became so lost, he never returned, nor did he leave that house by another way. He died lost.

The House of Cold had a very icy and strong wind inside it that froze everything that entered it. It was cold for the heart and cold for the feelings. What was human in humans was killed there.

The House of Jaguars had nothing but jaguars shut up inside it, ravenous and ferocious. These jaguars crept into the souls of anyone who stayed in the house, and they filled their souls with hatred for everything and everyone. So it killed with hate.

The House of Bats held nothing but bats who screeched and cried and bit, and in biting, they sucked the faith out of anyone who entered there, so he could no longer believe in anything and would die of skepticism.

The House of Knives had many sharp and keen blades inside it, and anyone who entered there would have his head or his thinking cut off, and so he would then thoughtlessly die a death of his understanding.

The House of Sorrow had nothing but sorrow, such a sorrow that anyone who stayed there would go mad and, in his sorrow, forget that there are others. Forgetting and forgetting, and dying a death without memory.

The House without Desire had an emptiness inside it that consumed all desire to live, to fight, to love, to feel, to walk, in anyone who entered there. Then he was left empty, dead in life, because to live without desire is to live death.

And these were the seven houses for the rebel, for anyone who wouldn't passively accept his blood fattening the powerful and his death would give life to the world of the dead.

A long time ago, there lived two rebels. Hunahpé and Ixbalanqué, they were called, and they were also called the hunters of the dawn. Evil lived in a deep hole named Xibalbé, out of which you would have to climb very high to reach the good earth. Hunahpé and Ixbalanqué were rebels against the evil gentlemen living in the great House of Evil. One day those evil gentlemen ordered Hunahpé and Ixbalanqué be brought to them through a trick, so they would come down into their evil dwelling.

And through trickery, the hunters of the dawn arrived, and the evil gentlemen shut them up in the House of Darkness, and they gave them a torch and two cigars for light. They told them they must pass the whole night inside the House of Darkness, and on the following day, deliver the torch and the two cigars back whole. And a guard would watch all night to see if the light from the torch and from the two cigars ever went out. If the torch and cigars weren't whole the next day, then Hunahpé and Ixbalanqué would die.

The two hunters of the dawn were not afraid, no. Seeming content, they said to the evil gentlemen that what they proposed was fine, and settled into the House of Darkness. And then they used their thinking and they called the macaw, the bird who guarded all the colors, and asked him to lend them red, and with it they painted the end of the torch so that from far off it looked as if it were burning. And Hunahpé and Ixbalanqué called the fireflies and asked two of them for their company, and they ornamented the ends of the two cigars with them so that from far off it really looked as if the two cigars were lit.

And dawn came and the guard informed the evil gentlemen that the torch had been lit all night long, and that the two hunters of the dawn had been smoking their cigars the whole time. And the evil gentlemen were happy because this would give them a good excuse to kill Hunahpé and Ixbalanqué, because they wouldn't be able to fulfill their agreement to deliver the torch and the two cigars whole. But when the two hunters of the dawn left the House of Darkness and handed over the torch and the two cigars whole, the evil gentlemen became very angry because they no longer had a good excuse to kill Hunahpé and Ixbalanqué. So, they said to each other: "These rebels are quite intelligent, very intelligent. Let's look, then, for another good excuse to kill them."

"Yes," they said, "Let them sleep now in the House of Knives, that way they will surely die, since it will cut off their understanding."

"That s not enough," said the other gentleman of evil, "because these rebels have so much understanding, they must be given a much harder task, one they won't be able to carry out, so that if the knives don't kill them, we will have another good excuse to do away with them."

"That's good," said the evil gentlemen. And they went to where Hunahpé and Ixbalanqué were, and said to them:

"Now you must go rest, so we will talk again tomorrow, but we are telling you now quite clearly that tomorrow at dawn you are to give us flowers." And the evil gentlemen laughed a little, because they had already warned the guardians of the flowers not to let anyone approach during the night to cut flowers, and if someone were to approach, to attack and kill them.

"Fine," said the hunters of the dawn, "And what colors do you want these flowers to be that we must give you?"

"Red, white and yellow, "responded the evil gentlemen, and they added: "We should make it quite clear to you that if you don't give us these red, white, and yellow flowers tomorrow, we'll be greatly offended and we shall kill you."

"Don't worry," said Hunahpé and Ixbalanqué. "Tomorrow, you'll have your red, white, and yellow flowers."

And the two hunters of the dawn settled into the House of Knives. The knives were about to cut them into many pieces when Hunahpé and Ixbalanqué stopped them and said: "Let's talk."

The knives stopped and listened. And this is what the two hunters of the dawn said, "If you cut us, you'll gain very little. On the other hand, if you do nothing to us, we will give you the flesh of all the animals."

And the knives agreed and did no harm to Hunahpé and Ixbalanqué. And ever since then, that is why knives have been used for cutting animal flesh, but if a knife cuts human flesh, then the hunters of the dawn pursue it to make it pay for its crime. And then Hunahpé and Ixbalanqué were quiet in the House of Knives, their thinking whole and lively. And they said to each other:

"Now what can we do to get the flowers the evil gentlemen want, since we already know they have alerted their guardians, and they will kill us if we go near to cut the flowers in their gardens?" And the two hunters of the dawn kept thinking, and then they realized they needed the support of the little ones, so they called on the leaf cutter ants and they spoke to them like this:

"Little sisters of the cutting ants. We need you to help us in our rebellion because the evil gentlemen want to kill our struggle."

"Very well," the cutting ants told them, and they asked: "How can we help your struggle against the evil gentlemen?"

"We are asking you, please, to go to the gardens and cut red, white, and yellow flowers and bring them here. We can't go because the guards have orders to attack us. But you, since you are little, they won't even see you and they will pay you no attention."

"Fine, then," the ants said, "We are happy to do it, indeed, because we little ones have our own ways of fighting the evil gentlemen, no matter how great or powerful they may be."

And the cutting ants left, and they were very many but very little, and they went into the gardens and the guardians did not see them, because the ants were so very little. And then the ants began cutting and carrying the flowers; some cut while others carried, and some cut and carried red flowers, and others cut and carried white flowers, and others cut and carried yellow flowers. And they finished quickly and quickly, they bore the flowers to where the two hunters of the dawn were.

On seeing the flowers, Hunahpé and Ixbalanqué became very happy, and this is how they spoke to the cutting ants:

"Thank you very much, little sisters. Although you are small, your power is great, and because we are so grateful to you, you shall always be many, and nothing big will ever be able to attack you." And that is why they say that ants always resist, and no matter how big their attackers are, they can't be defeated.

The next day the evil gentlemen came, and the two hunters of the dawn gave them the flowers they wanted. Now the evil gentlemen were surprised to see that the knives hadn't cut them, but they were even more surprised when they saw the red, white, and yellow flowers Hunahpé and Ixbalanqué gave them, and then those evil gentlemen grew very angry and set about looking for more excuses to do away with the rebel hunters of the dawn.

86

The Words That Walk Truths

I'D LIKE YOU TO LET me to tell you a story, a story having to do with seven, with sacrifice, with ancestors, with the land, and with the word.

The story I am going to tell you comes from very far away. And I am not speaking of distance or time but of depth, because the stories that gave birth to us don't walk through time or space. No, they're just there, being. And by being, life goes on above the stories and doubles the skin over them, because life and the world are like that, with history wrapping itself up in the skin, to stay warm and to be. And that's just how stories gather together, one above the other, so the very oldest are quite deep, and very far away. That is why when I say that the story I am going to recount to you comes from very far away, I am not speaking of many miles or years or centuries.

When the eldest of the elders of our peoples speak of stories that come from far away, they point to the earth to show us the place where the words that walk truths are. Dark is the earth, and dark is the dwelling where the first word, the true word, rests. That is why our very first fathers and mothers had dark skin. That is why those who carry history on their shoulders go about with faces the color of night.

The history of the worlds that make this world comes from very far away. You can't find it hanging from a book or painted on a tree. It isn't in the flowing of a river or in the flight of a cloud. You can't read the history of the worlds in our filled-up calendars. The history of how we were born and how we were made isn't hidden behind letters or within them. But it isn't the history of this world in which so many worlds walk that I am going to recount to you. Or maybe it is. Perhaps all histories are the daughters and mothers of the first history, the most distant, the most profound, the most true.

The eldest of the elders who live in these mountains tell that there were already many men and women living in this world before there was day. Large was the number of people, and everything was still night and water. The sky seemed as if it were sleeping, and it seemed asleep because the greatest of gods, those who gave birth to the world, the very first, were sleeping. These first gods had worked for a very long time. Making a new world is very tiring. They were sleeping, then, the most great gods, and the sky kept company with them in their sleep. The very first gods dreamed on beds of night and water. They had already made the mountains, the first earth they had plucked from the water. And some were even, and others were torn and thus there were mountains, valleys, and breaks. The first earth was mountains. That is why, say the eldest of the elders, it is in the mountain where the very first history lives, the one that is farthest away.

When the men and women grew tired of so much water and night, they started complaining and quarreling a lot. These men and women who were many made a big ruckus, yes, but they were the first who walked the world, and there were already many colors painting their skins and words. Such a confusion of noise woke up the first gods, the most great, and they asked the men and women living in the world why they were yelling so much. All of them began speaking at once, and shouted and grabbed the word and fought to see who could talk the most and the loudest. And so they carried on.

They didn't understand much of this, the first gods who were great and had given birth to the world. They couldn't understand what the men and women wanted, because they weren't speaking, just yelling and fighting. And the first gods lost more and more sleep until they called out to the men and women, who had been made of corn, the true ones, and asked them what was going on.

The men and women of corn had hearts made of the word, and they understood that the word doesn't walk with shouting or fighting, in order to embrace men and women. For when the flower of the word was born, the most great gods, those who gave birth to the world, the very first, planted it in the hearts of these men and women of corn, knowing that truth is good soil for cultivating and growing the word. But that is another story.

It turns out that these men and women of corn went to speak with the first gods.

"So here we are," they said.

And the gods asked: "Why do those men and women fight so much? Don't they know that all that noise they are making isn't letting us sleep? What do they want then?"

"They want light," said the true men and women to the great gods.

"Light," said the first gods.

"Light," repeated the true men and women.

The gods looked at each other, and you could clearly see they were pretending not to know anything, because certainly one of them had to know about light, but they didn't say anything.

"Wait," the great gods asked the true men and women, and they went off to have a meeting. They were at it for some time, perhaps because it simply takes a long time to reach great accords, because light was no small thing; it was, after all, light. When the gods returned, they told the true men and women: "The light is just beyond, but there isn't any here."

"So where is the light, then?" asked the men and women of corn.

"There," said the gods, pointing to the seven points that guide the world. And the seven points that mark the world are in front and behind, to one side, and first. The gods pointed to one of the sides, and their word followed: "The light is very heavy. That is why we didn't bring it with us. It is still there. It weighs a lot. Not even we who are the first gods could carry it and bring it here. That is why it is still there." The first gods were silent and sad because even though they were the most great, those who gave birth to the world, they hadn't been able to carry the light that the men and women needed to walk the worlds that make the world. And the saddest of all was Hurakán, also named Caculhá Hurakán, which means "bolt with one foot" or "lightning," because, even though he was very great and powerful, he hadn't been able to carry the light because he only had one foot.

The men and women of corn, the true ones, kept thinking. But since the shouting of the men and women was so loud, they went up a mountain and there they kept quiet to seek the word, and in silence they found it. And the word spoke to them and said that they needed to make something that could carry the light, even though it was very heavy, so it wouldn't just stay on the other side.

"That is it, then!" said the true men and women. "We just need to make something that will carry the light and bring it here. All right, then," the men and women of corn said once more.

And then they set about thinking how to make that something that could carry the light and bring it from very far away to this side. And they thought about what they could make that something out of, and they saw that the earth was good. But the earth crumbled when they just put a bit together. And then they threw water on it, and then it held together for a little, but when it dried, it crumbled apart again. And then they grabbed a bit of earth and threw a bit of water on it, and they brought it close to the fire, and it became strong and durable for a while, but then the heat of the fire itself broke it. Then they got the idea of blowing on it to cool it while it was by the fire. And they saw that in that way the earth held together well, with the help of the water, fire, and wind. And ever since, that is why clay has served to carry and hold things. And that is why the true men and women carry the light from very far away.

And then they set about thinking what shape to give the something that would bring the light to this side. And then they thought that, of all the things that walked and were in the world, the human being had the best form, and then they thought to give that something the shape of a human being, that something which would carry the light to bring it to the world for everyone. And so they made a head, two legs, and two arms for it. And the men and women of corn became very happy, because now the cart that would bring the light, carrying it from afar, had substance and shape.

But because everything was just night and water and was very dark, that something would certainly become lost on the road, and the true men and women grew very unhappy. But then came Hurakán, the Heart of the Sky, as they also call the lightning, the thunder, and the storm who walks on his one foot, but who is strong and shines. And the Heart of the Sky, also called Hurakán, carved something into the skin of the dark to give it the brightness of his one foot, and he carved it deep until he scratched the Heart of the Sky, and finally that something shone. But now his shape was no longer one head with two arms and two legs; all that scraping had sharpened it, and now it had five points: one where the head had been, two where the arms had been and two more where the legs had been. But that something with five points still shone a little. And the true men and women became happy, because that bit of brightness would ensure that it wouldn't become lost on the road, while going to carry back the light that was far away and so heavy.

And it was strong, and it even looked pretty with its five points, but it didn't walk. And the true men and women gave it quite a few pushes, but it just stayed right there. "Now what?" asked the men and women of corn. "We'll see," they answered, and they scratched their heads to see if that would make an idea come out, and because of that, ever since then, when men and women don't know something, they will scratch their heads to see if the idea is stuck there, or sleeping. But no matter how much they scratched, they did not find their idea. And they went to ask the eldest of the elders of their community. And this is what the eldest of the elders told them: "That something doesn't walk because it doesn't have a heart. Only things with hearts walk."

And then the true men and women became happy, because now they understood why what they had made wasn't walking. And then they said, "Let's put a heart in what we have made, so it can walk and go to bring the light that is far away and weighs so much." But they did not know how, or from what to make the heart for that something, and then each one of them ripped out the hearts that every one of them carried in their chests, and they put all the hearts together to make one very large heart, and they put it in the center of the five points of the something they had made. And that something began to move, and the men and women of corn were very happy, because even though they had given up their hearts, they had made the something move.

But the something walked from one side to the other, and it came and went and made turns and leaps, and no matter how much they pushed it and pointed out the side it should be walking on, it just wouldn't head out or stay on the path for good. And, after more head-scratching, the true men and women despaired a bit, and they went once again to ask the eldest of the elders of their village: "It is moving now because we gave it a heart, but it walks this way and that way. It doesn't head out on the good path we want it to. So what are we to do?" they asked.

And the eldest of the elders responded: "Things that have hearts move, but only things that think can have a destiny and a path."

And once again the men and women of corn became happy and said to each other: "Now we know how to give a destiny and a path to what we made. Yes," they said, "Let's give it thought from the same place where we found feeling." And from their breasts they pulled out the good word, the true one. And they went and kissed that something that moved so much with it, and, sure enough, that something stood still for a bit and then it spoke and asked:

"Where should I go and what should I do?"

The true men and women applauded, because they had now given birth to what would carry the light that weighed so much and was so far away and bring it to illuminate all the men and women of all the worlds. And thus something was made that was very great and powerful, and seven were the elements that formed it: earth, water, fire, air, lightning, heart, and word. And ever since then, seven are the elements that give birth to and make new and good worlds. And then the men and women of corn applauded, and then they told the something where it should go and what it should do, and they even gave it a tumpline to help it, because they understood that the light was so heavy that not even the greatest gods, those who gave birth to the world, the very first, had been able to carry it.

And the something left, and it was gone for some time. And sitting in the mountain, the true men and women also passed some time, looking out now this way and now that way. And night went on and nothing moved. But the men and women of corn didn't despair. They were calm because they knew well that the light would come; that is why they had given heart and word to the one who would have to carry and bring the light, no matter how far away and how heavy. And so it passed that some time later, that something could be seen far off, slowly returning. Step by tiny step, it was coming over to this side, walking the sky. And, once it arrived, more time passed and the light came right behind it. Then there was sun and there was day, and the men and women of the world were joyful and they stayed on their path, seeking with the light, seeking who knows what, because, although certainly everyone is seeking something, what is important is that everyone is seeking.

This is the story I wanted to recount to you, the story of how light came to this world. Perhaps you think this is just a story or a legend, like those who inhabit the mountains of the Mexican Southeast. Perhaps. But if you were to keep vigil in the night that embraces our lands, you could see at daybreak, to the east, a star. She announces the day. Some call her "dayspring" or "the morning star." Scientists and poets have called her Venus. But our most ancient ones called her Icoquih, which means "she who carries the world on her shoulders," or "she who carries the sun on her back." We name her "the morning star" because she announces that night is ending and another morning is coming. This star, made by the men and women of corn, the true ones, walks with feeling and thought, and, faithfully, it comes at daybreak.

And I recount this story to you, not to divert you and take away from the time you need to look at all the things that you have to look at in this meeting. No. I'm telling it to you because this story that comes from so far away reminds us that it is through thinking and feeling comes the light that helps us to seek. With heart and head we must be bridges, so that the men and women of all the worlds may walk from night to day.

PART THREE

Old Don Antonio

87

The Story of Colors

Old Don Antonio points at a macaw crossing the afternoon sky. "Look," he says. I see this burning streak of colors on the gray mist that foreshadows a rainstorm. "It doesn't seem real, so many colors for just one bird," I say on reaching the hilltop. Old Don Antonio is sitting on a little knoll, above the mud that has taken over this main path. He catches his breath while he rolls a new cigarette. I walk a few steps farther on and realize that he's stayed behind. I go back and sit beside him. "Do you think we'll get to town before it starts raining?" I ask him, lighting my pipe. Old Don Antonio doesn't seem to hear me. Now, a flock of toucans has caught his eye. In his hand, the cigarette waits for a flame to commence its slow smoky drawing. He clears his throat, lights the cigarette and gets comfortable to begin, slowly:

The Story of Colors

THE MACAW WASN'T ALWAYS like that. It barely had color. It was gray all over and had stubby little feathers, like a wet chicken's. It was just one more of the many birds that came to the world, nobody knows how, because even the gods didn't know who made them. That's just how it was. The gods woke up after the night said, "This is far enough," to the day, and the men and women were sleeping or making love, which is a beautiful way to grow tired to sleep well. The gods were fighting. These gods were always fighting because they were very quarrelsome, not like the first ones, the seven gods who gave birth to the world. And the gods were fighting because the world was very boring, painted in just two colors. And their anger was just because only two colors shared in the world: one was the black sent by the night, and the other was the white that walked by day. There was a third that wasn't really a color. It was the gray that paints dusk and dawn so the black and white won't bump up against each other. So these gods were quarrelsome, but they were also wise. They had a meeting, and they decided to make more colors, so that walking and making love would be more pleasurable for the bat men and women.

One of these gods began walking in order to think his thoughts better. He thought his thoughts so hard that he didn't look where he was going. He tripped on a rock that was so big he banged his head and blood poured out. After swearing and shouting for quite a while, he saw his blood and noticed that it was different from the other two colors. He ran to where the other gods were and showed them the new color and they named it "red," the third color to be born.

Later, another god was looking for a color for painting hope. He found it, even though it took a while, and went to show it to the assembly of the gods. They named this color "green," the fourth to be born. Another one started digging deep in the earth. "What are you doing?" the other gods asked him. "I am looking for the earth's heart," he replied, throwing dirt all over the place. Soon, he came upon the earth's heart and showed it to the other gods. They named this fifth color "brown."

Another god went straight up as high as he could "I'm going to see what color the world is," he said, and he climbed and he climbed. When he was quite high up, he looked down and saw the color of the world, but he didn't know how to bring it back down to where the other gods were. He just kept looking at it for the longest time until he grew blind with looking because by then the color of the world was stuck in his eyes. He got down as best he could, tripping all the way, and went where the assembly of gods was and told them, "I'm carrying the color of the world in my eyes." They called the sixth color "blue."

Another god was looking for colors when he heard a child laugh. Quietly, he drew closer and when the child wasn't paying attention, in a flashing second he snatched the child's smile away and left him crying. That's why they say children can be laughing one second and crying the next, because of how suddenly the god stole the child's laugh. The god took away the child's smile and they named this seventh color "yellow."

By then the gods were tired, so they went off to drink some *pozol*[1] and sleep, leaving the colors in a little box they threw beneath the ceiba tree.

The little box wasn't shut very tight so the colors got out and began to play and make love to each other, and different and new colors appeared. The ceiba tree looked at them all and sheltered them so the rain couldn't wash all the colors away. When the gods came back, there were no longer just seven colors but many more. The gods looked at the ceiba tree and said, "You gave birth to the colors. You will take care of the world. And from your crown, we will paint the world."

They climbed to the top of the ceiba tree, and from there, they began flinging the colors all around, just like that. The blue stuck partly to the sky and partly to the water; the green fell on the trees and plants; the brown, which was heavier, fell on the earth; and the yellow that was the child's laugh flew all the way up to paint the sun. The red dropped into peoples' and animals' mouths, who ate it so it painted the insides of their mouths red. And the black and white were already in the world. The way the gods were tossing around the colors, not even looking where they were throwing them, made a real mess. Some colors splashed on people, and that's why people are different colors and think differently.

After a while, the gods grew tired and wanted to go to bed again. These gods weren't like the first ones, the ones who gave birth to the world. These gods always wanted to sleep. So, because they didn't want to forget the colors or lose sight of them, they looked for a way to keep them safe. And they were thinking about how to do that with all their hearts when they saw a macaw. They grabbed it and began putting all the colors on it, having to stretch its feathers so all the colors would fit. And that's how the macaw got its colors. Now it strolls around in case men and women forget that there are many colors and ways of thinking in the world, and how happy the world will be when all the colors and ways of thinking have a place.

NOTE

1.   *Pozol* is a corn drink.

88

The Story of the Mirrors

JUNE 9–11, 1995

I want you as a glass
Never as a mirror

——PEDRO SALINAS

May 1985. The moon looks into the mirror surface of the lake, and jealous, with her waves the lake wrinkles her face. Midway between the shores we navigate in a dugout canoe, which is as stable as my resolve to cross this lake. Old Don Antonio has invited me to try out his dugout canoe. For twenty-eight days, between the new moon and the full moon, old Don Antonio has carved, with a sharp-edged machete and an ax, a long cedar log. The boat is seven meters long. He explains to me that a dugout canoe can be made from cedar, caoba, huanacastle, or bariy, and points out each type of tree to me. He is bent on showing me each tree, but I cannot tell the difference; to me all trees are tall. But that was during the day. Now it is dawn, as law dictates, and we are row-ing in this little cedarwood boat that Old Don Antonio has named the Malcontent.

"In honor of the moon," says Old Don Antonio, while rowing with a long and nar-row pole. We are in the middle of the lake. Like a comb, the wind curls the waves on the water and the canoe sways up and down. Old Don Antonio says we must wait for the wind to settle down, and lets the boat drift.

"Any one of these waves can capsize the canoe," he says, while with his burning cigarette he makes the smoke spiral like waves into the wind. By the light of the full moon, one can make out in the distance the large islets that dot Lake Miramar. From a spiral of smoke, Old Don Antonio beckons an old story. I am more worried about capsizing (I am still caught between being nauseous and being terrified), so I am in no mood for stories. Apparently, my state does not concern Old Don Antonio. Lying on the bottom of the canoe, he begins to recount . . .

The Story of the Mirrors

THE MOST OF ANCIENT of the ancients say that the moon was born right here in the jungle. They say that many worlds ago, the gods had fallen asleep, tired

376

from so much playing and so much doing. It was quiet. But a low whimpering started to come from the mountain. It turns out that the gods had left a lake forgotten in the middle of the mountain. When they parceled out those things belonging to the Earth, it appears that this small lake was left over. Not knowing what to do with it, they left her stranded among peaks so high that no one ventured there. And so the little lake was crying because she was alone. And as she was crying, the Mother Ceiba, she who sustains the world, her heart was saddened by the lake's crying. Lifting up her white skirts, the ceiba went to the little lake.

"Well, what's the matter?" the ceiba asked the bit of water, which now was just a little puddle after so much crying.

"I don't want to be alone," said the little lake.

"Then I will stay here by your side," said the ceiba, she who sustains the world.

"I don't want to stay here," said the little lake.

"Then I will take you with me," said the ceiba.

"I don't want to be down here, stuck to the earth. I want to be up high, like you," said the little lake.

"Then I will lift you to my head, but only for a bit. The wind is ill-humored and could blow you away," said the ceiba.

And doing what she could, Mother Ceiba gathered up her skirts, and bent down to lift the little lake into her arms. Carefully, since she was a mother, she placed the little lake upon the crown of her head. Slowly, Mother Ceiba stood up again, making sure that not one drop of water should spill from the little lake, because Mother Ceiba could see that the little lake was very shallow. When the little lake was finally up high, she exclaimed:

"It's really great up here! Take me to see the world! I want to see everything!"

"The world is too large, my girl, and you can fall from up there," said the ceiba.

"I don't care! Take me!" insisted the little lake, and she made like she was going to cry again.

Mother Ceiba did not want the little lake to cry, so she started to walk, holding herself very straight, with the little lake on her head. Ever since then, women have learned to walk with water jugs up on their heads without spilling a drop. Like Mother Ceiba, the women from the jungle walk high, when they bring water from the stream. Straight back, head up, and a step like a summer cloud. That's how a woman walks when she carries, up top, the soothing water.

Mother Ceiba was a good walker, for in those days the trees did not stand still but moved from place to place, having children, filling the world with trees. But the wind was hanging around, bored and whistling. When he saw Mother Ceiba, he wanted to play at lifting her skirts with the swing of his hand. But the ceiba got angry and told him:

"Be silent, wind! Can't you see I am carrying on my head a crying and willful little lake?"

Then the wind looked up and saw the little lake peering from above, nestled in the ceiba's crown of wavy hair. And he saw she was pretty and thought to make her fall in love with him. And so the wind went up to the ceiba's head and started whispering sweet words into the little lake's ears. Flattered, the little lake said to the wind:

"If you take me around the world, I will go with you!"

The wind didn't have to think twice about it. With some clouds he made himself a horse and went off with the little lake sitting behind him. All this happened so fast that Mother Ceiba never noticed that the little lake was no longer on her head.

For a long while the little lake traveled with the wind. The wind would tell the little lake how good-looking she was. Who wouldn't be satisfied to drink her water? One could go deep into her, the wind would say to the little lake, hoping to convince her to make love with him in the corner of some early dawn. And the little lake believed everything the wind said to her. And each time they would fly above a puddle or a lake, the little lake wouldn't miss the chance to look at her reflection, and she would fuss with her wet hair, gaze with her liquid eyes, make flirtatious faces with the small waves on her round face.

But what the little lake wanted was to go from place to place; she wanted nothing to do with the little corner of dawn and making love. And it seems like the wind was offended. He took her high up and made the horse buck, sending the little lake into a fall. And because she was up so high, it took a long time for the little lake into fall. And certainly she would have taken a good thump if it were not for some stars who saw that she was falling and, as best as they could, fastened the little lake to their pointed arms. Seven stars held her by her sides, like a sheet, and once again lifted her to the sky. The little lake was very pale from the fright of her fall. And since she did not want to go back down to the earth, she asked the stars if she could stay with them.

"All right," said the stars, "but you'll have to go wherever we go."

"Yes," agreed the little lake, "I will go with you."

But the little lake became sad always going to the same places, and she began her crying again. And the gods woke up with the crying and went to see what was going on, and they saw the little lake being pulled by seven stars, crossing the night. When they heard her story, they were angered because they had not made the lakes to hang around in the skies, but to be on the earth. They went to the little lake and said:

"You will no longer be a lake. Lakes don't live in the skies. But, since we can't lower you down again, you must remain here. Now your name will be 'moon' and for being flirtatious and conceited, your punishment will be to reflect forever the well in which the earth's light is kept."

As it turns out, the gods had put away the light inside the earth and had made a deep, round hole so that the stars could come and drink when their light and spirits went out. And so the moon has no light, but it is a mirror. When she appears full, she reflects the large hole with light, where the stars come to drink. A mirror of light, that is the moon. That is why, when the moon strolls over a lake, the mirror looks at itself in the mirror. And no matter what, the moon is never happy or sad, she is malcontent . . .

Mother Ceiba was also punished by the gods for all her pampering. She was forbidden to walk, so she would not go from place to place, and they made her carry the world. And they made her skin thicker, so she would not feel sorry when she heard the crying around her. Ever since then, with a skin as hard as stone, Mother Ceiba stands without moving. If she were to walk even a little bit, the world would fall down.

"And that's how it was," said Old Don Antonio. "Ever since then, the moon reflects the light that is kept inside the earth. That is why, when she finds a lake, the moon stops to make up her face and fix her hair. That is also why when women see a mirror, they stop to look at themselves. It was a gift from the gods: each woman was given a little piece of the moon, so she could fix her hair and makeup her face, so she wouldn't want to journey and lift herself up to the skies."

THE STORY ENDED, but the wind hasn't let up, and the waves still threaten the little boat. But I say nothing, and it's not because I am thinking about Old Don Antonio's words, but because I am sure that if I open my mouth I will throw up, perhaps even my liver, into the agitated mirror where the moon rehearses her coquetry . . .

89

The Story of Dreams

DECEMBER, 1995

P.S.

TO TEACH IS THE SAME AS TO STRUGGLE. Old don antonio was sharpening his machete and smoking in the doorway of his cabin. I was sleeping at his side, blanketed by exhaustion and the chirping of crickets. And just like ten years before and ten years after the sharp-edged smoke from Old Don Antonio's cigarette, the sky was a night sea so enormous that you couldn't see it begin or end. The moon had appeared a few moments earlier. A cloud of light marked the crest of the hill that could be a balcony for a silver-plated coquetry, a springboard for a clean heart-thrust, the platform for a maiden voyage. A golden blade barely winking at the expectant valley. Then, there was a road of gold turning to silver turning to mother of pearl. Then a mended sail filled and billowed upward. The night sailed past. Below, silence and nostalgia waited.

December. Nineteen seventy-five, 1985, 1995; the sea ever opening westward. It wasn't raining, but the cold dampened our clothes and seeped into the unquiet dreams of the restless sleep of slow asphyxiation. Out of the corner of his eye, Old Don Antonio saw I was awake and asked me:

"What did you dream?"

"Nothing," I answered, looking for my pipe and tobacco in the cartridge belt.

"That's no good. You dream and get to know yourself," came his reply as he returned to the slow caress of file against the metal-plated tongue.

"What's no good about it?" I asked, lighting my pipe.

Old Don Antonio stopped working and after checking the edge, set down the machete. With hands and lips, he started up a cigarette and a story:

The Story of Dreams

"NO ONE TOLD ME what I'm going to tell you. Well, my grandfather told me, but he said I wouldn't understand it until I dreamed it myself. So I'm going to

380

tell you the story I dreamed, not the story my grandfather told me." Old Don Antonio stretches out his legs and rubs his tired knees. He lets out a billow of smoke that obscures the moon's reflection on the steel leaf resting on his lap. He continues:

"In every wrinkle on the faces of the great-grandparents, our gods go on living and waiting. The old times reach down to us. It's through time that our ancestors' reason reaches us. The great gods speak through the eldest elders and we listen. When the clouds cover the earth, barely clinging to the hills with their little hands, the first gods come down to play with men and women and teach them the truth. You don't always recognize them because they're wearing the faces of the night and the clouds. We dream dreams to make ourselves better.

"It's through dreams that the first gods speak to us and teach us. The man who doesn't know how to dream is terribly alone and has to hide his ignorance in fear. The first gods taught the men and women of corn to dream so they could speak, so they could know and be known, and they gave them *nahuals*[t] to walk with them throughout their lives. The *nahuals* of the true men and women are the jaguar, the eagle, and the coyote: the jaguar to fight, the eagle to give flight to dreams, and the coyote to be able to think and to see through the lies of the powerful.

"In the world of the first gods, of those who made the world, everything is dream. The earth where we live and die is a great mirror of the dream in which the gods live. The great gods all live together. Birds live with them. No one is above or below. It's the injustice governments create that disorders the world and sets a few above the many below. The world isn't naturally like this. The true world, the great mirror of the dream of the first gods, those who gave birth to the world, is very big, and everyone is free as a bird. It's not like the world is now, shrunk so that a few can be above the many below. Right now, the world is flawed. It doesn't reflect the dream world where the first gods live.

"That's why the gods gave the men of corn a mirror called dignity. In it, men are equal and rebel if they are not equal. That's why our first grandparents rebelled, and that's why they die inside us today so that we may live. The mirror of dignity destroys the demons who deal in darkness. Seen in the mirror, the lord of darkness reflects the nothingness from which He's made. Being nothing, he melts into nothingness before the mirror of dignity, the lord of darkness, the divider of the world.

"The gods made four points upon which to lay the world, not because they were tired, but so that men and women could walk as free as birds, so that every-one could work together, and so no one would be set above anyone else. The gods made two more points for flying and walking on the earth. And the gods made another point from which the true men and women could set out walking. Seven points give sense to the world and purpose to the true men and women: ahead and behind, one side and the other, above and below, and the seventh is the path we dream, the destination of the men and women of corn, the true ones.

"The gods put a moon in the breast of the mothers, to feed the dream of the new men and women in whom history and memory live. Without them, death and oblivion feast. The earth, our great mother, has two breasts so that men and women can learn to dream. Learning to dream, they learn to grow. Finding dignity, they learn to struggle. That's why when the true men and women say, 'We're going to dream,' it means, 'We're going to struggle.'"

OLD DON ANTONIO fell silent. He fell silent, and I fell asleep. I dream that I'm dreaming, I dream that I know, I dream that I understand . . .

Above, the moon's breast poured milk on the road to Santiago. The night was queen, and all was still to be made, to be dreamed, to be struggled for.

EL SUP, PACKING MEMORIES AND A FIELD . . .

NOTE

1. A *nahual* is a kind of alter-ego for a person or deity, in the shape of an animal. Usually a person with a very strong personality—a sorceror or a king—could assume this animal shape. Belief in the *nahual* extends through Mesoamerica.

90

The Story of the Seven Rainbows

The evening was about to exhaust itself. There was a brilliant gray that also announces dawn. Old Don Antonio finished setting down two sacks of pergamino coffee and sat next to me. I waited for a connection to help me cross some settlements where there were no compañeros. The crossing had to be by night. With dawn came January and 1986. It was still a time to be hidden, to conceal ourselves from those we would become a part of later. I looked toward the west and, fortressed behind the pipe's smoke I tried to dream of a different morning.

Old Don Antonio remained silent and barely made the necessary noise to roll one of those cigarettes that announced smoke and stories. But Old Don Antonio did not speak. He stayed there looking toward where I was looking and waited, patiently, for me to speak.

"Until when will we be hiding from our people?" I said, while the last mouthful of smoke escaped through the bowl of the pipe. Old Don Antonio cleared his throat and decided, finally, to light the cigarette and the word. Slowly, like one who loosens hope, Old Don Antonio relight the evening with . . .

The Story of the Seven Rainbows

"IN THE VERY EARLY beginning of the worlds, where later our oldest grandfathers walked, the greatest gods, those who gave birth to the world, the first, came down to speak to the men and the women of corn. It was an evening just like this, cold, blinking rain and sun. The first gods sat to talk with the men and women of corn to agree on the path to be walked by the true men and women, since these gods, who gave birth to the world, were not bossy like the gods who came later. They sought a good agreement with the men and women of corn. They always sought to take a good path together, seeking agreement and good words. So this evening, which was one of the first of that very early world, the greatest gods were speaking with the men and women of corn, with their equals.

"They agreed to seek the accord with other men and women, who spoke other languages and had other thoughts. The men and women of corn had to walk very far within their heart to seek the words that other men and women, with other colors and other hearts, would understand.

"So they came to agree on the work for the men and women of corn to make a good world. They agreed that seven were the very first tasks, the most important to make us new. And the first seven gods spoke, those who gave birth to the world, saying that seven were the tasks that should be accomplished so that the world is made good, because seven were the winds or the skies that gave shelter to the world and, as such, the first gods said that these were the seven skies. The seventh wind was Nohochaacyum, of the great father Chaac. The sixth was the wind of the *Chaacob*, the gods of rain. The fifth wind was the Kuilob Kaaxob, masters of the wilderness. The fourth wind was the guardians of animals. The third wind was of the bad spirits. The second was the wind of the gods. And the first wind, immediately on top of the earth, was of the *balamob*, guardians of the crosses for the village and the *milpas*. In the depths was Kisin, the god of tremor and fear—the devil.

"The first gods also said that there were seven colors, and seven was the number used to count them. I have already told you the story of the colors, and later I will tell you the story of the seven tasks, if there is time for you to listen and for me to tell it," Old Don Antonio adds hurriedly, while the last glow of his cigarette is extinguished.

Then comes the silence in which Old Don Antonio conjures up more smoke and dreams. A small flashing light of the match in his hand and the glow reappears: "So the men and women of corn agreed to fulfill the seven tasks so that the world was made good. And they looked to where the sun and the moon take turns to sleep and asked the first gods how much they should walk in order to fulfill the seven tasks that serve to make the world new. So the first gods said that seven times seven they would walk seven, because that is how the number came about which reminds us that not everything comes in pairs and that there is always room for the other. So the men and women of corn said good and turned their gaze to the mountain, which was the small box where Mother Earth's breasts were held, taking turns one by, day the other by night. And in seeing this, the men and women of corn asked themselves how would they know how many times is seven times seven walking the number seven; and the first gods said that they did not know either because they were the first gods, but they did not know everything and they also had to study a lot; and that is why they would not leave but remained with the men and women of corn so that they would think together and together find the path to make the world new.

"And so there they were, that is thinking themselves, that is knowing themselves, that is speaking themselves, learning themselves— that is, being—when the rain hung right in the middle of the afternoon without falling or rising, was just there; and the men and women of corn and the first gods looked and saw how a bridge of light and clouds began to paint itself, how the bridge came from the mountain to the valley. They could see clearly that the bridge of colors, clouds, and light did not go anywhere, nor did it come from anywhere, but it was just there, on top of the rain and the world. And they were happy all of them who were thinking and knowing themselves, and they understood that it was good, this bridge for the good worlds to come and go, the new worlds that we make. And quickly the musicians brought out their instruments and quickly the first gods and the true men and women of corn pulled out their feet and they began to dance, because the had been thinking themselves, and knowing themselves, and speaking themselves and learning themselves. And now that they finished danc-ing, they met again and found that seven times seven meant that seven rainbows with seven colors had to be made by walking so that the seven main tasks could be fulfilled. And it was also understood that after making the seven rainbows there would be seven more, because the bridges of clouds, colors, and light do not come nor go, they have no beginning and no end, they do not start or stop, but continue to cross from one side to the other.

"And that is the agreement arrived at by the first gods and the men and women of corn, the true ones. And ever since that afternoon of happiness and knowing, they spend their lives making bridges, and also making bridges in death. The bridges are always made of colors, of clouds and of light to go from one place to the other, to carry out the tasks that give birth to the new world, that makes us good seven times seven walking seven, the men and women of corn, the true ones. Making bridges, they live, making themselves bridges, they die . . . "

OLD DON ANTONIO becomes quiet. I stare at him and am about to ask him what all this has to do with my question about how long will we be hiding, when a light catches his gaze and, smiling, he points west to the mountain. I turn around and see a rainbow that does not come or go, that is just there, bridging worlds, bridg-ing dreams . . .

The Story of Noise and Silence

IT WAS RAINING HEAVILY. The sea slept off the fatigue, a gift of lovemaking, and on the little cassette player, Mercedes Sosa[1] was unreeling the song that goes, "I thank life, it's given me so much . . ." It was dawn, and the airplane had already brandished death over the dark mountains of the Mexican Southeast. I was remembering Neftali Reyes, the self-named Pablo Neruda, when he said:

> . . . may the hour
> come in the pure fullness of its own time,
> and may the people fill the empty streets
> with their fresh, firm bodies.
> Here is my tenderness for then.
> You already know it.
> I bear no other flag.

The clock of war read "February 14, 1997." Ten years earlier, in 1987, it had been raining the same way. But then there was no sea, or tape recorder, or airplane, but dawn was circling our guerrilla camp. Old Don Antonio had stayed to chat. He had come, bringing in the evening and a sack of tostadas. There was no one else but him and me in the camp kitchen. A pipe and a hand-rolled cigarette vied with the smoke coming from the embers of the fire. Even so, we could speak only by yelling. It seemed to be quiet, but the rain shredded every corner of the night, and there wasn't an undisturbed place anywhere. The rain's noise dripped from the roof of trees, cloaking the mountain, and more rain noise splashed from the ground. The noise form the rain was double, below there was the sound of tree-filtered rain from above, and there was the noise that squelched the ground. In the middle, there was another sound, where the plastic tarps we used for roofs were talking the February rain in the jungle. Noise above, below, in the middle. There was no corner for a word. That's why I was surprised when I heard Old Don Antonio's voice clearly. Without losing the rolled cigarette on his lips, he began to tell a story . . .

The Story of Noise and Silence

"ONCE THERE WAS A TIME when time wasn't measured. During that time, the greatest gods, the ones who gave birth to the world, were walking the way gods do: dancing, of course. There was a lot of noise during that time. Voices and yells came from every direction. There was a lot of noise, and you couldn't understand any of it. And that noise was not meant for understanding anything, but for *not* understanding anything. At first, the first gods thought the noise was dance music, and they quickly chose partners and began to dance like this." Old Don Antonio stood up and did a dance step where you stand first on one foot and then on the other.

"But, as it turned out, the noise wasn't music or a dance. It was just noise, and you couldn't dance well to it or stay happy. Then the great gods stopped and listened carefully, because they wanted to know what the noise was saying, but they couldn't make anything out because it was just noise. And since you can't dance to noise, the first gods, the ones who gave birth to the world, couldn't walk anymore because they could only walk by dancing.

"They were sad at having to stop because the first gods were avid walkers, the first ones. And if one of the gods tried to walk or dance to the noise by himself, he couldn't, because he'd lose his steps and run into yhe others, tripping and falling over rocks and trees, and hurt himself." Old Don Antonio stopped to relight the cigarette the rain and noise had put out. After the flame came the smoke, and after the smoke came the word.

"Then the gods looked for silence to so they could get their bearings again, but they couldn't find it any anywhere. They didn't know where silence could have gone to. And the gods became desperate at not finding the silence that kept the path. So, in an assembly of gods, they came to an agreement. It was very difficult because of all that noise, but they finally agreed that each one should look for a quiet place to find himself. They looked high, they looked low, they looked all around but they couldn't find any. Finally, since there wasn't any other place left to find silence, they looked inside themselves, and when they looked for silence there, they found it, and found one another and found their path again, those great gods who gave birth to the world, the first ones."

Old don antonio was silent, and the rain was silent too. It was a short silence. Quickly, the crickets came, ripping that night of ten years past into little pieces.

Dawn was on the mountain when Old Don Antonio said good-bye with, "Well, I have arrived."

I REMAINED, smoking little pieces of silence that dawn had abandoned on the mountains of the Mexican Southeast.

NOTE

1. Mercedes Sosa is an Argentine singer with a tremendous following throughout Latin America. Her songs center around political resistence and love. *Gracias a la vida* (*Thanks to Life*) was written and originally sung by Violetta Parra, a folk singer/songwriter from Chile.

Making the Bread Called Tomorrow

OLD DON ANTONIO used to say that the ingredients needed to bake the bread we call tomorrow are many.

"One of them is pain," Old Don Antonio adds now, while he piles firewood up next to the oven.

We go out into an afternoon, shimmering after one of those rains that July uses to paint the earth green. Doña Juanita has stayed behind, preparing the sweet cornbread that around here they call *marquesote*, the loaf shaped by its sardine-can-baking pan.

I don't know how long Old Don Antonio and Doña Juanita have been together, and I have never asked . Today, in this jungle afternoon, Old Don Antonio speaks about pain as an ingredient of hope, and Doña Juanita bakes him a loaf of bread to prove it.

For several nights, illness has troubled Doña Juanita's sleep, and Old Don Antonio, unable to sleep in his devotion to her, relieves her pain with stories and games. This very dawn, Old Don Antonio had set up a grandiose show: Playing with his hands and the light from the hearth, he creates a multitude of shadow-puppet jungle animals. Doña Juanita laughs at the night-walking *tepescuintle*, at the restless whitetail deer, at the hoarse howler monkey, at the vain peacock and the loud parrot that Old Don Antonio paints on the canvas of his hut.

"It didn't cure me, but I laughed a lot," Doña Juanita tells me. "I didn't know the shadows were so happy."

That afternoon Doña Juanita bakes a *marquesote* for Old Don Antonio, not to thank him for the useless medicine during a night of joyful shadows. And she didn't bake it to make him happy either . . . She baked it as evidence that a pain shared brings relief and casts a joyful shadow. That's why Doña Juanita bakes bread, that her hands and Old Don Antonio's firewood birth inside an old sardine can.

And so that it shouldn't go to waste, we ate the evidence of Doña Juanita and Old Don Antonio's shared pain with some hot coffee, we ate the pain turned into shared bread and light . . .

WHAT WE ARE TELLING you happened long, long ago, that is, today . . .

The Story of the Others

Old Don Antonio used to say; "Life without those who are different is empty and damns you to stagnation." What does this have to do with the intercontinental struggle for humanity and against neoliberalism? Well, in order to explain it, I'd . . . Well . . . . I'd have to tell you . . .

It's dawn again. Beneath a menacing plane, the sea tries to read a book of poems with the faint help of a tiny candle stump. I scribble a letter to someone I don't know personally, who probably speaks another language, has a different culture, is from another country, is a different color, and for sure has a different history. The plane goes by, and I pause a little to listen and then a lot more to give myself time to deal with the difficulty of writing a letter to "those who are different."

Just then, from out of the highland mist, unnoticed by the sea, Old Don Antonio appears at my side, and giving me a few little taps on the shoulder, lights his cigarette and recounts . . .

The Story of the Others

"THE OLDEST OF THE OLD ones who settled in these lands said that the greatest gods, those who gave birth to the world, did not all think the same way. That is, they weren't all of one mind; but each felt his own thoughts, and among themselves, they listened to each other and respected each other. The eldest of the elders say that's the way it was. If it hadn't been so, the world would never have been born, because the first gods would have spent all their time fighting, since the thoughts they felt were different. The eldest of the elders say that's why the world came up with so many shapes and colors, as many as the thoughts the first, the greatest gods had.

"Seven were the greatest gods, and seven were the thoughts each one of them had, and seven times seven are the shapes and colors in which they dressed the world. Old Don Antonio tells me that he asked the eldest of the elders how the first gods were able to come to an agreement and talk to each other, if the thoughts they felt were so different. Old Don Antonio recounts that the eldest of the elders told him there was a meeting between the seven gods and the seven different thoughts each one had, and that at that meeting, they came to an agreement.

"The eldest of the elders told Old Don Antonio that the assembly of the first gods, those who gave birth to the world, was a long time before yesterday, that it happened when there was not yet time. And they said that during that assembly each one of the first gods said his piece and then they all said: 'My thoughts are different than those of others.'

"Then the gods were quiet for a bit and realized that when each one of them said 'the others,' they were talking about others as different. After they had been quiet for a while, the first gods realized that they already had a first agreement: that there were others, and that those others were different from who each one was. So the first agreement the very first gods had was to recognize difference and accept the existence of the other. And what else could they do anyway? Since they were all gods, all first, they had to accept this, because there wasn't one who was more or less than the others. They were different, and that is how they had to move along.

"After this first agreement came a discussion, because it's one thing to recognize that there are others who are different and a very different thing to respect them. So they spent quite a while talking and discussing just how one was different from the others, and they didn't mind spending a lot of time talking about it because there was no time yet. Afterward, they all kept quiet, and each one of them spoke about his difference and each of the other gods, who were all listening, realized that by listening and learning about the difference of the other, he could understand better what was different in him.

"Then they were very happy and started to dance. They danced a long time, but they didn't care because at that time, time didn't exist. After the dance, the gods agreed it's a good thing that there are others who are different, and that one must listen to them to know oneself. After that agreement, they went to sleep, tired from so much dancing. These first gods, who gave birth to the world, didn't tire from talking, because it so happens they were very good at talking, but they were just beginning to learn how to listen."

I DIDN'T NOTICE when Old Don Antonio left. The sea was already asleep, and a shapeless spot of wax was all that was left of the little candle stump. Up above, the sky began thinning its blackness with the morning light . . .

94

The Tale of the Lion and the Mirror

JULY 1998

Old Don Antonio says that when he was young, his father Don Antonio taught him how to kill a lion without a gun. Old Don Antonio says that when he was Young Antonio and his father was Old Don Antonio, his father told him the story that he now whispers in my ear so the sea will only be able to learn it from my lips.

The Story of the Lion and the Mirror

FIRST, THE LION TEARS its prey apart. Then he drinks the blood, eats the heart, and leaves the rest for the vultures. There's nothing that can overwhelm the lion's strength. There's no animal that can confront him, nor any man who doesn't flee from him. Only a force just as brutal, bloodthirsty, and powerful can defeat a lion.

The Old Don Antonio of then rolled his cigarette and, pretending to mind the logs forming the bright star of the campfire flames, looked out of the corner of his eye at the Young Antonio. He didn't have to wait long before the Young Antonio asked him:

"And what is this force great enough to defeat a lion?"

The Old Don Antonio handed the Young Antonio a mirror.

Me?" asked the Young Antonio, looking at himself in the round mirror.

Old Don Antonio smiled good-humoredly (that is what the young Antonio says) and took the mirror from him. "No, not you," he responded. "By showing you the mirror, I meant the strength which can defeat the lion is the lion's own strength. Only the lion himself can defeat the lion."

"Ah!" said the Young Antonio, just to be saying something.

Old Don Antonio understood that the Young Antonio hadn't understood a thing, so he went on with his story.

"When we understood that only a lion could defeat a lion, we began to think of how to make the lion confront himself. The eldest of the elders in the community said that you had to know the lion and they named one boy to get to know him."

"You?" interrupted the Young Antonio. Old Don Antonio's silence became his confirmation, and after rearranging the logs on the fire, he continued:

"They took the boy up to the top of a ceiba and left a tied-up calf at its base, and they went away. The boy was supposed to watch what the lion did with the calf, wait for the lion to go away, and then return to the community to tell them what he'd seen. And that is what he did. The lion came, killed and tore the calf apart, and afterward he drank its blood, ate its heart, and left as the buzzards were circling, waiting for their turn. The boy went back to the community and told them what he'd seen. The eldest of the elders thought for a while, and said:

"Let the death the predator inflicts be his death," and they gave the boy a mirror, some nails, and a calf.

"Tomorrow will be the night of justice," said the elders, and they went back to their thoughts.

The young boy did not understand. He went to his hut and stayed there for a good while, watching the fire. And that's where he was when his father came and asked him what was happening; the boy told him everything. The boy's father sat silently next to him, and after a while, he spoke. The boy began to smile as he listened to his father.

The next day, when the afternoon had already turned to gold and the gray of night had draped itself over the treetops, the boy left the community and walked to the ceiba carrying the calf. When he reached the foot of the Mother Tree, he killed the calf and took out its heart. Then he broke the mirror into lots of little pieces and stuck the pieces into the heart with some of the blood. Then he opened the heart again and put the nails inside. He put the heart back in the calf's chest and made a frame with stakes to keep the calf on its feet as if it were still alive. The boy climbed up to the top of the tree and waited there above. While the night let itself fall from the trees to the ground, he remembered his father's words: "The same death the predator inflicts."

It was night when the lion returned. The animal approached, and with one leap attacked the calf and tore it apart. When he licked the heart, the lion became suspicious because the blood was dry, but the broken mirror shards cut his tongue and made it bleed. The lion thought the blood from his own mouth was from the calf's heart. Excited, he chewed up the whole heart. The nails made him bleed even more, but the lion still thought the blood in his mouth was the calf's. He chewed and he chewed, and the more the lion cut himself, the more he bled, and the more he bled, the more he chewed. The lion kept chewing until he bled to death. The boy returned with the lion's claws strung in a necklace, and he showed it to the eldest of the elders in the community. They smiled and told him, "It isn't the claws you should keep as a trophy of the victory, but the mirror."

THAT'S HOW OLD DON ANTONIO says the lion killed himself. But along with the mirror, Old Don Antonio always carries his old flint rifle.

"Just in case the lion doesn't know his history," he tells me, smiling and winking an eye. On my other side, the sea adds: "In case the lion doesn't know . . .

The Fish in the Water

OLD DON ANTONIO tells a story that the eldest of the elders in his community once told him. He says once upon a time there was a very beautiful fish who lived in the river. The lion saw the fish and had a sudden craving for it. But when the lion reached the river, he realized that he couldn't swim and get to the fish. So the lion asked the opossum for advice, who told him:

"It's very simple. Fish can't live out of water. All you have to do is drink all the water out of the river. The fish will be left high and dry and then you can catch him and eat him."

The lion was very pleased with the opossum's advice and rewarded him with a position in his kingdom. The lion went to the edge of the river and began to drink. He died when all that water burst him into pieces. The opossum became unemployed.

Tan-tan.

95
The Story of the Measure of Memory

AUGUST 1998

NOTHING NEW AROUND HERE, an abundance of planes and helicopters promising war, rains promising sowing, and dignities which promise a future. The children continue being children, and little Pedrito has rebaptized me as "Up" (an easy abbreviation for "Sup", as I understand), while he tries to find out if my pipe is made of chocolate, just like some cigarettes he had been given.

While the sea dreams with me in the womb, I remember that in the next few days (August 28?), the Ladies will be celebrating the twentieth anniversary of an act which, like everything that comes from below, began small and then grew.[1] Twenty years ago, a group of determined and inconvenient (for the Power) women and men began a hunger strike demanding the liberation of political prisoners and an accounting of the disappeared.

We, and others without memory, owe these women of foolish tenderness many things. One of these things, and not the only one, is that tomorrow that is and has been promised us by those who, like the Ladies, know that memory does not rest nor yield, and that dignity has no age or size.

And then Old Don Antonio comes with a gift for the sea, and he recounts, just for the sake of recounting . . .

The History of the Measure of Memory

THE ELDEST OF OUR ELDERS tell that the first gods, those who gave birth to the world, parceled out memory among the men and women who walked in the world. "Memory is good," the greatest gods said and told, "because it is the mirror that helps us understand the present and promises the future."

The first gods measured out memory with a small cup in order to parcel it out, and every man and woman came by to receive a measure of memory.

But some of the men and women were larger than the others, so the measure of memory seemed not equal to the rest. In the smaller persons, memory shone clearly, and in the larger persons it was made opaque. That's why it is said that memory is greatest and strongest in the small people, and it is difficult to find in the powerful. That is why they also say that men and women become smaller and smaller when they grow old, so that memory will shine more brightly. They say that it is the work of the eldest of the elders to make memory great. And they also say that dignity is nothing more than memory that lives. That's what they say.

NOTE

1.   The Ladies are the women who founded the Eureka Committee twenty years earlier, in 1978, demanding that the government account for the fates of political prisoners and the disappeared.

96

The Story of One and All

IT WAS A DAWN IN DECEMBER. In December, mountain dawns are cold and rainy. The fog clings to the trees, giving them new shapes and shadows. So I am keeping watch over the solitary smoke rings of my pipe, hoping that maybe the sea will come to give harbor to the cloud issuing from my lips, when a form frees itself from a nearby tree, and I half-hear:

"Wisdom does not consist in knowing many things or in knowing much about one thing."

I tremble, partly with the cold, partly from the fog, but mostly from what I hear, and even more from surprise at recognizing Old Don Antonio by the brief lightning flash of his match at his creased cigarette. I do what I usually do in these cases: I rub my knees, clench my pipe, and say a wise "Mmmh." Old Don Antonio sits by me, fixing his cigarette in the left corner of his mouth and, muttering, gives shape, color, and warmth to . . .

The Story of One and All

ONCE THERE WAS A TIME when there was no time. It was the time of the beginning. It was about dawn. It was neither night nor day. Time was just there, without going anywhere or coming from anyplace. There was no light but it wasn't dark either. It was the time when the great gods were alive, the ones who gave birth to the world, the very first ones. The eldest of our elders say that those first gods were seven, and each was two. The eldest of our elders say that seven is the number the ancients used for the whole, and that one is always two so as to be able to walk together. That's why they say that the very first gods were born wise and great. They were small, and there weren't many of them. But they sure talked a lot; and talked to themselves a lot, Those first gods were full of hot air. They talked to themselves a lot and they all spoke at once, so they couldn't understand each other.

Although they spoke a lot, these gods didn't know very much. But who knows how or why, there came a moment when they all fell silent at the same time.

Then one of them spoke and said and told himself that it would be a good thing if whenever one of them spoke, the others wouldn't speak, because that way the one who spoke could be heard and the others who didn't speak could hear him, and that what they must do is to take turns speaking. The seven who are two in one agreed. And the eldest of our elders say that was the first agreement in history, that of not just speaking, but listening.

The gods looked in the corners of that dawn when there was no day or night or world or men or women or animals or anything yet. They looked and realized that every bit of that dawn was speaking truths and that one person alone couldn't listen to all the nooks and crannies of it, so they divided up the job of listening to dawn. That's how they were able to learn everything that the world of that time, that wasn't yet a world, had to teach them.

And that's how the very first gods saw what was needed for learning, and working, and living and loving. But they also saw that not one but all are needed to make the world turn. And that's how the first gods became wise, the greatest, the true gods, those who gave birth to the world. They learned how to talk to each other and how to listen. And they were wise. Not because they knew many things or because they knew a lot about any one thing, but because they understood that one and all are necessary and sufficient.

Old Don Antonio leaves. I stay remain, awaiting, expecting the sea and the wheat, knowing they must come . . . because they haven't left.

97

The Dawn Is Heralding Heat and Flashes

MAY 10, 1999

Dawn!

Brothers and sisters:

IT IS MAY, AND THE DAWN is heralding heat and flashes. But it is not this May, nor this dawn, no. Well, yes, it is this May and this dawn, but it is ten years earlier. The light from the campfire is painting shadows and lights on the walls of Old Don Antonio's hut. Old Don Antonio has been silent for some time, just looking at Doña Juanita, who is looking at her hands. I am to one side, sitting in front of a cup of coffee. It has been some time since I arrived.

I came to bring Old Don Antonio a deerskin, to see if he knew how and could tan it. Old Don Antonio had scarcely looked at the skin; he continued looking at Doña Juanita, looking at her hands. They were waiting for something. I mean, Old Don Antonio was waiting for something from looking so long at Doña Juanita, and Doña Juanita was waiting for something from looking so long at her hands. I chewed on my pipe and waited as well, but, of all of us who were there, I was the only one who didn't know what we were waiting for. Suddenly, Doña Juanita sighed deeply and raised her face and gaze to Old Don Antonio, saying:

"The water is coming on time."

"It is coming," Old Don Antonio said, and right then he took out his roller and began rolling a cigarette. I knew what that meant, so I quickly filled my pipe, lit it, and made myself comfortable in order to listen to and to remember, and so now I can tell you . . .

The Story of the Calendar

THE ELDEST OF THE ELDERS among our peoples tell that during the first times, time was completely disorganized, and it stumbled about like a drunk at the Santa Cruz fiesta. Men and women lost many things and lost themselves, because time did not pass evenly but rather sometimes hurried up and sometimes went by slowly, dragging along almost like an old lame person. Sometimes the sun was a great skin that covered everything, and other times it was just water, water above, water below, and water in between. Everything was absolute chaos and one could barely plant, hunt, or fix the straw on the roofs or the sticks and mud on the walls of the huts.

And the gods looked at everything and they looked, because these gods, who were the very first, those who gave birth to the world, were just strolling about and catching crayfish in the river and chewing sugarcane and sometimes they also helped separate the kernels from the maize for the tortillas. And so they looked at everything, these gods, those that gave birth to the world, the very first. And they thought. But they did not think quickly; rather they took a long time, because these gods were not hasty, and so they spent a long time just watching time go staggering about the land. After putting it off like that, then they did indeed think.

After they had thought then, because they also took their time in thinking, the gods called on the Mama they called Ixmucane, and they just said to her:

"Mama Ixmucane, this time that goes about the lands is not doing well and it just skips about and runs and drags, sometimes ahead, and sometimes backwards, and so one can absolutely not plant, and you will see that neither can they harvest when they want to and the men and women are growing sad and now many of us battle with each other in order to find the *maxcabil* and the sugarcane is not where we left it and so we are telling you, we do not know what you thought, Mama Ixmucane, but it is not good that time just goes about like this, without anyone being able to orient themselves as to when and where they must go and what is going on. This is what we are thinking, Mama Ixmucane, we do not know what you are going to tell us about this problem that we are telling you about."

Mama Ixmucane sighed for a good bit, and then she said:

"It is not good that time is just out of control like that, wreaking havoc and ruining things for all these good people."

"Yes, that is right, it is not good," said the gods. And they waited a bit, because they well knew that Mama Ixmucane had not finished speaking, she had barely begun. That is why, ever since then, it seems that mamas have already finished when they have barely begun talking to us.

Mama Ixmucane was sighing for another while, and then she continued speaking:

"Up there, in the sky, is the tale that time should follow, and time will pay attention if someone is reading the tale to it and telling it what comes next and how and when and where."

"If it is there and if it pays attention," said the gods.

Mama Ixmucane sighed more and at last she said; "I am willing to read time the tale so that it learns how to run straight, but my eyes are not good now, and I can scarcely look at the sky, I cannot."

"You cannot," said the gods.

"See, if I could," Mama Ixmucane said, "then I would straighten out time, but I cannot look at and read the sky, because my eyes are not good."

"Mmmh," said the gods.

"Mmmh," said Mama Ixmucane.

And so they remained, the ones and the other, just saying 'mmmh," until the gods finally began thinking again, and they said:

"Look, Mama Ixmucane, we do not know what you are thinking, but we think it would be good if we brought you the sky down here below and then you could see it up close very well and read and put aright the passing of time."

And Mama Ixmucane sighed heavily when she said, "Perhaps I have someplace to put the sky? No, no, no. Can you not see how small my hut is? No, no, no."

"No, no, no," said the gods. And they remained a good bit longer with their 'mmmh," "mmmh." And then the gods thought once more, and they said:

"Look, Mama Ixmucane, we do not know what you are thinking, but we think it would be good if we copy what is written in the sky and bring it to you so you can copy it and read it, and so you will set right the passing of time."

"That's good," said Mama Ixmucane.

And the gods went up and they copied the tale that the sky tells in a notebook and they came down once again, and they went to see Mama Ixmucane with the notebook, and they said to her:

"Look, Mama Ixmucane, here then is the tale that the sky tells, we wrote it down in this notebook, but it is not going to last, so you will have to copy it someplace else where the tale that will set right the passage of time will last forever."

"Yes, yes, yes," said Mama Ixmucane. "Copy the tale on my hands, and I will set the passing of time right so it goes straight and does not go about like an old drunk."

And on the palms and the backs of Mama Ixmucane's hands, the gods wrote the tale that is told in the sky in order to set right the passage of time, and that is why knowing mamas have many lines on their hands and they read the calendar on them, and that way they see that time runs straight and the harvest that history plants in memory is not forgotten.

OLD DON ANTONIO was silent and Doña Juanita repeated, looking her hands: "The water is coming on time."

98

The Story of the Milky Way

JUNE 24, 1999

Now the night of San Juan reigns in the mountains of the Mexican Southeast, that is, it's raining. The sea winds have blown a little box of memories to the top of this ceiba. Out of one of the corners of the open mouth of the little jewel case, a streamer of light protrudes, and with it, a story. Old Don Antonio suddenly appears, like this nocturnal rain, and as if nothing were going on, asks me for a light to fire his cigar and his memory. Old Don Antonio's words rise above the rough drumming of the rain on the nylon roof, with memories and luminous streamers to recount:

The Story of the Milky Way

BEFORE THE RAIN UNDRESSES the mountain, a long path of dusty light is seen up above. It comes from there, and it goes yonder, Old Don Antonio says, with a slight gesture of his head from one side to the other:

"They say it is called the Milky Way, or they also name it 'The Road to Santiago.' They say there are many stars, and they have joined together, so tiny, making themselves a slender opening, a narrow path in the already star-riddled sky. They say, but they also say it is not like that. The eldest of our elders say that which is seen above is a wounded animal." Old Don Antonio pauses, as if waiting for the question I do not ask:

"A wounded animal? How long ago?"

"When the very first gods had already created the world and they were lying around, men and women lived on the earth, working it, and throwing it around. But, they say that one day there appeared in a town a serpent who fed on men. Or rather, he only ate males; he did not eat women. And then when he had eaten all the men in a town, he went to another town and did the same thing. The towns quickly let each other know of this great horror that was coming to them. They spoke fearfully of the great snake, which was so fat and long that it managed to surround an entire town like a wall, not allowing anyone to enter or to leave. He said that if they did not give him all the males to eat, he would not let anyone leave. So some of them surrendered and others fought, but the snake's strength was great, and he always won.

"The towns lived in fear, merely waiting for the day that it would be their turn for the great snake to come and to eat all the men and swallow them whole. They say that there was a man who managed to escape from the serpent and he went to take refuge in a community that had already been attacked. There, in front of only women, the man spoke of the snake and said they must struggle to defeat it, because it was doing much damage in these lands. The women said, 'What are we going to do, since we are just women? How are we going to fight him with-out men? How are we going to attack him if it does not come here now because there are no longer any men, since he ate them all?'

"The women left, very discouraged and sad. But one remained and approached the man and asked him how he thought they could fight the snake. The man said he did not know, but he would have to think. And together, the man and the woman set to thinking, and they made a plan and they went to call the women, to tell them of the plan and everyone was in agreement. And then it came to pass that the man began to show himself freely about the town, and the serpent saw him from afar, because he had very good eyes. And then the serpent came and surrounded the town with his large body and told the women to bring him that man who was walking about, or otherwise he would not let anyone enter or leave. The women said they would bring him, but they would have to meet in order to make an agreement. 'That is fine,' said the snake.

"And then the women made a circle around the man, and since there were many of them, the circle was growing larger and larger, until the circle touched the very ring that the serpent's body had made around the town. Then the man said, 'That is good, deliver me.' And he walked to the serpent's head, and when the snake was occupied with eating the man, all the women picked up sharp sticks and began jabbing the snake all over his body. Since there were so many women about the place, and his mouth was full with the man he was eating, the serpent could not defend himself. He had never thought that the weak would attack him in such a thorough way. Quickly weakened and defeated, the serpent said; 'forgive me, do not kill me.' 'No,' said the women, 'we are going to kill you anyway, because you have done much evil eating up all of our men.' 'Let's make a deal,' said the snake, 'if you do not kill me, I will return your men to you because I have them in my belly.'

"And then the women thought that was good, they would not kill him, but that the great serpent could no longer live in those lands and would be expelled. Then the snake said, 'But, where am I going to live and what am I going to eat? No. There is no deal.' And then they were there with this problem, when the first woman said they would have to ask the man who had come, to see what he thought. So she said to the snake: 'Release the man you have just eaten, and we will see if he has an idea of what we can do.'

"The serpent released the man, who was half dead and half alive and spoke with difficulty. Then the man said he would have to ask the first gods to see what could be done, and that he could go to look for them because now he was half alive and half dead. And the man went and he found the first gods sleeping under a ceiba, and he awoke them and told them of the problem. The gods met together in order to think and to reach a good accord, then they went to see the serpent and the women and they listened. The women said the serpent was to blame and he should be punished, that he should give back the men he had swallowed and he would not die. Then the snake brought up all the men from all the towns, and the gods said the serpent would have to go and live on the highest mountain. But if the serpent could not fit on just one mountain, he would then have to use the two highest mountains in the world, and rest his tail on one and his head on the other; he would have sunlight for food, and the thousands of wounds the warrior women had given him would never close. Then the gods left, and the great serpent went sadly to the two highest mountains and put his head to rest on one and his tail on the other. His large body reached from one side of the sky to the other, and from then on by day he feeds on sunlight, and by night that light spills out through all the little holes of his wounds.

"The serpent is pale, that is why he is not seen by day, and that is why by night the light can be seen that falls from him and leaves him empty until, the next day, the sun feeds him once again. That is why they say that the large line that shines by night up above, is nothing but a wounded animal." That is what Old Don Antonio recounted to me, and then I understood that the Milky Way is nothing more than a long serpent of light, that feeds by day and bleeds by night.

IT HAS STOPPED RAINING on this night of San Juan. The sky clears and quickly turns dark. Above one can see that a serpent of light hangs from the thick body of a thousand wounds which stretch from end to end, to each corner of the horizon. The silver teardrops fall softly on the top of that ceiba, and drizzles into another rain below. There, the brightness bounces from a faceless mirror and turns the corner into a shadow where it can rest.

99

The Story of the False Light, the Stone, and the Corn

AUGUST 13, 1999

Old Don Antonio had just arrived, saying the good-bye that runs through his lungs. In spite of the cough that I had to share (not just in solidarity; I have one as well, although not as deep as the Old One's; my throat and chest really did hurt and sought relief), we both lit up the tobacco we were carrying—a cigarette for him, the well-gnawed pipe for me. Then we started the bridge, which is how we also name the word here. And, since the dancing light of a candle was illuminating us, and history came from light, and before that from the sun and from the morning, the word will be this, then . . .

The Story of the False Light, the Stone, and the Corn

LONG, LONG AGO, when time was still waiting for time to make time, the greatest gods, those who gave birth to the world, the very first, went about just the way they always went about: racing around in a big rush. It just so happened that these first gods had taken a lot of time with their dancing and singing and were late making the moon and the sun, whose work it was to give light and shadow to the world, which was moving very slowly. Then Vucub-Caquix, the seven-times keeper of the seven first colors, began to think that he was the sun and the moon, since the colors in which he dressed were many and beautiful, and because he flew very high, his vision reached far. So it seemed to him that it could reach everything.

Men and women were already moving about the land, but they hadn't turned out very well. For the first gods had already made men and women several times, and they just weren't very good at it. It was as if the greatest gods were learning, smudging the world and correcting the men and women they were creating. They hadn't as yet had time to make the men and women of corn, the true ones. Busy as they were, the first gods also didn't know that Vucub-Caquix was going around saying that he wanted everyone to worship him like the luminous light.

When they learn about it, the greatest gods had a wonderful idea. They would call on two young gods and two old ones to put Vucub-Caquix in his place. The two boys were called Hunabku and Ixbalanque, which are also the names borne by the hunter of the dawn. The two old gods were ZaquiNin-Ac and Zaqui-Nima-Tziis, the creator couple. With their blowpipe, Hunabku and Ixbalanque wounded in the mouth the false sun-moon, who boasted of his great light. Vucub-Caquix's pain was great, but he didn't fall. Then the old creators went and offered to heal his mouth. They took out his beautiful teeth and replaced them with kernels of corn, so Vucub-Caquix's face fell, and they blinded his eyes so he would forget his lust for nobility and remain exactly as he is now, flying the disordered flight of the macaw over these mountains.

And just as it was then, there have been and there are now among the people those who believe themselves to be the sun and moon, and boast of their great and powerful light. This is also true, of gold, money and political power praised as a path and destiny. Their light blinds and transforms, makes the false appear true, and conceals the truth behind double faces. When money was turned into a false god across the land, false priests made governments and armies so that the lie might endure. And so it is today; history keeps suffering and hoping that the young and the old will agree to wound money in its lying mouth and to knock out its bloody teeth. With stones and corn for weapons, young and old will strip power, and the stone will come to rest among other stones, and the men and women among the other men and women who walk the land. This struggle will be called "war," even if it is only to denounce and unmask the lie, and to put out the false and vain light that reigns from above.

Old Don Antonio becomes silent, shakes my hand and, saying, "I'm done," takes his leave. In my hand, Old Don Antonio had left a small stone and a solitary kernel of corn.

SPREAD ACROSS THE NIGHT's long negligee, thousands of lights wait and await . . .

The Night Is Ours

This is the story of how all was in suspense, calm and silent, how all was motionless and still, and how the expanse of the heavens was empty.

This is the first story, the first talk. Man didn't yet exist, nor the animals, birds, fish, crabs, trees, stones, caves, ravines, grasses or forests. There was only the heavens. The face of the earth had not yet appeared. There was only the calm sea and the expanse of the sky. There was nothing brought together, nor anything that could move, or quicken, or make a noise in the heavens.

There was nothing standing, only the calm water, the placid sea, alone and tranquil. Nothing existed.

There was only stillness and silence in the dark night. Only the Creator, the Maker, Tepeu, Gucumatz, the forefathers, were in the water surrounded by light. They were hidden beneath green and blue feathers, so they were called Gucumatz. They were great sages, great thinkers by nature. This was how the heavens were, and also the Heart of Heaven. That's how they told it.

And then came the word. Tepeu and Gucumatz came together in the darkness, in the night, and talked together. They talked and considered. They agreed, uniting their words and their thoughts.

And then as they considered, it became clear to them than when dawn broke, man must appear. Then, they planned the creation and the growth of woods and thickets, the birth of life and the creation of man. That's how it was arranged in the darkness of the night by the Heart of Heaven who is called Hurakán.

—POPOL VUH

THIS AUGUST DAY, we've harvested the biggest night in the world. But in another August, in the mountains of the Mexican Southeast, Old Don Antonio slowly sharpens his two-edged machete. The light of the cooking fire picks out orange and blue sparks on the long lead mirror he holds in his hands, while Doña Juanita pulls tortillas, one after another, from the *comal*.[1] I wait, sitting in the corner, smoking. Tonight, we're going hunting. I guess that Old Don Antonio is planning to be out on the mountain until dawn, because he's asked Doña Juanita to make tortillas and *pozol* for us. Between sighs, she's ground corn, kneaded dough, and already has a stack of big piping hot tortillas. On the fire, licked by the lusty flames, the coffee steams in a little pot.

I fall asleep to the rhythmic grinding of the stone on the double-edged machete and to the smell of Doña Juanita's tortillas. Suddenly, Old Don Antonio gets up saying: "Well, I'm off."

"All right, then," says Doña Juanita, wrapping the big ball of *pozol* in banana leaves, and packing it and the tortillas in Old Don Antonio's game bag. Carefully, she pours the coffee into an old plastic bottle and places it between the *pozol* and the tortillas.

I stir myself and join him. We're already going out the door when I notice that Old Don Antonio hasn't brought his old 22.

"You forgot your gun," I tell him.

"I haven't forgotten it," he responds without stopping. "We don't need it tonight."

We enter the night. I know this expression, "enter the night," is figurative, but it is more than figurative here. When we were in Old Don Antonio's cabin, it seemed as if the night were standing outside, as if it hadn't been invited to the knife-sharpening ceremony, the coffee making and the tortilla cooking. Although the little hut's rickety door was open, the night couldn't come in. It only reached toward the doorway, as if it knew it couldn't stay, that this wasn't its place. So when we left the cabin and went outside, we entered night.

We walked on the big road for quite a while. It had just rained heavily, but already the fireflies were playing like swift serpents of light in the branches and vines. August splashed puddles and mud in every direction, and sometimes it was impossible to keep from sinking knee-deep. After a while, we took an overgrown side path, seldom traversed and therefore not quite so muddy. I want to explain that the woods were massive and dense, and it was as if we sank even deeper into the night, a night within the night.

I was wondering what we were going to hunt, since Old Don Antonio had left his .22 at home. But it wasn't the first time that going out with him had began with a mystery and ended in a revelation, just like the dark night giving way to the sun, as it climbs up the back of the hills. I said nothing and followed his footsteps silently. It must have been after midnight when the path was lost in the thick bush that heals wounds for men and storms alike. Still, we kept walking. From time to time, Old Don Antonio used his machete to open the way where the vines wove a wall in front of us.

Although I was using my flashlight the whole time, Old Don Antonio only lit his every so often, casting his beam from side to side for just a moment as if he were looking for something. Suddenly, he stopped and pointed his light at the forest floor for a long time. I shone mine there too, but couldn't distinguish anything special, just some fallen branches, vines, grass, plants, and the knots and humps of roots protruding through the earth.

"Here it is," murmured Old Don Antonio, and sat at the base of a tree, some ten yards from where he'd been shining his flashlight moments before.

We sat there a good while, waiting. When I saw Old Don Antonio rolling a cigarette, I realized three things. First, that we weren't waiting for any animal (the tobacco smell would scare it off). Second, that it was okay for me to smoke, and third, that Old Don Antonio would begin talking at any moment. So I took out my pipe, puffing out big clouds to try to smoke out the biting gnats, and waited for Old Don Antonio to tell me a story, just as I would tell it to the Sea, and I'm now telling it to you.

The Story of the Night

"IGNORANT PEOPLE SAY that the night holds many great dangers, that the night is a den of thieves, a place of shadow and fright. The people who say this don't know anything. But you should know that the wicked and the bad no longer walk concealed in the black folds of the Night or skulk in dens. No, the wicked and the bad walk in broad daylight, unpunished. The wicked and the bad live in the great palaces of Power, own factories, banks, and big trading centers. They dress as senators and deputies; they are the presidents of those countries where the land is ailing, and who speak as if they weren't the wicked and bad speaking. The wicked and the bad cloak their gray pestilence with a thousand colors and walk in whatever colors they choose.

"Yes," says Old Don Antonio, puffing out smoke, "the wicked and the bad no longer hide. They show themselves and even make up the government. But it wasn't always like this. There once was a time when the wicked and the bad didn't walk in broad daylight. What's more, nobody walked in broad daylight because the day didn't exist yet. This was the time of night and water, and everything was inside the Night. The eldest elders tell how all beings were in the Night, and all they could do was cross through it from one shore to the other, never passing through to the other side, not because they didn't want to, but because there was no other side yet, only the great and silent Night.

"They also tell how it was in this Night that the greatest gods met for the first time, the first ones who gave birth to the world. Some say their first accord was to make the Day, because they understood perfectly that there had to be day, and that the night would follow it. But that's not how it was. No, the first gods' first accord was to drive the wicked and the bad out of the night. The eldest of the elders tell how the first gods had many good reasons for their decision to drive the wicked and the bad out from Night's house. They say that Tepeu, winner of all battles, spoke and clearly stated that neither the night or the newborn world were places for the wicked and the bad, and that even though it would take a long time, they'd have to struggle to drive the wicked and the bad out.

"Gucumatz the most wise, with quetzal feathers covering her long body, said the night was for doing good, and that the wicked and the bad got in the way of this. The first seven gods, the greatest, who were twice seven in one, spoke at length. Their final accord was that the wicked and the bad should be driven out of the night and flung so far off that even memory and recollection wouldn't be able to reach them. This is what the greatest gods agreed upon, those who gave birth to the world, the earliest. This was before the earth, the day, or anything existed, when everything was nothing more than night and silent black water. This is what the eldest of the elders say, from whom the communities learn their stories. In the oldest towns, the repositories of that which we now speak, the men and women of the corn keep the stories of how and why everything was made.

"And the eldest of the elders tell how the first accord was followed by the first problem: there was no place to drive the wicked and the bad to, because in this time before time everything was night and water. Nothing was made yet, nothing existed. Everything was waiting for its time. So the first gods returned to their councils and saw that first they'd have to make things and places, and only then would they have a way to drive out the wicked and the bad.

"That's how everything came into being. The day was born from the night, and so were the men and women of corn. And the birds and animals and fish were made, and there was movement on the earth, in the sea and the sky. And the world started stirring because of the heavy weight with which her long journey was beginning. And the first gods were tired, because they had given birth to so much, well, the whole world! And inside this world, they made many more worlds, each different and distinct, and yet all worlds belonging to the world!

"But the greatest gods were so exhausted they forgot their accord to drive off the wicked and the bad, to send them far beyond the reach of memory and recall. Then the first gods remembered they'd forgotten, and hunted for the wicked and the bad, to drive them and their magnificence out. They looked all through the night and couldn't find them. They checked every nook and cranny but couldn't turn up anything wicked or bad! The eldest of the elders explain how the wicked and the bad took advantage of the confusion of the creation of the world to escape through a crack in the night into the day, where they hid behind the guise of government. Every once in a while, from time to time, in whatever time Time takes, the wicked and the bad change clothes, so that without having to abandon Power and Government, they can seem like something other than what they are, themselves.

"The night is still here with its edges and doors and windows. It came alive itself and went around making the lights that hang in the dark water. Certainly, the night has its shadows, but they are shadows in the shadow, the men and women who live in and care for the mountains, who have their own light and shine in their own way. The eldest of the elders say this. And they say that the first gods are still looking for the wicked and the bad all through the night, that often you can run across them lifting up a stone, or shaking out some solemn cloud, or poking at the moon, or scratching at the stars to see if the wicked and the bad haven't hidden there.

"They also say that when they grow tired of looking, the first gods get together and amass a ton of stars over the black fire of the mountains, and with blue and mother-of-pearl light prepare a place to dance and sing, and ready the marimba made of bone, wood, and light, and they play, filling the night that is born in the mountains of the Mexican Southeast. They do this, they say, because the wicked and the bad don't like dancing and singing. They say that they flee from the joy that is stirred up from the dancing ground.

"And the eldest of the elders tell how the first gods chose a group of men and women to search through the world for the wicked and the bad, to find them and cast them far away. And so that no one would know, they hid the greatness of these men and women in little bodies and painted them brown, so they could walk the night without fear, and by day be as earth of the earth. And so they would not forget that the night is the mother, the beginning, the house and place of the first gods, they gave them black masks to wear so they could go without faces, so that, even by day, they could carry a piece of the night in their memories.

"The eldest of the elders say this," said Old Don Antonio, rolling a new cigarette. After lighting it, he returned to the story.

"These men and women of whom so much is told are called the true ones, and they began searching for the wicked and bad alongside the first gods. But at some point, they'll have to go out into the day and look there too for the wicked and the bad. They'll have to go out and enter the night through the best door, the dawn."

Old Don Antonio falls silent. Above, darkness is yielding to the sun's inevitable march. One last breath of light illuminates the last dark corner and, leaving its claw marks on the hill, climbs to a higher slope. He rises, stretches his legs, examines his double-edged machete, and says, "Well, let's go."

"Go? I ask. "But weren't we going to hunt some animal or something?"

"No," answers Old Don Antonio, without pause. "We weren't hunting any animal. We were looking for the wicked and the bad."

We quickly retrace our path. When we come out into the pastures, midway down the slope, the day had enveloped the whole glen, the last drops of rain have run off, and a ton of roosters not so much sing as crow. Old Don Antonio stops for a moment and, pointing to the distance in the west, says,

"This is the hour the wicked and the bad rule. They aren't hiding now; they walk in the daylight, and in the daylight they corrupt whatever they touch. But not in the night, no. The night, the night is ours."

Old Don Antonio falls silent, and in the silence we cover the last leg separating us from the cabin. When we arrive, Doña Juanita is arriving too, with a bundle of wood on her back. As she puts it down, she asks us:

"So, did they show up?"

"No," responds Old Don Antonio.

"We'll have to keep watching, then," says Doña Juanita, piling up a few glowing coals and stoking the fire.

"Yes, we'll have to keep watching," says Old Don Antonio, again sharpening the double-edged machete on the stone.

OUTSIDE, THE DAY KEEPS gaining ground. But, it does not enter Old Don Antonio's cabin, as if it knows that the vigil for the wicked and the bad goes on inside, as if it fears that the fire that Doña Juanita feeds forges another day, "the new morning."

NOTE

1. A *comal* is a flat earthenware round which is placed on the fire and heated up to make tortillas.

The Story of the Questions

THE COLD IS SQUEEZING these mountains. Ana Maria and Mario are with me on this expedition, ten years before the dawn of January. The two have just joined the guerrillas. I am an infantry lieutenant, and it is my turn to teach them what others taught me: to live in the mountains. Yesterday I ran into Old Don Antonio for the first time. We both lied. He said he was on his way to check out his milpa, I said I was hunting. Each knew he was lying, and we both knew we knew it. I left Ana Maria to continue her expedition and followed the path toward the river to try, with the help of a clisimeter, to locate on the map the tall mountain before me, and perhaps to bump into Old Don Antonio. He must have been thinking the same thing, because he showed up on the same spot where we had found each other before.

Like yesterday, Old Don Antonio sits on the ground, and leans against a moss green huapac and begins to roll a cigarette. I sit in front of him and light the pipe. Old Don Antonio begins:

"You're not hunting."

"You're not on the way to the milpa, " I answer. Something made me speak in the proper tense, with respect, to that man of undetermined age and cedar skin, who I was seeing for the second time in my life. Old Don Antonio smiles and adds:

"I've heard of you. In the canyons they say you are bandits. In my village, they're upset because you are here."

"And you, do you think we're bandits?" I ask.

Old Don Antonio releases a puff of spiraling smoke, coughs, and shakes his head. I'm encouraged and ask him another question:

"So who do you think we are?"

"I would prefer if you told me," he says and looks into my eyes.

"It's a long story," I say. So I begin to talk about the times of Zapata and Villa, and the revolution, and the land, and the injustice, and hunger, and ignorance, and sickness, and repression and everything. And I finish by saying: "We are the Zapatista National Liberation Army." I wait for some sign from Old Don Antonio, who has not taken his eyes from my face.

"Tell me more about Zapata," he says, after more smoke and a cough.

I start with Anenecuilco, then with the Plan de Ayala, the military campaign, the organization of the villages, the betrayal at Chinameca. Old Don Antonio continues to stare at me until I finish.

"It wasn't like that," he says.

I'm surprised, and all I can do is babble. "No?"

"No. I'm going to tell you the real story of Zapata."

Taking out tobacco and rolling paper, Old Don Antonio begins his story, which merges and confuses modern times with old times, just like the smoke from my pipe and his cigarette now mingle and converge on one another.

"Many stories ago, when the very first gods, the ones who gave birth to the world, were still roaming the night, they say there were two gods who came from one, Ik'al and Votán. When one turned, the other could be seen, when the other turned, the one could be seen. They were opposites. One was like the light, like a May morning in the river. The other was dark, cold, like a night in a cave. They were the same. One was two, because one made the other. But they didn't walk, they were always stationary, these two gods who were one. 'So what do we do? Life is sad like this,' they lamented, the two who were one. 'The night won't go,' said Ik'al. 'The day won't go,' said Votán. 'Let's walk,' said the one who were two. 'How?' said the other. 'Where?' said the one.

"First by asking, 'Why?' and then by asking, 'Where?' they saw they moved a little bit. Happy was the one who was two. Then both of them decided to move, and they couldn't. 'How do we do it, then?' One would show himself first, and then the other would show himself. So they agreed that in order to move, they had to do so separately. No one could remember who moved first, but they were just happy that they moved and said, 'What does it matter who is first as long as we move?' The two gods, who were the same one, laughed, and the first deal they made was to agree to have a dance, and they danced, one little step behind the other, and they danced a long time because they were happy they had found each other.

"Then they tired of all the dancing and asked what else they could do and saw that the first question had been, 'How do we move?' and that it brought the answer of 'Together but separately and in agreement.' They didn't care so much about this answer because they were already moving and that brought them to the next question, when they realized that there were two roads. The one was very short and they could see the end of it, so they decided not to go down this road which you could see was short, And because they were so happy they could move, they decided to choose the long road, which then brought them to another question: 'Where does the road go?' It took them a long time, but the two, who were one, finally decided that they would never know where that long road took them unless they moved. So they said to one another; 'Let's walk it, then.'

"And they began to walk, first one and then the other. They found it was taking them a long time, and then came another question: 'How will we walk for such a long time?' Ik'al declared he did not know how to walk by day and Votán declared that by night he was afraid. So they cried for a long time, and when all the crying stopped, they finally agreed and understood that Ik'al could walk by night and Votán by day, and that Ik'al would walk Votán through the night.

"That's how they answered the question of how to walk all the time. Since then, the gods walk with questions, and they never stop. They never arrive, and they never leave. So that is how the true men and women learned that questions help to walk, and not to stand still. Since then, true men and women walk by asking, and to arrive they say good-bye, and to leave they say hello. They are never still."

I chew on the now-short stem of the pipe, waiting for Old Don Antonio to continue, but he never does. In fear that I will disrupt something very serious I ask, " . . . and Zapata?"

Old Don Antonio smiles.

"You've learned now that in order to know and walk, you have to ask questions." He coughs and lights another cigarette, and out of his mouth come these words that fall like seeds on the ground.

"Zapata appeared here in the mountains. He wasn't born, they say. He appeared just like that. They say he is Ik'al and Votán, who came all the way over here in their long journey, and so as not to frighten good people, they became one. Because, after being together for so long, Ik'al and Votan learned they were the same and could become Zapata. And Zapata said he had finally learned where the long road went, and that at times it would be light, and times it would be darkness, but that it was the same. Votan Zapata and Ik'al Zapata, the black Zapata and the white Zapata, they were both the same road for the true men and women."

Old Don Antonio took from his backpack a little nylon bag. Inside there was a very old picture of Emiliano Zapata from 1910. In his left hand, Zapata has his sword raised to his waist. In his right hand, he has a pistol. Two bandoliers cross his chest, one from left to right, the other from right to left. His feet are placed as if he's standing still, or as if he's walking. And in his gaze there is something that says, "Here I am," or "There I go." There are two staircases. One emerges from darkness, with dark-skinned Zapatistas, as though they were coming from the depths of something. The other staircase, which is lighted, is empty, and one cannot tell from where it comes and where it goes. I would be lying if I told you that I noticed all those details. It was Old Don Antonio who pointed them out. Behind the picture is written:

Gral. Emiliano Zapata, Jefe del Ejercito Suriano.
Gen. Emiliano Zapata, Commander-in-Chief of the Southern Army.
Le General Emiliano Zapata, Chef de l'Armée du Sud.
Photo by: Agustin V. Casasola. C.1910.

OLD DON ANTONIO TELLS ME, "I have asked a lot of questions of this picture. That is how I came to be here." He coughs and tosses the cigarette butt. He gives me the picture. "Here," he says. "So that you learn how to ask questions . . . and how to walk. It's better to say good-bye when you arrive. That way it's not so painful when you leave," he says, giving me his hand as he leaves, while he tells me he is arriving. Since then, Old Don Antonio says hello by saying, "Good-bye," and leaves by saying, "Hello."

Chiapas, The First Postmodern Revolution
ANA CARRIGAN

Echoes From the Past: The Legacy of Emiliano Zapata

THE DIRT ROAD LEADS OUT of the valley, away from the fertile ranch lands that surround the provincial capital of Ocosingo. It follows the path of a narrow ravine through the foothills, climbing between forests of pine trees, headed eastward for the Lacandon Rain forest. This is the road down which two regiments of the Zapatista Army traveled on the afternoon of Friday December 31, 1993 on their way to attack San Cristobal de las Casas and Ocosingo. In every village they passed as they came down from the mountains, carrying their weapons and their hand-made uniforms concealed in backpacks and coffee sacks, their numbers swelled.

In January 1994, the international press, among them many veterans of the Central American conflicts of the 1980s, came to these indigenous territories looking for the past— and found the future. Who had ever heard a revolutionary movement announce it had no interest in power? Or met a guerrilla leader who insisted that the rebels had "neither the desire nor the capacity" to impose their own program, and that they had taken up arms to establish, "not the triumph of a single party, organization, or alliance of organizations," but to create "a democratic space, where the confrontation between diverse political points of view can be resolved." Such pronouncements disclosed a dramatic break with the dogmas and romantic machismo of all previous Latin American guerrillas and it soon emerged that these masked descendants of the ancient Mayan culture had produced the first postmodern revolution.

The Zapatista rebellion is an explosion, rising from the submerged roots of Mexico's forgotten past, caused by a modernization program that menaced the indigenous population with the destruction of everything they hold essential to their way of life. The youthful Zapatista leaders are not seeking to create some imaginary utopia. Their goals are firmly rooted in Mexico's past. Their Magna Carta is the Mexican Constitution of 1917, with its recognition of the indigenous right to self-government and its radical agrarian reform. Their historical model is the indigenous and peasant revolt of the second decade of this century, led by the legendary figure whose name they have appropriated, Emiliano Zapata.

"From the beginning," writes John Womack, "the [Zapatista] movement had been a deliberate enterprise by country chiefs to restore the integrity of the state's villages, to gain local rights of participation in national progress." For Emiliano Zapata and his chiefs, "Tierra y Libertad!"—the rallying call of the peasant army—was no rhetorical slogan; by giving the indigenous land and the freedom to decide at the local village level how it should be cultivated, Zapata aimed to restore the essential features of the indigenous agrarian tradition. The chief aim of today's Zapatistas is the restoration of the lost democratic agrarian ideal for which Emiliano Zapata fought and died, which was appropriated and betrayed after his death by the Institutional Revolutionary Party (PRI).

The current Zapatista revolution differs from its 1911 precursor, however, in one crucially important respect. The presence at the revolution's core of the fair-skinned, urban, university educated poet-warrior-spokesman, Subcomandante Marcos has created, a unique fusion between "the two Mexicos": the one white/mestizo, modern and western, the other traditional and Mesoamerican. When Subcomandante Marcos speaks for the indigenous people "who are my bosses," the poet-philosopher-warrior of the Zapatista movement opens the map of Mexico at a faded, almost obliterated page. Charting the contours of the Mayan experience for his countrymen, he traces the paths along which he invites them to follow him into this neglected world. With his mastery of both idioms, Marcos has built bridges between the remote indigenous villagers of the rain forest and the white/mestizo dwellers of the cities so that, for the first time, the "two Mexicos" have become accessible to each other.

In 1994, Marcos's messages from the excluded fringe of Mexican life reverberated on two fronts: for the indigenous population, the Zapatista rebellion legitimized their commitment to determine their own history; for the country at large, the Zapatista call for the dismantling of the links between the PRI and the government projected the indigenous people into the center of a national debate on the need to democratize the political system.

I. Origins of the Rebellion

We used to have laws in the Republic of Mexico. For example: Article 27. Emiliano Zapata and his soldiers imposed that law with their lives and their blood, and in a few hours, without consulting the peasants, Salinas de Gortari wiped them out. When we knew that our land could be sold or taken from us, when we heard that there would be no more land for us, that nearly finished us. At that moment my brothers wanted to rise up.

—EZLN Commander Major Mario, Lacandon Jungle, January 30, 1994.

THE ZAPATISTAS MADE THEIR FIRST, spectacular public appearance in San Cristobal de las Casas in 1992. On October 12 of that year, amid demonstrations marking "The Year of the Indian, 500 Years of Resistance," 4,000 young men and women armed with bows and arrows suddenly appeared out of the crowd. Marching in military formation, they advanced to the central plaza where they attacked the monument to the founder of San Cristobal, the sixteenth century Spanish *encomendador*, Diego de Mazariegos. As the symbol of 500 years of oppression crashed from its pedestal, the Indians hacked it to pieces and pocketed the fragments before disappearing. In the annals of indigenous resistance, the toppling of Mazariegos's statue had a symbolic resonance equivalent to the destruction of the Berlin Wall.

The next time the Zapatistas came to the city was on New Year's Day, 1994. They had replaced their bows and arrows with assault rifles and exchanged their traditional dress for homemade army uniforms and ski masks. But the anticolonial message was the same: "We are the product of 500 years of struggle," they declared. "NAFTA [North American Free Trade Agreement] is a death sentence for the Indians."

The origins of the Zapatista rebellion are rooted in the unequal distribution of land. Other key factors are the brutal repression of the independent peasant and indigenous organizations throughout the 1980s and the economic devastation of the Indian communities caused by the economic policies of the preceding decade. Yet the primary cause was the state's refusal to grant land to the indigenous, as mandated in Article 27 of the Mexican Constitution. All other ills, including the destruction of the Lacandon Jungle, derive from the state's corrupt and discriminatory system of land distribution. Successive state administrations have ignored or circumvented the land reforms that, during the Mexican Revolution, Emiliano Zapata won for the indigenous and poor peasants early in the century. In 1916, at the height of the revolution, 8,000 of the largest families owned three million hectares of the best land—almost half of the land surface of the state. In 1990 the same proportion of the land was in the hands of 6,000 landowners—most of them cattle ranchers—while a million indigenous *ejidatarios* (villagers who own and manage their land collectively) struggled to survive on the remaining 3 million acres of poor, marginal land, only 41 percent of which was officially classified as suitable for farming.[1]

When the fighting stopped in 1920, Mexico had a populist agrarian law based on Emiliano Zapata's ideas and designed to meet the needs of the nation's indigenous population. In Zapata's home state of Morelos, new agrarian laws placed precise limits on the size of large estates; restored traditional communal lands to their original owners; recognized "the traditional and historic right" of the villages and communities to administer "their fields of communal distribution and common use (*ejidos*) in the form which they judge proper"; affirmed "the unquestionable right which belongs to every Mexican of possessing and cultivating an extension of land, the products of which permit him to cover his needs and those of his family"; and provided legal protection against any intrigues between corrupt village leaders and speculators by making the government grants permanent. The Revolutionary Agrarian Law of 1915, drafted by Zapata's legal advisers, stated: "The farms which the Government cedes to communities or individuals are not alienable, nor can they be mortgaged in any form, all contracts which tend to go against this disposition being null."² Thus Zapata ensured that the collectively owned and farmed Indian *ejido* lands, once granted, could never be taken away.

But these laws were never enacted in Chiapas. For seventy-five years they remained on the national statute book, establishing the principle of indigenous rights to land ownership and legitimizing indigenous struggles. The original Article 27 embodied the Mexican State's most sacred pact with the indigenous population, and the demand for its restoration is a preeminent priority for the new generation of Zapatista rebels.

By the time the 1911 revolution ended, Emiliano Zapata, already a legend in his lifetime, had become a mythic hero. In 1919, when news of his murder reached Mexico City, the editorials of various newspapers warned the postrevolutionary leaders that to destroy his myth "would require reforms to destroy the injustices that had generated him."³ Seventy-five years later, when the Zapatista National Liberation Army seized San Cristobal in 1994, the injustices of that earlier time were still virtually intact. "Why Zapata? Didn't Zapata come from the state of Morelos?" a tourist with a camcorder asked a young guerrilla on the street in San Cristobal on New Year's night, 1994. The young Zapatista answered: "Because Zapata, even though he's dead, is the food of the Indians. His fight made us grow. He is the fertilizer of the people of the land, the one that nourishes us, and makes us strong."⁴

II. Chiapas: Backdrop to the Rebellion

I watched my father die because there was no money in our village to buy him medicine for his stomach. That's why I went with the Zapatistas . . . I decided to fight because if we're all going to die it might as well be for something.

—RAUL HERNANDEZ, (seventeen years old, Zapatista prisoner, quoted in *Expresso*, February 8, 1993)

THE STATE OF CHIAPAS is the eighth largest in Mexico and one of the richest in natural resources. It has oil, gas, timber, and hydroelectric power. Three major dams produce 55 percent of the nation's electricity, and eighty-six oil wells pump out more than 25,000,000 barrels of crude oil annually and more than 500 billion cubic feet of natural gas per day; oil and natural gas production account respectively for 21 percent and 47 percent of national production. The state is the largest coffee producer in the country—35 percent of all the coffee grown in Mexico comes from Chiapas—and is the second largest producer of beef.[5] It is the second largest producer of corn, bananas, honey, melons, avocados, and cocoa, all sold for export. In the decade prior to the Zapatista rising, local politicians and businessmen, among them a recent state governor, acquired immense fortunes by exploiting the rain forest's precious woods, mahogany and tropical cedars; between 1981 and 1989, 7 million cubic meters of these woods were harvested, the net profit from these logging operations amounting to $8 million in 1988 alone.[6] In 1989, exports from Chiapas were valued at $200 million.

Yet despite these resources, over 70 percent of the population—2,200,000 indigenous and mestizo peasants—live below the poverty line, compared to only 6 percent nationwide.[7] The lack of basic services for the population places Chiapas on a par with any poverty-stricken Third World country. The education system is a travesty: Chiapas has the lowest literacy rate in Mexico (30 percent statewide, almost 50 percent in the conflict zone).[8] In the rain forest communities, where 52 percent of the population is under fifteen years of age, there are only 217 primary schools for almost 65,000 school-age children; in the municipalities of Ocosingo and Las Margaritas—both focal points of the conflict zone—40 and 33 percent of school-age children, respectively, never attend school (the national rate is 14 percent). In the rain forest, 39 percent of the population has never been to school, 41 percent cannot read, and 36 percent speak no Spanish.[9]

Chiapas also suffers from an abysmal lack of infrastructure. In spite of the state's energy resources, between 70 and 80 percent of the houses in the villages and towns of eastern Chiapas have no access to electricity or gas; 62 percent have no clean drinking water; more than 85 percent no drainage; over 80 percent have mud floors.[10] The state's transportation system is also minimalist; just two-thirds of the municipalities have paved or partially paved roads, and twelve thousand rural communities can only be reached by mountain trails. Only two railroad lines exist, both date from the early 1900s.

Chiapas also has the lowest level of health services in the country: There is one doctor for every 1,500 residents—one-half the national average—and only 0.4 hospital beds per thousand inhabitants, one-third the level of Mexico as a whole. Infant mortality in the rain forest is over 10 percent. These statistics help explain why the major causes of death in the Indian villages of Chiapas have not changed in fifty years; in 1994 malnutrition, cholera, tuberculosis, dysentery, and other poverty-related, curable diseases accounted for an estimated 15,000 Indian deaths each year.[11]

The state holds the record for the highest unemployment rate (50 percent) and the lowest salaries paid to rural workers in a region where 6 out of 10 employed work in agriculture. One-fifth of the population lives outside the money economy, and 40 percent of workers receive less than the minimum wage. Subsistence farmers traditionally supplemented their incomes by hiring themselves out as day workers on large estates, but unemployment has increased dramatically since the early 1980s, when large coffee farmers began employing Guatemalan refugees at substantially lower wages than their Mexican counterparts; since 1980 the average real wages of rural day workers have fallen by 51 percent.[12] In short, the indigenous communities of the rain forest have virtually no access to markets, credit, technical support services, tractors, education, clean water, or health services. These realities, created by a policy of official neglect amounting to a penalization of the indigenous population for its independence from the PRI, are the catalysts of the Zapatista rebellion.

Chiapas has been an unstable state, run by corrupt PRI authorities who protect the interests of the PRI's main supporters—large landowners and cattle ranchers, who monopolize 2 million hectares, or one-third of the state's total farmland, for cattle grazing.[13] In Chiapas, all economic and political power is based on land ownership; from the governor's office to the smallest local courtroom, the sheriff in charge is almost always a landowner or a cattleman. The second most important pillar of the political machine is the network of *caciques*, indigenous political bosses who administer the state programs and have a monopoly on transport, markets, and access to credit. The *caciques* control the official peasant and indigenous organizations, recruit informers to infiltrate independent organizations, and hire the cattlemen's enforcers, the Guardias Blancas (White Guards)—paramilitary mercenaries who invade and seize indigenous land, create havoc in indigenous villages, massacre civilians, and "disappear" or assassinate indigenous and peasant leaders.[14] Frequently, the White Guards are accompanied on their forays by state and federal police or troops of the Mexican army.

The federal government, however, is jointly responsible for this anti-indigenous apartheid. Historically, electoral fraud in Chiapas provided the PRI with its largest percentage (98-99 percent) of the vote statewide; in the 1991 local elections, 50 of the villages in the conflict zone reported a 100 percent turnout for the PRI. Consequently, the Mexican government has been unwilling to challenge the methods of political and economic leaders who consistently deliver such powerful regional support. "The government is in a trap," Mexican analyst Jorge Castaneda told the magazine *Proceso* in January 1994. "Like every authoritarian system it cannot afford to fight against the structures that provide its life force . . . Its true base of political support [in Chiapas] is not in the electorate, it is in the economic and social sectors—the business sectors and the *caciques*—whom it cannot attack because it depends on them for its life."

III. The Arrival of Marcos

THE HISTORY OF THE ZAPATISTA movement is inseparable from the history of the disorderly colonization of the Lacandon rain forest, which over the course of the last thirty years has been transformed into a human and ecological nightmare. The current generation of indigenous rebels are the descendants of a diaspora that began in the 1930s, when, under pressure from President Lazaro Cardenas to comply with the land reform laws, the state authorities began sending landless indigenous to establish *ejidos* in the virgin Lacandon Jungle. Their decision to hand over state lands evaded the problem of redistributing the land of the large estates, as mandated by law. Pursuing the indigenous dreams of land and autonomy, thousands of the very poorest of the indigenous, released from debt peonage, fled their serflike conditions as *acasillados* ("the attached") of the large estates, and trekked into the Lacandon Jungle in search of a better future. When the first wave of migrants arrived, the rain forest covered 13,000 square kilometers of almost unpopulated territory, stretching eastward from the towns of Ocosingo, Altamirano, and Las Margaritas to the Usumacinta River and the Guatemalan border. Since 1960, the population of the rain forest has increased from 6,000 to 300,0000, nearly three-quarters of the forest has been cleared and burned for milpas and cattle pastures, and an additional 2,500 square kilometers have been seized for oil and gas exploration. Today, only 3,400 square kilometers of virgin rain forest have survived, protected in the Montes Azules Biosphere Reserve.[15]

Historically, Mayan identity and culture varies from village to village; the village is the embodiment of the traditions, the history, and the ethnic identity of each community. But an indigenous village without land is an aberration, and since the 1930s, successive waves of migrants abandoned everything that was familiar to them to claim the promised new lands and establish new communities in an alien environment. They came from a variety of ethnic groups; some even came from neighboring states that the authorities wanted to clear of the indigenous. As each new group arrived, they penetrated still deeper into the jungle. In the 1960s, local timber merchants bulldozed roads into the heart of the rain forest to begin extracting truckloads of precious woods, and additional waves of indigenous migrants followed in their wake. But after the indigenous had cleared the land and planted their milpas with corn, beans and coffee, cattlemen from out of state drove down these same roads, seized the new *ejidos*, converted them to pasture, and pushed the indigenous ever farther into the rain forest.[16] So began decades of vicious land conflicts with the cattlemen.

When Marcos and a small group of revolutionaries came to the rain forest in 1984 to create an indigenous guerrilla force, they found that for twenty years, Bishop Don Samuel Ruiz Garcia and the church workers of the San Cristobal diocese had been intensely involved in indigenous community life. Bishop Ruiz was the greatest defender of Indian rights in Latin America since his sixteenth-century forebear, the first bishop of San Cristobal, Fray Bartolome de las Casas. In the 1960s he participated in the preparations for the Second Vatican Council, and on his return from Rome, he brought Pope John's "preferential option for the poor"—the source of liberation theology—to the rain forest. It must have seemed extraordinary for the indigenous people to find the new bishop turning up on foot to visit their isolated villages, talking with them in their own languages, sleeping on their mud floors, and sharing their beans and dry tortillas. "I came to San Cristobal to convert the poor, but they ended up converting me," Ruiz told historian John Womack many years later.[17] As he learned about the indigenous culture, the bishop introduced Christian concepts in a language that related to indigenous daily life, giving the Indians hope in a better future.

Bishop Ruiz and his diocesan coworkers set out to unify and build a sense of collective security and community among this fragmented and disparate population. They used the Bible and a forestwide system of radios to foster communication, solidarity and a shared identity. Translated into indigenous dialects, the Book of Exodus helped the Indians understand the serfdom from which they had escaped and offered a vision of the freedom they yearned for in their own version of the "Promised Land." The radios created a network for organizing and training community leaders. So, gradually, with the persistent guidance and support of the bishop's diocese, the isolated communities united and forged a new identity, through which they rediscovered and reinvented their ancestral traditions. Church workers trained catechists and deacons from whose ranks emerged a network of community and regional leaders throughout the rain forest. The Church sponsored and promoted the development of indigenous organizations, and Church protection and support legitimized the indigenous struggle for the four essentials of community life: land, education, health, and access to markets. By 1984 the indigenous had already developed an acute awareness of their rights, and had been analyzing and confronting their problems, in their own languages, with their own leaders, in their own independent organizations for the better part of a decade.

The guerrilla newcomers came from out of state. All were veterans of a small, clandestine and urban revolutionary force from the northeastern city of Monterrey—the Forces of National Liberation. Their influences were the classic political-military ideologies of the Latin American left—Leninist-Maoist and Guevarist. They listened to the revolutionary messages broadcast by Radio

Sandino from Nicaragua and by the FMLN Radio Venceremos from El Salvador; their self-image was cast in the romantic history of "El Che" and the victorious guerrillas of Cuba and Nicaragua; they saw themselves in the role of a revolutionary vanguard, arriving in the rain forest to inspire and lead "the prolonged popular war" at the head of an indigenous guerilla force. Their goal was the overthrow of the Mexican state-party system and the installation of a revolutionary and socialist people's republic. But when the newcomers met the indigenous world, they discovered they had to relearn everything from scratch. ("Our square conception of the world and of revolution was badly dented in the confrontation with the indigenous realities of Chiapas").[18]

At first the revolutionaries approached the Church, hoping to convince the bishop to sponsor their presence in the communities, but the bishop turned them away. "From the moment we arrived there was friction," Marcos told reporters from *Proceso* magazine in San Cristobal, in February 1994. "The Church said armed conflict was not possible in Mexico, that the change had to come peacefully, through mass democratic mobilization. The work of the Church was always in direct opposition to our work."[19] So the guerrillas withdrew into the mountains, where they learned to survive clandestinely in a hostile environment, until, just as Marcos had predicted, external violence changed the political dynamic inside the communities and began to erode the influence of the Church. "The Church was committed to change through open political participation," said Marcos, "and the communities tried to do that by every means possible. But the state kept strangling them; the numbers of deaths kept rising. We always knew the state was on our side, in the sense that it would prove [the Church's way] was not enough . . . that a different way forward was necessary."[20] The Zapatistas' arrival in Chiapas had coincided with a regional expansion of cattle ranching that brought with it increased violence, brutality and state repression. As the landowners needed more acreage to convert their estates to pasture, they invaded villages to seize *ejido* lands. When the indigenous and peasant organizations mobilized protests, their leaders were systematically killed or thrown in jail without legal recourse. It was then that the indigenous communities sought Marcos's help to create self-defense units to protect them against the landowners' mercenaries, the Guardias Blancas.

"We found each other," says Marcos, "and we began to speak in two different languages. They needed military instruction and we needed the support of a social base."[21] Marcos and his group quickly realized they would get nowhere without the support of a consensus within the communities. In short, any indigenous army that the Zapatista organizers might recruit would have to submit to the collective decision-making authority of the village assemblies. If the civilians were going to be calling the shots, the classical, vertical structure of a revolutionary guerrilla movement would not work. Some entirely new form of political-military structure would have to be invented. Only Marcos and a very few of his companions met the challenge. But in the ensuing collaboration between the nonindigenous, urban leftists, and the traditional indigenous peasants in their isolated rain forest communities, both sides learned from each other and were changed by each other.

The resulting revolutionary movement defies categorization. The unique collaboration between the indigenous and the outsiders produced a military force commanded by a collective indigenous civilian leadership, the Clandestine Indigenous Revolutionary Committee (CCRI), whose members are elected by the civilians in their democratic village assemblies and who themselves obey the decisions of the villagers. Through that first small nucleus of self-defense units, the Zapatista organizers slowly won the trust of the communities.

Before the Zapatistas came, the most effective force in the region had been the Church-sponsored indigenous organization known as Union de Uniones (UdU), which represented 6,000 families and concentrated on developing small-scale economic projects and education and health programs. As the Zapatistas secretly began recruiting and organizing in the villages, the inevitable competition with the UdU leaders led to conflicts. Over time, some of the communities split their loyalties and eventually the UdU leadership was infiltrated by the PRI. As the Zapatistas grew and consolidated their strength, Bishop Ruiz's dream of uniting the indigenous population from one end of the rainforest to the other in a single, mass movement disintegrated.

Eventually, too, the Zapatistas infiltrated the Church infrastructure and the Union de Uniones through the Bishop's network of youthful indigenous catechists. Every village had two or more catechists, the people Bishop Ruiz described as "those who gather and harvest the community thought." Their disaffection with the Church and disavowal of the Bishop's authority would be key elements in the acceptance of the Zapatistas by the communities. The EZLN (Zapatista National Liberation Army) also ran vaccination campaigns for the children; organized programs to help the young indigenous women to break free from the submissiveness so deeply ingrained in their culture; and banned alcohol among their members. By infiltrating the leadership of the Union de Uniones, they converted several thousand of their members to the Zapatista cause. In 1991, they also organized a radical civilian front organization, the Asociación Nacional de Campesinos Indigenas Emiliano Zapata (ANCIEZ), which carried the fight for land throughout Chiapas and was responsible for the attack on Diego de Mazariegos's monument in San Cristobal de las Casas during the "Year of the Indian, 500 Years of Resistance" celebrations.[22]

Meanwhile, the rebel army continued to grow. Recruitment was conducted person by person, at night, in one-on-one interviews. Each new recruit was escorted to one of the clandestine training camps in the mountains only after he or she had signed a formal oath of loyalty and secrecy. The EZLN soldiers, who never left their villages for more than a few days or nights at a time, trained secretly, carrying out their daily farming activities until a few days before the rebellion began. Consequently, most of the non-Zapatista members among the indigenous population—as well as the cattlemen and the PRI—believed that the "armed groups," which everyone knew were training in the mountains, were still preparing solely for purposes of self-defense. But in the summer of 1992, after the Mexican government amended the agrarian law, there was a dramatic shift of mood throughout the rain forest. Now the younger members of the Zapatista army began agitating for insurrection, and the leaders initiated consultations with the villagers. When the members of the CCRI put the question to the village assemblies, the majority in the communities voted for war. The CCRI began to prepare for an uprising by the end of 1993, and the tempo of the recruiting drive accelerated.

Marcos also never ceased lobbying the indigenous to adopt the wider political objectives of unseating the PRI and so open a national political space for a pluralistic multiethnic democracy. To this end the Zapatistas held courses among the young recruits in Mexican history and the Spanish language and promoted Mexico's national heroes as legitimate symbols of a joint Mexican/indigenous heritage. These efforts successfully shrank the gulf between the indigenous and the country at large and ultimately forged the pan-indigenous nationalism that distinguishes the Zapatista rebellion from all previous indigenous uprisings. Ultimately the population adopted the dual agendas of the Zapatista revolt: the regional, indigenous demands on the one hand, and the national objectives of democracy, justice, and liberty in a pluralistic multiethnic society on the other.

IV. A Revolution Foretold

The Mexican State, liberal, republican and federal, of equality before the law, is one that has always had to be a [state] of justice. When, at the beginning of the twentieth century, [the state] forgot this, the people, rising in their revolution, reminded it.

—PRESIDENT CARLOS SALINAS, address to the nation, early in 1989

We rose up, not to kill or be killed, but so that they would listen to us.

—SUBCOMANDANTE MARCOS, San Cristobal. February 1994

In Mexico, the past reappears because it is a hidden present.

—OCTAVIO PAZ, "Critique of the Pyramid"

IN 1992 "EVERY MAN, woman and child who was still awake at the end of the assembly," according to Marcos, voted to instruct the Zapatista army to prepare for war. Once again, as in 1911, the Indian rising was precipitated by the impact of an economic reform and modernization program, imposed from above and driven by the perceived exigencies of a foreign model of development. No one disputes the credit due to President Carlos Salinas for rescuing Mexico from the financial ruin brought on by the debt crisis of 1982. Yet while his economic reform policies attracted billions of dollars of foreign investment (much of it speculative investment in the booming Mexican stock exchange), controlled the national debt, stabilized the peso, and brought down triple-digit inflation to 7 percent, these policies also produced an unprecedented concentration of wealth in the hands of a minuscule corporate and industrial elite; in 1990, a little over 2 percent of the Mexican population controlled 78.5 percent of the nation's wealth.[23] In Salinas's Mexico, once again, the historic divisions based on wealth and land ownership, exacerbated by the racial fault line between the nonindigenous landowners and the indigenous peasants, intensified exponentially.

Judging from the government's reaction, the small ski-masked figures who appeared on the streets of San Cristobal de las Casas on New Year's night might have been aliens, dropping in on the NAFTA celebrations from some other planet. Yet none of the self-evident causes of the rebellion—the misery, the hunger, the repression, the utter neglect and abandonment of the Mayan communities of Chiapas—was news to anyone. Interviewed just days after the insurrection, the Chiapaneco playwright Carlos Olmos told *Proceso* magazine, "It has been an open secret that there were guerrillas in Chiapas. Peace in Chiapas has been a sham for centuries."[24]

Yet, the Mexican army, members of President Salinas's cabinet, and the president himself also knew that there were guerrillas in Chiapas. In March 1993, on an official visit to Ocosingo, President Salinas was petitioned in person by leaders of the local Cattlemen's Association, who pleaded with him for government intervention to deal with guerrillas training in the mountains just beyond the town.[25] Two months later, just seven months before the Zapatistas seized San Cristobal and three other towns in the region, the Mexican army accidentally stumbled on a Zapatista training camp. According to news reports at the time, troops from out of state sealed all the access roads into the rain forest, ransacked villages, and arrested and tortured non-Zapatista peasants.[26] Yet when the army withdrew to barracks three weeks later, the military Commander of the region publicly stated that "there are no guerrillas in Chiapas." To drive home the point, the state attorney general added that anyone who saw fit to challenge this assertion would be seeking to damage Mexico's image.[27]

After the revolt it was widely reported, in Mexico and abroad, that the government's failure to forestall the uprising resulted from Salinas's decision to avoid engaging in a counterinsurgency campaign during the U.S. Congress debates on NAFTA. This understandable reluctance to scuttle the image of Mexico in the United States on the eve of major economic legislation affecting both countries does not, however, explain the government's failure to address the festering misery and mounting frustration in Chiapas. As long as the macro-economic indicators remained healthy, it appears that the president and his team of young Harvard- and Yale-educated economists were too busy stoking the transformation of the Mexican economy to assess the social effects of their policies on the people who had to pay the price for the tight fiscal controls, the closures of state owned businesses, (according to government statistics, 150 million people lost their jobs in 1993), or the cancellations of subsidies to poor farmers.[28] As they drove Mexico down the fast track toward ratification of NAFTA, the Mexican political and economic elite shared certain sanguine convictions: they believed that revolution was an anachronism and that modern Mexico had outgrown the era when peasants and indigenous would rise up against the state to challenge the status quo. They also saw political reforms as unnecessary. Mexicans, it was commonly said, were apathetic, would put up with anything, and would always vote for the PRI.

So when the government deregulated coffee prices in 1989, and the price of coffee beans fell by 50 percent in a single year, the government's answer to the economic dislocation in Chiapas was to cut subsidies and disband the only state agency that provided marketing and technical assistance to small growers. In a single year, the Indians' domestic market share fell from 16 percent to 3.4 percent.[29] In 1991, when required to institute radical reforms in the agricultural sector in order to qualify for NAFTA and meet the World Bank's terms for a $300,000,000 development loan, President Salinas terminated Mexico's traditional system of land tenure, the cherished legacy of the Mexican Revolution. In 1989 the president had declared that the "essential condition for achieving the modernization of rural Chiapas is the direct participation of the peasants as the protagonists of their own reality."[30] Yet in 1992 he removed existing restrictions on the size of the large estates and abolished the Ejido Law in order to clear the way for privatization of the land and thus allow national and foreign agribusiness to grow cash crops for export, violating the inalienability of ejido lands in Article 27 of the Mexican Constitution of 1917.[31]

The discovery that it was the forgotten Mayan villages of the Lacandon Jungle who had taken up arms shook the president and his cabinet colleagues to the core. When the president unleashed the Mexican Army with orders to "capture the leaders" and "eliminate the problem," the EZLN's strategy of surprise attacks followed by rapid withdrawals that melted into the civilian population, made a mockery of the army's attempts to encircle and crush them.[32] The original ambition of the rebels to seize the largest military base in the state, outside San Cristobal, supply themselves with weapons and ammunition, and proceed to the state capital of Tuxtla Gutiérrez, failed. Nevertheless, with only limited ammunition, several thousand poorly armed, undernourished young indigenous men and women launched eight frontal attacks in as many consecutive days on the base and drove 12,000 heavily armed troops backed with tanks, armored cars, rocket-firing helicopters and fighter planes onto the defensive. For ten days the national army was reduced to the humiliating spectacle of shelling the hills of Chiapas.

After twelve days, the threat of a violent upheaval at home and the realization that the images from Chiapas were playing to an international audience—especially to Mexico's new NAFTA partners—had made the price of sustaining the offensive unbearable. Yet the true message of the rebellion had still not reached the government. In the Presidential Palace, experts determined that whatever the true origins of the Zapatista National Liberation Army might be, it was not indigenous. To the fury of the Zapatista leaders, the government's descriptions of the rebel force changed from "a couple of hundred transgressors of the law" to "a professional, violent, and well-trained extremist organization" whose leaders were Guatemalans, Nicaraguans, or some other variant of the "leftover mercenaries of the exhausted Central American conflicts of the eighties," while the rebels' "indigenous component" was dismissed as naive, manipulated young "cannon fodder" for its cynical "foreign comandantes."[33]

By the time the shooting war stopped, the television cameras and reporters had broadcast far and wide the images and statistics of misery in Mexico's forgotten Southeast. The international media, whose glowing reports had promoted Salinas's "Mexican Miracle" as a regional blueprint for Latin America's emerging democracies, finally began to ask the tough questions that cast doubt on the nature and progress of Mexico's development. They awakened a new generation of grassroots activists in Mexican society from "the long and lazy dream that 'modernity' imposes on everyone and everything."[34] When they did so, "they realized," says Jorge Castenada, "that the fundamental national problems so many people thought had been dealt with—inequality, injustice, lack of democracy— had never been resolved at all."

Overnight, the "local conflict in four small municipalities of Chiapas" had ignited a national debate on globalization, agrarian policies, indigenous rights, Mexican racism and democracy.[35] Above all, as primarily mestizo, modern

Mexico was forced to confront traditional, indigenous Mexico, the debate increasingly focused on the nation's tormented identification with the sixty-five year-old ruling political state-party system, raising profound questions about its future stability and reliability as an economic partner. "This country today," said the writer Carlos Montemayor, "is a sounding box of political tensions. Historically, the rural areas have always been the launching pad for political change because of the Mexicans, especially the Indians, who regard the land as a living entity . . . In Mexico, we can't play around with the land, or pretend that it's a chemically inert property that can change ownership without affecting the deepest fibers of traditional Mexico. Chiapas represents the most urgent warning Mexico has known, a reminder that there exists a traditional population that cannot be ignored as we move into the new century."[36]

V. Conversations in the Cathedral

The EZLN came to this dialogue in the true spirit of being heard and explaining all the reasons that obliged us to take up arms so as not to die an undignified death . . . .We encountered attentive ears that were willing to hear the truth . . .The dialogue of San Cristobal was real. There were no tricks or lies. There was no buying or selling of dignities. Now that we have a response that reflects the sincere interest of the gentleman commissioned as Peace Envoy, it is our obligation to reflect well on what his words say. We must now speak to the collective heart that commands us. We must listen to its voice in order to start again; from them, from our people, from the indigenous people in the mountains and canyons, will come the decision on the next step to take along this road whose destiny will, or will not, be peace with justice and dignity."

—JUAN, a member of the Clandestine Revolutionary Indigenous Committee at the conclusion of the Dialogue for Peace and Reconciliation, March 2, 1994.

IT WAS A SUNDAY, a lovely sunny day in late February in 1954 when the Zapatista leaders returned to San Cristobal to open peace talks with President Salinas's personal envoy, Manuel Camacho Solís. The town where the war had begun, Camacho Solís had said the night before, should be the town where the message of peace would first be heard.

The Bishop Don Samuel Ruiz would mediate the talks, and he had opened the doors of the great, sixteenth-century baroque Cathedral of San Cristobal de las Casas to provide a safe sanctuary to the participants. The scene was a set piece of political theater. Below the altar steps, against the backdrop of the Mexican flag, was a long, baize-covered table, jammed with microphones, was presided over by the bishop, Peace Commissioner Camacho, and Subcomandante Marcos (the latter wearing his black ski mask with two bandoliers crossing his chest). Masked members of the women and men of the CCRI flanked the three men on either side. In the background, other Zapatista soldiers stood motionless, like medieval statues, lit by shafts of light falling from a great height to pierce the dark, cavernous spaces of the vast cathedral. Facing this scene, standing behind rows upon rows of television cameras, several hundred members of the international press corps would attend a daily presentation each evening to learn of the progress of the talks.

All week, Marcos dominated this scene. It was from here that he told the Mexicans why the indigenous rebels had come and asked the awkward questions: "Why," he demanded, "is it necessary to kill and to die so that you should listen to Ramona, seated here beside me, tell you that Indian women want to live, want to study, want hospitals, want medicines, want schools, want food, want respect, want justice, want dignity?" The most electrifying moment came on about the third or fourth day of the talks, as Marcos turned to the diminutive Ramona, then silently drew from her satchel an immense silk Mexican flag, and draping it across his chest offered one corner to the Peace Commissioner to assist him hold it up for the cameras. "This," he announced, " is the flag for which we became soldiers." His speech that day put an end to live radio broadcasts from the cathedral for the rest of the week, but it was too late. For there was Marcos on prime time national television, star, author and impresario of a script entitled "Bringing the Revolution from the Rain Forest to the Nation," and there has been nothing comparable in the history of Latin American revolutionary politics.

It was in the cathedral that Marcos and the citizens of Mexico's tentative civil society first met. Two weeks before the talks began, the Zapatistas had written to Mexican non-governmental organizations nationwide asking them, with great respect, if they would provide security for the Zapatista leaders when they came to town. Civil society is not comfortable with armed movements; even when the cause is just. It is not the role of civil activists to support violent revolution. Yet in Mexico in 1994, something new, something manifestly different, was in the air. From all over the country people answered the Zapatistas' call; the young and the old, men and women, students and retired couples, came to put their bodies on a peace line by creating a human security cordon around the cathedral twenty-four hours a day, thus protecting the group of ski-masked indigenous leaders who had come to talk about making peace. It was the start of a relationship of trust between the Zapatistas and Mexico's civilian opposition to the government's policies.

On January 11, 1994, while the war between the rebels and the Mexican army was still being fought (the cease-fire would come twenty-four hours later), a courageous small independent daily newspaper in San Cristobal de las Casas called *El*

Tiempo published the first Zapatista communiqué: "We are not asking you to agree with us or with the choice we have made," Marcos wrote, "but my companions . . . have asked me to approach you. They hope, that since you represent the only honest and objective journalism left in Chiapas, you will give them the opportunity to tell their story." Between the January 12 cease-fire and the opening of the first peace talks in the last week of February, Marcos ran an extraordinary press campaign in a selection of national newspapers to introduce the indigenous rebellion to his countrymen. His communiqués brought Mexicans a startling new voice. By the time the Zapatistas came to the first peace talks in the San Cristobal Cathedral, Marcos had already laid the foundations for a relationship between Mexico's emerging civil society and the indigenous rebellion.

The Zapatistas had been taken by surprise by the cease-fire. They had not been expecting the mass mobilizations for peace that had forced President Salinas to call off the Mexican army when the rebel forces were retreating at the end of the twelve-day war. Encouraged by the prevailing sense that the PRI was crumbling, the Zapatistas shared with their supporters an irrationally optimistic belief that civil society, that decentralized coalition of many small, disparate groups, organized around concrete local issues, could be quickly transformed into a coordinated national political movement capable of moving into the open space created by the rebellion. While Manuel Camacho and Bishop Ruiz were secluded behind closed doors, negotiating with the collective leadership of the CCRI, Marcos pursued a separate, parallel strategy. Within the cavernous interior of the cathedral he lobbied delegations from all over the country, striving to mobilize a mass movement behind the fundamental demand for democracy that Salinas had excluded from the talks. Marcos's message to everyone who trooped in to see him was consistent with everything he had been saying since the cease-fire: "We know our limits . . . We don't see the armed struggle in the classic sense of all the previous guerrillas, that is, as the one and only way forward, as the only all-powerful truth around which everything else is subordinated . . . We're not saying, 'Here is how we believe the country should be and we'll shoot anyone who doesn't agree with our views.' And we can't solve all the problems of Mexico. What we're saying is 'Let's make a deal to create a democratic space. If our program wins out in that space, fine . . . If not, let someone else's [program] win. What matters is that the space must exist.'"[37]

For most of Mexico's progressive middle class, however, it was one thing to support the Zapatistas and quite another to mobilize behind an overt challenge to the legitimacy of the PRI government. Put to the test, the alliance faltered, and when it did, Marcos blamed himself for asking too much: "It was too big a thing to expect," he said of his failure to inspire mass mobilization behind the Zapatista's demand for Salinas's resignation and the creation of a transition government to dismantle the links between the PRI and the government and open the way to pluralistic democratic elections.

When the talks ended, the peace plan the indigenous leaders took back with them to submit to the villagers included an explicit admission that, all previous denials to the contrary, the agrarian laws had indeed never been complied with within Chiapas. The government now promised to investigate the large estates and redistribute the illegally held land, but it avoided the two central demands—the return to the original Article 27 legislation and full political autonomy for the indigenous population. Instead, it offered a new Indigenous Bill of Rights, which recognized community practices and customs, and the provisions to address the land issue were only applicable within the state of Chiapas. This new Indigenous Bill of Rights, worked out with Camacho and sanctioned by Salinas, was not enough to persuade the rebels to put down their guns. Nevertheless, there was a real sense that progress toward "peace with justice and dignity" had been made. Relationships of trust had been forged between Camacho and the indigenous leaders; "If Camacho is not sincere then he deserves an Oscar," Marcos told the press. Juan, the spokesman for the CCRI, also spoke warmly of Camacho and especially of the bishop and his team, whom, he said, had mediated "not in the middle of war and peace, but in the middle of two voices who are trying, still, to find each other. If some tranquility blossoms in these lands," he continued, "it will be due, above all, to their peace-making work."

Three weeks later, the villages of the rain forest were in the midst of their consultations on the peace proposals when Luis Donaldo Colosio, President Salinas' handpicked candidate for the presidential elections in August, was assassinated in Tijuana. Overnight, Mexico was a different country. The bullet that killed Colosio also assassinated the political career of Manuel Camacho—there were insinuations of Camacho's involvement in the murder. Colosio's only rival within the PRI, Camacho was also the only national politician with credibility among the Zapatistas and the political courage and will to confront the risks of a negotiated and sustainable peace in Chiapas. In the rain forest, the consultations were put on hold. The Zapatista Army went on red alert, anticipating a military attack. It was June before the Zapatistas announced the result of the village consultations: 97.88 percent of the indigenous had voted to reject the government's offer.[38] Two years later, Marcos told Yvon Le Bot, French scholar and director of Latin American research at the Centre National de la Recherche Scientifique in Paris, "All this process of dialogue went to hell March 23rd when Colosio was assassinated. . . .The bullet that killed Colosio killed the possibility of a peace accord with the EZLN. We can't sign any pact with someone who isn't even capable of guaranteeing the life of his heir. Why would he guarantee that of his enemy? Also it reflected a political crisis so deep that we couldn't have reached any result." Once again, President Salinas imposed the PRI's replacement candidate, naming a little-known technocrat, Ernesto Zedillo, by personal fiat. The San Cristobal dialogue was dead. The hour of the Chiapas counterrevolution had arrived.

VI. The Zedillo Years, 1995-2000

The Indians arrived to give a lesson in modernity . . . to the technocrats piloting the ship of Mexican authoritarianism and put in question the national identity and the legitimacy of the political system.

—ROGER BARTRA, in *La Jornada*, June 29, 1994

IN POST-ZAPATISTA MEXICO everything had changed, yet nothing had changed. The Zapatista rebellion had triggered a struggle in the center of the ruling party around the urgent need to reform a system whose internal contradictions were tearing it apart. Colosio was dead, gunned down in the dry heat and dust of Tijuana, but six years later the PRI had not managed to find and punish his assassin. The national secretary of the PRI was dead too, shot at point-blank range in full daylight in Mexico City just six months after the murder of Colosio. Yet in 1994, nothing could upset the PRI's electoral machine. Not yet. That was coming. But after the August 1994 presidential elections, the Mexican left, so energized and united by the Zapatista rebellion, disintegrated once again. Throughout the Zedillo presidency, political reform within the ruling party was fiercely resisted, and in Chiapas corrupt local bosses were given a free hand to intensify the militarization and paramilitarization of the indigenous territories.

So change, but no change. During the presidency of Ernesto Zedillo, the army engaged in a low-intensity counterinsurgency war in Chiapas. The Mexican army increased its forces from 10,000 to 60,000 men and expanded its military occupation to over half of the states' municipalities. By 2000, the army had 300 camps strategically located around the state and 30 military bases inside the rain forest. To repress the rebellious civilian Zapatista population, at least nine paramilitary groups, trained by the army and police and recruited by the cattlemen and their allies among the loyal "good" indigenous in the PRI-controlled peasant organizations, have been operating against the Zapatista communities with complete impunity.

When in 1995 President Zedillo had to decide how he would deal with the growing menace of ungovernability and civil war in Chiapas, it soon became evident that he was either not willing or not capable of exerting control over the federal government's Zapatista policy, which, as always, would remain hostage to other interests. In February 1995, just a few weeks after the EZLN had reconfirmed its promise to sustain an indefinite, unilateral cease-fire, and while his envoys were holding talks with the Zapatista leaders about reopening the peace negotiations, President Zedillo went on national television to reveal the identity of Marcos and some other nonindigenous Zapatista leaders, and accused the EZLN of plotting to destabilize the Mexican State and stockpiling an arsenal in the rain forest. He then dispatched the army to seize control of Zapatista territory in the rain forest, with warrants for the arrest of the leaders. Zedillo's army failed to capture Marcos; all they found was his pipe, still smoking and warm. Thirty thousand troops launched a military offensive into Zapatista territory searching for nonexistent arms stockpiles as well as terrorizing and displacing tens of thousands of civilians.

Zedillo never tried to explain his abrupt about-face, but the entire operation backfired on him as Mexican civil society awoke from its postelectoral lethargy and 100,000 people marched in Mexico City. Through e-mail (the Zapatistas are credited as the first revolutionary movement to understand and effectively use the power of the Internet) there were immediate solidarity demonstrations in Europe and the United States that revealed the astonishing scope of international support for the Zapatistas. Five days later, Zedillo was forced to back down and call off the army, and by April the government and the Zapatistas had agreed to resume peace talks in the indigenous village of San Andres Larrainzar.

It took ten months for the talks to produce an agreement on the first point in the agenda, but on February 16, 1996, the delegates on both sides signed the text of a remarkable new accord on indigenous rights and culture that recognized the indigenous in the Mexican Constitution and committed the state to constructing a new juridical framework guaranteeing political, jurisdictional, and cultural rights and autonomy to Mexico's indigenous population. The Zapatistas' call for administrative and political autonomy had always included official recognition of self-government in all indigenous territories, villages, and municipalities nationwide, at the level of the state. The Zapatista vision of decentralized, autonomous political authority had been articulated nearly eighty years ago by their hero, Emiliano Zapata: "Municipal liberty," wrote Zapata, "is the first and most important of democratic institutions, since nothing is more natural or worthy of respect than the right that the citizens of any settlement have of arranging by themselves the affairs of their common life, and of resolving, as best suits them, the interests and needs of their locality."[39]

In January 1996, five weeks before finalizing an agreement with the government in San Andres on legislation intended to radically reform relations between the state and Mexico's indigenous population, the Zapatistas sponsored a special forum on indigenous rights and culture in San Cristobal de las Casas, at which over 500 representatives from thirty-five indigenous groups reached a consensus on the demands that they wanted to see included within the terms of any new accord arrived at in the negotiations. For the Zapatistas, their ability to deliver the government's commitment to meet these demands within the terms of a document that, as spelled out in the language of the concluding section, committed the Mexican government to build "a new social pact that reforms at the roots the existing social, political, economic, and cultural relations with indigenous peoples" signified a huge step forward. Effectively, the San Andres Accords on Indigenous Rights and Culture represents a historical breakthrough for Mexico's indigenous with its promise for "recognition and promotion of the multicultural nature of the nation . . . " its acceptance of the principle that, "the development of the nation must be based on plurality, understood as peacefully, productively, respectfully and equitably living together in diversity."

But once again President Zedillo did a u-turn and refused to sign the accords. Months later, when he disavowed the legal draft prepared by members of the official Commission of Concordance and Peace (COCOPA) for presentation to Congress, even after the text had been amended to deal with his objections and the changes accepted by the Zapatista negotiators, in September 1996 the Zapatistas withdrew from the peace negotiations.

By then, as the army continued to tighten the circle around the EZLN and the repression and dirty war of the paramilitaries intensified, life inside the rain forest under an army of occupation had become so violent that the men no longer dared leave their communities to work their crops, and hunger now stalked the rain forest, while in northern Chiapas an increasingly polarized and tense situation, stoked by an open alliance of police and paramilitaries, had created a situation of ungovernability. As the rebellion entered its third year, the number of those who had been killed or wounded in the undeclared, low-intensity war exceeded the number who died during the twelve-day war. Despairingly, the bishop warned that PRI paramilitaries, operating against opposition Partido Revolucionario Democrático (PRD) members and Zapatistas with the blatant complicity of the police and the army, were fomenting a fratricidal war. But the president had long since decided to back the local extremists, who had demanded the bishop's head, and the federal government permitted the criminal situation to fester. Northern Chiapas was a tinderbox. In December 1997 it exploded. The Christmas week massacre of forty-five unprotected refugees in the little village of Acteal was a tragedy foretold.

Two weeks prior to the massacre, a delegation from Mexico City had visited the area where the killings were to take place. The catalyst for their visit was a Mexican television report that had documented killings by progovernment paramilitaries in the region. The camera had documented the plight of thousands of displaced families, driven from their villages by the violence during the preceding months and weeks and living in makeshift camps—without food, medicine, access to clean drinking water, or adequate shelter from the bitter rains and freezing fogs of the December nights. *Chiapas: Witness to an Atrocity* had also exposed the fact that while rampant impunity protected the paramilitaries, even flight offered no guarantees of safety to the refugees. Isolated and surrounded by the same paramilitary troops who had driven them from their homes, burned their houses, stolen their animals and all their possessions, and were now harvesting their coffee crop—their sole source of income for the year ahead—the refugees lived in terror of further attacks.

The broadcast aired nationally in prime time on Sunday evening, December 7, 1997. The delegation came to Chiapas to see the conditions in the refugee camps for themselves four days later, accompanied by the press. In the days immediately preceding the December 22 massacre, there were many disturbing reports. One report described the delegates' visit to the village of Pechiquil, very close to Acteal, where paramilitaries had kidnapped twenty families and had been holding them hostage. "They have not been permitted to talk [to us] or to move about," the report explained. "Patrolling the area are men with various official uniforms, from those of the army, the Judicial Police (a federal police force), to men in brown and black with red bandanas imitating the uniform of the Zapatista National Liberation Army. The observers had to leave the area quickly," the report continued, "faced with the hostility of the village authorities. . . The twenty families, some incomplete because other members have been able to flee, could be dead right now. They are at the mercy of gunmen."

But it was not the hostages in Pechiquil who died. It was those members of their families who had managed to escape and had subsequently been given refuge by the community of nearby Acteal. When the progovernment killers struck, most of the women and small children they attacked and murdered had already been driven from their homes and had seen their families shattered in the process. But although they knew they were prime targets of the paramilitary strategy to "cleanse" the area of Zapatista sympathizers and ought to have left the area for their own safety, the women refused to move away from their men trapped in Pechiquil. "We are Las Abejas, [the Bees]," the refugees had told journalists two weeks earlier; "We have organized as a civil society with the help of the Church. We are not EZLN. We don't want guns. We have to conduct our fight [for our rights] peacefully. That is why we painted our houses and our churches white and put up signs which say *NEUTRAL ZONE*."

"But," they explained, "we are also civilian supporters of the Zapatistas. We look, and we see that like them we are following the same path for a better

Mexico, a Mexico with justice for all of the people." Two weeks before the tragedy, the people in Acteal defined their role in relation to the Zapatista rebellion's struggle for indigenous rights: "We are the cushion between the government and the Zapatistas," they said. "If there is going to be an attack against them, we, as the civil society, are the ones who can resist. But, if this cushion tears, then it is easier for the government to attack our brothers in the Zapatista Army." On December 22, 1997, the protective "cushion" of Las Abejas was torn to shreds when a uniformed paramilitary force, armed with AK-47 and R-15 assault rifles loaded with army issue ammunition (soft-nose or expanding bullets), went on an obscene four-hour killing spree in Acteal.

Within days of the attack, the Mexican army was advancing deep into Zapatista rain forest territory south and east of Acteal. Spokesmen for the Mexican minister of defense said the military were searching for Zapatista weapons. Soldiers in the rain forest told indigenous villagers they had orders from the president to find and arrest the EZLN leaders.Twice before, in January 1994 when the rebel army was retreating to the rain forest, and again in February 1995, when President Zedillo ordered the army to arrest the entire Zapatista leadership who had assembled to study the government's latest proposals for restarting the peace talks, mass mobilizations by Mexican and international Zapatista supporters had forced the government to back away from a military solution. This time, the president intensified the military pressure.

And then, suddenly, the magical Zapatista ability to inspire the solidarity and affection of a largely apolitical and anti-ideological generation on a global scale kicked in. In Mexico City, several hundred thousand people marched. Thousands of artists, academics, writers and entertainers signed pledges of support. There were dozens of concerts and aid convoys all across Mexico, and volunteers packed and shipped hundreds of tons of supplies for the Chiapas refugees. Twelve hundred Roman Catholic catechists from the San Cristobal Diocese made a pilgrimage across the country to build support for the bishop's blueprint for peace; 1,111 Mexico City women, symbolizing the number of rebellious, Zapatista self-governing communities that had organized in accordance with the San Andres Accords, drove to Chiapas to support Zapatista women and children who were resisting the army's incursion armed with sticks and stones. Dozens of human rights organizations traveled to Chiapas from all over the country to participate in one of the Church-sponsored Peace Camps established by the bishop's diocese to monitor the military presence in twenty-six Zapatista villages that had remained particularly vulnerable after the army's 1995 offensive.

Abroad, meanwhile, in 130 cities, in twenty-seven countries, on five continents, Zapatista supporters marched in cities across Europe, Latin America, the United States, Australia, and Africa. In Italy, 60,000 Italians took to the streets in nine cities. The same outpouring took place in Spain, Catalonia and the Basque country; while Mexican consulates in Hamburg, San Francisco, Quito, Venice, and Ancona were among the long list of Mexican government and travel offices abroad occupied by Zapatista sympathizers. Resolutions of support for the Zapatistas and calls on the Mexican government to withdraw the army from Chiapas and restart the peace talks poured in from organizations and individuals as diverse as Spanish Judges for Democracy, the Fiat Motor Workers' Union, the pope, the Swiss Parliament, the French Unions, and the Parliament of the European Union. On January 27, the Italian Parliament's Foreign Affairs Commission suspended the Mexico-European Union Trade Agreement, and in mid-February a delegation of 170 European politicians, intellectuals, and human rights observers traveled to Chiapas on a fact-finding mission, and once again the military solution was averted.

VII. Zapatismo

Zapatismo is not an ideology,
it is not a bought and paid for doctrine.
It is . . . an intuition.
Something so open and flexible that
it really occurs in all places.
Zapatismo poses the question:
"What is it that has excluded me?"
"What is it that has isolated me?"
. . .In each place the response is different.
Zapatismo simply states the question
and stipulates that the response is plural,
that the response is inclusive . . .

—MARCOS

SIX YEARS AGO, when the rebellion was still young, a graffiti went up in San Cristobal de las Casas: "We Are Not Guerrillas. We Are Revolutionaries." At the time, the distinction was unclear to many people. In hindsight, that statement said everything Mexicans needed to learn about the Zapatistas.

In those early days, the people who came to Chiapas to meet and find out about the Zapatistas were Mexican citizens from a white/mestizo, urban progressive minority who wanted to democratize Mexico's antiquated, corrupt political system, but wanted change to come non-violently. In those earliest contacts between the indigenous rebels from Mexico's forgotten past and the nonindigenous citizens of modern Mexico, each brought something to the dialogue the other needed. The citizens brought the unlimited power of access to the world beyond the poverty-stricken ghetto of the rain forest. The revolutionaries from the excluded Mesoamerican country brought the agenda: democracy, justice, liberty, pluralism, and indigenous rights.

To discover the moment when the Zapatista National Liberation Army began the process of transformation from the military vanguard of an armed indigenous and peasant socialist revolution, to an open-ended revolutionary, democratic civilian phenomenon that defies and challenges conventional, political analysis, one needs to go back to the first encounter, in February 1994, between the Zapatista leaders and the Mexican activists who came to San Cristobal to create a human security cordon around the cathedral during the San Cristobal talks. "When they formed that absurd and marvelous cordon of peace, Marcos told Yvon Le Bot two years later, "[it] took us completely by surprise. They were hungry, taking risks, getting photographed [by the army] . . . they could lose their jobs. All that just because they believed in it. It was our first contact with them . . . I wouldn't call it Zapatismo yet. It's a movement barely emerging, people of all classes, from high to low, who sympathize with certain ideas of Zapatismo and who come to see, who want to meet us, get to know us."

From such beginnings, through the series of meetings with Mexican and international civil society in the rain forest; through the National Convention for Democracy in August 1994, at which the Zapatistas inaugurated the first of five civil society encounter forums and resistance centers named Aguascalientes in honor of the village where Zapata and Francisco Villa met in 1917 to write the revolutionary agrarian laws; through the convocation of the Movement for National Liberation, the first and second *encuentros* for humanity and against neoliberalism, and the formation of the Zapatista Front for National Liberation, or FZLN, Zapatismo has remained faithful to the EZLN's original vision to give the political landscape "not just another political organization," but "something truly new."

Zapatismo is not a party, nor a guerilla force. It is a catalyst, an instigator, a creator of possibilities. It provides a platform for the widest possible convergence of democratic forces, multiethnic, multiparty, multicultural, ageless, classless, all contributing to a vast, inchoate movement that would return power to society. Zapatismo seeks a transformation of the future through the radicalization of democracy. The graffiti that said, "We Are Not Guerrillas. We Are Revolutionaries," used old words in new ways. It said to the Mexicans that the revolution to which the Zapatista movement aspires is a radical, democratic dialogue, not a violent rebellion. This is what makes the Zapatistas so threatening to their enemies and so challenging and attractive to their supporters: "The only thing that we proposed to do was to change the world."

NOTES

1. Neil Harvey, "Chiapas: de la concertación a la violencia," La Jornada del Campo, 25 Jan. 1994.

2. John Womack Jr., *Zapata and the Mexican Revolution*, 1968.

3. Ibid.

4. "Interview with Shulamis Hirsch," *Sintesis*, Jan. 5, 1994, p13.

5. Onecimo Hidalgo, *Economia del Estado de Chiapas*, Centro de Información y Análisis de Chiapas A.C., 1988.

6. Marcos, *Chiapas: The Southeast in Two Winds, a Storm and a Prophecy* (Mexico City: Mexican Press, 1994).

7. Julio Moguel, *"Salinas' Failed War on Poverty,"* NACLA Report on the Americas, 28, no. 1, Aug. 1994.

8. Julio Moguel, "Chiapas y el Pronasol."

9. Ibid.

10. Ibid.

11. Ibid., See also "En esta hora de gracia," Pastoral Letter of Bishop Samuel Ruiz to Pope John Paul II, Aug. 1993.

12. Julio Moguel, "Salinas' Failed War."

13. *Agenda Estadistica del Gobierno del Estado de Chiapas* (1991), quoted in Neil Harvey, "Chiapas: del congreso indigena a la guerra campesina," *La Jornada del Campo*, 25 Jan. 1994.

14. Areceli Burguete Cal y Mayor, *Chiapas: Cronología de un etnocidio reciente. Realidad social violenta y violatoria a los derechos humanos*, (1988); and Minnesota Advocates for Human Rights, *Conquest Continued: Disregard for Human and Indigenous Rights in the Mexican State of Chiapas*,(Minneapolis: Minnesota Advocates for Human Rights, 1992).

15. James D. Nations, "The Ecology of the Zapatista Revolt"; Xochtil Leyva Solano, "Militancia politico-religiosa e identidad en la Lacandona," address to the II Mayan International Congress, 1992.

16. Rodiles, "Las Canadas: radiografia social y productiva de una region en conflicto"; Frank Cancian and Peter Brown, "Who is Rebelling in Chiapas?" *Cultural Survival Quarterly*, Spring 1994; and Solano, "Militancia politico-religiosa."

17. Womack, *Zapata and the Mexican Revolution*.

18. Guillermo Correa, "Hay guerrilleros en Chiapas desde ocho años: grupos radicales infiltration a la inglesia y a las comunidades," *Proceso*, Sept. 13, 1993. Also Ignacio Ramirez, "Grupos de izquierda de Torreon utilizaron la infraestructura religiosa y radicalizaron a los catequeistas: Samuel Ruiz," *Proceso*, Feb. 28, 1994.

19. "Interview: Subcomandante Marcos," *Proceso*, Feb. 21, 1994.

20. Ibid.

21. Interview in the Selva Lacondona with Marcos, by Salazar Devereaux (Haitian Information Bureau), Ana Laura Hernandez and Gustavo Rodriguez (Amor y Rabia, Mexico), Eugenio Aguilera (Nightcrawlers Anarchist Black Cross), *Peacenet*, May 11, 1994.

22. Author's interview in San Cristobal (March 1994) with leader of the Church-sponsored Independent Indian Organization (ARIC), aka Union de Uniones.

23. Moguel, "Salinas' Failed War on Poverty."

24. Hector Rivera, "Solución politica, no el uso de la fuerza militar, clama el dramaturgo Carlos Olmos," *Proceso*, 10 Jan. 1994.

25. Francisco Lopez Ardinez, President of the Ocosingo Cattlemen's Assoc., interviewed by Elio Enriquez, *La Jornada*, 27 May 1993.

26. "The eight peasants they've arrested are innocent. If they were guerrillas they wouldn't be so stupid to go to their houses, they'd have fled." Lazaro Hernandez, spokesman for the Union de Uniones, interview in *La*

Jornada, June 1 and 2, 1993. See also Ramon Vera, "Relaciones peligrosas," Ojaresca, July 1993.

27. Joaquin Armendariz Cea, quoted in *La Jornada*, July 11, 1993.

28. Statistics from the Bank of Mexico and the Ministry of Labor, *Proceso*, April 11, 1994.

29. Author's interview in Mexico City with Luis Hernandez Navarro, adviser to the National Coordinating Committee of Coffee Cooperatives (CNOC) and researcher at the Center for the Study of Change in the Mexican Countryside (CECCAM), Jan. 22, 1994.

30. Inaugural address of President Carlos Salinas, December 1988.

31. Womack, *Zapata and the Mexican Revolution.*

32. Author's interview with (anonymous) former "insider" source, Mexico City, January 1994.

33. Interview with Bishop Aguirre Franco of Tuxtla Gutierrez, *La Jornada*, January 4, 1994; see also report from the Ministry of the Interior, January 7, 1994, and various announcements by President Carlos Salinas.

34. Communiqué from Marcos to the Mexican press, January 20, 1994.

35. Homero Campa, "Omision deliberada o ineptitud del gobierno ante la evidente existencia de la guerrilla: Jorge G. Castaneda?" *Proceso*, January 10, 1994.

36. Pascal Beltran del Rio, "Inalcanzable, la solución militar: la capacidad del EZLN muestra que cuenta con el apoyo de incontables comunidades: Carlos Montemayor," *Proceso*, January 10, 1994.

37. Marcos in interviews with radio reporters in San Cristobal, February 22, 1994.

38. "The EZLN Says No," response from the CCRI to the government's peace proposals, June 10, 1994.

39. Womack, *Zapata and the Mexican Revolution.*

Zapatista Timeline

TOM HANSEN AND ENLACE CIVIL

Beginning of history—Mayans settle area now known as Chiapas, Mexico.

1524–27 Spaniards conquer Mayan people, beginning five centuries of exploitation and repression.

Late 1500s Mayan population reduced by 50 percent through disease and repression. Population doesn't begin to recover until mid-seventeenth century.

1712 Indigenous Tzeltal rebellion brought on by Spanish tribute demands and crop failures. The Tzeltals are brutally held down.

1824 Chiapas separates from Guatemala to join a weak Mexican state, allowing relative autonomy for local elites, and beginning decades of Liberal/Conservative struggles for control over land and indigenous labor. Both liberals and conservatives accrue huge landholdings, displacing indigenous owners, and many indigenous people are forced into virtual slavery.

1867–70 Indigenous communities rebel over taxation, control of markets, and religious freedom in Chamula. Violent repression again defeats the rebellion.

1876–1910 Dictatorship of Porfirio Diaz oversees accumulation of immense landholdings by local mestizos. Chiapas economy is opened to international trade, with coffee, cacao, and mahogany as the major exports.

1910–1920 Mexican Revolution. In Chiapas the fight is over control of land and indigenous labor. When General Alvaro Obregón becomes president in 1920, regional *caciqués* declare loyalty in exchange for autonomy to govern Chiapas. Mexico's ensuing agrarian reform has limited impact in the state.

1928 Calles created the National Revolutionary Party (PNR), the precursor of the Institutional Revolutionary Party (PRI)—in power for seventy-one years, until its defeat in the July 2, 2000 elections.

1934–1940 The populist presidency of Lázaro Cárdenas proclaims a common struggle with indigenous communities. Many indigenous Chiapanecos assume positions in PRI-controlled labor unions and peasant organizations. Although Cárdenas's populism largely ends with his presidency, many indigenous political structures remain under PRI control for decades.

1940–70 Land reform under the *ejido* system (communally owned land) continues to lag in Chiapas, while large landowners consolidate their holdings. Cattle ranching becomes an important business as roads penetrate the state. Pressure for land from a booming indigenous population results in over 100,000 Indians migrating to the Lancandon Jungle.

1960 Samuel Ruiz Garcia is named Bishop of San Cristobal de las Casas. After the Medellin Council of Latin American Bishops in 1968, Ruiz begins to promote liberation theology and an indigenous-centered Catholicism.

1968 Student movement in Mexico City is brutally repressed, with hundreds murdered by government agents in the Tlatelolco massacre. The repression convinces many activists to carry their struggles underground. Over the next decade, more than two dozen urban guerrilla groups develop throughout Mexico. The most active period of guerrilla activity is between 1971 and 1975. Most movements disintegrate under brutal repression and a dirty war, which leave hundreds of activists "disappeared" and over one thousand dead.

1970s Pressure for land precipitates organized local revolts against indigenous *caciqués* aligned with the PRI. Over the next two decades, 50,000 Indians are expelled from their communities for resisting local power structures, with many settling around large cities or in the Lacandon Jungle.

1974 The Indigenous Congress is organized by the Diocese of San Cristobal at the invitation of the state governor. Over 1,200 delegates representing 300 communities demand land reform, education in native languages, health care, and labor rights. The congress proves to be a historical juncture for indigenous grassroots organizing.

1979 Founding meeting of the National Coordinating Committee's "Plan de Ayala." Two dozen peasant organizations declare themselves independent of the government.

1982 General Absalón Castellanos Domínguez becomes governor of Chiapas and oversees a dramatic increase in militarization to control land struggles. During his administration, 102 campesinos are assassinated, 327 are disappeared, 590 are imprisoned, 427 are kidnapped and tortured, 407 families are expelled from their homes, and 54 communities are overrun by security forces.

1983 Marcos and other activists from the National Liberation Forces (FLN) arrive in Chiapas. The Zapatista National Liberation Army (EZLN) is born on November 17 with three indigenous and three mestizos.

1985 Earthquake destroys large sections of Mexico City. Inadequate and corrupt response by government officials forces civil society to organize itself, marking an important break in PRI's control.

1986 EZLN enters first indigenous community at invitation of local leaders.

1988 Fraudulent presidential elections on July 6 bring PRI candidate Carlos Salinas de Gortari to power. Opposition candidate Cuauhtemoc Cárdenas is ahead in polling when vote-counting computers suddenly crash. Three days later, Salinas is declared the winner.

1989 EZLN grows to over 1,300 armed members.

1992 President Salinas reforms Article 27 of the Mexican Constitution, ending seventy-five years of land reform and allowing for privatization of *ejidos*.

1993 Zapatista communities approve a military offensive by the EZLN and form the Clandestine Indigenous Revolutionary Committee—General Command (CCRI-CG) to lead the struggle.

1994

JANUARY: NAFTA is implemented on January 1. On the same day, 3,000 members of the EZLN occupy six large towns and hundreds of ranches in an armed uprising. Within twenty-four hours the army responds, bombing indigenous communities and killing at least 145 indigenous people. Mexican civil society responds with massive demonstrations calling for an end to military repression. A cease-fire is declared on January 12.

FEBRUARY: Peace talks begin, but the government peace proposal is rejected by Zapatista communities.

AUGUST: The Zapatistas organize the National Democratic Convention. Over 6,000 people representing a broad range of civil society gather at Aguascalientes, a meeting place carved out of the jungle.

Ernesto Zedillo is elected president, and Eduardo Robledo Rincón is elected governor amid widespread charges of fraud. Amado Avendano Figueroa, the PRD candidate, declares a "government in rebellion."

DECEMBER: On December 19, the Zapatistas declare the civil authority of thirty-eight autonomous indigenous municipalities, representing a serious challenge to local PRI power structures.

The Mexican peso tumbles, losing more than half of its value during the next two months. A U.S./International Monetary Fund bailout of $50 billion does not mitigate dramatic increases in unemployment and loss of living standards during the following year. The majority of Mexicans suffer, while the elite enjoys the fruits of privatization and NAFTA.

1995

JANUARY: The Chase Manhattan Bank issues a report calling for the Mexican government to "eliminate the Zapatistas." At this point, dozens of communities have publicly defined themselves as Zapatistas, representing well over 50,000 civilians.

FEBRUARY: On February 9, the army mounts a massive invasion in Zapatista areas of influence, implementing a strategy of low-intensity warfare (also known as civilian-targeted warfare). Among other things, the army displaces almost 20,000 campesinos, destroys Aguascalientes, and turns it into an army base. The Zapatistas respond by constructing five new Aguascalientes (centers of indigenous resistence). During the next five years, over 60,000 army troops occupy nearly every corner of the state, establishing army encampments just yards from most of the well-established Zapatista communities, disrupting the lives, economy and culture of Indigenous communities.

APRIL: Peace talks resume.

AUGUST: The Zapatistas hold the first international *consulta*. Over a million people vote, calling on the EZLN to transform itself into a new independent political force.

OCTOBER: Talks begin in San Andres Larrainzar on indigenous rights and culture.

1996

FEBRUARY: The EZLN and the government sign the San Andres Accords, out-lining a program of land reform, indigenous autonomy, and cultural rights. March: Talks begin on democracy and justice, concluding with no agreement on August 12, as government representatives refuse to discuss Zapatista pro-posals and present nothing substantial of their own.

JULY/AUGUST: the Zapatistas organize the first Intercontinental *Encuentro* for Humanity and Against Neoliberalism. Several thousand people attend from Mexico and around the world to discuss the role of civil society in confronting neoliberalism.

AUGUST: On August 30, the EZLN suspends peace talks, demanding that gov-ernment representatives actually be empowered to negotiate. December: President Zedillo formally rejects the San Andres Accords.

1997

JULY: The July 6 midterm elections mark significant gains for opposition parties; inside the "conflict zone" in Chiapas, however, abstention reaches 80 percent. Chiapas' elections are notoriously fraudulent, and the high rate of abstention reflects a general mistrust of government in indigenous communities.

SEPTEMBER: On September 12, Zapatistas arrive in Mexico City for the found-ing of the unarmed Zapatista National Liberation Front (FZLN), the civil politi-cal arm of the indigenous movement.

DECEMBER: On December 22, a paramilitary group affiliated with the PRI attacks a church in the community of Acteal, killing 45 Indigenous campesinos, mostly women and children. Paramilitary activity has been grow-ing throughout the state for several years as part of the strategy of civilian-tar-geted warfare. Local PRI officials and army officers are implicated, but the intellectual authors are never brought to justice. Shortly thereafter, the Zedillo administration denies the existence of paramilitaries in Chiapas, and the army begins a campaign to disarm the EZLN, but not the paramilitary groups.

1998

FEBRUARY: In a twisted response to the Acteal massacre, February marks the beginning of a campaign to expel foreign human rights observers from Chiapas, as the Zedillo administration tries to hide the truth from the world. Over 150 are expelled during the coming two years.

Peace talks are still suspended, and the government continues to increase military presence throughout the state.

APRIL: The army begins to dismantle autonomous Zapatista communities. Over 1,000 troops and police invade four communities, destroying records and arresting community leaders.

JUNE: The army's campaign to dismantle rebel communities culminates in the predawn invasion of San Juan de Libertad in June. At least eight civilians and one policeman are killed. The resulting outcry from civil society puts a temporary halt to the army's offensive.

Bishop Samuel Ruiz ends his efforts to mediate a peace, accusing the government of preferring the path of war and repression.

1999

MARCH: The Zapatistas organize a *Consulta* on Indigenous Rights and Culture. Over 5,000 civilian Zapatistas conduct a week-long program of popular education throughout the country. On March 21, over 3 million Mexicans vote at thousands of polling places, agreeing that the San Andres Accords should be implemented.

APRIL: State police occupy the autonomous community of San Andres Sakamch'em, site of the historic San Andres Accords, and install a PRI mayor. The following day, 3,000 unarmed Zapatistas nonviolently force the police to leave the town and re-install their elected representatives.

MAY: The second National *Encuentro* of Civil Society draws 2,000 participants to discuss the March *consulta*.

AUGUST: The military deploys paratroopers and forces to occupy the remote village of Amador Hernandez, the final link in plans to build a road that will encircle the Zapatistas in the Lacandon Jungle. The community resists with nonviolent protests, but the military encampment remains.

2000

Zapatista communities register to vote in historic numbers, and the national election commission announces at least 100 new polling places in these communities.

JULY 2: Vincente Fox (of the conservative PAN party) is elected president, rupturing seventy-one years of PRI control.

Bibliography

Asturias, Veduccia Miguel Angel and J.M. Gonzalez de Mendola. *Pupol-Vuh*. Buenos Aires: Editorial Losado, 1965.

de Cervantes, Miguele. *Don Quixote*. Oxford University Press, 1992.

Chiapas El alzamiento. Mexico: La Jornada Ediciones, 1994.

Harvey, Neil, *The Chiapas Rebellion, The Struggle for Land and Democracy*, Duke University Press, 1998.

Katzenberger, Elaine, ed. *First World, Ha Ha Ha! The Zapatista Challenge*. City Books, 1995.

de Leon, Antonio Garcia, Carlos Monsivais and Elena Poniatawska. *EZLN: Documentos y Comunicados 1; 1 de enero / 8 de agosto de 1994*. Mexico: Ediciones Era, 1994.

de Leon, Antonio Garcia and Carlos Monsivais. *EZLN: Documentos y Comunicados 2; 15 de agosto de 1994 / 29 septiembre de 1995*. Mexico: Ediciones Era, 1995.

——*EZLN: Documentos y Comunicados 3; 2 de octobre 1995 / 24 de enero de 1997*. Mexico: Ediciones Era, 1997.

Marcos, Subcomandante Insurgente. *Relatos de El Viejo Antonio*. Mexico: CIACH, 1998.

——*Conversations with Durito: Shine for a Stories for a Sleepless Solitude*. AZ Editorial Collective–Book Abstract, June 1999.

——*Don Durito de la Lacandona*. Mexico: CIACH, 1999.

——*La Revuelta de La Memoria*. Mexico: CIACH, 1999.

——*Cuentos para una soledad desvelada*. Mexico: Ediciones del Frente Zapatista de Liberacion Nacional, 1997.

——*Desde las Montanas del Sureste Mexicano*. Mexico: Plaza & Janes Editores, 1999.

Ruggiero, Greg, Shahulka, Stewart eds., The Zapatistas, *Zapatista Encuentro: Documents from the 1996 Encounter for Humanity and Against Neoliberalism*, The Open Media Pamphlet Series, Seven Stories Press, 1998.

Subcomandante Insurgente Marcos et al., *Shadows of Tender Fury*. Monthly Review Press, 1995.

Torres, Yolotl Gonzalez. *Diccionario de Mitologia y Religion de Mesoamerica*. Mexico: Larousse, 1999.

Dark Night Field Notes #7, #8, #10, #12/13

WEB RESOURCES

Noticias (News). www.sccs.swarthmore.edu/~justin/ezln/NEWS.html

Ya Basta! www.icf.de/YaBasta/

Enlace Civil. www.enlacecivil.org.mx/index.html

Zapatista Front of National Liberation. www.ezln.org.fzln/

www.mexconnect.com/mex_/history.html

OTHER TRANSLATIONS OF SOME OF THESE WRITINGS HAVE APPEARED IN:

Zapatistas! Documents of the New Mexican Revolution, by Subcomandante Marcos and Members of the
     EZLN (Autonomedia)

Zapatistas—Spreading the Hope for Grassroots Change, by Marc Cooper (Open Media Pamphlet Series)

*Shadows of Tender Fury: The Letters and Communiques of Subcomandante Marcos and the Zapatista Army
     of National Liberation*, by Subcomandante Marcos, et al.

Dark Night Field Notes

Extra! (Paper Tiger Television)

Subcomandante Insurgente Marcos is a guerrilla spokesperson and strategist for the Zapatistas, an indigenous insurgency movement based in Chiapas, Mexico. He is the author of several books translated into English, including *Shadows of Tender Fury* (Monthly Review Press) which featured early letters and communiques, and a children's book *The Story of Colors* (Cinco Puntos), which won a Firecracker Alternative Book Award. Marcos lives and works from "the mountains of the Mexican southeast" in the state of Chiapas.

Ana Carrigan worked in film and video in El Salvador and Nicaragua throughout the 1980s. She is the author of *Salvador Witness: The Life and Calling of Jean Donovan* and *The Palace of Justice: A Colombian Tragedy*. She is a freelance reporter and an editorial contributor to *The Nation* and *In These Times*. She reports from Colombia for *The Irish Times* and *The Sunday Boston Globe*. She lives in New York City and is currently writing a memoir for Seven Stories Press.

Tom Hansen is the National Coordinator of the Mexico Solidarity Network, a coalition of 88 organizations supporting struggles for justice, dignity, democracy and human rights in Mexico and the US. He also serves as co-Director of the Chiapas Media Project, a bi-national partnership that develops alternative media capacities with indigenous communities in Chiapas, Mexico.

Juana Ponce de León, a writer, literary critic, and editor, was the founder of Cronopios Books in Amherst, Massachusetts. She was a project officer for Fifty Communities Awards Program for Friends of the United Nations, and a co-editor *of Creating Common Unity*. She was editor of *LS*, the literary supplement for the *Advocate Weekly Newspapers*. She has written extensively on Latin American and Hispanic literature. Her articles have appeared in many publications including *The New York Times Book Review*, *The Washington Post Book World*, *The Village Voice Literary Supplement*, *Latina*, *Hipsanic*, *Publishers*

Weekly, and *Sí*. She edited *Dream With No Name: Contemporary Fiction from Cuba*. She is Editor-in chief of Siete Cuentos Editorial, the Spanish-language imprint of Seven Stories Press.

Gregory Rabassa teaches at Queens College, CUNY, and has translated forty novels by Latin American and Portuguese writers. His latest translation is *Doña Inés Versus Oblivion* (Louisiana State University Press, 1999) a novel by Ana Teresa Torres, winner of the Pegasus Prize.

José Saramago was born in 1922 in Azinhaga, Portugal. His first major literary success did not come until he was 60. His writings are a blend of magic realism, myth, history, and sharp-edged political comment. His communist affiliation and his belief in a greater union between his country and Spain have not endeared him to the Portuguese establishment. He has lived in the Canary Islands since 1993. He was awarded the Nobel Prize for Literature in 1998. His major works include: *Manual de Pintura e Caligrafia* (*Manual of Painting and Caligraphy*), *Memorial do Convento* (*Baltasar and Blimunda*), *O Año da Morte de Ricardo Reis* (*The Year of the Death of Ricardo Reis*), *A Jaganda de Pedra* (*The Stone Raft*), *Historia do Cerco de Lisboa* (*The History of the Seige of Lisbon*), *Ensaio Sobrea a Cegueira* (*Blindness: a novel*).